Quicken 99

THE OFFICIAL GUIDE

Quicken 99

THE OFFICIAL GUIDE

Maria Langer

Osborne/**McGraw-Hill**

Berkeley   New York   St. Louis   San Francisco
Auckland   Bogotá   Hamburg   London   Madrid
Mexico City   Milan   Montreal   New Delhi   Panama City
Paris   São Paulo   Singapore   Sydney   Tokyo   Toronto

Osborne/**McGraw-Hill**
2600 Tenth Street
Berkeley, California 94710
U.S.A.

For information on translations or book distributors outside the U.S.A., or to arrange bulk purchase discounts for sales promotions, premiums, or fund-raisers, please contact Osborne/**McGraw-Hill** at the above address.

Quicken 99: The Official Guide

1234567890 AGM AGM 90198765432109

ISBN 0-07-211889-X

Publisher
    Brandon A. Nordin
Editor in Chief
    Scott Rogers
Acquisitions Editor
    Joanne Cuthbertson
Project Editor
    Ron Hull
Editorial Assistant
    Stephane Thomas
Technical Editor
    Gordon Hurd
Copy Editor
    Luann Rouff

Proofreader
    Stefany Otis
Indexer
    Jack Lewis
Computer Designers
    Jani Beckwith
    Ann Sellers
    Jean Butterfield
Illustrator
    Lance Ravella
Series Design
    Jill Weil
Cover Design
    Regan Honda

To my uncle, Bob Kleinhans,
with love and best wishes.

Contents At A Glance

Part Four   Saving Money on Big-Ticket Items

Part Five   Achieving Your Goals

Contents

Part Four   Saving Money on Big-Ticket Items

Part Five   Achieving Your Goals

Acknowledgments

A book is the final product of a lot of imagination and hard work by many people. This book is no different. I'd like to thank the people who were involved with this project.

First, thanks to Joanne Cuthbertson at Osborne/McGraw-Hill, for developing the concept for this book. Joanne worked with me and the folks at Osborne and Intuit to make sure the book's content and design were exactly what everyone wanted. She worked very hard, worried a lot, and did a great job. She should be proud of this book and the rest of the Quicken Press series.

Next, thanks to Jeremy Judson at Osborne/McGraw-Hill for suggesting me as a potential author for this book. He helped me convince Joanne that I was the right candidate for the project. Now if he'd only stop working on those Oracle books so I can work with him again…

For the technical side of things, I need to thank a bunch of people at Intuit, starting with Mike Barden and Rod Cherkas. These two guys made sure I had everything I needed to write the book, and then made sure everything I wrote was correct. Other folks at Intuit that deserve thanks are Leigh Chapman, Gregg Simard, Dave Bruno, Shannon Stubbo, Anders Martinson, James Hackleman, Sean Martin, Jenny Robertson and the entire Quicken 99 Product Development team.

For production, I need to thank some folks on the Osborne/McGraw-Hill side of the project: Gordon Hurd, yet another technical reviewer; Ron Hull, the project editor; Luann Rouff, the copy editor; and all the production people who laid out pages and painstakingly positioned all those callouts and callout lines. (It wasn't *my* idea—I swear!) Finally, a big thanks to Stephane Thomas, the editorial assistant who managed the countless FedEx packages and e-mails between me, Joanne, Mike, Ron, and Gordon. She's one of the few people whose smiling face can be seen in just about every e-mail message she writes.

The last thanks goes to Mike, for not minding so much when I skipped vacation to write this book. As usual, he listened sympathetically to all of my complaints about changing betas and difficult deadlines. Well, the book is done now. How about taking the motorcycles up to Colorado for a week or two?

Introduction

Choosing Quicken to organize your finances was a great decision. Quicken has all the tools you need to manage your personal finances. Its well-designed, intuitive interface makes it easy to use. And its online and automation features make entering transactions and paying bills a snap. But if that isn't enough, Quicken also offers features that can help you learn more about financial opportunities that can save you time and money—two things there never seems to be enough of.

Choosing this book to learn Quicken was also a good decision. As the Official Guide, it has Intuit Corporation's "seal of approval"—which means that Intuit, the developer of Quicken, was involved throughout the book's planning, writing, and production stages. The book was even reviewed for accuracy by the folks at Intuit's Technical Support Department.

This Introduction tells you a little about the book and a little about me—so you know what to expect in the chapters to come.

About This Book

Throughout this book, I tell you how to get the most out of Quicken. I start by explaining the basics—the common, everyday tasks that you need to know just to use the program. Then I go beyond the basics to show you how to use Quicken to save time, save money, and make smart financial decisions. Along the way, I'll show you all of Quicken's features, including a bunch that you probably didn't even know existed. You'll find yourself using Quicken for far more than you ever dreamed you would.

Every book is based on certain assumptions, presents information in a certain order, and uses certain conventions to communicate information. This book is no different. Knowing the book's assumptions, organization, and conventions can help you understand how to use this book as a learning tool.

Assumptions

In writing this book, I had to make a few assumptions about your knowledge of your computer, Windows, Quicken, and financial management. These assumptions give me a starting point, making it possible for me to skip over the things that I assume you already know.

What You Should Know About Your Computer and Windows

To use this book (or Quicken 99, for that matter), you should have a general understanding of how to use your computer and Windows. You don't need to be an expert. As you'll see, Quicken uses many standard and intuitive interface elements, making it easy to use—even if you're a complete computer novice.

At a bare minimum, you should know how to turn your computer on and off and how to use your mouse. You should also know how to perform basic Windows tasks, such as opening and exiting programs, using menus and dialog boxes, and entering and editing text.

If you're not sure how to do these things, check the manual that came with your computer or try working through the Windows Tour. These two resources can provide all the information you need to get started.

What You Should Know About Quicken and Financial Management

You don't need to know much about either Quicken or financial management to get the most out of this book: I assume that both are new to you.

This doesn't mean that this book is just for raw beginners. I provide plenty of useful information for seasoned Quicken users—especially those of you who have used previous versions of Quicken—and for people who have been managing their finances with other tools, such as other software (welcome to Quicken!) or pencil and paper (welcome to the 90s!).

Because I assume that all this is new to you, I make a special effort to explain Quicken procedures, as well as the financial concepts and terms on which they depend. New concepts and terms first appear in italic type. (They also appear in the glossary that you'll find in Appendix A.) By understanding these things, not only can you better understand how to use Quicken, you can communicate more effectively with finance professionals such as bankers, stock brokers, and financial advisors.

Organization

This book is logically organized into five parts, each with at least three chapters. It starts with the most basic concepts and procedures, most of which involve specific Quicken tasks, and then works its way up to more advanced topics, many of which are based on finance-related concepts that Quicken makes easy to master.

I want to stress one point here: It is not necessary to read this book from beginning to end. Skip around as desired. Although the book is organized for cover-to-cover reading, not all of its information may apply to you. For example, if you're not in the least bit interested in investing, skip the chapters related to investing. It's a simple as that. When you're ready for the information that you skipped, it'll be waiting for you.

Now here's a brief summary of the book's organization and contents.

Part I: Quicken Setup and Basics

This part of the book introduces Quicken's interface and features and helps you set up Quicken for managing your finances. It also provides the information you need to set up and test Quicken's online features. If you're brand-new to Quicken, I highly recommend reading at least the first two chapters in this part of the book.

Part I has three chapters:

- Chapter 1: Getting to Know Quicken
- Chapter 2: Setting Up Accounts and Categories
- Chapter 3: Online Setup

Part II: Organizing Your Finances

This part of the book is primarily how-to information about using Quicken to record, organize, and manage your finances. Because not all Quicken users take advantage of its online features, this section provides details about features you can use without connecting to the Internet, an online service, or a financial institution. But as you read through the chapters in this section, you'll learn some of the ways Quicken's online features can make organizing your finances quicker or easier to do.

There are seven chapters in Part II:

- Chapter 4: Paying Bills and Managing Your Checkbook
- Chapter 5: Automating Transactions
- Chapter 6: Tracking Credit Cards
- Chapter 7: Tracking Investments
- Chapter 8: Reports and Graphs
- Chapter 9: Budgeting and Forecasting
- Chapter 10: Preparing for Emergencies

Part III: Saving Time with Online Features

While Part II only mentions Quicken's online features, Part III provides the details you need to use them to their fullest. In its chapters, you'll learn about the Quicken.com Web site and how to take advantage of the convenience of online banking, bill pay, credit card tracking, and investing.

Part III has five chapters:

- Chapter 11: Exploring Quicken.com
- Chapter 12: Banking and Paying Bills Online
- Chapter 13: Tracking Credit Cards Online
- Chapter 14: Tracking Investments Online
- Chapter 15: Accessing Quicken Data on the Web

Part IV: Saving Money on Big-Ticket Items

This part of the book helps you to save money where savings are needed most: on big-ticket items such as income taxes, insurance, and the purchase of a home or car. Although Quicken can't pay for these things, it can help you gather the information you need—or organize the information you already have—to make smart, money-saving decisions.

Part IV has three chapters:

- Chapter 16: Saving Money at Tax Time
- Chapter 17: Insurance
- Chapter 18: Buying a Home or Car

Part V: Achieving Your Goals

In Part V, you'll learn how to use Quicken to help achieve your goals. Whether you want to make the most of your invested funds; have financial security in your retirement years; or save up for the down payment on a house or college education for your children, Quicken can help you.

Part V has three chapters:

- Chapter 19: Maximizing Investment Returns
- Chapter 20: Planning for Retirement
- Chapter 21: Saving for the Future

Appendix

If twenty-one chapters of information aren't enough for you, there's more. Appendix A, "Managing Quicken Files," explains how to back up, restore, and otherwise maintain Quicken files.

Conventions

All how-to books—especially computer books— have certain conventions for communicating information. The following sections outline the conventions I use throughout this book.

Menu Commands

Quicken, like most other Windows programs, makes commands accessible on the menu bar at the top of the application window. Throughout this book, I tell you which menu commands to choose to open a window or dialog box or to complete a task. I use the following format to indicate menu commands: Menu | Submenu (if applicable) | Command.

So, for example, if I wanted you to choose the One Step Update command under the Online menu, I'd tell you to choose Online | One Step Update. If I wanted you to choose the Register command from the Options submenu under the Edit menu, I'd tell you to choose Edit | Options | Register.

Keystrokes

Keystrokes are the keys you must press to complete a task. There are two kinds of keystrokes.

Keyboard Shortcuts   Keyboard shortcuts are combinations of keys you press to complete a task more quickly. For example, the shortcut for "clicking" a Cancel button may be to press the Esc key. When instructing you to press a key, I provide the name of the key in small caps, like this: ESC. If you must press two or more keys simultaneously, I separate them with a dash, like this: CTRL-P. Finally, if you must press two or more keys simultaneously, and then press another key or key combination, I separate the keystrokes with a comma, like this: ALT-F4,T.

Literal Text   Literal text is text that you must type in exactly as it appears in the book. Although there aren't many instances of literal text in this book, there are a few. I display literal text in bold type, like this: **Checking Acct**. If literal text includes a variable—text you must substitute when you type—I include the variable in bold italic type, like this: ***Payee Name***.

Icons

I use icons to indicate a wide variety of useful information.

Shortcut   Like most other Windows programs, Quicken often offers more than one way to complete a task. The Shortcut icon identifies a method for completing a Quicken task more quickly than other methods.

Tip   A tip is a little something extra that you don't really *need* to know. Tips can help you get more out of Quicken when you're ready to go beyond the basics.

Caution   A caution is vitally important information that can protect you from data loss or other serious consequences. Don't skip the cautions!

Save Time   The Save Time icon identifies Quicken features that can save you time. Don't confuse these with shortcuts—while shortcuts can save you time when working with a specific feature, a Save Time icon identifies specific features that can save you time. For example, as you'll see in Part III of this book, online credit-card tracking can save lots of time spent entering transactions.

Save Money   The Save Money icon identifies Quicken features that can save you money.

Get Smarter   The Get Smarter icon identifies Quicken features that can help you learn more about a concept. You'll find that the Get Smarter icons can help you make better, more informed decisions.

Quicken Quotes

If you're brand-new to Quicken, you probably don't know much about it. Or, you may have some incorrect notions about what it does and how it works. The Quicken Quotes sidebars will set you straight by providing interesting tidbits on how some of the over 10 million Quicken users out there take advantage of Quicken's features to save them time, save them money, or help them make better, more informed decisions. These real-life stories will give you plenty of ideas about how you can make Quicken work harder for you.

About the Author

Finally, let me tell you a little bit about me.

I graduated from Hofstra University with a BBA in Accounting in—well, you don't really need to know *when*. I worked as an accountant, auditor, and financial analyst over the next eight years. Then I realized that I really didn't like what I was doing every day and took the necessary steps to change careers. I've written 20 computer books since the change, many of which are about business and productivity software such as Word, Excel, and FileMaker Pro.

I use Quicken. I've been using it for years. I use it to manage four bank accounts and two credit card accounts, to track my mortgage, and to pay all my bills (online, of course). I also use its investment features to track my portfolio and research the companies in which I invest. While I don't use all Quicken features regularly, I've used them all at least once to save time, save money, make important financial decisions, or help me plan for my future.

Frankly, I can't imagine not using Quicken. And I'm glad to have the opportunity to show you why you would agree.

Quicken Setup and Basics

This part of the book introduces Quicken's interface and features. It explains how to install Quicken and set up accounts, categories, and online access. It has three chapters:

Chapter 1:   Getting to Know Quicken

Chapter 2:   Setting Up Accounts and Categories

Chapter 3:   Online Setup

Getting to Know Quicken

In This Chapter:

- *An Overview of Quicken*

- *Installing Quicken*

- *Starting Quicken*

- *The Quicken Interface*

- *Online Help*

If you're brand-new to Quicken, get your relationship with Quicken off to a good start by properly installing it and learning a little more about how you can interact with it.

In this chapter, I provide a brief overview of Quicken, explain how to install and start it, take you on a tour of its interface, and show you how to use its extensive Online Help feature. Although the information I provide in this chapter is especially useful to new Quicken users, some of it also applies to upgrading users.

What Is Quicken?

On the surface, Quicken is a computerized checkbook. It enables you to balance your accounts, and organize, manage, and generate reports for your finances. But as you explore Quicken, you'll learn that it's much more than just a computerized checkbook. It's a complete personal finance software package—a tool for taking control of your finances and making your money work harder for you.

What Quicken Can Help You Do

At the very least, Quicken can help you manage your bank accounts and credit card accounts. You can enter transactions and have Quicken generate reports and graphs that show where your money went and how much is left.

Quicken can also help you manage investment accounts. You can enter transactions and have Quicken tell you the market value of your investments. Quicken can also help you organize other data, such as the purchase price and current worth information for your possessions, and vital information you may need in the event of an emergency.

With all financial information stored in Quicken's database, you can generate net worth reports to see where you stand today. You can also use a variety of financial planners to make financial decisions for the future. And Quicken's Tax Deduction Finder helps you find deductible expenses for tax time.

With Quicken's online features, you can automate much of your data entry. You can also explore a whole world of up-to-date information that you can use to shop for the best bank accounts, credit card accounts, loans, and insurance. You can read news and information about investment opportunities and advice offered by financial experts. You can get in touch with other Quicken users to see how they use Quicken to manage their money.

Now tell me, can the paper check register that came with your checks do all that?

Save Time, Save Money, Get Smarter

Quicken and this book have an underlying theme: save time, save money, and make informed financial decisions. You'll see plenty of examples of how Quicken can do this throughout this book, but here are a few simple examples to whet your appetite:

 SAVE TIME   Entering transactions into registers can be tedious. But Quicken offers several features for speeding up this process, including memorized transactions, QuickFill, and the ability to download transactions from a bank, credit card company, or brokerage firm.

 SAVE MONEY   Many of the organizations you pay every month—credit card companies, banks, and utilities—charge a late fee when payment is received after the due date. Quicken's reminders and Billminder features help you remember when payments are due. Its online payment and scheduling features can work together to automatically pay bills when they are due. Making timely payments saves money.

 GET SMARTER   Buying a home is a big purchase decision that is based on many smaller decisions. How much can you afford to spend on a home? What are the current interest rates and other loan terms? What will your monthly payments be? Which loan is right for you? Quicken can help answer all of these questions by providing access to up-to-date information via QuickenMortgage and a variety of planning tools such as the Loan Planner.

These are just a few examples. Quicken is full of smart features like these. It takes the drudgery out of organizing and managing your finances and rewards you by helping you make the most of your money.

Quicken Basic vs. Quicken Deluxe

Two versions of Quicken are covered in this book: Basic and Deluxe.

Quicken Basic is an entry-level product designed for people who are new to personal finance software. As its name suggests, it includes basic features to track bank accounts, credit cards, investments, budgets, and loans. It also enables you to use online account access and payment, shop for insurance and mortgages, and download investment information for a brokerage account.

Quicken Deluxe is more robust. Designed for people who want to take a more active role in financial management, investments, and planning, it includes all the features in Quicken Basic plus the financial alerts feature, money-saving features for tax time and debt reduction, free access to investment information, and the Emergency Records Organizer and Home Inventory features.

Getting Started

Ready to get started? In this section, I explain how to install, open, and register Quicken. If you're upgrading from a previous version of Quicken, be sure to consult the section titled "Upgrading from a Previous Version."

Installing Quicken

Quicken uses a basic Windows setup program that should be familiar to you if you've installed other Windows programs. Following are the step-by-step instructions to install Quicken.

Starting the Installer

Insert the Quicken 99 CD into your CD-ROM drive. A dialog box like the one shown here should appear:

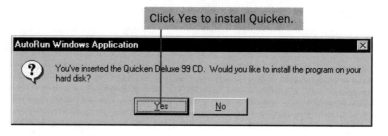

Click Yes to install Quicken.

AutoRun Windows Application

You've inserted the Quicken Deluxe 99 CD. Would you like to install the program on your hard disk?

Yes   No

If this dialog box does not automatically appear, you can start the installer by following these steps:

1. Click the Start button on the task bar.
2. Click Settings.
3. Click Control Panel.
4. Double-click Add/Remove Programs.
5. Click Install.
6. Click Next.
7. Click Finish.

A Welcome window appears next. Read the information in the window and click the Next button. The Software License Agreement window appears. Read the agreement and, if you agree to the terms, click Yes. (As noted in the window, you must click Yes to install Quicken.)

Choosing a Destination Location

The Choose Destination Location window, which indicates the default location for installing Quicken, appears next:

If desired, click Browse to select a different destination folder.

Choose Destination Location   ×

Setup will install Quicken Deluxe 99 in the following folder.

To install to this folder, click Next.

To install to a different folder, click Browse and select another folder.

You can choose not to install Quicken Deluxe 99 by clicking Cancel to exit Setup.

Destination Folder
C:\QUICKENW   Browse...

< Back   Next >   Cancel

Click Next to continue the installation.

Tip   Because the default directory for all recent versions of Quicken is C:\QUICKENW, if you want to keep a previous version of Quicken installed on your computer, you will probably have to install Quicken 99 into a different directory. These instructions, however, assume that you are installing into the default directory location.

When you click Next, a dialog box may appear, asking whether you want to create a new directory. If so, click Yes.

Selecting the Type of Installation and Installation Components

Next, the installer displays the Type of Installation window:

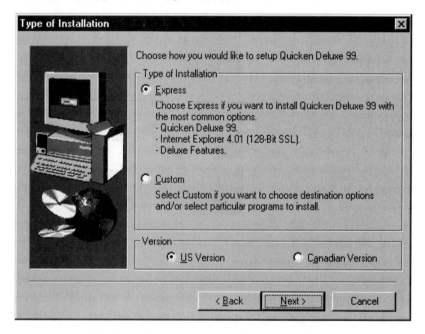

Here you must make two selections:

- **Type of Installation** offers a choice of Express or Custom. An Express installation installs Quicken 99's common options. A Custom installation enables you to select the options that you want to install. Select the appropriate option button.

- **Version** lets you choose the US or Canadian version of Quicken 99. Select the option button for the version you want.

Tip If you're not sure which Type of Installation option to select, select Express. That's the installation I use and discuss throughout this book.

If you select the Custom option in the Type of Installation window, the Select Installation Components window appears next:

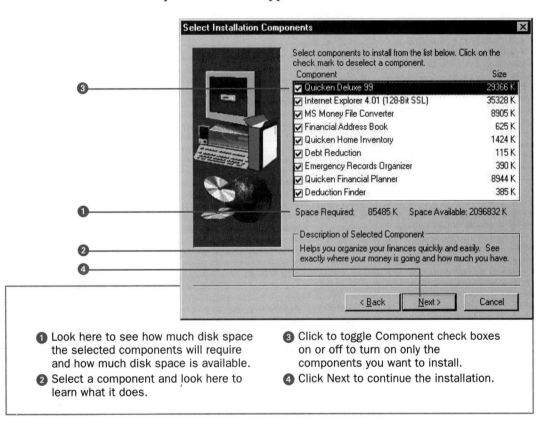

❶ Look here to see how much disk space the selected components will require and how much disk space is available.

❷ Select a component and look here to learn what it does.

❸ Click to toggle Component check boxes on or off to turn on only the components you want to install.

❹ Click Next to continue the installation.

When you select the Custom option in the Type of Installation window, you can also select the Program Folder in which Quicken will appear on the Start menu. You do this in the Select Program Folder window, shown here:

The default Program Folder name is Quicken (which makes sense to me), but you can either enter a new name here, or click one of the existing folders in this list to select it.

Click Next to continue the installation.

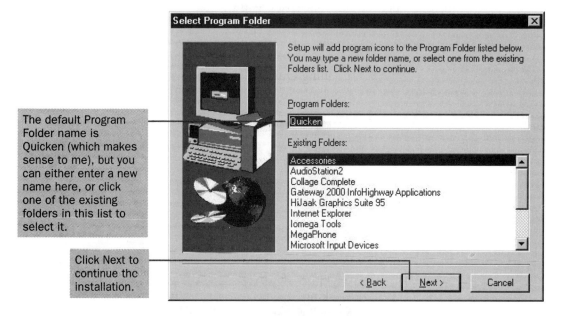

Checking and Confirming Settings

The Check Settings window, which lists the installation components and location, appears next:

Check this list to make sure it lists the components you want to install.

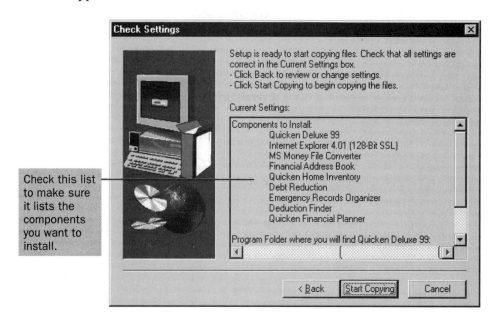

Finishing Up

When the Quicken installer is finished, you may be prompted to restart your computer. Do so. You'll then be ready to start working with Quicken.

Upgrading from a Previous Version

To upgrade from a previous version of Quicken, begin following the instructions in the section titled "Installing Quicken." The message that appears when you insert the CD-ROM disk looks like this:

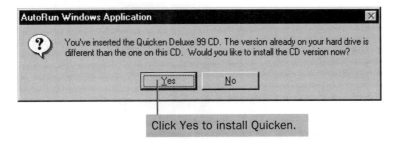

Later in the installation process, after choosing a location for Quicken, a dialog box may appear, asking if you want to uninstall the previous copy of Quicken. Click Yes. You will then be prompted to confirm that you want to remove the previous version of Quicken. Click Yes again.

Follow the prompts in the Uninstaller windows that appear to remove the previous version of Quicken from your computer. When the Uninstaller is finished, click OK. Then continue following the instructions in the section titled "Installing Quicken."

Opening Quicken

You can open Quicken several different ways. Here are the two most common methods.

Opening a Quicken Shortcut

An Express installation of Quicken places one or two shortcuts on your Windows desktop, depending on the version and components of Quicken you have installed:

Quicken 99 or Quicken Deluxe 99   Double-clicking this shortcut opens the version of Quicken you have installed on your computer.

QuickEntry 99   Double-clicking this shortcut opens QuickEntry, a program that enables you to enter transactions into Quicken without opening Quicken itself. QuickEntry is part of Quicken Deluxe and is not available in Quicken Basic. I tell you more about QuickEntry in Chapter 4.

Opening Quicken from the Task Bar

You can also use the Windows task bar's Start button to open Quicken and other Quicken components, such as QuickEntry (if installed):

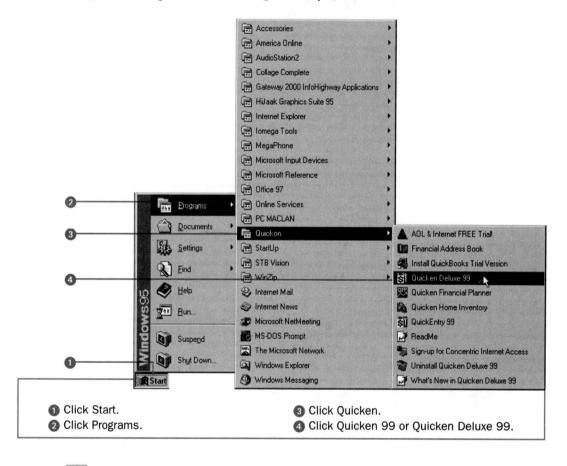

❶ Click Start.
❷ Click Programs.
❸ Click Quicken.
❹ Click Quicken 99 or Quicken Deluxe 99.

Registering Quicken

The first time you open Quicken, the Product Registration window appears. It tells you about the benefits of registering Quicken. Because some Quicken features will not work unless you register, it's a good idea to register right away.

Click the Register button and follow the instructions that appear onscreen to register online or by telephone. It takes only a few minutes and doesn't cost a thing.

New User Setup

If you're a brand-new Quicken user, after registering Quicken, the Quicken New User Setup window appears. It offers a quick way to set up Quicken so you can get right to work. I explain how to use Quicken New User Setup in Chapter 2.

Converting Existing Data

If you upgraded from a previous version of Quicken, when you first start Quicken 99, it displays a dialog box telling you that it needs to upgrade your data file. Click OK. Quicken saves a copy of the data in C:\QUICKENW\ Q98FILES—this makes it possible to go back to the previous version of Quicken if necessary. It then converts the data file for use with Quicken 99, and the default Quicken Home Page window appears (see Figure 1-1). I tell you more about the Home Page window a little later in this chapter and in Chapter 8.

The Quicken Interface

Quicken's interface is designed to be intuitive and easy to use. It puts the tools you need to manage your finances right within mouse pointer reach. You never have to dig through multiple dialog boxes and menus to get to the commands you need most.

In this section, I tell you about the components of the Quicken interface and explain how you can use them to make your work with Quicken easy.

Features and Commands

Quicken offers a number of ways to access its features and commands, including standard Microsoft Windows elements such as menus and dialog boxes, and Quicken elements such as the Activity bar and Button bar.

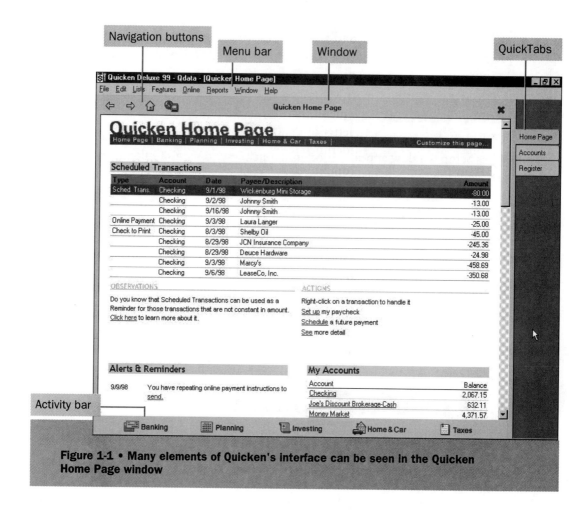

Figure 1-1 • Many elements of Quicken's interface can be seen in the Quicken Home Page window

Menus

Like all other Windows programs, Quicken displays a number of menus in a Menu bar at the top of the screen (see Figure 1-1). You can choose commands from the menus in three ways:

- Click the menu name to display the menu. If necessary, click the name of the submenu you want (see Figure 1-2), and then click the name of the command that you want.

- Press ALT to activate the Menu bar, and press the keyboard key for the underlined letter in the menu that you want to open. If necessary, press the key for the underlined letter in the submenu that you want to open, and then press the key for the underlined letter in the command that you want.

- Press the shortcut key combination for the menu command that you want. A command's shortcut key, if it has one, is displayed to the right of the command name on the menu.

Shortcut Menus

Shortcut menus (which are sometimes referred to as *contextual* or *context-sensitive* menus) can be displayed throughout Quicken. Point to the item for which you want to display a shortcut menu and click the right mouse button. The menu,

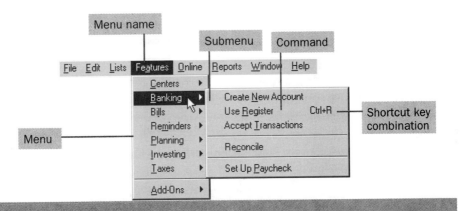

Figure 1-2 • A menu and submenu

which includes only those commands applicable to the item, appears at the mouse pointer:

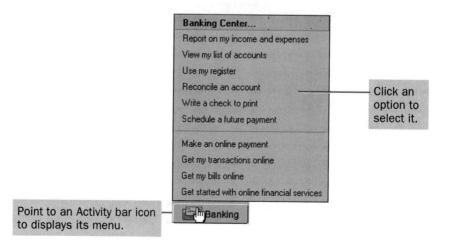

Activity Bar

The Activity bar is a row of icons across the bottom of the screen (refer to Figure 1-1). It organizes commonly accessed Quicken features and tasks. To use an Activity bar icon, point to it. A menu pops up:

Button Bar

The Button bar is a row of textual buttons and menus that appears near the top of many windows. The items on the left side of the window, which vary from window to window, are buttons; simply click one to access its option. The items with triangles beside their names on the right side of the window are menus:

- **Report** displays a list of reports related to the active window:

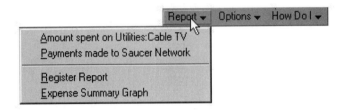

- **Options** displays a list of commands specific to the active window:

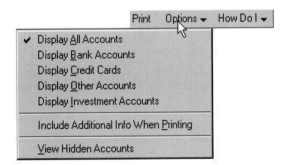

- **How Do I** displays a list of tasks related to the active window:

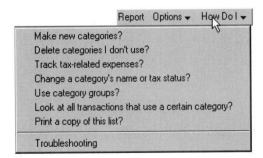

Menu names on the right side of the Button bar are generally the same from one window to another. One exception is the Print command, which will sometimes replace or appear beside the Report menu. The options these menus offer differ depending on the active window.

Dialog Boxes

Like other Windows applications, Quicken uses dialog boxes to communicate with you. Some dialog boxes display a simple message, while others include text boxes, option buttons, check boxes, and drop-down lists you can use to enter information. Many dialog boxes also include a Help button that you can use to get additional information about dialog box options.

Windows

Quicken displays information in windows. It has different types of windows for the different types of information it displays.

Quicken Home Page

The Quicken Home Page (shown in Figure 1-1) provides information about your financial status. Other Financial Information Centers are similar in design and appearance. If you're using Quicken Deluxe, you can customize this window's view or create new views to show the things that interest you most. I tell you how in Chapter 8.

List Windows

A list window (see Figure 1-3) shows a list of information about related things, such as accounts, categories, classes, and scheduled transactions. You can open a list window by choosing it from the Lists menu.

Register Windows

You use the register window (see Figure 1-4) to enter and edit transactions in an account register. You can open the register window by choosing Features | Banking | Use Register or pressing CTRL-R.

Button bar

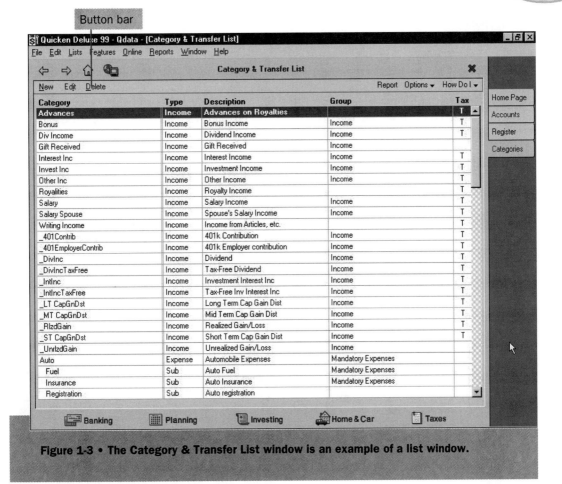

Figure 1-3 • The Category & Transfer List window is an example of a list window.

QuickTabs

QuickTabs are buttons you can click to quickly switch from one open window to another. They appear on the right side of the screen in the order in which the windows were opened. The register window also has account tabs along the bottom of the window to switch from one account's register to another's. You can see both kinds of tabs in Figure 1-4.

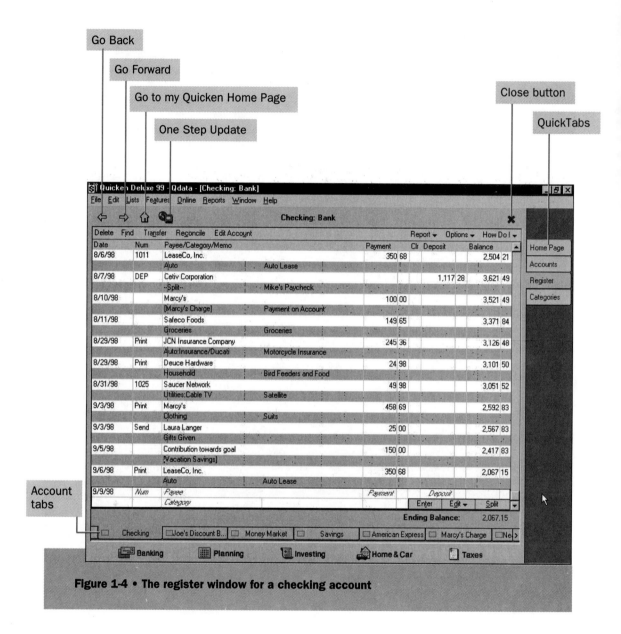

Figure 1-4 • The register window for a checking account

Tip   You can change the order of QuickTabs by dragging one to a new position in the row of tabs.

Navigation Buttons

Navigation buttons along the top of the window (see Figure 1-4) enable you to move from one window to another, or to close a window.

- **Go Back** displays the previous open window.
- **Go Forward** displays the next open window.
- **Go to my Quicken Home Page** displays the Quicken Home Page window.
- **One Step Update** connects to the Internet to update all your online information at once.
- X closes the active window.

Online Help

In addition to the How Do I menu in Quicken windows, and the Help button in dialog boxes, Quicken includes an extensive Online Help system to provide more information about using Quicken while you work. You can access most Help options from the Help menu:

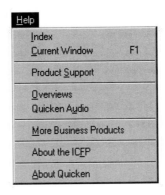

Here's a brief summary of some of the components of Quicken's Online Help system.

Quicken Help

Quicken's Online Help uses the same Help engine as most Windows programs. You can open it by choosing Help Index from the Help menu. It displays a window with three tabs for getting help:

- **Contents** lists Help topics organized in "books":

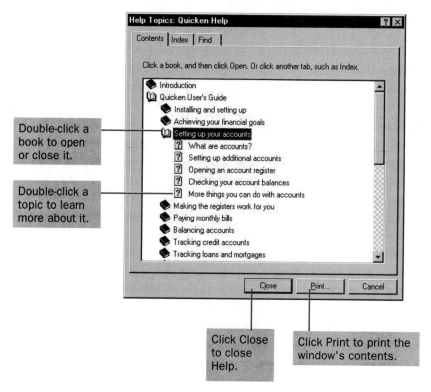

Double-click a book to open or close it.

Double-click a topic to learn more about it.

Click Close to close Help.

Click Print to print the window's contents.

- **Index** lists Help topics alphabetically:

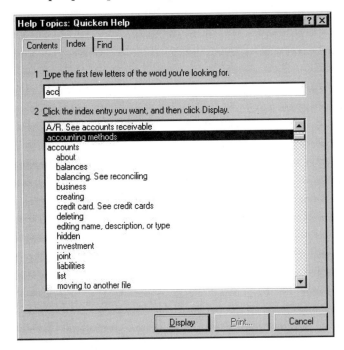

- **Find** enables you to search for information about a topic:

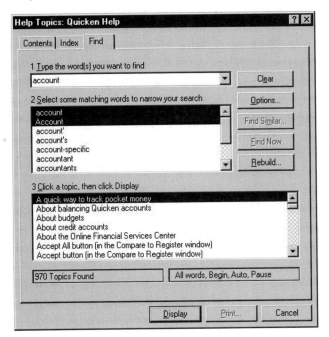

Tip The first time you use the Find feature, you must use the Find Setup Wizard to create a searchable word list for Help topics. (Just follow the prompts that appear on screen.)

When you view a Help topic, it appears in a small window with a yellow background:

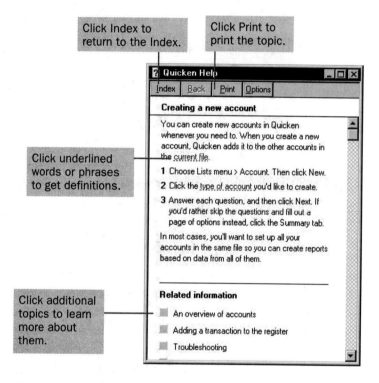

Click Index to return to the Index.

Click Print to print the topic.

Click underlined words or phrases to get definitions.

Click additional topics to learn more about them.

Context-Sensitive Help

The Current Window command on the Help menu opens a Help topic with information about the active window. This is probably the quickest way to get information about a specific topic or task with which you are working. This command even has its own shortcut key: F1.

Product Support

The Product Support command on the Help menu opens the Product Support
window:

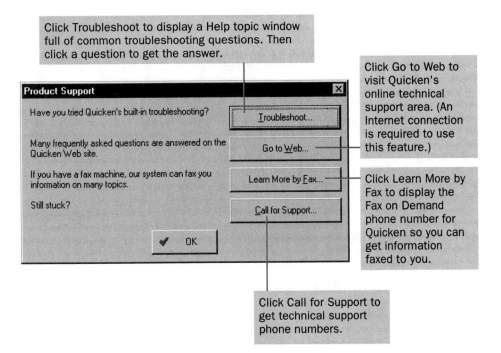

Click Troubleshoot to display a Help topic window
full of common troubleshooting questions. Then
click a question to get the answer.

Click Go to Web to
visit Quicken's
online technical
support area. (An
Internet connection
is required to use
this feature.)

Click Learn More by
Fax to display the
Fax on Demand
phone number for
Quicken so you can
get information
faxed to you.

Click Call for Support to
get technical support
phone numbers.

Overviews

Quicken Overviews provide text and video information about using Quicken.
Although some information is stored on your hard disk when you install
Quicken, other information, such as videos, are only available when the Quicken
CD-ROM is inserted in your CD-ROM drive.

The Quicken Overviews main window appears right after you complete the
Quicken New User Setup. This makes it easy to learn more about Quicken's

features before you begin working. You can also open Overviews at any time by choosing Overviews from Quicken's Help menu. Here's an example of a Quicken Overviews window with a video:

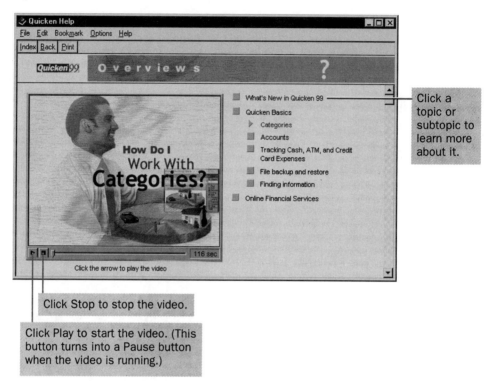

Click a topic or subtopic to learn more about it.

Click Stop to stop the video.

Click Play to start the video. (This button turns into a Pause button when the video is running.)

QuickenAudio

QuickenAudio provides verbal instructions for completing tasks. You enable this feature by inserting the Quicken CD-ROM and choosing QuickenAudio from the Help menu. (A check mark indicates that it is turned on.) The tiny QuickenAudio window appears:

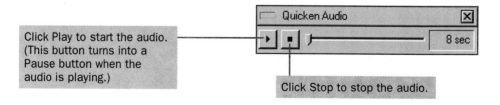

Click Play to start the audio. (This button turns into a Pause button when the audio is playing.)

Click Stop to stop the audio.

Tip   If QuickenAudio is enabled, when you work with a feature for which QuickenAudio instructions exist, a narrator automatically provides instructions.

Customizing Quicken's Interface

Quicken's Window menu, which is depicted here, offers a number of commands you can use to customize Quicken's interface and appearance.

- **Show QuickTabs** controls the display of QuickTabs (refer to Figure 1-1).
- **Show Activity Bar** controls the display of the Activity bar along the bottom of the window (refer to Figure 1-1).
- **Show Top Iconbar** displays a row of icons, like the one shown next, for accessing Quicken features.

- **Show Progress Bar** displays the Progress bar along the bottom of the screen. I tell you about the Progress bar in Chapter 9.
- **Use Fly-Over Menus** enables you to display Activity bar icon menus by pointing to them. With this option disabled, you must click an Activity bar icon to display its menu.

- **QuickTabs on Right** displays QuickTabs along the right side of the window. With this option disabled, QuickTabs appear on the left side of the window.
- **Color Schemes** displays a submenu of predefined color schemes you can apply to Quicken's windows and other interface elements.
- [**Window name(s)**] at the bottom of the menu offer access to open windows. You may find this handy to switch from one window to another if you have the Show QuickTabs option disabled. Otherwise, it's probably quicker to switch to a window by clicking its QuickTab.

A check mark beside a menu command indicates that it is turned on or enabled. Choosing the command from the menu toggles the check mark setting.

Exiting Quicken

When you're finished using Quicken, choose Exit from its File menu. This saves your data file and closes the Quicken application.

Tip   Sometimes, when you close Quicken, you'll be asked if you want to back up your Quicken data file. I tell you about data files, including how to back them up, in Appendix A.

Setting Up Accounts and Categories

In This Chapter:

- *Overview of Data Files, Accounts, and Categories*

- *Quicken New User Setup*

- *Setting Up Accounts*

- *Working with the Account List*

- *Setting Up Categories and Subcategories*

- *Working with the Category & Transfer List*

To make the most of Quicken, you must properly set it up for your particular financial situation. There are two parts to the setup process:

1. Use Quicken New User Setup to quickly create a primary bank account and a basic set of categories. This takes about five minutes and must be completed when you first set up Quicken.
2. Add accounts and categories as necessary to meet your specific needs. This takes only a minute or two for each account or category. You'll probably want to do this when you first start using Quicken, but you can do it any time you like.

In this chapter, I explain how to set up the Quicken accounts and categories you'll use to organize your finances.

Before You Begin

Before you start the setup process, it's a good idea to have an understanding of how data files, accounts, and categories work. You should also gather together a few documents to help you properly set up your accounts.

Data Files

All the transactions you record with Quicken are stored in a *data file* on your hard disk. This file includes all the components—accounts, categories, and transactions—that make up your Quicken accounting system.

Although it's possible to have more than one Quicken data file, it isn't usually necessary. One file can hold all your transactions. In fact, it's difficult (if not downright impossible) to use more than one Quicken file to track a single account, like a checking or credit card account. And splitting your financial records among multiple data files makes it impossible to generate reports that consolidate all the information.

When would you want more than one data file? Well, you could use two data files if you wanted to use Quicken to organize your personal finances and the finances of your business, which has entirely separate bank, credit, and asset accounts. Or if you're using Quicken to track the separate finances of multiple individuals.

I tell you more about working with Quicken data files in Appendix A.

Accounts and Categories

There are two primary components to every transaction you record in Quicken: account and category.

An *account* is a record of what you either own or owe. For example, your checking account is a record of cash on deposit in the bank that is available for writing checks. A credit card account is a record of money you owe to the credit card company or bank for the use of your credit card. All transactions either increase or decrease the balance in one or more accounts.

A *category* is a record of where your money comes from or goes. For example, salary is an income category for recording the money you earn from your job. Dining is an expense category you might use to record the cost of eating out. Categories make it possible to track how you earn and spend money.

If you know anything about accounting, these concepts should sound familiar, even if the names don't match what you learned in school or on the job. Accounts are what you'd find on a *balance sheet;* categories are what you'd find on an *income statement.* Quicken can produce reports like these; I tell you how in Chapter 8.

What You Need

To properly set up accounts, you should have balance information for the accounts that you want to monitor with Quicken. You can get this information from your most recent bank, investment, and credit card statements. It's a good idea to gather these documents before you start the setup process so they're on hand when you need them.

If you plan to use Quicken to replace an existing accounting system—whether it's paper-based or prepared with a different computer program—you may also find it helpful to have a *chart of accounts* (a list of account names) or a recent income statement. This way, when you set up Quicken accounts and categories, you can use familiar names.

Quicken New User Setup

The Quicken New User Setup main window appears when you start Quicken for the first time as a new user or you create a new Quicken data file:

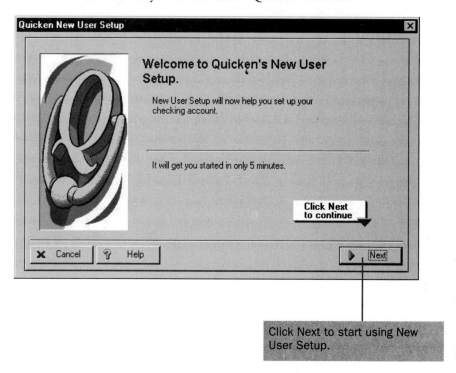

Click Next to start using New User Setup.

Next, Quicken New User Setup asks you four questions to determine which categories you'll need to record transactions. Select the appropriate option buttons to answer the questions and click Next to continue.

Select the appropriate option buttons to answer these four questions.

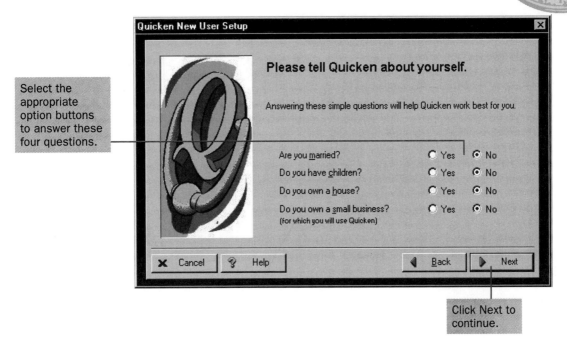

Click Next to continue.

The next window prompts you to enter a name for your checking account. Enter a name and then click Next to continue.

Quicken New User Setup then asks if you have your last checking account statement. Select the Yes or No option button and click Next. The window that appears next varies depending on which option you have selected in the previous window:

- If you have selected No, Quicken tells you that it will open the account with a balance of $0.00 starting on today's date.
- If you have selected Yes, a window like the following appears:

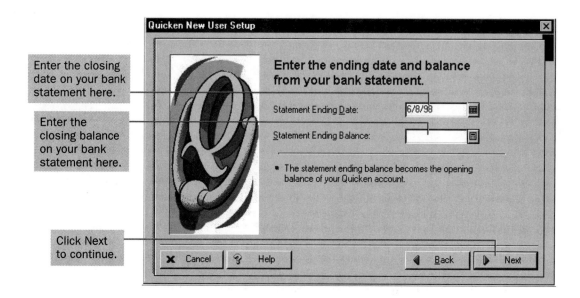

Enter the closing date on your bank statement here.

Enter the closing balance on your bank statement here.

Click Next to continue.

The next window confirms the information you entered about your checking account:

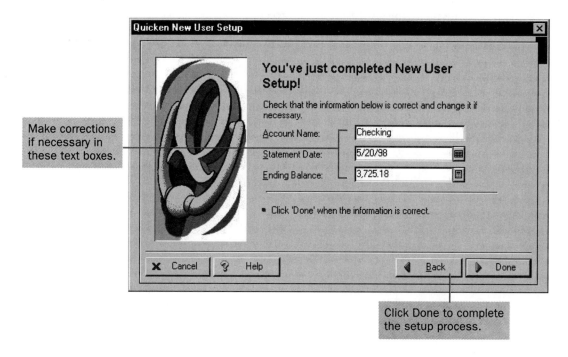

Make corrections if necessary in these text boxes.

Click Done to complete the setup process.

When the setup process is finished, the Quicken New User Setup window disappears and the Overviews window takes its place. You can use Overviews to get a general idea of how different Quicken features work. (This is covered in Chapter 1.) When you're finished looking at Overviews, click the close button to close the Overviews window.

You're now ready to start using Quicken.

Customizing Setup

Quicken New User Setup performs the bare minimum setup: one account (checking) and a collection of categories based on options you selected. But in many cases, you'll want to customize the setup to add accounts and add or remove categories. In this section, I tell you more about accounts and categories and explain how you can customize the default setup.

Accounts

While the majority of your expenditures may come from your checking account, you probably have more than one account that Quicken can track for you. By setting up all your accounts in Quicken, you can keep track of balances and activity to get a full picture of what you own and what you owe.

Types of Accounts

Quicken Deluxe offers nine different kinds of accounts for tracking what you own and what you owe:

What You Own   In accounting jargon, what you own are *assets*. In Quicken, an asset is one type of account, but there are several others:

- **Checking** is for tracking checking account activity.
- **Savings** is for tracking savings account activity.
- **Cash** is for tracking cash inflows and expenditures.
- **Money Market** is for tracking money market account activity.
- **Asset** is for tracking items that you own such as a house, property, automobile, or money owed to you by others. I tell you more about setting up asset accounts for a house, car, or recreational vehicle in Chapter 18.
- **Investment** is for tracking the stocks, bonds, and mutual funds in your investment portfolio. I discuss investment accounts in detail in Chapter 7; you may want to consult that chapter when setting up an investment account.

- **401(k)** is for tracking retirement investments that have special tax advantages, such as 401(k) and 403(b) plans. I also tell you about 401(k) accounts in Chapter 7.

What You Owe   The accounting term for what you owe is *liabilities*. Quicken offers two kinds of accounts for amounts you owe:

- **Credit Card** is for tracking credit card transactions and balances.
- **Liability** is for tracking mortgages or other loans.

Setting Up Accounts

To create a new account, click the Accounts icon at the bottom of the window and choose Create a New Account from its pop-up menu. The Create New Account window appears, as shown here. Use it to select the type of account you want to create.

Select the option button for the type of account you want to create.

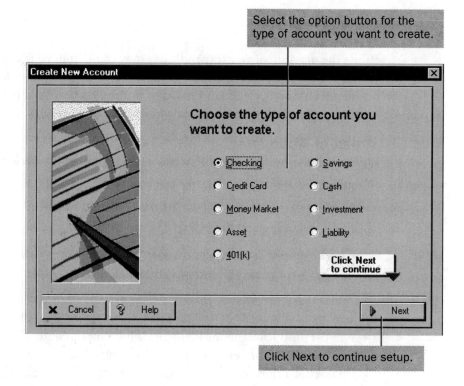

Click Next to continue setup.

The EasyStep tab of the Account Setup window appears next. You have two options for completing the account setup, as you can see in the following illustration:

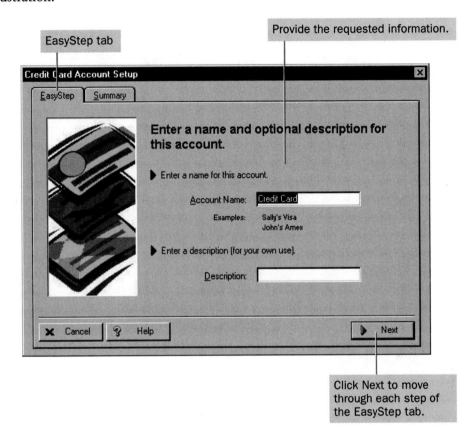

EasyStep tab

Provide the requested information.

Click Next to move through each step of the EasyStep tab.

- Follow the prompts in the EasyStep tab of the Account Setup window to enter information about the account. This works very much like the checking account setup part of Quicken New User Setup.
- Click the Summary tab at the top of the Account Setup window to display all options for the account so you can enter them all at once. The following illustration shows the options under the Summary tab:

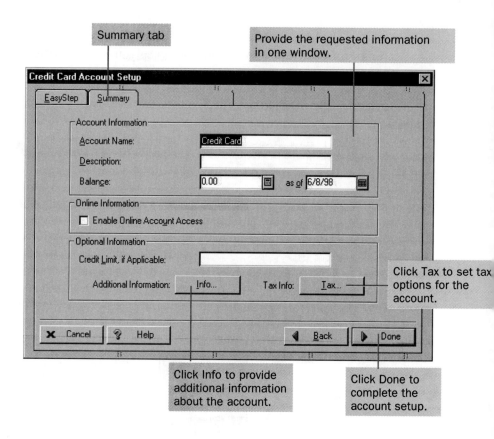

The type of information you're asked to provide varies slightly with the type of account. The following sections describe the kind of information you'll need for most accounts; because Investment and 401(k) accounts are radically different, I discuss them in Chapter 7.

Account Information The account information includes the account name, an optional description, the account balance, and the date of the account balance. Almost every type of Quicken account requires this information. If you don't know the balance of an account, you may set it to $0.00 and make adjustments later, either when you get a statement or reconcile the account.

Online Information Quicken offers two kinds of online privileges for accounts. *Online account access* enables you to download account transactions and balances. This automates transaction entry. *Online payment* enables you to send payment instructions to your bank for paying bills and making other payments. This eliminates the need to write and mail checks. I tell you how to set up and use Quicken's online features in Part III of this book.

Optional Information   In addition to required information, you can also use Quicken to store other information about the account. When you click the Info button in the Summary tab of the Account Setup window, the Additional Account Information window appears:

Enter additional information about the account as desired in each text box.

Additional Account Information

Financial Institution:

Account Number:

Contact:

Phone Number:

Comments:

Interest Rate:

Print Extra Information:

Click OK to return to the Summary tab of the Account Setup window.

OK   Cancel   Help

Tip   By consistently storing this information in Quicken for all your accounts, it's easy to find when you need it.

When you click the Tax button in the Summary tab of the Account Setup window, a Tax Schedule Information window appears. I tell you about it in Chapter 16.

Working with the Account List

You can view a list of your accounts at any time. Choose Lists | Account or press CTRL-A. The Account List appears (see Figure 2-1). For each account, it displays the account name, type, description, number of transactions, balance, and number of checks.

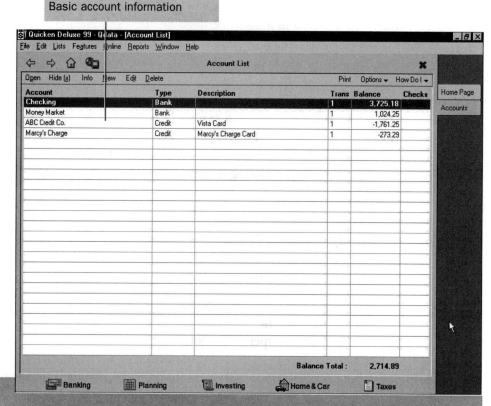

Basic account information

Figure 2-1 • **Use the Account List to view information about and modify accounts.**

The Account List offers a quick and easy way to maintain your accounts. Click an account to select it, and then click one of the buttons on the Button bar to perform a task:

- **Open** opens the register for the account. I tell you about using registers in Chapter 4, too.
- **Hide** removes the account from view so it does not appear in lists and cannot be used in transactions. This is a good way to get an inactive account out of the way without deleting it and its transactions.
- **Info** displays any additional information you may have entered for the account.
- **New** displays the Create New Account window so you can create a new account.

- **Edit** displays the Edit Account window, which looks and works just like the Summary tab of the Account Setup window. You can use this window to edit information about the account.
- **Delete** enables you to delete the account. It displays a dialog box you can use to confirm that you want to delete the account. You must type **yes** into the dialog box and click OK to delete the account.

Caution   When you delete an account, you permanently remove all of its transactions from your Quicken data file. To get the account out of sight without actually deleting it and its data, consider hiding it instead.

Categories

Quicken New User Setup automatically creates dozens of commonly used categories based on your answers to questions. Although these categories might completely meet your needs, there may be times when you'll want to add, remove, or modify a category to fine-tune Quicken for your use.

Types of Categories

There are basically two types of categories: income and expense.

Income   *Income* is incoming money. It includes things such as your salary, commissions, interest income, dividend income, child support, gifts received, and tips.

Expense   An *expense* is outgoing money. It includes things such as insurance, groceries, rent, interest expense, bank fees, finance charges, charitable donations, and clothing.

Subcategories

A *subcategory* is a subset or part of a category. It must be the same type of category as its primary category. For example, the Auto category may be used to track expenses to operate your car. Within that category, however, you may want subcategories to record specific expenses, such as auto insurance, fuel, and repairs. Subcategories make it easy to keep income and expenses organized into manageable categories, while providing the transaction detail you might want or need.

Displaying the Category & Transfer List

You can view a list of your categories at any time. Choose Lists | Category/
Transfer or press CTRL-C. The Category & Transfer List appears (see Figure 2-2).
For each category, it displays the category name, type, description, group, and tax
status. (I tell you about groups, which are used primarily for budgeting, in
Chapter 9.) You can use the Category & Transfer List to create, edit, and delete
categories.

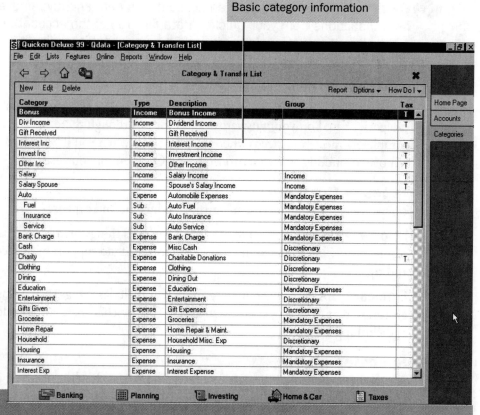

Figure 2-2 • Use the Categories & Transfer List to view and modify categories.

Creating a New Category

To create a new category, start by displaying the Category & Transfer List. Then click the New button on the Button bar. The Set Up Category window appears, as shown next. Enter information about the category into the window and click OK.

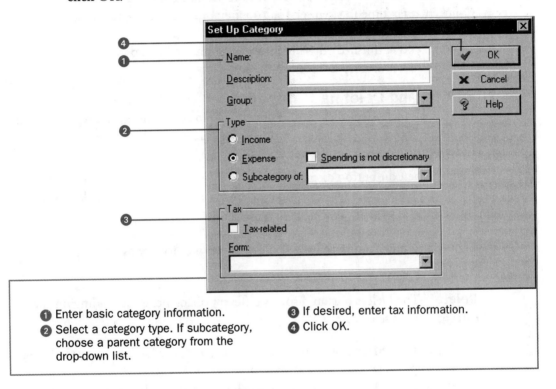

① Enter basic category information.
② Select a category type. If subcategory, choose a parent category from the drop-down list.

③ If desired, enter tax information.
④ Click OK.

Here's a quick summary of the kind of information you should provide for each category:

Category Information   The basic category information includes the category name, which is required, and the description and group, which are optional. Groups are used primarily for budgeting, so I discuss them in Chapter 9. For now, you can either leave the edit box empty or choose an existing group from the drop-down list.

Type   The type information enables you to select the type of category: Income, Expense, or Subcategory. If you select Subcategory, you must choose a category from the drop-down list beside it. If you have complete control over spending for an expense category, you can turn on the "Spending is not discretionary" check box. This option is also used primarily for budgeting.

Tax You can use the tax area options to specify whether a category is tax-related and, if so, what tax form it appears on. I tell you more about using Quicken at tax time in Chapter 16. You are not required to enter anything in this area.

When you're finished entering information in the Set Up Category window, click OK. The category is added to the list.

Editing and Deleting Categories

You can also use the Category & Transfer List to edit or delete a category. Select the name of the category you want to edit or delete, and then click the Edit or Delete button on the Button bar.

Edit The Edit button displays the Edit Category window, which looks and works just like the Set Up Category window. You can use this to make just about any change to a category.

Tip You can "promote" a subcategory to a category by changing its type.

Delete The Delete button displays different dialog boxes depending on the category that is selected:

- If you selected a category with no subcategories, the Delete Category dialog box appears, as shown in Figure 2-3.
- If you selected a category with subcategories, a dialog box tells you that you can't delete a category with subcategories.
- If you selected a subcategory, a dialog box offers to merge the subcategory with its parent category.

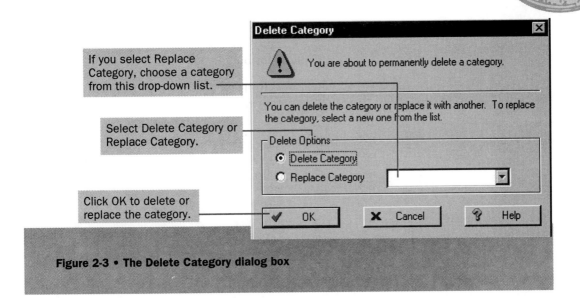

If you select Replace Category, choose a category from this drop-down list.

Select Delete Category or Replace Category.

Click OK to delete or replace the category.

Figure 2-3 • The Delete Category dialog box

Caution   When you delete a category without replacing it with another category, or delete a subcategory without merging it with its parent category, you permanently remove the category or subcategory from all of the transactions that referenced it, resulting in uncategorized transactions.

Online Setup

In This Chapter:

- Benefits of Going Online with Quicken

- What You Need to Connect to the Internet

- Setting Up an Internet Connection

- Testing Your Connection

- Troubleshooting Connection Problems

Chapter 3

49

Many of Quicken's features work seamlessly with the Internet. If you have access to the Internet, either through a direct connection to an Internet Service Provider (ISP) or through a connection to an online service such as America Online or CompuServe, you can take advantage of these online features to get up-to-date information, automate data entry, pay bills, and obtain Quicken maintenance updates automatically.

In this chapter, I tell you why you might want to take advantage of Quicken's online features. Then I explain how to set up Quicken to go online.

What? You don't currently have Internet access? No problem! I tell you what you need to know to sign up with an ISP, too.

Why Go Online?

Before I go any further, I want to remind you that you don't *have* to go online to use Quicken. Quicken is a good financial management software package, even without its online features. But Quicken's online features make it a *great* financial management software package. In this section, I tell you why.

The best way to explain the benefits of going online is to list a few of the features online users can take advantage of.

If You Have a Bank Account, You Can Benefit

Throughout the month, you write checks and mail them to individuals and organizations. You enter these transactions in your checking account register. At month-end, you reconcile the account. You can do all this without going online. I tell you how in Chapter 4.

But if you register for online account access with your bank, you can download all bank account activity on a daily basis so you know exactly when the transactions hit your account—even the ATM and debit card transactions you always forget to enter. If you register for online payment, you can pay your bills without licking another envelope or pasting on another stamp. I explain how all this works in Chapter 12.

Quicken Quote

"I do all of my banking on my PC with Quicken. Quicken's online banking and bill payment is a huge time-saver for me. I never have to go to the bank, almost never order checks, never buy postage stamps, never have to go to the post office, and I don't have to worry about the post office losing my outgoing bills. I can reconcile my account with the paper statement in a three-minute period. Overall, I don't want to ever go back to the old-fashioned way of doing things. Quicken saves me valuable time."

Sean Belger, *El Cajon, CA*

If You Have Credit Cards, You Can Benefit

Do you have credit cards? Then you may take advantage of Quicken's credit-card tracking features, which I cover in Chapter 6, to keep track of your charges, payments, and balances. You don't need to go online.

But if you sign up for online account access, all your credit card charges can be downloaded directly into Quicken, eliminating the need for time-consuming data entry, while giving you an up-to-date summary of your debt. Online account access can even tell you when your bills are due and prepare the transactions for payment. I tell you more about this in Chapter 13.

If You Invest, You Can Benefit

Quicken can keep track of your investments, whether they are 401(k) accounts, mutual funds, or stocks. You can enter share, price, and transaction information into Quicken and it will summarize portfolio value, gains, and losses. It'll even keep track of securities by lot. You don't need to go online to track your investments. I explain how in Chapter 7.

But with online investment tracking, Quicken can automatically obtain quotes on all the securities in your portfolio and update its market value. Depending on your brokerage firm, you may also be able to download transactions, account balances, and holdings. I tell you about all this in Chapter 14.

GET SMARTER   But wait, there's more! You can also get valuable, up-to-date research information and news about securities that interest you. You can "chat" with other investors to see what's hot—and what's not. This helps you make informed investment decisions. You can learn more in Chapter 19.

If You Want to Save Money, You Can Benefit

Car insurance. Mortgages. Car loans. Bank accounts. All of these things have one thing in common: Their rates vary from one provider to another. Shopping for the best deal can be a lot of time-consuming work—wading through newspaper and magazine ads, making calls, visiting banks. Quicken can help you understand the basics of insurance, loans, and banking. Its planners can help you evaluate the deals you learn about, and all without going online.

But with the help of Quicken's built-in Internet links, you can shop for the best deal online, without leaving the comfort of your desk, getting newspaper ink all over your hands, or spending an afternoon listening to music while on hold. Up-to-date rates are only a mouse click away with an Internet connection and Quicken to guide you.

Enough Already!

If all this doesn't convince you that going online with Quicken can help you save time, save money, and get smarter, stop reading and move on to the next chapter. You'll probably never be convinced. I will say one more thing, however: After using Quicken's online features for more than two years now, I can't imagine using Quicken any other way.

Security Features

Perhaps you're already convinced that the online features can benefit you. Maybe you're worried about security, concerned that a stranger will be able to access your accounts or steal your credit card numbers.

You can stop worrying. The folks at Intuit and the participating banks, credit card companies, and brokerage firms have done all the worrying for you. They've come up with a secure system that protects your information and accounts.

PINs

A *PIN*, or *Personal Identification Number*, is a secret password you must use to access your accounts online. If you have an ATM card or cash advance capabilities through your credit card, you probably already have at least one PIN, so the idea shouldn't be new to you. It simply prevents anyone from accessing the account for any reason without first entering the correct PIN.

An account's PIN is initially assigned by the bank, credit card company, or brokerage firm. Some companies, like American Express, require that your PIN consist of a mixture of letters and numbers for additional security. You can change your PINs to make them easier to remember—just don't use something obvious like your birthday or telephone number. And don't write it on a sticky note and attach it to your monitor! If you think someone might have guessed your PIN, you can change it.

Tip   It's a good idea to regularly change all *your PINs and passwords— not just the ones you use in Quicken.*

Encryption

Once you've correctly entered your PIN, the instructions that flow from your computer to the bank, credit card company, or brokerage firm are encrypted. This means they are encoded in such a way that anyone able to "tap in" to the transactions would "hear" only gibberish. Quicken does the encryption using, at a minimum, the 56-bit single Data Encryption Standard (DES). Quicken is also capable of encrypting data with stronger methods, including the 128-bit RC4 or 168-bit triple DES. Once the encrypted information reaches the computer at the bank, credit card company, or brokerage firm, it is unencrypted, and then validated and processed.

Encryption makes it virtually impossible for any unauthorized party to "listen in" to your transaction. It also makes it impossible for someone to alter a transaction between the moment it leaves your computer and the moment it arrives at your bank, credit card company, or brokerage firm for processing.

Other Security Methods

Quicken also takes advantage of other security methods for online communications, including Secure Sockets Layer (SSL) encryption, digital signatures, and digital certificates. Together, all of these security methods make online financial transactions secure—even more secure than telephone banking, which you may already use!

What You Need

To take advantage of Quicken's online features, you need a connection to the Internet. There are different ways to connect and different organizations that can provide the connection. In this section I explain your options.

Tip   If you already have a connection to the Internet or online service, you may already have everything you need. Read on to make sure.

Internet Service Provider (ISP)

An *ISP* is an organization that provides access to the Internet, usually for a monthly fee. These days, there are literally thousands of ISPs that can provide the access you need for Quicken's online features. Here's a partial list:

- America Online (version 3.0 or higher)
- AT&T WorldNet
- CompuServe
- Concentric Network (CNC)
- Earthlink/Sprint

- Erol's Internet
- GTE
- Internet MCI
- Microsoft Network
- Mindspring
- Netcom
- Pac Bell
- Prodigy

If you don't already have an account with an ISP, you must set one up before you can configure Quicken to use its online features. Consult the information that came with your copy of Quicken for special deals on Internet accounts through America Online, Concentric Network, and other Quicken-preferred ISPs.

Internet Connection Methods

You can connect to the Internet in either of two ways: with a direct connection or a dial-up connection.

Direct Connection   A *direct* or *network* connection directly connects your computer to the ISP, usually via a network. This is common in office environments these days, but it is still uncommon for households because it's expensive and can be difficult to set up.

Dial-Up Connection   A *dial-up* or *modem* connection uses a modem to connect to an ISP via a telephone line. The modem dials a telephone number, connects to your ISP's computer, exchanges some ID and protocol information, and connects to the Internet. This is the most common connection method for households because it's inexpensive and easy to set up.

Keep two things in mind if you use a dial-up connection:

- If you have only one phone line, that phone line will be in use while you are accessing Quicken's online features (or any other Internet feature). That means you can't accept incoming calls. And if someone picks up an extension while you're online, there's a good chance you'll be disconnected. If you spend a lot of time online, whether using Quicken or just "surfing the 'net," you might want to consider adding a second line to your house. It's not as expensive as you might think. Just don't let the phone company talk you into a special data phone line for modem connections. You don't need a special line, and you certainly don't need to pay for one.

- If you have call waiting, you must disable it when you connect to the Internet. Otherwise, the call waiting tone that sounds when there's an incoming call can disconnect you. You can automatically disable call waiting by entering specific digits—usually *70—before dialing the phone. If you have call waiting, check with the phone company to see what the codes in your area are.

More About Modems

If you know that modem stands for *mo*dulator/*dem*odulator I'm impressed! But do you need to know that? No. Modem connections are so easy to set up and use that you don't need to know the geeky terminology for the things that make it work.

Anyway, a dial-up connection requires a modem. Here are some things to consider when shopping for a modem:

- If you have a 9,600 bps modem lying around, give it away (if you can find someone to take it). Although it will be fast enough to exchange data for online account access, online payment, and online quotes, you'll fall asleep if you try to use it to view Web pages. A 14.4 Kbps modem is (barely) okay; a 28.8 Kbps modem is better. If you buy a new modem, don't buy anything slower than 33.6 Kbps if you expect it to last more than a few years. These numbers, in case you haven't caught on, refer to speeds; the higher the number the better.
- Modem prices are way down these days—you should be able to get a good 33.6 Kbps or 56 Kbps fax-modem for well under $200. And, yes, I did say fax-modem. That means you can use it to send and receive faxes, too. (It isn't worth buying a modem that can't handle faxes, even if you could find one.)
- Modems can be internal or external. If internal, the modem plugs into a slot on your computer's main circuit board. That means you (or your friendly neighborhood computer guru) must open the computer's case and install it. If external, the modem plugs into your computer's serial port. That means you must have an available serial port.

Modems really are easy to set up. Read the manual that comes with yours. It'll tell you everything you need to know—and more.

Fringe Benefits

One more thought I'd like to share with you here: If you set up an Internet account, you can use it for a wide variety of things—not just Quicken. Use it to exchange e-mail with friends and family members. Use it to search the Internet for information about your hobbies and interests, your next vacation, or the local weather. Shop online. Chat. Download shareware, freeware, or the latest updates to commercial software products.

Heck, if you have it, you may as well use it. Just remember to go outside once in a while.

Setting Up an Internet Connection

To use Quicken's online features, you need to set up Quicken for your Internet connection. You do this with Internet Connection Setup. In this section, I provide step-by-step instructions for setting up a connection.

Getting Started

Choose Online | Internet Connection | Setup. The Internet Connection Setup window appears, as shown here. Select the option that best describes your Internet connection situation.

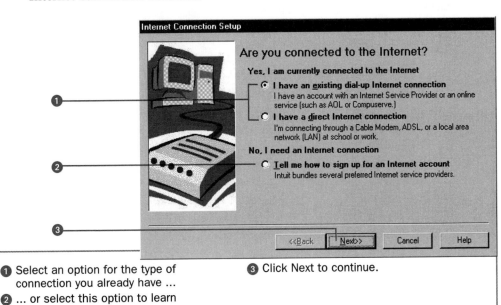

❶ Select an option for the type of connection you already have ...

❷ ... or select this option to learn more about setting up an account with an ISP.

❸ Click Next to continue.

Setting Up an Existing Connection

If you selected the first option in the Internet Connection Setup window, when you click Next, Quicken scans your Windows setup, looking for Internet connection configurations. It lists all of them, in a window like this:

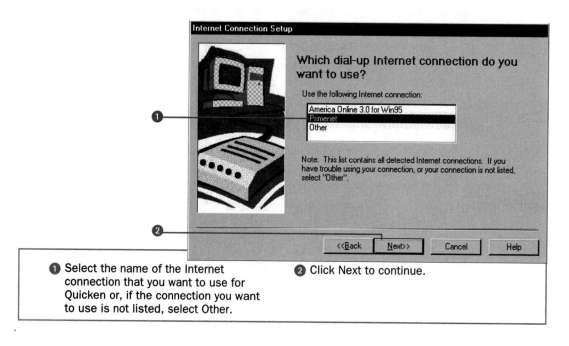

❶ Select the name of the Internet connection that you want to use for Quicken or, if the connection you want to use is not listed, select Other.

❷ Click Next to continue.

If you choose Other, the Internet Connection Setup window displays a message with instructions. It tells you to complete the setup, connect to your ISP in the usual way, and then access the desired Quicken online feature. Be aware that you may have to do this each time you want to use an online feature.

No matter what kind of connection you have, a message with information about the Web browser appears next. It tells you that although you can use any Web browser you like with Quicken, two features—Interactive Billing and What-If Planners—require Microsoft Internet Explorer version 3.0 or later. Because Internet Explorer version 4.0 is installed with Quicken, it's a good idea to select that as the browser for use with Quicken. This will enable you to display

Web pages for Quicken features right within Quicken. You can still use other browsers outside of Quicken.

Tip   If you decide not to use Internet Explorer, Quicken will automatically launch your browser when it needs to display a Web page.

Click Next to display a window with a list of installed browsers. Select the one you want to use with Quicken, and then click Next.

If you have a direct connection to the Internet, a window like the following one appears, prompting you to enter Proxy Server information:

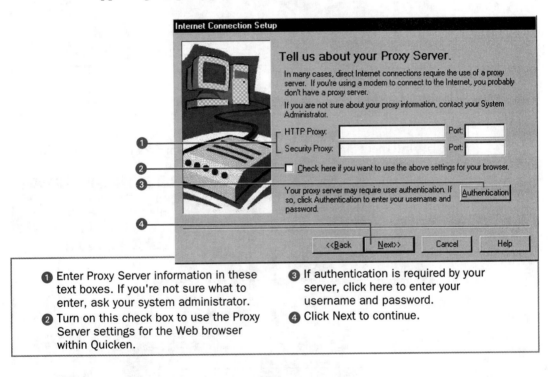

1 Enter Proxy Server information in these text boxes. If you're not sure what to enter, ask your system administrator.

2 Turn on this check box to use the Proxy Server settings for the Web browser within Quicken.

3 If authentication is required by your server, click here to enter your username and password.

4 Click Next to continue.

You have the option of sending diagnostic data to Intuit during your Internet sessions. The data you send—which is completely transparent to you—helps Intuit improve Internet access for its software products. The window that appears explains all this:

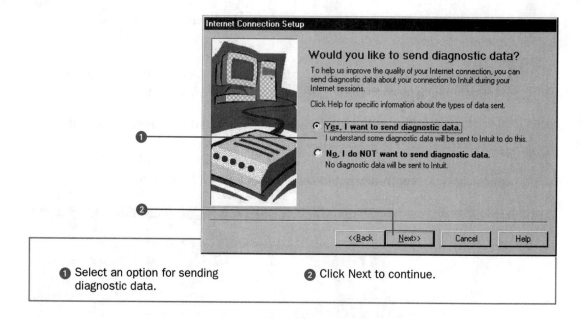

1 Select an option for sending
diagnostic data.

2 Click Next to continue.

The last Internet Connection Setup window summarizes your setup options:

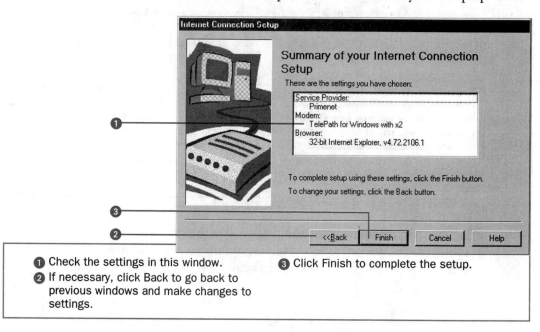

1 Check the settings in this window.

2 If necessary, click Back to go back to
previous windows and make changes to
settings.

3 Click Finish to complete the setup.

The Internet Connection Options dialog box appears next. Use it to set your preferences for the Internet connection. I tell you more about this dialog box in the section titled "Setting Internet Connection Options" below. Skip ahead to that section now.

Tip You can change these options at any time. Just follow the preceding instructions again.

Setting Up a New Internet Account

If you don't already have an Internet account, you'll have to set one up. Your Quicken software package includes information about special deals for Intuit-preferred ISPs. Be sure to check them out.

Of course, you don't have to use any of the ISPs listed with Quicken literature or in this book. You can use any ISP you like. Shop around and find the ISP that best meets your needs. (If you live in a remote area, as I do, you may find only one or two within your local calling area.)

Contact the ISP and set up an account. The ISP should provide all the instructions you need. (If it doesn't, find another ISP—one that can provide technical support when it's needed.) Then, when your computer is set up to access the Internet, return to the Internet Connection Setup window, choose one of the first two options, and follow the instructions appropriate to setting up Quicken for your connection.

Setting Internet Connection Options

At the end of the Internet Connection Setup process, the Internet Connection Options dialog box appears:

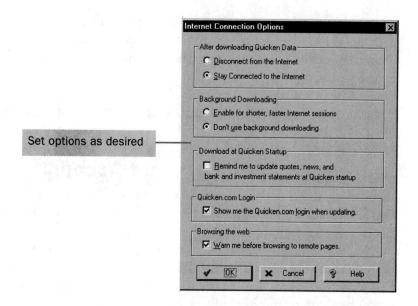

Set options as desired

Tip   You can also open this dialog box to check or change settings by choosing Online | Internet Connection | Options.

Here's a quick rundown of the options in the Internet Connection Options dialog box:

Connection Options   The After downloading Quicken Data section of the dialog box offers two options for your Internet connection once Quicken has finished obtaining the data it needs:

* **Disconnect from the Internet** tells Quicken to sever your Internet connection. You might find this option especially useful if you don't use many online features, or if you have a dial-up connection with only one telephone line that you don't want to tie up.

- **Stay Connected to the Internet** tells Quicken to maintain your Internet connection. You might find this option useful if you use many online features or use Quicken's online features as part of a daily online routine. Because I have a dedicated phone line for my dial-up connection and tend to do all my online work at once—e-mail, Web browsing, and online financial work with Quicken—I use this option. Keep in mind, however, that if you use this option with a dial-up connection, you eventually have to manually disconnect from the Internet to free up your phone line.

Background Downloading Options   The Background Downloading section of the dialog box offers two options to set the way Quicken downloads or retrieves information from the Internet:

- **Enable for shorter, faster Internet sessions** enables the Quicken Download Agent, which will run automatically whenever you start your computer. This feature uses an Internet connection to download information such as program patches, even if Quicken isn't running. Because this feature works in the background, you probably won't even notice it. When the Download Agent is active, however, a Q appears on the far right side of the task bar at the bottom of your screen.

Tip   You can disable the Download Agent for the current session by right-clicking the Q when it appears in the task bar.

- **Don't use background downloading** disables the Quicken Download Agent. This means you will only receive Quicken patches and other information when you specifically request them.

Startup Option   A check box in the Download at Quicken Startup section of the dialog box instructs Quicken to remind you to get updates to all the information you track with online features. When this check box is turned on, each time you start Quicken, it displays a dialog box like the following:

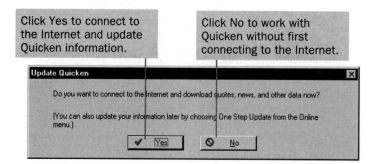

Click Yes to connect to the Internet and update Quicken information.

Click No to work with Quicken without first connecting to the Internet.

Update Quicken

Do you want to connect to the Internet and download quotes, news, and other data now?

(You can also update your information later by choosing One Step Update from the Online menu.)

✔ Yes   🚫 No

Tip   You can quickly update all your Internet information by clicking the One Step Update button at the top of most Quicken windows.

Quicken.com Login Option   The "Show me the Quicken.com login when updating" check box instructs Quicken to display the Quicken.com login screen when you connect to Quicken.com. With this option turned off, Quicken can automatically enter your saved login information if, when you registered with Excite or Quicken.com, you selected the option to save your login information and are connecting with the same computer.

Browsing the Web Option   The "Warn me before browsing to remote pages" check box tells Quicken to display a warning dialog box like the one shown next when you choose a menu command or click a link that displays a Web page on the Internet. You may want to keep this check box turned on if you have a dial-up connection to the Internet and want to be warned before Quicken makes a connection.

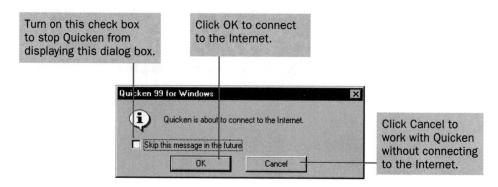

Turn on this check box to stop Quicken from displaying this dialog box.

Click OK to connect to the Internet.

Quicken 99 for Windows

ⓘ   Quicken is about to connect to the Internet.

☐ Skip this message in the future

OK   Cancel

Click Cancel to work with Quicken without connecting to the Internet.

Testing Your Connection

Once you've set up Quicken for an Internet connection, you're ready to test it. Here are two simple tasks to get you started.

Tip   I show you how to set up and connect for online account access and other features in Part III of this book.

Visiting Quicken.com

A good connection test is a visit to Quicken.com, Intuit's feature-packed financial Web site for Quicken users and other visitors. I tell you all about Quicken.com in Chapter 11, but for now, let's just connect to it to make sure your Internet connection works.

Choose Online | Quicken on the Web | Quicken.com. Quicken attempts to connect to the Internet using the ISP you selected in the Internet Connection Setup window.

What you see during the connection process will vary depending on your ISP. If you use an online service such as America Online, CompuServe, or Prodigy, the service's access software may start automatically to make the connection. You may be prompted to enter a username or password. Other windows may appear. It may be necessary to switch from connection software back to Quicken by clicking the Quicken button on the Windows task bar.

When the connection is complete, Quicken requests the Quicken.com home page. It appears in an Internet window (see Figure 3-1).

Tip   If you were already connected to the Internet when you accessed one of Quicken's online features, you won't see the connection happening. Instead, the Quicken.com page will simply appear in the Internet window.

Disconnecting from the Internet

To manually disconnect from the Internet when you are finished using Quicken's online features, choose Online | Disconnect. One of two things will happen:

- If you are connected via an online service such as America Online, CompuServe, or Prodigy, Quicken may tell you that it cannot disconnect from the Internet. Switch to the online service's access software by clicking its name in the task bar, and then use that software to disconnect from the Internet.

- If you are connected via another ISP, Quicken may display a dialog box offering to disconnect from the Internet. Click Yes to disconnect.

Tip Once you have successfully completed the Internet connection setup process, Quicken reminds you to disconnect from the Internet each time you exit the program. The dialog box that appears even offers to disconnect for you.

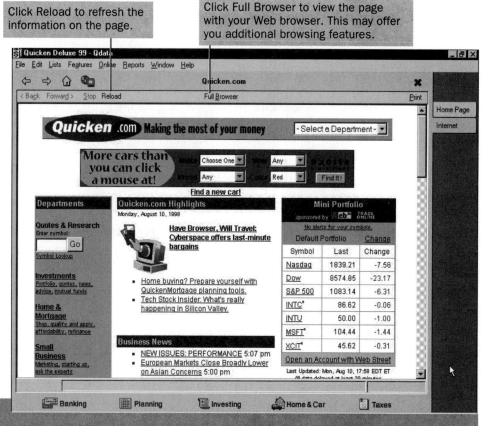

Figure 3-1 • The Quicken.com home page. This page changes daily to offer new information and features.

Troubleshooting

If you follow the instructions I provided throughout the chapter, you shouldn't have any trouble connecting to the Internet with Quicken. But things aren't always as easy as they should be. Sometimes even the tiniest problems can prevent you from successfully connecting and exchanging data.

In this section, I provide some troubleshooting advice to help you with connection problems you may experience. Check this section before you start pulling out your hair and cursing the day computers were invented.

Setup Problems

To determine whether the problem is a Quicken setup problem or a general Internet setup problem, exit Quicken and try connecting to the Internet from another program, such as your regular Web browser or e-mail program.

- If you can connect to the Internet from another program but not from Quicken, the problem may be with Quicken's Internet connection setup. Go back to the section titled "Setting Up an Internet Connection" earlier in this chapter and repeat the setup process.
- If you can't connect to the Internet from any other program or with Dial-up Networking (for dial-up connections), the problem is with your Internet setup for Windows, your modem (for dial-up connections), or your network (for direct connections). You must fix any problem you find before you can successfully set up and connect with Quicken.

Modem Problems

Problems with a dial-up connection may be related to your modem. Try each of the following, attempting a connection after each one.

- Check all cables between your computer and your modem (if you have an external modem), and between your modem and the telephone outlet.
- Check the telephone line to make sure it has a dial tone and that it is not being used by someone else or another program.
- Turn off your modem, and then turn it back on. Or, if you have an internal modem, restart your computer. This resets the modem and may resolve the problem.

If you can connect but have trouble staying connected, try the following:

- Make sure no one is picking up an extension of the phone line while you are online.
- Make sure call waiting is disabled by entering the appropriate codes for the dial-up connection.
- Have the phone company check the line for noise. If noise is detected, ask the phone company to fix the problem. (It shouldn't cost you anything if the line noise is the result of a problem outside your premises.)

Network Problems

Problems with a direct connection may be related to your network. Try these things, attempting a connection after each one:

- Check all cables between your computer and the network hub or router.
- Check to make sure the correct Proxy Server information was entered into Quicken's Internet Connection Setup window, which I discuss earlier in this chapter.
- Restart your computer. Sometimes resetting your computer's system software can clear network problems.
- Ask your system administrator to check your network setup.

ISP Problems

Intuit has identified some problems with specific ISPs and has developed workarounds so you can successfully connect with Quicken. Following is a brief list, by ISP.

Tip   You can get up-to-date information about known ISP problems by using the Help Index to open the Internet Troubleshooting topic. I tell you how to use Online Help in Chapter 1.

All ISPs

If you don't save your username and password information for your ISP in its connection or dial-up software, you may be prompted to enter it when you access an Internet feature. This could cause Quicken to cancel your request for access to an online feature. If this happens, when you have successfully connected to the Internet, simply switch back to Quicken and re-access the online feature.

America Online
Make sure you have the 32-bit version of America Online 3.0 (or later) software installed on your computer. You can obtain this software for free from America Online.

CompuServe
Make sure you have CompuServe version 3.01 (or later) software and the Dial-up Scripting Tools installed. (Quicken's Internet Connection Setup process should prompt you to install the tools if they are required.) If you want to use CompuServe's Spry Mosaic Web browser within Quicken, make sure Spry Mosaic version 4.0 (or later) is installed.

Microsoft Network
If you're a Microsoft Network user, its sign-on dialog box may appear when you attempt to connect to the Internet from within Quicken, even if you did not select it for your Internet connection. To fix this, open Microsoft Network and select the Connect using other dial-up Internet access provider option in its Settings dialog box.

Netcom
Netcom's Netcruiser browser is incompatible with Quicken 99 so it doesn't appear in the Internet Connection Setup window as a browser option. Use Internet Explorer instead.

When connecting via Netcom, you may be prompted to enter your username and password in a dialog box. The username in the dialog box begins with #. Be sure to leave this required character in the dialog box when entering your username and password.

If you get an invalid phone number when attempting to connect via Netcom, you must copy the correct phone number from the Netcom application to the Netcom Dial-up Connection Properties. Locate the correct phone number in the Netcom application. Double-click My Computer on your desktop, and then double-click Dial-up Networking. Right-click Netcom and enter the correct phone number.

Organizing Your Finances

This part of the book explains how to use Quicken to organize your finances—manage your checkbook, track credit cards and investments, generate reports and graphs, create budgets and forecasts, and record information in case of emergency. It has seven chapters:

Part Two

Paying Bills and Managing Your Checkbook

Chapter 4

In *This* Chapter:

- *Writing Checks*

- *Entering Payments and Other Transactions*

- *Transferring Money*

- *Using QuickEntry*

- *Using Splits and Classes*

- *Working with Existing Transactions*

- *Reconciling Accounts*

- *Setting Up and Printing Checks*

- *Setting Check and Register Options*

73

At Quicken's core is its ability to manage your bank accounts. This is probably Quicken's most-used feature. You enter the transactions and Quicken keeps track of account balances and the source and destination of the money you spend. Quicken includes a number of features to automate transaction entries and to remind you when payments must be made. It can also do all the math when it comes time to balance or reconcile accounts. If desired, you can even have Quicken print checks for you.

Tip   Quicken's Online Account Access and Online Payment features can save you time and money. Once you understand the basics of entering transactions as discussed in this chapter, be sure to consult Chapter 12 to see how Quicken's online features can make transaction entry easier.

Recording Transactions

Generally speaking, transactions can be broken down into two broad categories: payments and deposits.

Payments   *Payments* are cash outflows.

- You write a check to pay your electric bill.
- You withdraw money from your savings account to buy a gift for your mother.
- You use your ATM card to withdraw spending money from a bank account.
- You use your debit card to buy groceries.
- You pay a monthly checking account fee.

Tip   Quicken's Online Payment feature enables you to send a check to anyone, without actually writing or mailing the check. I tell you about this feature in Chapter 12.

Deposits   *Deposits* are cash inflows.
- You deposit your paycheck in your checking account.
- You sell your old computer and deposit the proceeds in your savings account.
- Your paycheck or social security check is deposited into your bank account as a direct deposit.
- You earn interest on your savings account.

To make the most of Quicken, you must be willing to spend a little time entering transactions like these for the account(s) you want to track. There are different ways to enter transactions, based on the type of transaction you want to enter:

- Use the *Write Checks window* to record and print checks.
- Use *registers* to record payments or deposits for any bank account.
- Enter *transfers* to transfer money from one account to another.
- Use *QuickEntry* to enter transactions without opening Quicken.

In this section, I cover all of these techniques.

Writing Checks

Quicken's Write Checks window uses a basic check-like interface to record checks. You enter in the window the same information that you would write on an actual check. You then tell Quicken to print the check based on the information you entered.

Tip   To use this feature, you must order compatible check stock from Intuit or another check printer. I tell you how and explain how to print checks near the end of this chapter.

Using the Write Checks Window

To begin, choose Features | Bills | Write Checks, or press CTRL-W. The Write Checks window appears, as shown next. Use it to enter the necessary information for a check and record the transaction.

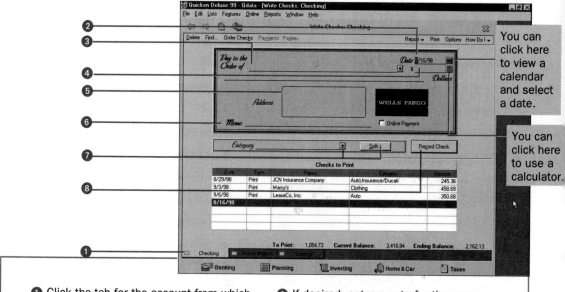

You can click here to view a calendar and select a date.

You can click here to use a calculator.

① Click the tab for the account from which you want to write the check.

② Enter the date that you want to appear on the check.

③ Enter the payee name or select one from the drop-down list.

④ Enter the amount of the check.

⑤ If desired, enter the payee address.

⑥ If desired, enter a note for the memo line of the check.

⑦ Select a category or subcategory from the drop-down list, or click Split to enter more than one category for the transaction.

⑧ Click Record Check to add the check to the Checks to Print list.

Write Checks Window Tips

Keep a few things in mind when using the Write Checks window:

- You can press the TAB key to move from one text box to another.
- If you enter the name of a payee that is already in Quicken's data file, Quicken may fill in the entire payee name and most recent transaction for you. This is Quicken's QuickFill feature, which I tell you about in Chapter 5.
- If you enter an address on the check, you can mail the check using a window envelope. The address is automatically added to the Quicken Financial Address Book, which I tell you about in Chapter 10.
- To enter more than one category for a check, click the Split button. I tell you about splits later in this chapter.
- If you enter a note on the memo line of a check, it might be visible if you mail the check in a window envelope.

- The Online Payment check box only appears if online payment is enabled for the account for which you are writing a check. I tell you about online payments in Chapter 12.

Entering Manual Checks, Other Payments, and Deposits

If you prefer to write checks manually or need to enter other payments or deposits, you can use Quicken's registers. As the name suggests, these electronic registers are very similar to the paper checking-account register that comes with your checks.

Using the Register

To open your register, choose Features | Banking | Use Register, or press CTRL-R. The account register window appears, as shown here. Use it to enter and record transactions.

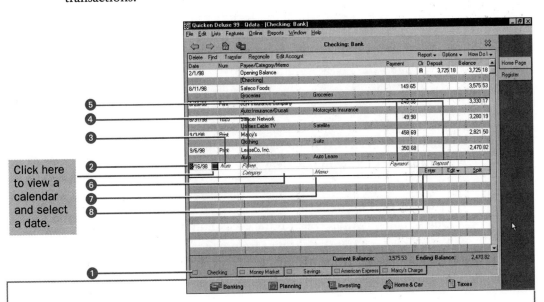

Click here to view a calendar and select a date.

❶ Click the tab for the account for which you want to enter the transaction.

❷ Enter the date of the transaction.

❸ Enter or choose a transaction number or Num code.

❹ Enter the name of the payee (for a payment) or payer (for a deposit).

❺ Enter the payment or deposit amount.

❻ Select a category or subcategory from the drop-down list, or click Split to enter multiple categories for the transaction.

❼ If desired, enter a note for the transaction.

❽ Click Enter to record the transaction.

Register Tips

Here are a few things to remember when using the register window:

- You can press the TAB key to move from one text box to the next.
- If you enter the name of a payee or payer that is already in Quicken's data file, Quicken may fill in the entire name and most recent transaction for you. This is Quicken's QuickFill feature, which I tell you about in Chapter 5.
- To enter more than one category for a transaction, click the Split button. I tell you about splits a little later in this chapter.
- When the Payment or Deposit text box is active, a calculator icon appears. You can click it to use a calculator.

About the Num Field

The Num field is where you enter a transaction number. You can enter any number you like or use the drop-down list to display a list of standard entries:

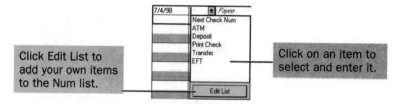

- **Next Check Num** automatically increments the most recently entered check number and enters the resulting number in the Num field.
- **ATM** is for ATM withdrawals.
- **Deposit** is for deposits.
- **Print Check** is for transactions for which you want Quicken to print a check. Quicken automatically records the check number when the check is printed.
- **Transfer** is for a transfer of funds from one account to another.
- **EFT**, which stands for Electronic Funds Transfer, is for direct deposits and similar transactions.

Tip You can press the + or − key on the keyboard to increment or decrement the check number while the Num field is active.

Transferring Money

You can also record the transfer of funds from one account to another. This feature makes it easy to record telephone transfers offered by many banks.

SAVE TIME Online account access enables you to transfer money from one account to another by simply entering the transaction. There's no need to call or visit your bank or submit any paper forms.

Using the Transfer Dialog Box

Click the Transfer button on the Button bar in the account register window. The Transfer dialog box appears:

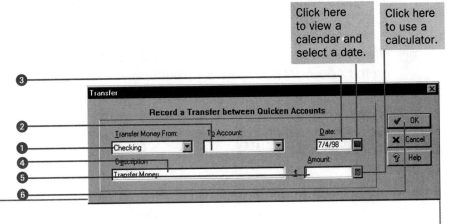

Click here to view a calendar and select a date.

Click here to use a calculator.

❶ Choose the account from which you want money moved (the source account).

❷ Choose the account into which you want money moved (the destination account).

❸ Enter the transaction date.

❹ Enter a description for the transaction.

❺ Enter the amount of the transfer.

❻ Click OK to record the transaction.

Transfer Tips

Here are a few tips for using the Transfer dialog box and making transfers:

- You can press the Tab key to move from one text box to the next.
- You can also record a transfer in the account register window of either the source or destination account. Simply choose the other transfer account from the Categories drop-down list:
- When you select Transfer (TXFR) from the Num drop-down list, accounts appear in the Categories drop-down list.

Using QuickEntry

Quicken Deluxe users can also enter transactions with *QuickEntry*. This program, which works just like the account register feature of Quicken, makes it possible to enter transaction information without opening Quicken. Then, the next time you open Quicken, you can review and either accept or reject the QuickEntry transactions.

Tip   You might find QuickEntry useful if both you and your spouse want to track payments and deposits, but only you know how to use Quicken. This prevents your spouse from accidentally changing the financial records, while enabling him or her to help you enter transactions.

Opening QuickEntry

To use QuickEntry, open it by double-clicking its icon on the desktop or choosing it from the Quicken submenu in the Programs folder on the Windows task bar. As shown next, QuickEntry looks just like Quicken's account register. It works the same way, too.

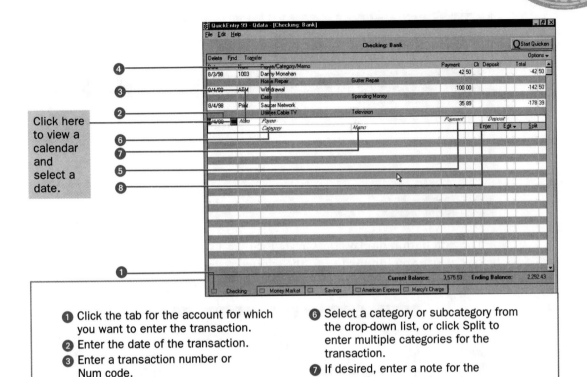

Click here to view a calendar and select a date.

1. Click the tab for the account for which you want to enter the transaction.
2. Enter the date of the transaction.
3. Enter a transaction number or Num code.
4. Enter the name of the payee (for a payment) or payer (for a deposit).
5. Enter the payment or deposit amount.

6. Select a category or subcategory from the drop-down list, or click Split to enter multiple categories for the transaction.
7. If desired, enter a note for the transaction.
8. Click Enter to record the transaction.

When you're finished entering information in QuickEntry, choose File | Exit. The transactions you entered are automatically saved for review the next time you use Quicken.

Reviewing QuickEntry Transactions

After using QuickEntry to enter one or more transactions, the next time you open Quicken, the Transaction Entry list automatically appears in the Accept Transactions window, shown next.

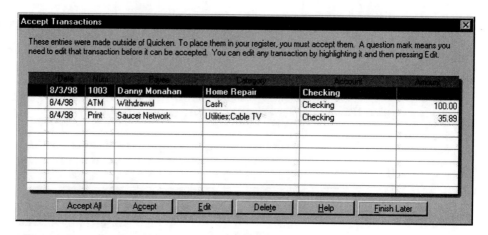

The Edit button displays the Create Register Transaction dialog box (shown below), which you can use to edit the selected transaction. The fields in this dialog box are the same as those used in QuickEntry and the account register.

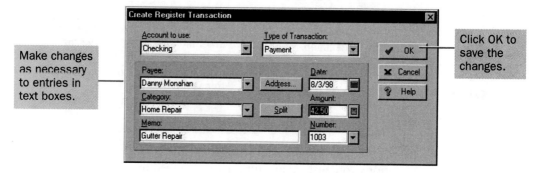

If you click Finish Later in the Accept Transactions Window, you can view the Transaction List again by choosing Features | Banking | Accept Transactions.

Using Splits and Classes

You can fine-tune your classification of payments or deposits by using *splits* and *classes*.

Splits

A split is a transaction with more than one category. For example, suppose you pay one utility bill for two categories of utilities—electric and water. If you want to track each of these two expenses separately, you can use a split to record each category's portion of the payment you make. This enables you to keep good records without writing multiple checks to the same payee.

To record a transaction with a split, click the Split button in the Write Checks window, the account register window, the QuickEntry window, or the Create Register Transaction dialog box. The Split Transaction Window appears, as shown here. It enables you to enter as many categories as you like.

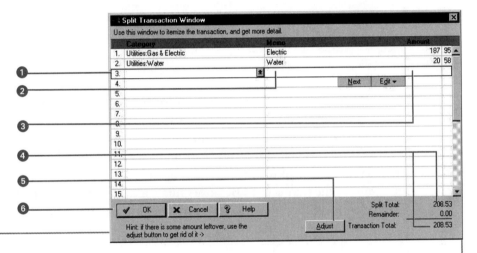

❶ Use the drop-down list to enter each category.

❷ If desired, enter a memo for each category entered.

❸ Enter the amount of the transaction to be assigned to each category.

❹ Check to be sure the Split Total is the same as the Transaction Total.

❺ If necessary, click Adjust to adjust the Transaction Total to match the Split Total.

❻ Click OK to save the split information.

When you complete the split, the word *Split* appears in the Category field of the transaction. Here's what it looks like in the account register window:

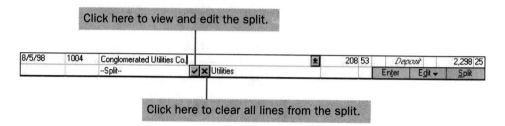

Click here to view and edit the split.

Click here to clear all lines from the split.

Caution Clearing all lines from a split permanently removes them.

Classes

A *class* is an optional identifier for specifying what a transaction applies to. For example, if you have two cars for which you track expenses, you can create a class for each car—for example, *Ford* and *Toyota*. Then, when you record a transaction for one of the cars, you can include the appropriate class with the category for the transaction. Because Quicken can produce reports based on categories, classes, or both, classes offer an additional dimension for tracking and reporting information.

Displaying the Class List

Quicken maintains a list of all the classes you create. You can display it by choosing Lists I Class, or by pressing CTRL-L. The next illustration shows an example with some classes I created. The list shows the class name and description. You can use the Class List to create, edit, and delete classes.

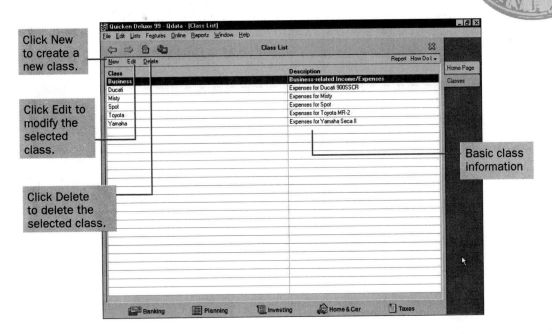

Click New to create a new class.

Click Edit to modify the selected class.

Click Delete to delete the selected class.

Basic class information

Creating a New Class

To create a class, display the Class List, and then click the New button on the button bar. The Set Up Class dialog box appears. Use it to enter information about the class:

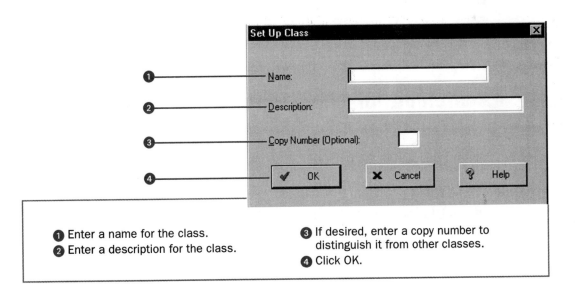

① Enter a name for the class.
② Enter a description for the class.

③ If desired, enter a copy number to distinguish it from other classes.
④ Click OK.

Only one piece of information is really necessary: the class name. You may want to make it short so it's easy to remember and enter. The description can be used to provide additional information on what the class is used for. The *copy number* enables you to associate different classes with different but similar activities. For example, if you have two separate businesses for which you report activity on two Schedule Cs, you can assign Copy 1 to one business's classes and Copy 2 to the other business's classes.

Including a Class in a Transaction

To include a class in a transaction, enter a slash (/) followed by the class name after the category. Here's an example in the register window:

| 8/5/98 | 1005 | Auto Repair Co, Inc. | | | 40 | 00 | *Deposit* | 2,258 | 25 |
| | | Auto:Service/Toyota | Oil Change | | | | Enter | Edit ▾ | Split |

Enter a slash and the class name after the category.

Tip If you enter a class name that is not on the Class List, Quicken displays the Set Up Class window so you can create the class on the fly.

Working with Existing Transactions

So far, this chapter has concentrated on entering transactions. What do you do when you need to modify a transaction you already recorded? That's what this section is all about.

Searching for Transactions

Quicken includes three primary commands to help you locate and work with transactions:

- **Find** enables you to search for transactions in the active account based on any field.
- **Find/Replace** enables you to find transactions based on any field and replace any field of the found transactions.

- **Recategorize** enables you to find transactions for a specify category and replace the category.

The following sections take a closer look at each of these commands.

Using the Find Command

To use the Find command, begin by clicking the tab for the account that you want to search in either the Write Checks window or the account register window. Then choose Edit | Find & Replace | Find, or click the Find button in the window, or press CTRL-F. The Quicken Find dialog box appears. Use it to search for transactions that match the criteria you enter. To use the Find dialog box: choose a Search field, enter search criteria, and choose a search condition. Click Find to find the first match, or click Find All to find all matches.

After setting up the search, if you click the Find button, Quicken selects the first match found in the window. You can then click the Find button again to find the next match. If you click the Find All button, Quicken displays the Quicken Find window, which lists all the matches it found.

Tip Quicken remembers a Find setup throughout the Quicken session. Later, to conduct the same search, you can choose Edit | Find & Replace | Find Next, or press SHIFT-CTRL-F.

Using the Find/Replace Command

The Find/Replace command works throughout Quicken—not just with the Write Checks or account register window active. To use it, choose Edit | Find & Replace | Find/Replace. The Find and Replace dialog box appears. The top part of the dialog box looks and works very much just like the Quicken Find dialog box. Once you set up the search and click the Find All button, a list of matches appears in the bottom half of the dialog box, as shown next. You can then enter replacement options.

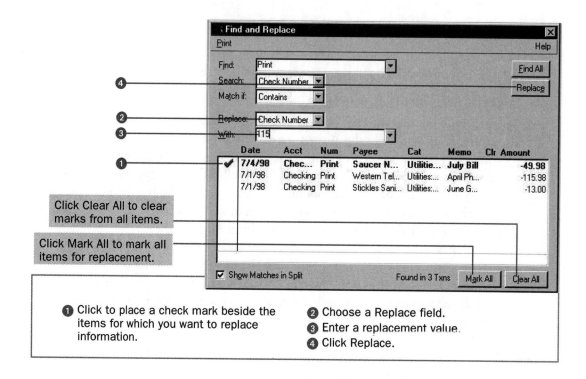

Click Clear All to clear marks from all items.

Click Mark All to mark all items for replacement.

❶ Click to place a check mark beside the items for which you want to replace information.

❷ Choose a Replace field.
❸ Enter a replacement value.
❹ Click Replace.

Using the Recategorize Command

The Recategorize command works like the Find/Replace command, but it finds and replaces only categories. For example, suppose you were using the Misc category a little more often than you should, and you know that some transactions could be recategorized. You can use the Recategorize command to find transactions with the Misc category, and then change some or all of them to a more appropriate category.

Choose Edit | Find & Replace | Recategorize to display the Recategorize dialog box. Choose a category from the Search Category drop-down list. Then click Find All to display a list of matches:

Use the Find menu to choose the type of transactions you want to search for.

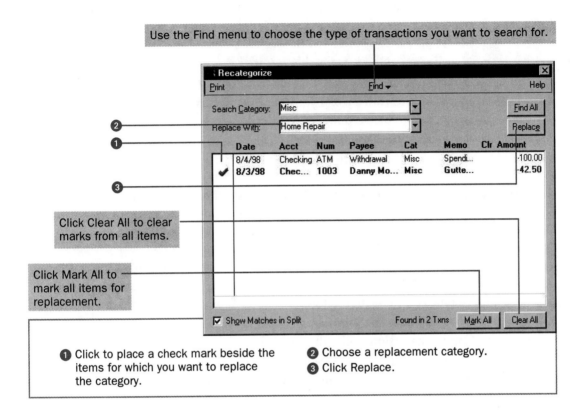

Click Clear All to clear marks from all items.

Click Mark All to mark all items for replacement.

❶ Click to place a check mark beside the items for which you want to replace the category.

❷ Choose a replacement category.
❸ Click Replace.

Changing Transactions

In my opinion, one of Quicken's best features is the ability to change a transaction at any time—even after it has been cleared. Believe it or not, some other financial management programs won't let you do this!

If all you want to do is change one of the fields in the transaction—such as the category, date, or number—simply find the transaction in the appropriate account register, make changes as desired, and click the Enter button to record them.

The Edit drop-down menu that appears in the account register window offers other options for working with a selected transaction:

- **Restore Transaction** enables you to change a transaction back to the way it was before you started changing it. This option is only available if you have made changes to the selected transaction.
- **New Transaction** enables you to create a new transaction for the account. (It does not affect the currently selected account.)
- **Insert Transaction** enables you to insert a transaction before the selected transaction in the account register.
- **Delete Transaction** deletes the selected transaction. This is the same as clicking the Delete button in the Button bar.

Caution   Deleting a transaction removes the transaction from the Quicken data file, thus changing the account balance and category activity.

- **Void Transaction** marks the selected transaction as void. This reverses the effect of the transaction on the account balance and category activity without actually deleting the transaction.
- **Memorize Transaction** tells Quicken to add the selected transaction to its list of memorized transactions.
- **Copy Transaction** copies the selected transaction.
- **Paste Transaction** pastes the last-copied transaction into the current account register. This option is only available after a transaction has been copied.

Tip   You might want to copy a transaction to paste it into another register if you realize that you entered it in the wrong register. You can then go back and delete the original transaction.

- **Go to Transfer** displays the selected transaction in the account register for the other part of a transfer. For example, if the selected transaction involves the checking and savings accounts and you are viewing it in the checking account register, choosing the Go to Transfer command displays the same transaction in the savings account register. This command is only available if the selected transaction includes a transfer.
- **Go to a Specific Date** enables you to move to a different date within the register. This does not affect the selected transaction.

Reconciling Accounts

One of the least pleasant tasks of manually maintaining a bank account is balancing or reconciling it monthly. If you're good about it, you faithfully turn over your bank statement each month and use the form your bank provides to balance the account. There's a lot of adding when it comes to totaling the outstanding checks and deposits, and the longer you wait to do the job, the more adding there is. And for some reason, it hardly ever comes out right the first time you try. Maybe you've even failed so many times that you've given up. I know someone who opens a new checking account once a year just so she can start fresh after twelve months of not being able to balance her account. That's *not* something I recommend.

Reconciling your checking account is very important. It enables you to locate differences between what you think you have in the account and what the bank says you have. It can help you track down bank errors (which do happen once in a while) or personal errors (which, unfortunately, seem to happen more frequently). Completely balancing your checking account and making adjustments as necessary can prevent you from accidentally bouncing checks when you think you have more money than you really do. That can save you the cost of bank fees and a lot of embarrassment.

If you keep track of all bank account activity with Quicken, reconciling your bank accounts is easy. You don't need to use the form on the back of the bank statement. You don't even need a calculator. Just use Quicken's reconciliation feature to enter beginning and ending bank balances, check off cleared transactions, and enter the transactions you missed. You'll find you're successful a lot more often with Quicken helping you out.

Getting Started

To reconcile a bank account, you must have the bank statement for the account. Bank statements usually come monthly, so you won't have to wait long.

With statement in hand, open the account register for the account you want to reconcile. Then click the Reconcile button in the Button bar. The Reconcile Bank Statement dialog box, which gathers basic statement information prior to reconciling the account, appears:

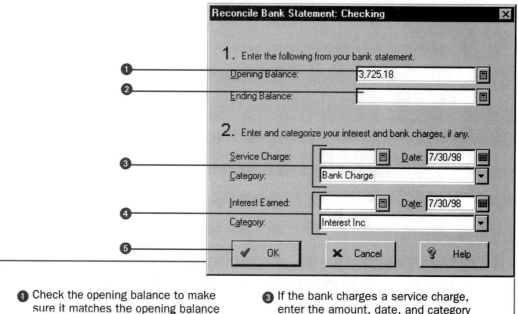

❶ Check the opening balance to make sure it matches the opening balance on your bank statement. If it doesn't, make changes as necessary.

❷ Enter the ending balance from the bank statement.

❸ If the bank charges a service charge, enter the amount, date, and category for the charge.

❹ If the account earned interest, enter the amount, date, and category for the interest.

❺ Click OK.

Comparing Transactions

The next step to reconciling the account is to compare transactions that have cleared on the bank statement with transactions in your account register. For this, Quicken displays the Reconcile Bank Statement window (shown next), which displays all payments, checks, and deposits. Your job is to check off the items that appear on your bank statement.

Click Statement to view or modify statement
information already entered.

Click to place a
check mark in the
Clr column for
items that appear
on your bank
statement.

When the
difference is
0.00, you have
successfully
balanced your
bank account.

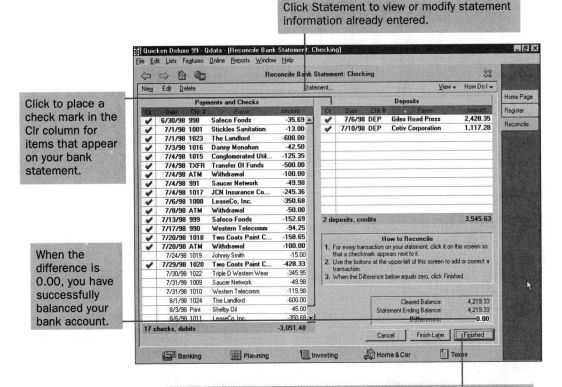

Click Finished to complete the reconciliation, or click Finish Later to
save your changes without completing the reconciliation.

While you're checking off items in the Reconcile Bank Statement window, be
sure to check off the same items with a pen on your bank statement. Any items
that appear on the bank statement but not in your account register are items that
you failed to enter. After checking off the items that do appear in your account
register, you have to add the items that don't. Switch to the appropriate account
register window to enter them. After entering these items, you can switch back to
the Reconcile Bank Statement window and check them off.

Finishing Up

When you reconcile a bank account with Quicken, your goal is to make the difference between the Cleared Balance and the Statement Ending Balance zero. You can monitor this progress at the bottom of the Reconcile Bank Statement window.

When the Difference Is Zero...

If you correctly checked off all bank statement items and the difference is zero, you've successfully reconciled the account. Congratulations. Click the Finish button.

If You Can't Get the Difference to Zero...

Sometimes, try as you might, you just can't get the difference to zero. Here are a few last things to check before you give up:

- Make sure all the amounts you checked off in your account register are the same as the amounts on the bank statement.
- Make sure you included any bank charges or earned interest.
- Make sure the beginning and ending balances you entered are the same as those on the bank statement.

If you checked and rechecked all these things and still can't get the difference to zero, click Finished. Quicken displays a dialog box that indicates the amount of the difference and offers to make an adjustment to your account register for the amount. Click Adjust to accept the adjustment. The amount of the adjustment will be applied to the Misc category.

But next month, don't give up!

Printing a Reconciliation Report

At the end of a reconciliation, Quicken displays a dialog box that offers to create a reconciliation report. If you click Yes, another dialog box enables you to set options for the report. Click Print to print the report.

Tip You may want to file the report with your bank statement and canceled checks.

Printing Checks

Quicken's ability to print checks enables you to create accurate, legible, professional-looking checks without picking up a pen. In this section, I tell you how to print the checks you enter in the Write Checks window that I discuss earlier in this chapter.

Getting the Right Checks

Before you can print checks from Quicken, you must obtain compatible check stock. Intuit offers checks in a number of different styles:

- **Voucher** checks pair each check with a similarly sized voucher form. When you print on a voucher check, the transaction category information, including splits and classes, can be printed on the voucher part.
- **Wallet** checks pair each check with a stub. When you print on a wallet check, the transaction information is printed on the stub.
- **Standard** checks print just checks. There's no voucher or stub.

In addition to these styles, you can get the checks in two different formats for your printer:

- **Sheet-fed** or **page-oriented** checks are for laser and inkjet printers.
- **Continuous** checks are for pin feed printers.

A catalog and order form for checks came with your copy of Quicken. You can use it to order checks. If you have an Internet connection, you can order checks online from within Quicken by choosing Features | Billing | Order Checks, or by clicking the Order Checks button in the Write Checks window.

Setting Up

Quicken must also be set up to print the kind of checks you purchased. You do this once and Quicken remembers the settings.

Choose File | Printer Setup | For Printing Checks to display the Check Printer Setup dialog box, shown here. Use it to set options for the check stock and your printer.

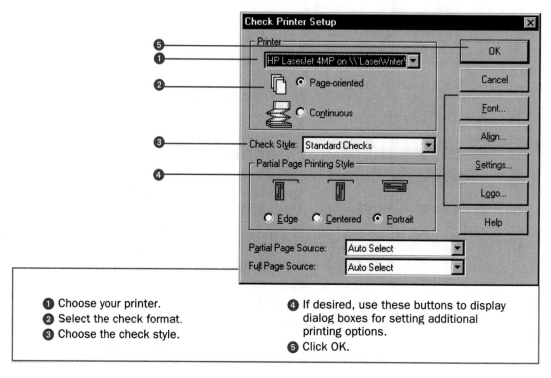

1 Choose your printer.
2 Select the check format.
3 Choose the check style.

4 If desired, use these buttons to display dialog boxes for setting additional printing options.
5 Click OK.

Partial Page Printing Options

If you select the Page-oriented option and either Standard or Wallet checks in the Check Printer Setup dialog box, you can also set options for Partial Page Printing Style. This enables you to set up the printer for situations when you're not printing an entire page of checks.

- **Edge** is for inserting the page against one side of the feeder. The left or right edge of the checks enter the feeder first.
- **Centered** is for centering the page in the feeder. The left or right edge of the checks enter the feeder first.
- **Portrait** is also for centering the page in the feeder. But in this case, the top edge of each check enters the feeder first.

If your printer supports multiple feed trays, you can also set the source tray for partial and full pages by choosing options from the Partial Page Source and Full Page Source drop-down lists.

Continuous Printing Options

If you select the Continuous option and either Standard or Wallet checks in the Check Printer Setup dialog box, the dialog box changes to offer two Continuous options:

- **Bypass the driver** should be turned on for a continuous printer that skips checks or prints nothing.
- **Use low starting position** should be turned on for a continuous printer that cuts the date or logo off your checks.

Checking the Settings for Page-Oriented Checks

If you're using Page-oriented checks, you can check your settings by printing a sample page. Here's how:

1. Click the Align button in the Check Printer Setup dialog box.
2. In the Align Checks dialog box that appears, click the Full Page of Checks button.
3. In the Fine Alignment dialog box, click the Print Sample button.
4. When the sample emerges from your printer, hold it up to the light with a sheet of check stock behind it. The sample should line up with the check.
5. If the sample does not line up properly with the check stock, set Vertical and/or Horizontal adjustment values in the Fine Alignment dialog box. Then repeat Steps 3 through 5 until the alignment is correct.
6. Click OK in each dialog box to accept your settings and close it.

Printing Checks

Once setup is complete, you're ready to print checks. Insert the check stock in your printer. Then choose File | Print Checks, or click the Print button in the Write Checks window. The Select Checks to Print dialog box appears, as shown next. Use it to set printing options and print checks.

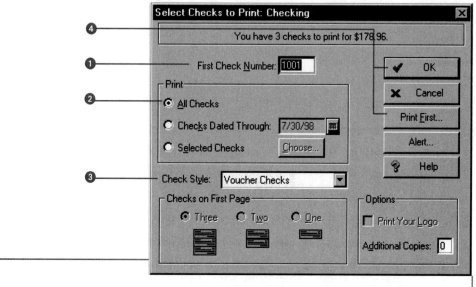

① Enter the first check number.
② Select the Print option to determine which checks to print.
③ Change the Check Style and other check printing options if necessary.
④ To print just the first check, click Print First, or click OK to print the selected checks.

If you select the Selected Checks option in the Select Checks to Print dialog box, you can click the Choose button to display a list of checks, and check off the ones you want to print. Click Done in that window to return to the Select Checks to Print dialog box.

Quicken sends the print job to your printer. It then displays a dialog box asking if the checks printed correctly.

- If all checks printed fine, just click OK.
- If there was a problem printing the checks, enter the number of the first check that was misprinted, and then click OK. You can then go back to the Select Checks to Print dialog box and try again.

Setting Check and Register Options

The Check Options and Register Options dialog boxes enable you to fine-tune the way the Write Checks and account register windows work. The options are similar in both dialog boxes, so I'll discuss them together.

To Set Check Options

To set Check options, begin by opening the Check Options dialog box. Choose Edit | Options | Write Checks, or click Options on the Button bar in the Write Checks window.

There are three categories of options: Checks, Miscellaneous, and QuickFill. Each set of options can be found on its own tab in the Check Options dialog box.

Check Options

Check options, shown here, affect the way the checks you enter with the Write Checks window appear when printed:

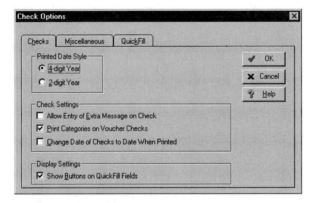

- **Printed Date Style** enables you to select a 4-digit or 2-digit date style. The 4-digit style is turned on by default.
- **Allow Entry of Extra Message on Check** displays an additional text box for a message in the Write Checks window (see the following illustration). The message you enter is printed on the check in a place where it cannot be seen if the check is mailed in a window envelope.

Enter an extra message here.

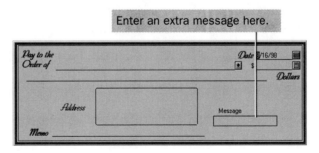

- **Print Categories on Voucher Checks** prints category information, including splits and classes, on the voucher part of voucher checks. This option only affects voucher-style checks. This option is turned on by default.
- **Change Date of Checks to Date When Printed** automatically prints the print date, rather than the transaction date, on each check.
- **Show Buttons on QuickFill Fields** displays drop-down list buttons on fields for which you can use QuickFill. I tell you about QuickFill in Chapter 5.

Miscellaneous Options

Miscellaneous options, shown here, affect the way you are notified about problems when you enter transactions in the Write Checks window. All of these options are turned on by default.

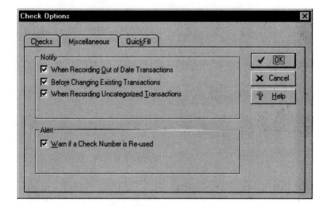

- **When Recording Out of Date Transactions** warns you when you try to record a transaction with a date after the current date.
- **Before Changing Existing Transactions** warns you when you try to modify a previously entered transaction.
- **When Recording Uncategorized Transactions** warns you when you try to record a transaction without assigning a category to it.
- **Warn if a Check Number is Re-used** warns you if you assign a check number that was already assigned in another transaction.

To Set Register Options

To set Register options, begin by opening the Register Options dialog box. Choose Edit | Options | Register, or choose Register Options from the Options menu on the Button bar in the account register window.

There are three categories of options: Display, Miscellaneous, and QuickFill. Each set of options can be found on its own tab in the Register Options dialog box.

Display Options

Display options, shown here, affect the way the transactions you enter appear in the account register window.

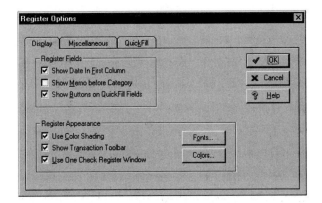

- **Show Date in First Column** displays the transaction date in the first column of the register. This option is turned on by default.
- **Show Memo before Category** displays the Memo field above the Category field.
- **Show Buttons on QuickFill Fields** displays drop-down list buttons on fields for which you can use QuickFill. This option is turned on by default. I tell you about QuickFill in Chapter 5.
- **Use Color Shading** displays each type of register with a different background color.
- **Show Transaction Toolbar** adds the Enter, Edit, and Split buttons to the currently selected transaction. This option is turned on by default.

- **Use One Check Register Window** displays each register in the same window, with account tabs along the bottom of the window to switch from one register to another. This option is turned on by default.
- **Fonts** displays a dialog box in which you can select the font for register windows.
- **Colors** displays a dialog box in which you can select the background colors for the various types of register windows.

Miscellaneous Options

Miscellaneous options, shown next, affect the way you are notified about problems when you enter transactions in the register and the way transactions are entered.

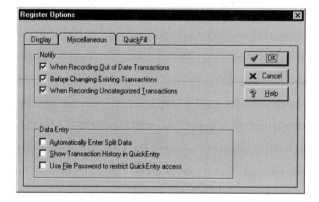

- **When Recording Out of Date Transactions** warns you when you try to record a transaction with a date after the current date. This option is turned on by default.
- **Before Changing Existing Transactions** warns you when you try to modify a previously entered transaction. This option is turned on by default.
- **When Recording Uncategorized Transactions** warns you when you try to record a transaction without assigning a category to it. This option is turned on by default.
- **Automatically Enter Split Data** turns the OK button in the Split Transaction window into an Enter button for entering the transaction.

- **Show Transaction History in QuickEntry** displays all transactions—including transactions entered into Quicken—in the account register within QuickEntry's window. This feature is only available in Quicken Deluxe.

- **Use File Password to Restrict QuickEntry Access** extends your Quicken password to protect QuickEntry as well. You must turn on the Show Transaction History in QuickEntry check box to use this feature. This feature is only available in Quicken Deluxe. I tell you about file passwords in Appendix A.

Automating Transactions

In This Chapter:

- *QuickFill*

- *Memorized Transactions*

- *Financial Calendar*

- *Scheduled Transactions*

- *Reminders*

- *Billminder*

- *Bank Account Alerts*

- *EasyStep Paycheck*

Chapter 5

Quicken includes a number of features to automate the entry of transactions. You got a glimpse of one of them, QuickFill, in Chapter 4. In this chapter, I tell you about QuickFill and the other features you can use to automate transaction entries or remind yourself when a transaction is due. I'm sure you'll agree that all of these features can make data entry quicker and easier.

Tip Before you read this chapter, make sure you have a good understanding of the data entry techniques covered in Chapter 4.

QuickFill and Memorized Transactions

As you enter transactions, Quicken is quietly working in the background, memorizing information about each transaction. It creates a database of memorized transactions, organized by payee name. It then uses the memorized transactions for its QuickFill feature.

Tip By default, the QuickFill feature is set up to work as discussed here. If it does not, check the QuickFill options to make sure they are properly set. I tell you how at the end of this section.

How It Works

QuickFill works in two ways:

- When you enter the first few characters of a payee name in the Write Checks or register window, Quicken immediately fills in the rest of the payee name. If you advance to the next text box or field of the window, Quicken fills in the rest of the transaction information based on the last transaction for that payee.
- You can select a memorized transaction from the drop-down list in the payee field of the Write Checks or register window. Quicken then fills in the rest of the transaction information based on the last transaction for that payee.

QuickFill entries include amounts, categories, and memos. They can also include splits and classes. For example, you might pay the cable or satellite company for television service every month. The bill is usually the same amount each month. The second time you create an entry with the company's name, the rest of the transaction is filled in automatically. You can make adjustments to the amount or other information as desired and save the transaction. It may have taken a minute or so to enter the transaction the first time. But it'll take only seconds to enter it every time after that.

Working with the Memorized Transaction List

If desired, you can view a list of memorized transactions, as shown here. Just choose Lists | Memorized Transactions, or press CTRL-T.

Click New to create a new memorized transaction.

Click Edit to modify the selected memorized transaction.

Click Delete to remove the selected memorized transaction from the list.

Click Use to enter a new transaction based on the selected memorized transaction.

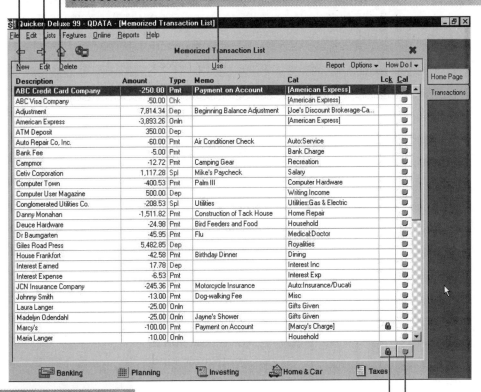

Description	Amount	Type	Memo	Cat	Lck	Cal
ABC Credit Card Company	-250.00	Pmt	Payment on Account	[American Express]		
ABC Visa Company	-50.00	Chk		[American Express]		
Adjustment	7,814.34	Dep	Beginning Balance Adjustment	[Joe's Discount Brokerage-Ca...		
American Express	-3,893.26	Onln		[American Express]		
ATM Deposit	350.00	Dep				
Auto Repair Co, Inc.	-60.00	Pmt	Air Conditioner Check	Auto:Service		
Bank Fee	-5.00	Pmt		Bank Charge		
Campmor	-12.72	Pmt	Camping Gear	Recreation		
Cetiv Corporation	1,117.28	Spl	Mike's Paycheck	Salary		
Computer Town	-400.53	Pmt	Palm III	Computer Hardware		
Computer User Magazine	500.00	Dep		Writing Income		
Conglomerated Utilities Co.	-208.53	Spl	Utilities	Utilities:Gas & Electric		
Danny Monahan	-1,511.82	Pmt	Construction of Tack House	Home Repair		
Deuce Hardware	-24.98	Pmt	Bird Feeders and Food	Household		
Dr Baumgarten	-45.95	Pmt	Flu	Medical:Doctor		
Giles Road Press	5,482.85	Dep		Royalities		
House Frankfort	-42.58	Pmt	Birthday Dinner	Dining		
Interest Earned	17.78	Dep		Interest Inc		
Interest Expense	-6.53	Pmt		Interest Exp		
JCN Insurance Company	-245.36	Pmt	Motorcycle Insurance	Auto:Insurance/Ducati		
Johnny Smith	-13.00	Pmt	Dog-walking Fee	Misc		
Laura Langer	-25.00	Onln		Gifts Given		
Madelyn Odendahl	-25.00	Onln	Jayne's Shower	Gifts Given		
Marcy's	-100.00	Pmt	Payment on Account	[Marcy's Charge]	🔒	
Maria Langer	-10.00	Onln		Household		

Click the Lock button to toggle the locked setting. When locked, none of the information in the selected memorized transaction can be changed when it is used.

Click the Calendar button to toggle the Financial Calendar setting. When enabled, the transaction will appear on the Financial Calendar's Transaction List.

You can use buttons on the Button bar to add, modify, delete, or use memorized transactions:

- **New** displays the Create Memorized Transaction dialog box, which you can use to create brand-new transactions without actually entering them into any register of your Quicken data file. This dialog box looks and works very much like the Create Register Entry dialog box described in Chapter 4.
- **Edit** displays the Edit Memorized Transaction dialog box for the currently selected transaction. This dialog box looks and works like the Create Memorized Transaction dialog box.
- **Delete** displays a dialog box asking you to confirm that you really do want to delete the selected memorized transaction. If you delete the transaction, it is removed from the Memorized Transaction List only—not from any register in the Quicken data file.
- **Use** displays the appropriate register for entering the transaction and fills in the transaction's information for you. You must click Enter to accept the entry.

Tip   Quicken can remember the first 2,000 transactions you enter—that's 2,000 payees! After that, it stops memorizing transactions. You can use the Delete button in the Memorized Transaction List window to delete old transactions to make room for new ones.

Setting QuickFill Options

You can customize the way QuickFill works by setting options in the Register Options and Write Checks Options dialog boxes. These settings affect the way the QuickFill feature works in the account register and Write Checks windows.

To set QuickFill options for account register windows, choose Edit | Options | Register. Click the QuickFill tab to see the dialog box shown in the following illustration. To set QuickFill options for the Write Checks window, choose Edit | Options | Write Checks. In the dialog box that appears, click the QuickFill tab.

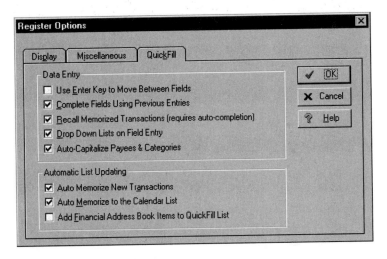

- **Use Enter Key to Move Between Fields** enables you to use both the Enter and Tab keys to move from field to field when entering data.
- **Complete Fields Using Previous Entries** enters transaction information using the information from previous entries. This option is turned on by default.
- **Recall Memorized Transactions** uses memorized transactions to fill in QuickFill entries. This option, which is not available if the Complete Fields Using Previous Entries option is disabled, is turned on by default.
- **Drop Down Lists on Field Entry** automatically displays the drop-down list when you advance to a field with a list. This option is turned on by default.
- **Auto-Capitalize Payees & Categories** automatically makes the first letter of each word in a payee name or category uppercase. This option, which is only available in the Register Options dialog box is turned on by default.
- **Auto Memorize New Transactions** tells Quicken to automatically enter all transactions for a new payee to the Memorized Transaction List. This option is turned on by default.
- **Auto Memorize to the Calendar List** tells Quicken to automatically add memorized transactions to the Transaction List in the Financial Calendar window. This option is turned on by default. You'll learn more about the Financial Calendar window in the next section.

- **Add Financial Address Book Items to QuickFill List** tells Quicken to add entries from the Financial Address Book to QuickFill drop-down lists. This feature, which I discuss in Chapter 10, is only available in Quicken Deluxe.

Financial Calendar and Scheduled Transactions

Quicken's Financial Calendar feature keeps track of all your transactions by date. It also enables you to schedule one-time or recurring transactions for the future.

Opening the Financial Calendar

To open the financial calendar, choose Features | Reminders | Financial Calendar. The Financial Calendar window appears:

Click Note to enter a note for the selected date.

Click Prev Month to view the previous month's calendar.

Click Go To Date to view a specific date.

Click Next Month to view the next month's calendar.

Drag this item to a date to create a new scheduled transaction.

Currently selected date; click a date to select it.

Memorized Transaction List

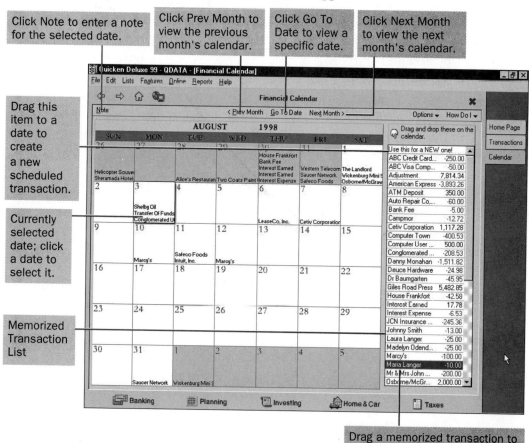

Drag a memorized transaction to a date to schedule it.

When you double-click a calendar date (or single-click a selected date), a window listing all the transactions for that date appears:

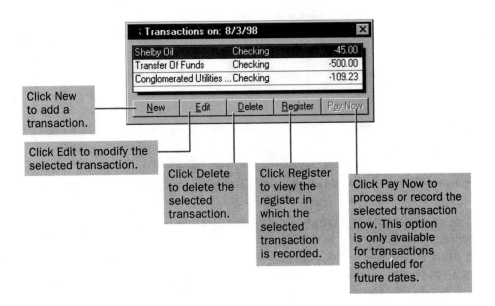

Click New to add a transaction.

Click Edit to modify the selected transaction.

Click Delete to delete the selected transaction.

Click Register to view the register in which the selected transaction is recorded.

Click Pay Now to process or record the selected transaction now. This option is only available for transactions scheduled for future dates.

Creating a Scheduled Transaction

You can create a scheduled transaction right from within the Financial Calendar window.

- To schedule a transaction based on a memorized transaction, drag a transaction from the Transaction List on the right side of the window to the date on which you want the transaction to occur.
- To schedule a transaction that is not based on a memorized transaction, drag the "Use this for a NEW one!" item from the Transaction List on the right side of the window to the date on which you want the transaction to occur.

The New Transaction dialog box appears, as shown here. It's a lot like the Create Memorized Transaction dialog box, but it has additional options for scheduling transactions.

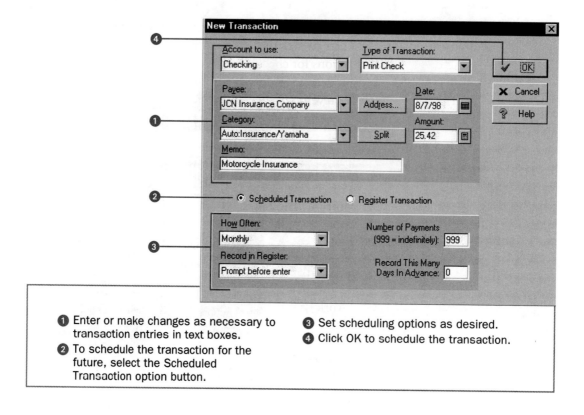

① Enter or make changes as necessary to transaction entries in text boxes.

② To schedule the transaction for the future, select the Scheduled Transaction option button.

③ Set scheduling options as desired.

④ Click OK to schedule the transaction.

When the Scheduled Transaction option button is selected, four scheduling options appear at the bottom of the dialog box:

- **How Often** enables you to specify how often the transaction should be recorded. Your options are Only Once (the default option), Weekly, Every two weeks, Twice a month, Every four weeks, Monthly, Every two months, Quarterly, Twice a year, and Yearly.

- **Number of Payments** is available if you choose any How Often option except Only Once. Enter the number of payments you want to schedule. For example, if you are scheduling a transaction for monthly payments on a four-year car loan and four payments have already been made, you'd choose Monthly from the How Often drop-down list and enter 44 in the Number of Payments text box.

- **Record in Register** enables you to specify how you want the transaction recorded. Your options are "Automatically enter" and "Prompt before enter" (the default option). If you choose "Prompt before enter," Quicken reminds you that a transaction must be recorded by displaying a message in the Quicken Home Page window shortly before payment is due.

- **Record This Many Days In Advance** enables you to specify how many days before the transaction date the transaction should be entered. For example, you might want transactions for checks and other payments to be entered a week in advance so your account balance reflects these items before they're actually paid. This can prevent you from spending money that will be needed for future transactions.

Caution Scheduling a transaction is not the same as recording it. You must record a transaction in order to have it appear in the appropriate register or print a check for it. Choosing the "Automatically enter" option from the Record in Register drop-down list is a good way to ensure that a scheduled transaction is properly recorded.

Working with the Scheduled Transaction List

The Scheduled Transaction List (shown here) displays a list of all future transactions. To view and work with the list, choose Lists | Scheduled Transaction, or press CTRL-J.

Click New to create a new scheduled transaction.

Click Edit to modify the selected scheduled transaction.

Click Delete to delete the selected scheduled transaction.

Click a tab to view a specific type of scheduled transaction.

Click Pay to enter the selected scheduled transaction into the appropriate register.

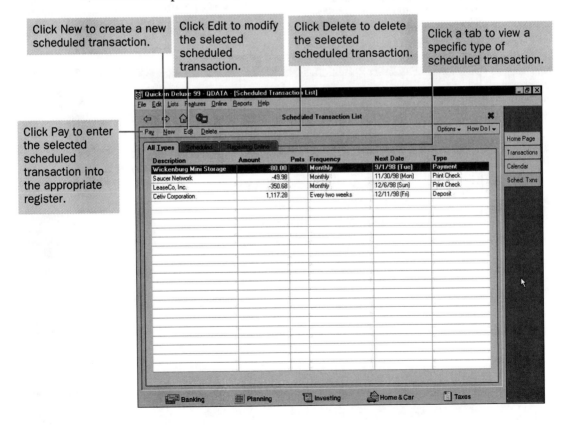

Use the Scheduled Transaction List to create, modify, delete, or enter scheduled transactions.

Using Reminders

Quicken offers three ways to remind you about upcoming scheduled transactions. One of them, the Reminders area in the Quicken Home Page window, was discussed earlier. In this section, I tell you about the others: the Quicken Reminders window and Billminder.

Working with the Quicken Reminders Window

The Quicken Reminders window (see the following illustration) lists all the scheduled transactions that are due to be recorded. You can open the window by choosing Features | Reminders | Reminders.

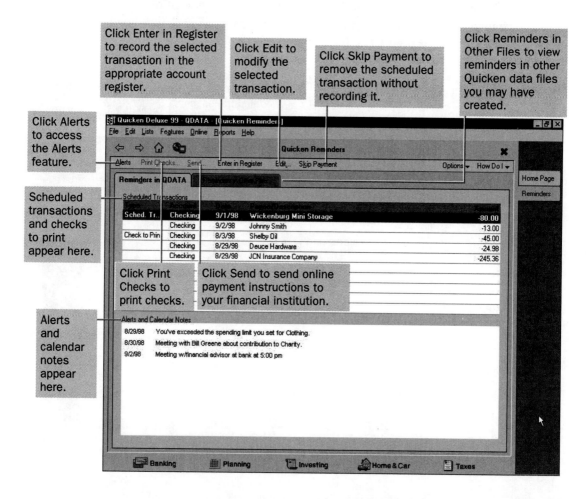

Working with Billminder

Billminder is a Quicken feature that reminds you of scheduled transactions and alerts when you first start Windows. Once enabled, a window like the following one appears when you start your computer on any day for which scheduled transactions are due to be recorded.

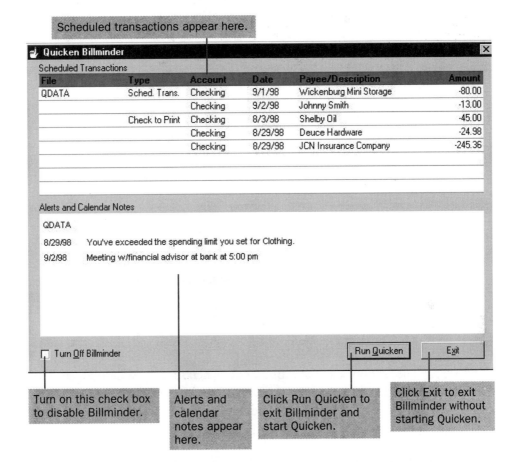

Scheduled transactions appear here.

File	Type	Account	Date	Payee/Description	Amount
QDATA	Sched. Trans.	Checking	9/1/98	Wickenburg Mini Storage	-80.00
		Checking	9/2/98	Johnny Smith	-13.00
	Check to Print	Checking	8/3/98	Shelby Oil	-45.00
		Checking	8/29/98	Deuce Hardware	-24.98
		Checking	8/29/98	JCN Insurance Company	-245.36

Alerts and Calendar Notes

QDATA

8/29/98   You've exceeded the spending limit you set for Clothing.

9/2/98   Meeting w/financial advisor at bank at 5:00 pm

☐ Turn Off Billminder   Run Quicken   Exit

Turn on this check box to disable Billminder.

Alerts and calendar notes appear here.

Click Run Quicken to exit Billminder and start Quicken.

Click Exit to exit Billminder without starting Quicken.

Setting Reminder and Billminder Options

You can fine-tune the way the Reminder and Billminder features work by setting options for them. Use the Options menu on the Button bar of the Quicken Reminders window to display submenus full of commands.

The Reminders submenu enables you to set general reminder options:

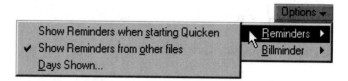

- **Show Reminders when starting Quicken** displays a dialog box with reminders when you first start Quicken.
- **Show Reminders from other files** displays reminders from other Quicken data files.
- **Days Shown** displays a dialog box that you can use to specify the number of days prior to a scheduled transaction to remind you about it and the time span for which calendar notes should be displayed.

The Billminder submenu, shown here, enables you to set options for the Billminder feature:

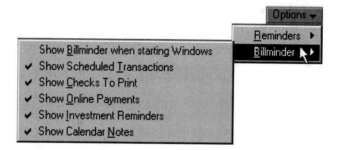

The first option, Show Billminder when starting Windows, enables Billminder. The other options let you specify what types of items should be included in the Billminder window.

Setting Bank Account Alerts

Quicken's Alert feature monitors your Quicken data file and displays alerts based on the options you set. The Alert feature is used throughout Quicken; in this section, I tell you about the alerts you can set for bank accounts.

Quicken Quote

"I think financial alerts are great. Timeliness makes money. It's good to have a reminder when you have a lot of things to keep track of."

Jeff Hall, City, ST

To set an alert, choose Features | Reminders | Alerts, or click the Alerts button on the Button bar in the Quicken Reminders window. The Set Up Alerts dialog box appears. If necessary, click the Accounts tab to display its options:

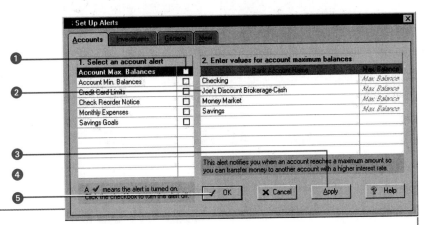

1. Turn on the check box for the type of alert you want to set.
2. Enter appropriate values in the left side of the window.
3. Click Apply to save your settings for the current alert.
4. Repeat Steps 1 through 3 for each type of alert you want to set.
5. Click OK.

- **Account Max Balances** enables you to enter maximum desired balances for each bank account.

- **Account Min Balances** enables you to specify the minimum balance for each bank account, along with the balance at which Quicken should remind you to add more money.

- **Check Reorder Notice** enables you to specify a check number at which Quicken should remind you to order more checks. When you use the check with that number, the reminder appears. This helps prevent you from running out of checks.

I tell you about other options in this dialog box throughout this book.

SAVE MONEY If an account that does not earn interest has a higher balance than necessary, you can move that money into an interest-bearing account to earn money on it. Use the Account Max Balances feature so you know when it's time to move your money. Likewise, many banks waive a monthly fee if your account balance remains above a certain amount throughout the month. Use the Account Min Balances feature to help keep your balances above the minimum, thus avoiding bank fees.

Using EasyStep Paycheck

The EasyStep Paycheck feature offers yet another way to automate transactions. You use it to enter information about your regular payroll check and its deductions. Then, when payday comes along, Quicken automatically enters the payroll deposit information based on the EasyStep Paycheck transaction.

Tip Although you can use EasyStep Paycheck to record payroll checks with varying amounts and deductions—such as a check with varying hourly wages or overtime pay—it can be a real time-saver if your paycheck is the same (or almost the same) every payday.

Start by choosing Features | Banking | Set Up Paycheck. The Paycheck Setup window appears. The first window provides general information about EasyStep Paycheck and how it works. Click Next to begin.

The Paycheck Setup window works a lot like the Create New Account window that I tell you about in Chapter 2. It begins by displaying the first step of the EasyStep tab, shown here. Use the check boxes in this tab to indicate the kinds of deductions that appear on your pay stub.

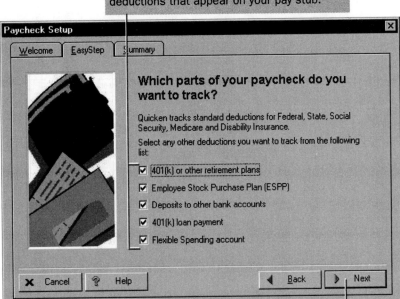

Turn on only the check boxes for the types of deductions that appear on your pay stub.

Click Next to continue.

The next window prompts you to enter a name for the paycheck and specify how often you're paid. The Paycheck name is simply an identifier—you can call it anything you like. When you're finished providing this information, click Next to continue.

You're now prompted to enter information about your most recent paycheck. Enter the date of the paycheck and the account to which you usually deposit it. Then click Next.

The next EasyStep window prompts you to enter three pieces of information:

- **Gross amount** is the amount of pay before any deductions.
- **Net amount** is the amount you actually deposit.
- **Category** is the Quicken category in which you want to record the source of paycheck funds. By default, the Salary category is selected, but you can choose any appropriate income category.

When you're finished entering information, click Next.

The next window (shown here) enables you to enter additional categories and corresponding amounts for the paycheck. This could include commissions, bonuses, tips, and advances.

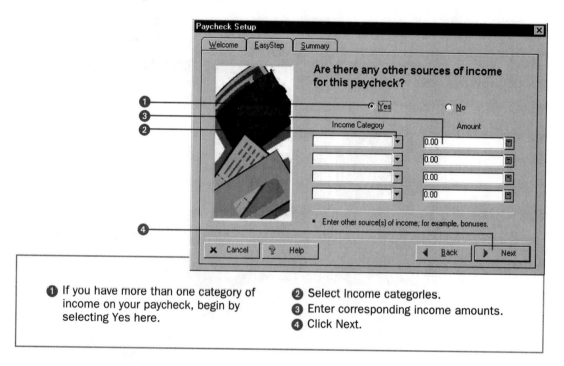

The next window works very much the same way, but it enables you to categorize and enter the different standard tax deductions taken out of your paycheck. Try not to get depressed when entering this information.

The next window is for entering additional taxes and their corresponding categories. If you need to enter this information, select the Yes option near the top of the window, and then select appropriate categories and enter amounts. When you're finished, click Next.

You're now prompted to enter information about other deductions you selected in the very first step of EasyStep Paycheck. The options that appear here vary depending on the options you selected. Choose accounts and enter amounts as necessary. Click Next to advance to the next window.

After entering the deductions you specified earlier, another window appears allowing you to enter categories and amounts for other deductions. When you're finished, click Next to continue.

Next, Quicken offers to remind you to enter paycheck information:

- Click Yes to have Quicken create a scheduled transaction with a split that includes all the deductions and other information you entered. Quicken reminds you to record this information on the date it is expected.
- Click No to enter the transaction just once. You might want to use this option if your paycheck varies greatly from one pay period to the next and you want to go through the EasyStep Paycheck process again each payday.

When you click Next, the Summary tab of the Paycheck Setup window appears (see the following illustration). It shows all the information you entered for the paycheck. Click Done to record the information in the appropriate register and close the Paycheck Setup window.

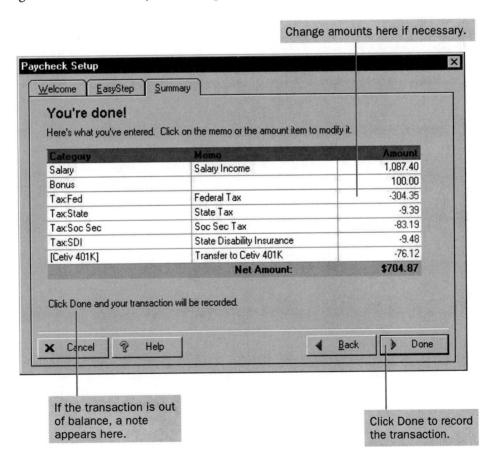

Change amounts here if necessary.

If the transaction is out of balance, a note appears here.

Click Done to record the transaction.

Tracking Credit Cards

Chapter 6

123

You can use either of two techniques for paying credit card bills and monitoring credit card balances:

- Use your checking account register or the Write Checks window (as discussed in Chapter 4) to record amounts paid to each credit card company. Although this does track the amounts you pay, it doesn't track how much you owe.
- Use a credit card account register to record credit card expenditures and payments. This takes a bit more effort on your part, but it tracks how much you owe.

Knowing how much you owe on your credit cards helps you maintain a clear picture of your financial situation. In this chapter, I explain how to use Quicken's credit card account register to track credit card charges and payments.

SAVE TIME   Quicken's Online Account Access feature enables you to download credit card charges right into Quicken, thus eliminating the need for time-consuming data entry. I tell you about online access for credit cards in Chapter 13.

Choosing Your Strategy

Before you get started, take a moment to think about the strategy you want to use for recording credit card transactions. Choosing the strategy that's right for you makes the job easier to handle.

Enter as You Spend

One strategy is to enter transactions as you spend. To do this, you must collect all the credit card receipts that are handed to you when you use your credit cards—which might be something you already do. Don't forget to jot down the totals for any telephone and online shopping you do. Then, every day or every few days, sit down with Quicken or QuickEntry and enter the transactions.

While this strategy requires you to stay on top of things, it offers two main benefits:

- Your Quicken credit card registers always indicate what you owe to credit card companies. This prevents unpleasant surprises at month-end, or at the check-out counter when you're told you've reached your limit. It also enables you to use Quicken Alerts to track credit card balances; I tell you about that later in this chapter.

- At month-end, you don't have to spend a lot of time entering big batches of transactions. All (or at least most) of them should already be entered.

I'll be the first to admit that I never was able to use this strategy. I just don't like holding onto those pieces of paper. Of course, since signing up for Online Account Access, all this information is entered regularly for me. And I don't have to save a single charge slip.

Enter When You Pay

The other strategy, which you may find better for you, is to enter transactions when you get your monthly statement. With this strategy, when you open your credit card statement, you'll spend some time sitting in front of your computer with Quicken to enter each and every transaction. If there aren't many, this isn't a big deal. But if there are many transactions, this could take some time.

Of course, the main benefit of this strategy is that you don't have to collect credit card receipts and spend time throughout the month entering your transactions. But you still have to enter them! This is the method I use for the one credit card I have that I cannot access online yet.

Recording Credit Card Transactions

Once you select a strategy, you're ready to enter the transactions. You have two ways to approach this, too:

- Use credit card account registers to enter charges and payments. Using this method, each charge or payment has its own entry in the register. This method is especially useful if you enter charges as you spend.

- Use splits in the Write Checks or checking account register window to enter payments, total charges, and the categories and amounts for individual charges. This method may be more useful if you enter charges when you pay your bill.

There's no right or wrong way. Take a look at both methods and decide which works best for you.

SAVE TIME   Quicken Deluxe users can use QuickEntry to enter credit card charges. This may be a little faster than entering them directly into Quicken. I tell you how to use QuickEntry in Chapter 4.

Creating Credit Card Accounts

No matter which method you use to enter transactions, you still need to create credit card accounts to track card balances. If you haven't already done so, do it now. I explain how to create accounts in Chapter 2, so you can consult that chapter if you need detailed instructions.

Here are a few tips for creating credit card accounts:

- Give the accounts names that clearly identify the account. For example, if you have two Visa cards, don't name them Visa 1 and Visa 2. Instead, include the credit card or bank name in the account name. This prevents you from accidentally entering a transaction in the wrong account register.
- Get the account's balance from your most recent credit card statement. Then be careful not to enter transactions that already appear on the statement.
- Click the Info button in the Optional Information area of the Credit Card Account Setup window to enter the credit card company or bank name, credit card number, and contact phone number. This information will come in handy if you ever lose the credit card and need to cancel it.

Entering Individual Charges in Credit Card Accounts

To enter individual charges in a credit card account, begin by opening the account register for the credit card account. Choose Features | Banking | Use Register, or press CTRL-R. In the register window that appears, click the account tab at the bottom of the window to display the credit card register you want to use (see Figure 6-1). Then enter the transaction information.

Shortcut   You can quickly open a register by clicking its account name in the Quicken Home Page window.

Tip   The credit card account register works very much like a bank account register, which I discuss in detail in Chapter 4. If you skipped Chapter 4, go back and read it now to learn more about the options in the account register window.

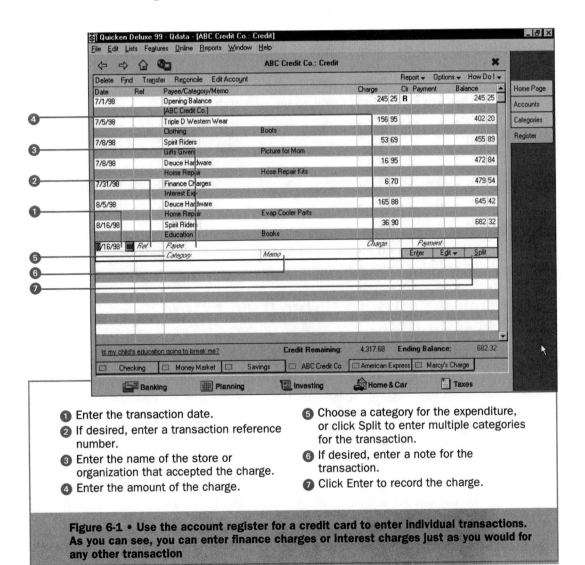

❶ Enter the transaction date.

❷ If desired, enter a transaction reference number.

❸ Enter the name of the store or organization that accepted the charge.

❹ Enter the amount of the charge.

❺ Choose a category for the expenditure, or click Split to enter multiple categories for the transaction.

❻ If desired, enter a note for the transaction.

❼ Click Enter to record the charge.

Figure 6-1 • Use the account register for a credit card to enter individual transactions. As you can see, you can enter finance charges or interest charges just as you would for any other transaction

When you're ready to make a payment on your account, you can write a check using the Write Checks or account register window, as I discuss in Chapter 4. Be sure to click the tab at the bottom of the window to enter the payment transaction in the appropriate checking account. When you get to the category field of the transaction, choose the credit card account from the list of accounts at the bottom of the Category drop-down list. This treats the payment as a transfer to the credit card account, while enabling you to write a check for it. The transaction might look like this in your checking account register:

8/5/98	1006	ABC Credit Card Company		50 00		2,208 25
		[ABC Credit Co.]	Payment on Account			

and like this in your credit card account register:

The amount of the payment shows up as a reduction in the credit card account balance.

8/5/98		ABC Credit Card Company		50 00	429 54
		[Checking]	Payment on Account		

Tip   You can also enter a payment transaction for your credit card account at the end of the credit card account reconciliation process, which I discuss near the end of this chapter.

Using Splits to Enter Credit Card Transactions

To enter charges in a split, begin by opening the account in which you want to record the transaction. In this example, I'm using my checking account register to record all charges and payments at once. If you prefer, you could use the Write Checks window or the credit card account register.

Choose Features | Banking | Use Register or press CTRL-R. In the register window that appears, click the account tab at the bottom of the window to display the account register you want to use. Enter the payment information: transaction date, transaction number or Num code, the name of the credit card company, and the amount of the payment. Then click Split.

Rather than enter a single category for the payment, click the Split button. The Split Transaction Window appears, as shown next. Use it to enter the individual charges, using the appropriate categories for each transaction.

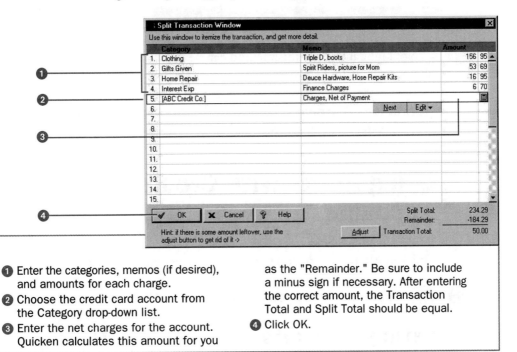

① Enter the categories, memos (if desired), and amounts for each charge.

② Choose the credit card account from the Category drop-down list.

③ Enter the net charges for the account. Quicken calculates this amount for you

as the "Remainder." Be sure to include a minus sign if necessary. After entering the correct amount, the Transaction Total and Split Total should be equal.

④ Click OK.

When you're finished, the account register transaction should look something like this:

and the corresponding transaction in the credit card account register should look like this:

The increase in the credit card account balance appears as a single item.

8/5/98	ABC Credit Card Company	184 29		429 54
	[Checking]			

No doubt about it—this method can be more confusing than simply entering all transactions into the credit card account register. (You may find that this method makes more sense when you pay all credit card charges each month, as you might for American Express.) But the end result is the same—purchases are properly categorized and credit card account balances are up-to-date.

Using Alerts with Credit Card Accounts

One good thing about tracking credit card account balances is that you can use Quicken Alerts to warn you before balances get out of control.

Tip I tell you more about Reminders and Alerts in Chapter 5.

Setting Up Alerts

To set up Alerts, choose Features | Reminders | Alerts. The Set Up Alerts dialog box appears. If necessary, click its Accounts tab to display its options (see Figure 6-2). Then set up alerts as desired.

You must enter Credit Limit amounts for any credit card for which you want to set Remind Me At values. This includes credit cards with no preset spending limits, such as American Express. For example, to be warned of a growing balance on a credit card that has no spending limit, enter a high Credit Limit value for the account so you can also set an appropriate Remind Me At value.

SAVE MONEY If your credit cards have different interest rates, set a lower Remind Me At value for the high-interest credit card. This helps prevent you from charging more on the more expensive card.

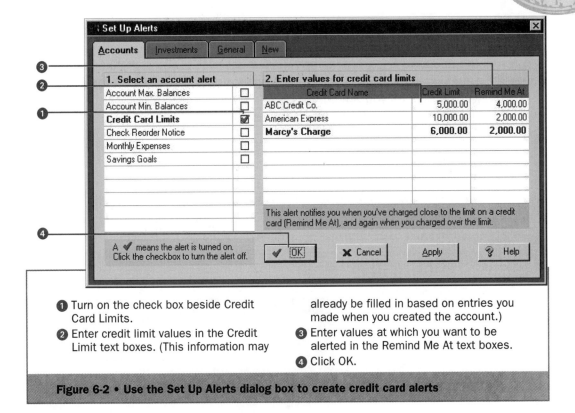

Figure 6-2 • Use the Set Up Alerts dialog box to create credit card alerts

① Turn on the check box beside Credit Card Limits.

② Enter credit limit values in the Credit Limit text boxes. (This information may already be filled in based on entries you made when you created the account.)

③ Enter values at which you want to be alerted in the Remind Me At text boxes.

④ Click OK.

Working with Alerts

Once you've set up credit card alerts, Quicken keeps an eye on your credit card balances. It displays an alert on screen if you enter a credit card transaction that meets either of two conditions:

- Your credit card balance is near the Remind Me At value you entered for it.
- Your credit card balance exceeds the Credit Limit value you entered for it.

Alerts also appear in the Quicken Home Page window, Billminder dialog box, and Quicken Reminders window. You learn about all of these things in Chapter 5.

Reconciling Accounts

You can reconcile a credit card account just as you would a bank account. This enables you to verify your account balance and find transactions you neglected to enter.

> **Tip**   If you enter credit card transactions right from your credit card statement at month-end, you probably don't need to reconcile your credit card account: The transactions in your account register should exactly match what's on your statement. Reconciling is useful when you enter transactions as you spend throughout the month, to make sure your records match the credit card company's.

Getting Started

With your credit card statement in hand, open the account register for the account you want to reconcile. Then click the Reconcile button in the Button bar. The Credit Card Statement Information dialog box appears (see Figure 6-3). Use it to enter basic information from your credit card statement.

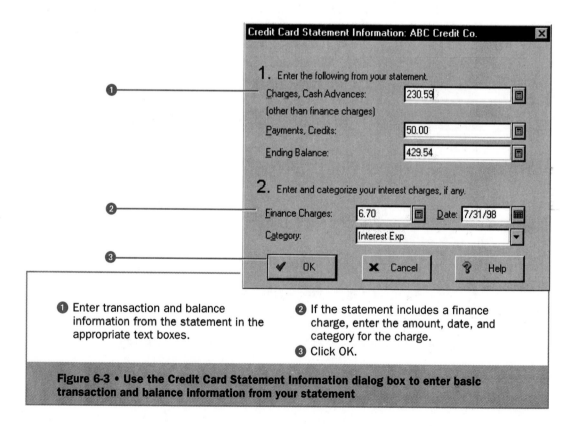

① Enter transaction and balance information from the statement in the appropriate text boxes.

② If the statement includes a finance charge, enter the amount, date, and category for the charge.

③ Click OK.

Figure 6-3 • Use the Credit Card Statement Information dialog box to enter basic transaction and balance information from your statement

Caution If you manually entered finance charges in your register, as shown earlier in this chapter, don't enter them again in the Credit Card Statement dialog box. Doing so will cause a duplicate entry.

Comparing Transactions

The next step to reconciling the account is to compare transactions on the credit card statement with transactions in your account register. For this, Quicken displays the Reconcile Credit Statement window (see Figure 6-4), which displays all charges, fees, and payments from your account register. Your job is to check off the items that appear on your credit card statement.

When the Difference is 0.00, you have successfully balanced your credit card account.

Click Statement to view or modify statement information already entered.

Click to place a check mark in the Clr column for items that appear on your credit card statement.

Click Finished to complete the reconciliation, or click Finish Later to save your changes without completing the reconciliation.

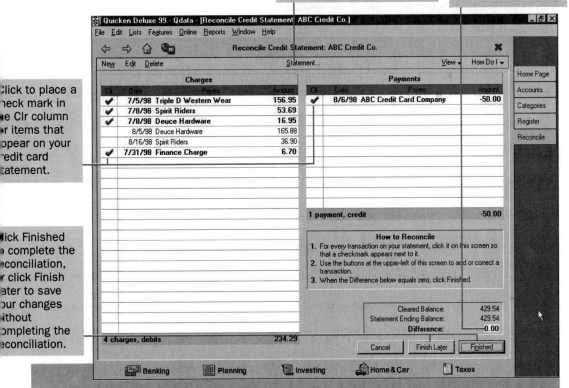

Figure 6-4 • Use the Reconcile Credit Statement window to check off items that appear on your credit card statement and in your account register

While you're checking off items in the Reconcile Credit Statement window, be sure to check off the same items on your credit card statement. Any items that appear on the credit card statement but not in your account register are items you failed to enter. After checking off the items that do appear in your account register, you have to add the items that don't. Switch to the appropriate credit card account register window to enter them, as instructed earlier in this chapter. After entering these items, you can switch back to the Reconcile Credit Statement window and check them off.

Finishing Up

When you reconcile a credit card account with Quicken, your goal is to make the difference between the Cleared Balance and the Statement Ending Balance zero. You can monitor this progress at the bottom of the Reconcile Credit Statement window (refer to Figure 6-4).

When the Difference Is Zero

If you correctly checked off all statement items and the difference is zero, you've successfully reconciled the account. Congratulations. Click the Finish button.

When You Can't Get the Difference to Zero

Sometimes, try as you might, you just can't get the difference to zero. Here are a few last things to check before you give up:

- Make sure all the amounts you checked off in your account register are the same as the amounts on the credit card statement.
- Make sure you included any finance charges and cash advances.
- Make sure the ending balance you entered is the same as the ending balance on the credit card statement.

If you checked and rechecked all these things and still can't get the difference to zero, click Finished. Quicken displays a dialog box indicating the amount of the difference, and offers to make an adjustment to your account register for the amount. Click Adjust to accept the adjustment. The amount of the adjustment will be applied to the Misc category.

Making a Credit Card Payment

At the end of a reconciliation, Quicken displays a dialog box that offers to make a payment on the credit card account:

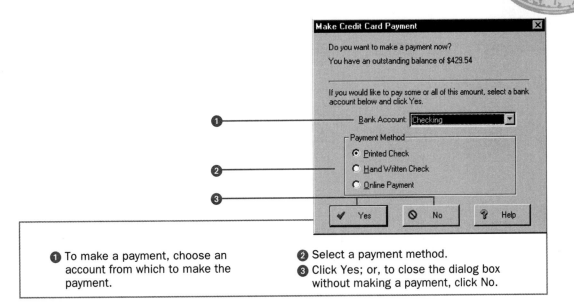

❶ To make a payment, choose an account from which to make the payment.

❷ Select a payment method.

❸ Click Yes; or, to close the dialog box without making a payment, click No.

Tip The Online Payment option shown here appears only if you have set up online payment for one of your bank accounts. I tell you more about that in Chapter 12.

If you click Yes, Quicken creates the payment transaction and displays it in the appropriate window for the account you selected. You can modify the transaction as desired, and then click Record Check or Enter to record it.

Tracking
Investments

In This Chapter:

- *Investment Basics*

- *Setting Up Investment Accounts*

- *Viewing Security Lists and Details*

- *Recording Investment Transactions*

- *Setting Up Watch List Securities*

- *Tracking the Market Value of Investments*

Chapter 7

137

Investments offer individuals a way to make their money grow. Although more risky than deposits made to an FDIC-insured bank, stocks, bonds, mutual funds, and other types of investments have the potential to earn more. That's why many people build investment portfolios as a way to save for future goals or retirement.

In this chapter, I tell you a little about investments and portfolio management, and then explain how you can use Quicken to keep track of the money you invest.

Quicken Investment Basics

Quicken enables you to record your investment transactions and track your portfolio value. With the information about your investments that you enter into Quicken, you can see how various investments perform, generate reports for tax time, and get a clear picture of what your investments are worth.

Before learning how to use Quicken to track your investments, here's a review of what investments and portfolios are.

Types of Investments

An investment is a security or asset that you expect to increase in value and/or generate income. There are many types of investments:

- **A certificate of deposit,** or **CD,** is an account with a bank or other financial institution. It earns a fixed rate of return and has a predetermined maturity date. Withdrawals before the maturity date normally result in penalty fees, which can exceed earned interest. CDs on deposit with a bank are normally FDIC-insured against loss.

- **A money market fund** is an account with a bank or other financial institution that earns interest based on short-term cash values.

- **Stocks** represent part ownership of an organization. Stock investments can earn you money by paying dividends.

- **Bonds** represent loans to an organization. Bonds can earn you money by paying interest either during the bond's term or at its maturity date.

- **Treasury bills** represent loans to the U.S. government. They are issued at a discount and redeemed at face value; the difference between the two prices are the earnings.

- **Mutual funds** consist of multiple investments owned by many people. When you buy into a mutual fund, you pool your money with other investors to buy stocks, bonds, or other securities. Mutual funds can earn you money by paying dividends and interest.

- **Annuities** are regularly funded accounts that earn interest or dividends paid in the future.
- **401(k)** and **403(b) plans** are employer-funded retirement investments. They can consist of stocks, bonds, mutual funds, or any other type of investment.
- **IRAs, SEPs,** and **Keogh accounts** are employee-funded retirement investments. They have special tax implications and rules for funding. They can consist of stocks, bonds, mutual funds, or any other type of investment.
- **Real estate** is land or buildings. Real estate investments can earn money from rental or lease income.

Most investments can also earn you money if you sell them for more than you paid for them. I provide more specifics about investments and retirement planning in Chapters 19 and 20 respectively.

Portfolio Accounts

The term *portfolio* refers to the total of all of your investments. For example, if you have shares of one company's stock, shares in two mutual funds, and a 401(k) plan account, these are the items that make up your portfolio.

Types of Portfolio Accounts

Your Quicken portfolio can include two types of Quicken accounts: investment and 401(k).

Investment   An investment account is for tracking a wide variety of investments, including stocks, bonds, mutual funds, and annuities. There are two types of investment accounts:

- **A regular investment account** is for tracking one or more securities or mutual funds. Similar to a brokerage account, it can track income, capital gains, performance, market values, shares, and cash balances.
- **A single mutual fund investment account** is for tracking a single mutual fund. It can track the share balance, market value, income, capital gains, and performance of the fund. It can't, however, track interest or miscellaneous income or expenses.

Tip Although you can always convert a single mutual fund investment account to a regular investment account, you can't convert a regular investment account to a single mutual fund investment account.

401(k) A 401(k) account is for tracking 401(k) or 403(b) accounts. It can track performance, market value, and distribution among investment choices. If you (and your spouse) have more than one 401(k) plan, you should set up a separate account for each.

You can have as many investment or 401(k) accounts as you need to properly represent the investments that make up your portfolio.

Quicken Quote

"401(k) tracking is an invaluable feature that allows me to watch my nest egg grow and grow. My company sends out statements only once a year so this lets me stay up-to-date on its current value."

George Thomason Jr., *Suisan City, CA*

Choosing the Right Type of Account

Sometimes it's not clear which kind of account is best for a specific kind of investment. Table 7-1 offers some guidance.

Tip When trying to decide between an investment account and an asset account, consider the value of the investment. Does its value change regularly? If so, you should use an investment account, which offers better tools for tracking changing values. If the value does not change regularly or you cannot obtain accurate estimates of changing values, an asset account may be better. You can always update the asset value when an accurate market value is available.

This chapter concentrates on investment and 401(k) accounts.

Type of Investment	Type of Account
Stocks in your possession	Regular investment account (either one per security or one for all securities)
Brokerage account with one or more securities, with or without an associated cash, checking, or interest-earning account	Regular investment account with linked checking account
Mutual fund account with no cash balance	Single mutual fund investment account (one per mutual fund)
401(k) or 403(b) plan	401(k) account
IRA, SEP, or Keogh account	Regular investment account
CDs	Regular investment or asset account
Money market funds	Money market account
Treasury bills	Regular investment or asset account
Variable annuities	Regular investment account
Fixed annuities	Regular investment or asset account
Real estate investment trusts (REITs) or partnerships	Regular investment account
Real estate	Asset account

Table 7-1 • Quicken Accounts for Various Investment Types

The Importance of Portfolio Management

At this point, you may be wondering why you should bother including investment information in your Quicken data file. After all, you may already get quarterly (or even monthly) statements from your broker or investment firm. What you may not realize, however, is how you can benefit from keeping a close eye on your investments. Take a look at what portfolio management with Quicken can do for you.

Centralizing Your Investment Records

Unless you have only one brokerage account for all your investments, you probably get multiple statements for the stocks, bonds, mutual funds, and other investments in your portfolio. No single statement can provide a complete picture of your portfolio's worth. Quicken can, however. By entering the transactions and values on each statement within Quicken, you can see the details of your entire portfolio in one place.

Knowing the Value of Your Portfolio on Any Day

Brokerage statements can tell you the value of your investments on the statement's ending date, but not what they're worth today. Or what they were worth on June 15, 1998. Quicken, however, can tell you what your portfolio is worth on any day for which you have entered security prices. And it can estimate values for dates without exact pricing information.

 SAVE TIME If you like to keep your portfolio's value up-to-date with the latest security prices, retrieve prices online. I show you how to take advantage of this feature in Chapter 14.

Keeping Track of Performance History

Manually compiling a complete pricing and performance history for an investment is no small task, especially for periods spanning multiple statements. If you consistently enter investment information in your Quicken data file, however, preparing performance charts and reports is as easy as choosing a menu command or clicking a button.

Calculating Your Return on Investment

Return on Investment varies from one investment to another. Quicken enables you to see the return on investment for each security you hold—all in one place!

GET SMARTER Use this feature to make better financial decisions. When you're ready to invest more money in your portfolio, it's easy to see which holding is doing the best—and may deserve more funding.

Calculating Capital Gains Quickly and Easily

Calculating the gain on the sale of an investment isn't always easy. Considerations include not only the purchase and selling price, but commissions, fees, stock splits, and purchase lots. Quicken can take all the work out of calculating capital gains—even if you're just considering the sale and want to know what its impact will be. This is extremely helpful at tax time, as I discuss in Chapter 16.

Setting Up Accounts

Ready to start tracking your investments with Quicken? The first thing you need to do is set up the accounts you'll need to do it right. This section tells you how.

Creating an Investment Account

You create an investment account with the Investment Account Setup window, which enables you to enter information for the account. When you're finished, Quicken automatically displays the Security Setup window, which enables you to enter information for each of the securities in the investment account.

Getting Started

Choose Lists | Account or press CTRL-A to display the Account List window. Then click the New button on the Button bar. In the Create New Account window that appears, select the Investment option button and click the Next button. The Investment Account Setup window appears, as shown in Figure 7-1.

Figure 7-1 • Use the EasyStep tab of the Investment Account Setup window to enter information step-by-step

You have two options for setting up the account:

- Enter appropriate information into each EasyStep window and click the Next button to continue. This guides you step-by-step through the creation of the account by asking simple questions. The last step displays your entries in the Summary window, giving you a last chance to change them before creating the account.
- Click the Summary tab to display and enter information into the Summary window, as shown in Figure 7-2. This method is quicker, but it might not be a good choice if this is the first time you're setting up an investment account.

Tip   I tell you more about entering tax schedule information for accounts in Chapter 16.

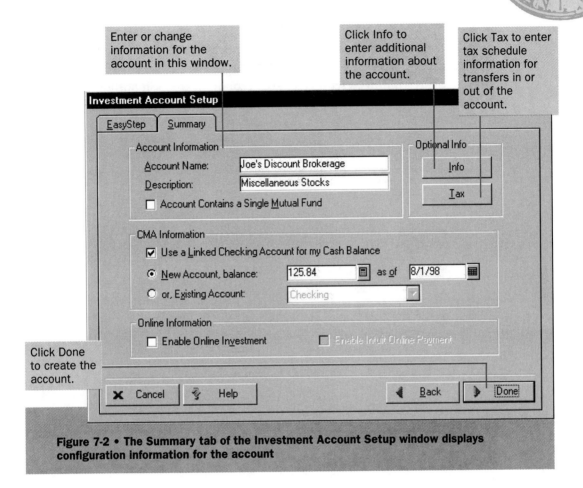

Enter or change information for the account in this window.

Click Info to enter additional information about the account.

Click Tax to enter tax schedule information for transfers in or out of the account.

Click Done to create the account.

Figure 7-2 • The Summary tab of the Investment Account Setup window displays configuration information for the account

To keep things simple, use the EasyStep tab for the first investment account you create. I'll walk you through the steps.

Entering Account Information

The first EasyStep window (refer to Figure 7-1) prompts you to enter an Account Name and Description. Enter the information in the appropriate text boxes and click the Next button.

The next window asks if you have applied for online services for the account. For now, select the No option button and click Next to continue. (I explain how to set up investment accounts for online account access in Chapter 14.)

Next, Quicken wants to know if the investment account allows you to write checks or use a debit card against its balance. Select the Yes or No option button and click Next. If you select Yes, Quicken displays a window like the one shown here. Use this window to set up a linked account for the cash portion of the investment account:

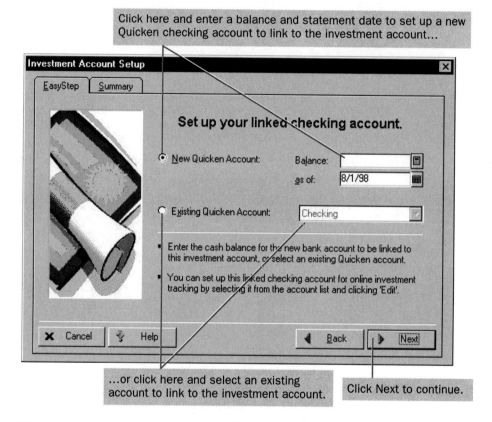

Click here and enter a balance and statement date to set up a new Quicken checking account to link to the investment account...

...or click here and select an existing account to link to the investment account.

Click Next to continue.

The next window enables you to specify whether the account will be for stocks, bonds, or multiple mutual funds (a regular investment account), or for one mutual fund (a single mutual fund investment account). Select the appropriate option button and click Next to continue.

Next, Quicken asks whether the account is tax-deferred or tax-exempt. Select the appropriate option button. If desired, you can also click the Tax Info button to enter tax return schedules for reporting transfers in and out of the account. (I tell you more about using Quicken's built-in tax features in Chapter 16.) When you're finished, click Next to continue.

The Summary window appears (refer to Figure 7-2). It shows all the information you entered for the account. You can make changes if necessary. You can also use the Info button to enter additional information about the account, such as the financial institution name, contact information, and account number. When you're finished, click Done.

Entering Securities in a Regular Investment Account

When you create a regular investment account, Quicken automatically displays the Security Setup window, which you can use to enter information about the securities you already own. Like EasyStep windows, the Security Setup window walks you through the entry of each security, step-by-step, providing lots of general information along the way.

Click Next in the window that first appears. Then use a window like the one shown here to enter general information about the security:

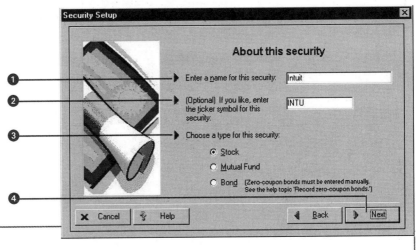

① Enter a name for the security.

② If desired, enter the security's ticker symbol.

③ Select the appropriate security type.

④ Click Next to continue.

> **Tip** You can modify the list of security types. Choose Lists | Investment | Security Type to display the Security Type List. Then use the New, Edit, and Delete buttons on the Button bar to modify the list.

When you click the Next button, the Security Setup window enables you to specify two optional pieces of information for organizing your investments:

- **Investment Goal** includes College Fund, High Risk, Low Risk, Income, and (none).
- **Asset Class** enables you to set one or a mix of asset types for the investment. When you click the Specify Asset Class button, the Asset Class Information dialog box appears (shown in the following illustration). If you select Single, you can choose one of the predefined classes: (none), Bonds, Domestic Bonds, Global Bonds, Stocks, Large Cap Stocks, Mid Cap Stocks, Small Cap Stocks, International Stocks, Money Market, Cash, or Other. If you select Mixture, you can use another dialog box to set the various classes.

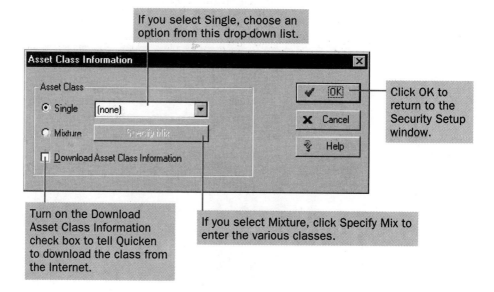

If you select Single, choose an option from this drop-down list.

Click OK to return to the Security Setup window.

Turn on the Download Asset Class Information check box to tell Quicken to download the class from the Internet.

If you select Mixture, click Specify Mix to enter the various classes.

Tip   You can modify the list of investment goals. Choose Lists | Investment | Investment Goal to display the Investment Goal List. Then use the New, Edit, and Delete buttons on the Button bar to modify the list.

SAVE TIME If you have access to the Internet, turn on the Download Asset Class Information check box in the Access Class Information dialog box and let Quicken retrieve this information for you based on the investment's ticker symbol. This saves you the bother of looking it up and entering it manually, and ensures that it is correct.

When you click Next in the Security Setup window, Quicken asks you to select a starting date for tracking the stock. There are three options:

- **Today** begins tracking an investment as of the current date. This is the quickest option.
- **The end of last year** begins tracking an investment as of the last day of the previous year. This enables you to generate accurate reports for the current year and the future.
- **The date you purchased this stock/mutual fund/bond** begins tracking an investment from the date you enter. Although this option may require a bit more work on your part, you should select it if you want to generate accurate reports—including capital gain/loss tax reports—for all years.

Select the appropriate option and, if necessary, enter a date. Then click Next. The next window enables you to enter the number of shares, cost per share, and commission or brokerage fee for the transaction. You can enter fractions for per share prices. For example, if a stock sells for 10 3/4, you can enter either **10 3/4**—with a space between the 0 and the 3—or **10.75**. Quicken converts fractions to decimal equivalents. Quicken will automatically calculate the total cost and display it in the window. When the amount is correct, click Next to continue.

Caution If you're interested in tracking stocks by lot, you must enter each purchase of a security separately. For example, suppose you purchased 50 shares of Intuit on 1/16/97, 50 more shares on 6/20/97, and 100 more shares on 5/1/98. Don't enter 200 shares with an average purchase price and total fee. Instead, enter each purchase lot separately to properly track their acquisition dates and prices. This makes it possible to take advantage of Quicken's Capital Gains Estimator feature, which I tell you about in Chapter 16.

Next, Quicken wants to know how you want to track the cost of securities. You have two options:

- **Lot Identification** enables you to track the cost of each security by its purchase lot. This is the most accurate way to track investment costs and performance. It also enables you to control capital gains timing by allowing you to choose the lot(s) you sell.
- **Average Cost** enables you to average the cost of all the purchases of a security. This method is commonly used for mutual funds reporting and has less bookkeeping requirements for tax purposes.

Tip Although you can switch methods at any time, the IRS requires that you stick to a method for a security once you have reported your first capital gain.

Select the desired cost tracking method and click Next. Quicken tells you that it has added the security to your account and offers to add another security. Click the Yes or No option button and click Next.

If you click Yes, the entire security setup process begins all over again. Follow the steps in this section to enter another security or another purchase lot of a security you already entered.

If you click No, Quicken displays a window listing all the securities you entered for the account.

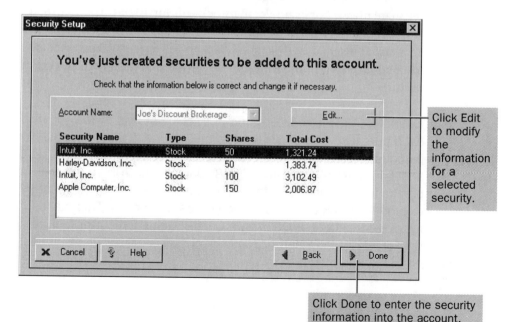

Click Edit to modify the information for a selected security.

Click Done to enter the security information into the account.

When you click Done, the window disappears. In the Account List window (see Figure 7-3), you can see the new investment account listed—as well as any linked bank account.

Adjusting the Balance of Cash Accounts

When you enter securities in an investment account, the cost of those securities may be deducted from a linked bank account, thus reducing the value of the linked account. You can see this in the Account List window (see Figure 7-3).

You can correct the balance in the linked account by entering an adjustment transaction in the misstated account (see Figure 7-4). Just be sure to use the same account name in the Category field. When you click Enter, Quicken warns you that you are recording a transfer back into the same account. Click Yes to accept

The linked bank account

The investment account

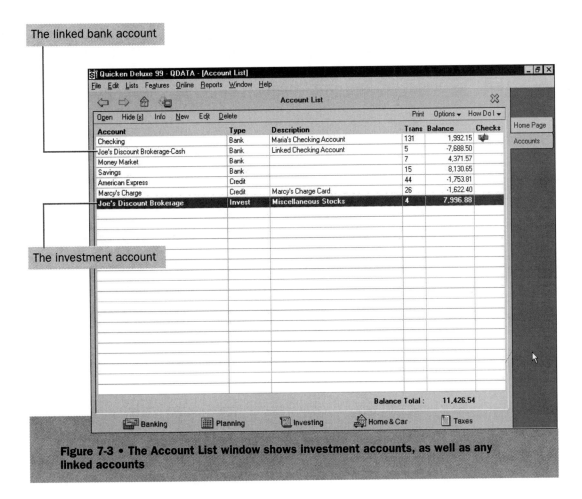

Figure 7-3 • The Account List window shows investment accounts, as well as any linked accounts

Entry for adjustment to opening balance

Entry for opening cash balance

Transactions for opening balance purchases

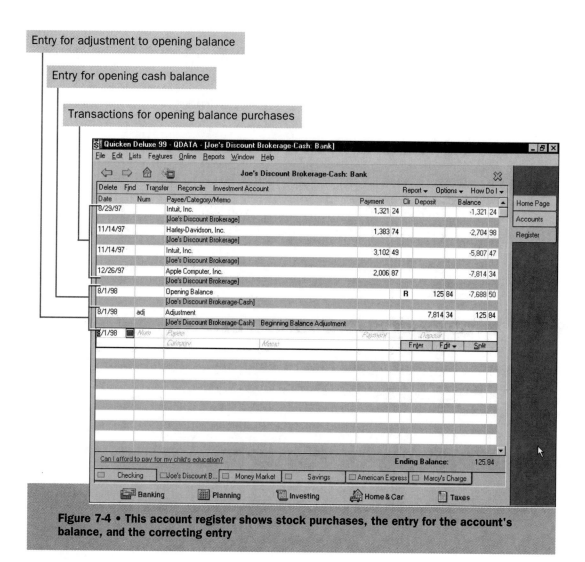

Figure 7-4 • This account register shows stock purchases, the entry for the account's balance, and the correcting entry

the transaction and correct the account balance. (I tell you more about using account registers in Chapter 4.)

Entering Mutual Fund Information for a Single Mutual Fund Investment Account

When you create a single mutual fund investment account, Quicken automatically displays the Set Up Mutual Fund Security dialog box, shown here, which you can use to enter information about the mutual fund in the account:

Enter information about the security in this area.

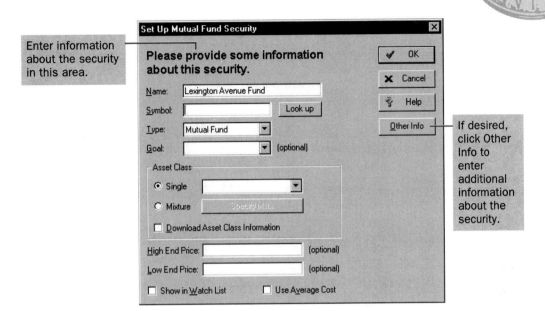

Set Up Mutual Fund Security

Please provide some information about this security.

Name: Lexington Avenue Fund

Symbol: [ ] Look up

Type: Mutual Fund ▼

Goal: [▼] (optional)

Asset Class

● Single [▼]

○ Mixture Specify mix...

☐ Download Asset Class Information

High End Price: [ ] (optional)

Low End Price: [ ] (optional)

☐ Show in Watch List   ☐ Use Average Cost

✓ OK
✗ Cancel
? Help
Other Info

If desired, click Other Info to enter additional information about the security.

This dialog box gathers the same kind of information that you enter in the Security Setup window. You can consult the section titled "Entering Securities in a Regular Investment Account" earlier in this chapter for details. I tell you about the other options in this window later in this chapter.

When you click OK to save the security information, the account appears in the Account List window.

Creating a 401(k) Account

You create a 401(k) account with the 401(k) Setup window, which enables you to enter information for the account. Before you begin, take out your most recent 401(k) statement. You'll need it to enter accurate information about the account's securities.

Caution   If you have already created a 401(k) account with EasyStep Paycheck, which I discuss in Chapter 5, don't set up another account for the same investment. Instead, edit the existing account. I tell you how later in this chapter.

Getting Started

Choose Lists | Account or press CTRL-A to display the Account List window. Then click the New button on the Button bar. In the Create New Account window that appears, select the 401(k) option button and click the Next button.

The 401(k) Setup window appears. Click its Next button to begin entering information about the account in the EasyStep tab, shown here:

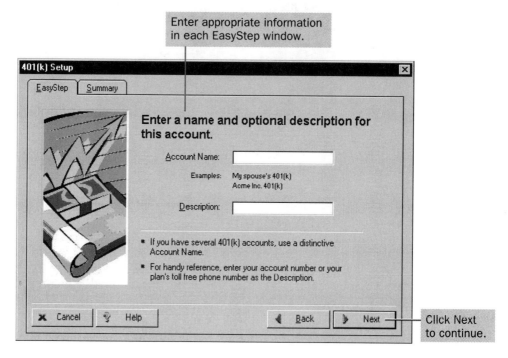

Enter appropriate information in each EasyStep window.

Click Next to continue.

Use the EasyStep tab of the 401(k) Setup window to enter information step-by-step.

Tip   Although it appears that you can click the Summary tab and enter all information at once (as you can for the Investment Account Setup window), you can't. The Summary tab is just a tease. You must work through each step of the EasyStep window before you can switch from one tab to the other.

Entering Account Information

The first EasyStep window prompts you for an Account Name and Description. Enter a unique name for the account. If you have more than one 401(k) account (for example, yours and your spouse's), make sure you give each one a distinctive name so you can tell them apart. Enter a description if desired. Then click Next.

The next window prompts you to enter information from the plan's most recent statement. Enter the statement's ending date and the number of different securities you own in the appropriate text boxes. Click Next.

Next, Quicken asks two questions regarding your statement: Does your employer contribute to your 401(k)? Does the statement list how many shares of each security you own? Select the Yes or No option button for each question and click Next to continue.

Quicken displays a window that enables you to enter the Security Name, Total Shares, and Ending Balance for a security that's part of your 401(k). Enter the information in the appropriate text boxes and click Next. Quicken will display the same window for the number of securities you entered earlier in the setup process. Provide the requested information and click Next until each security has been entered.

Finally, the Summary tab appears, as shown next. It displays the information you entered and enables you to edit it. When you're finished reviewing and changing information in the window, click Done to create the account. It appears in the Account List window.

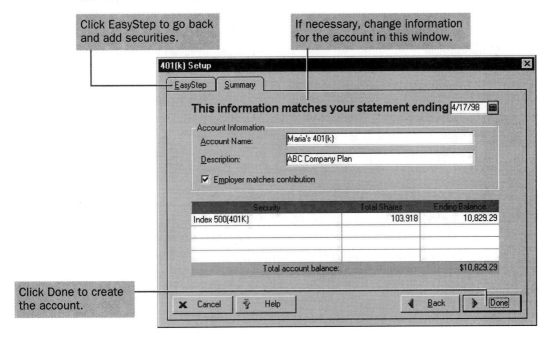

> **Tip** To add securities, you must use the EasyStep tab to change the number of securities, and then enter additional security information.

Editing an Existing 401(k) Account

If you created a 401(k) account as part of the Paycheck Setup process discussed in Chapter 5, part of the account creation process is already done. All you have to do is edit the account to provide details about the securities it contains.

Choose Lists | Account or press CTRL-A to display the Account List window. Double-click the name of the 401(k) account you already created. The 401(k) Setup window appears. Follow the instructions in the previous section to provide missing information for the account. When you click the Done button at the end of the process, the account is updated with the information you provided.

Viewing Your Investments

Quicken offers a number of ways to view your investment information. Each method also offers options to add transactions or edit securities. Here's an overview of each method so you know their options, benefits, and drawbacks.

Security List

The Security List window (see Figure 7-5) simply lists the securities in Quicken's data file. You can use this window to add, edit, delete, or hide securities, including Watch List securities—securities you don't own but want to monitor.

To open this window, choose Lists | Investments | Security or press CTRL-Y.

Investment Register

The Investment Register window, shown in Figure 7-6, looks similar to the Account Register window, but it shows only your investment and 401(k) accounts. It enables you to enter transactions for each investment account. It also provides buttons for opening other windows to work with investments.

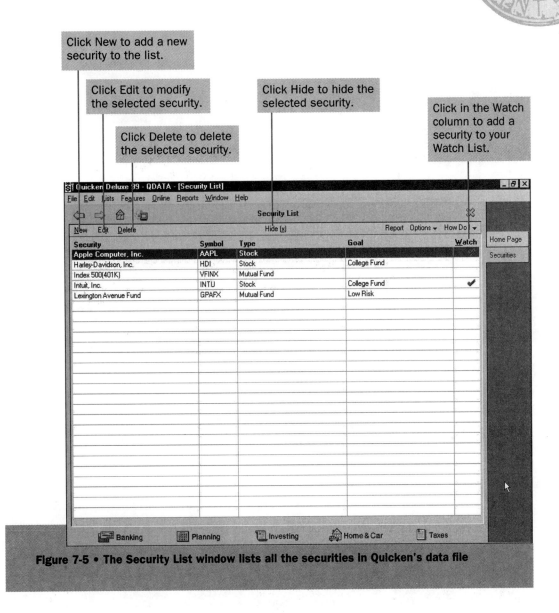

Click New to add a new security to the list.

Click Edit to modify the selected security.

Click Hide to hide the selected security.

Click in the Watch column to add a security to your Watch List.

Click Delete to delete the selected security.

Figure 7-5 • The Security List window lists all the securities in Quicken's data file

To open the Investment Register window, double-click any investment or 401(k) account in the Account List window (see Figure 7-3).

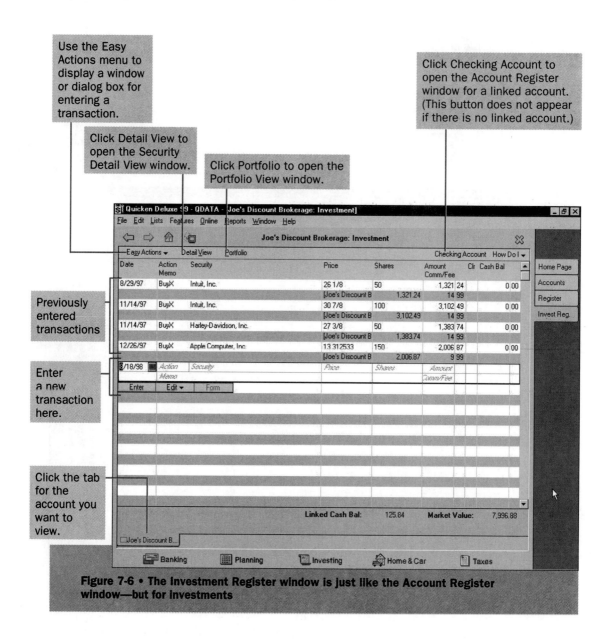

Use the Easy Actions menu to display a window or dialog box for entering a transaction.

Click Detail View to open the Security Detail View window.

Click Portfolio to open the Portfolio View window.

Click Checking Account to open the Account Register window for a linked account. (This button does not appear if there is no linked account.)

Previously entered transactions

Enter a new transaction here.

Click the tab for the account you want to view.

Figure 7-6 • The Investment Register window is just like the Account Register window—but for investments

Portfolio View

The Portfolio View window (see Figure 7-7) displays all of your investments in one place. Information can be viewed in a wide variety of ways to show you exactly what you need to see to understand the performance, value, or components of your portfolio.

You can open the Portfolio View window in a number of ways:

- Choose Features | Investing | Portfolio View or press CTRL-U.
- Click the Portfolio View button in the Investment Register window or the Security Detail View window, which is discussed later in this chapter.

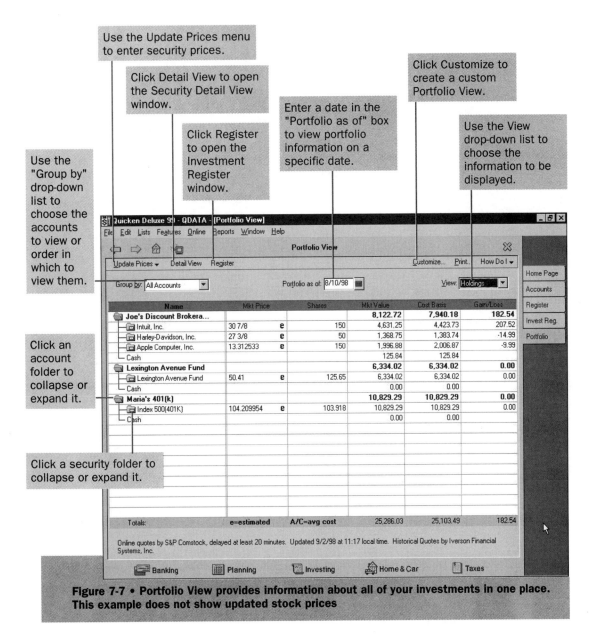

Figure 7-7 • Portfolio View provides information about all of your investments in one place. This example does not show updated stock prices

Quicken Quote

"I did not really appreciate or intelligently work with my investments until the arrival of Quicken 99. It makes the process of reviewing my portfolio even easier and comprehendible. Nice job!"

Michael Cassidy, *Oak Hill, VA*

Using Portfolio View Options

The real strength of Portfolio View is its flexibility. It can display information about your investments in a wide variety of ways. You can set the view by choosing options from the Group by and View drop-down lists. There are many view combinations—far too many to illustrate in this book. But the following section describes the options so you can explore the views on your own.

Using the Group by Options   The Group by options enable you to select the accounts that are displayed in the window or the order in which securities appear. The drop-down list offers eight options:

- **All Accounts** shows all accounts and all securities within them.
- **Selected Accounts** displays a dialog box you can use to select the accounts you want to appear and the order in which you want them to appear.
- **Security** displays only the securities. Account information is not provided.
- **Security Type** displays the securities organized by type: Bond, CD, Mutual Fund, and Stock.
- **Investment Goal** displays the securities organized by investment goal: No Goal, College Fund, High Risk, Income, and Low Risk.
- **Asset Class** displays the securities organized by Asset Class: No Asset Class, Domestic Bonds, Large Cap Stocks, Small Cap Stocks, Global Bonds,

International Stocks, Money Market, Other, Bonds, Stocks, Cash, Mid Cap Stocks, and Asset Mixture.

- **Watch List** displays investments on your Watch List, including those you do not own, but for which you want to track prices. I tell you more about creating Watch List items later in this chapter.
- **Individual Accounts** (listed by name) displays only the specific account's investments.

Using the View Options   The View options enable you to specify the information you want to view for the displayed securities. The drop-down list offers five options:

- **Holdings** displays the market price, number of shares, market value, cost basis, and gain or loss for each security.
- **Performance** displays the market price, number of shares, dollars invested, dollar return, and return on investment for each security.
- **Valuation** displays the market price, number of shares, dollars invested, dollar return, and market value for each security.
- **Price Update** displays the market price, number of shares, last price, market value, and market value change for each security.
- **Quotes** displays the ticker symbol, market price, change, high, low, and value for each security. This view is only useful if you enter—either manually or via Quicken's Online Quotes feature—the stock price information for the day.

Customizing Portfolio View

The View drop-down list in the Portfolio View window also offers two Custom options. You can customize any view (including either of the two Custom views) by clicking the Customize button in the Portfolio View window. Then use the Customize Portfolio dialog box shown here to select the columns you want to appear in the view. When you're finished, click OK to complete the customization.

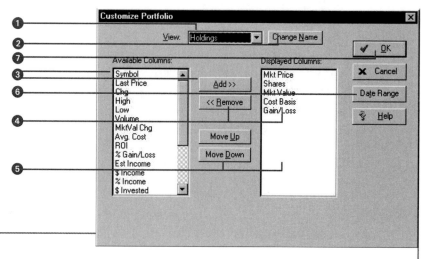

❶ Select the view you want to customize from the View drop-down list.

❷ If desired, enter a new name for the view and click the Change Name button.

❸ To add a column, click its name in the Available Columns list, and then click the Add button.

❹ To remove a column, click its name in the Displayed Columns list, and then click the Remove button.

❺ To move a column up or down in the Displayed Columns list, click its name to select it, and then click the Move Up or Move Down button.

❻ To specify a date range for the view, click the Date Range button.

❼ Click OK to save your settings.

Security Detail View

The Security Detail View window provides a wealth of information about a specific security, including value and performance information, transactions, and price or market value history. You can use this window to enter transactions, update prices, edit a security, or open the Portfolio View or Investment Register windows. If you have access to the Internet, you can click the News tab at the bottom of the window to view news stories about the security.

You can open the Security Detail View window (shown in Figure 7-8) in a number of ways:

- Choose Features | Investing | Security Detail & News.
- Click the Detail View button in the Investment Register or Portfolio View window.
- Double-click a security in the Portfolio View window.

Use the Easy Actions menu to display a window or dialog box for entering a transaction.

Use the Update menu to enter security prices.

Click Edit to modify the currently displayed security.

Click Portfolio to open the Portfolio View window.

Click Register to open the Investment Register window.

Previously entered transactions

Choose a security to display from this drop-down list.

Choose options from these drop-down lists to change the view.

Click News to display related news stories downloaded from the Internet.

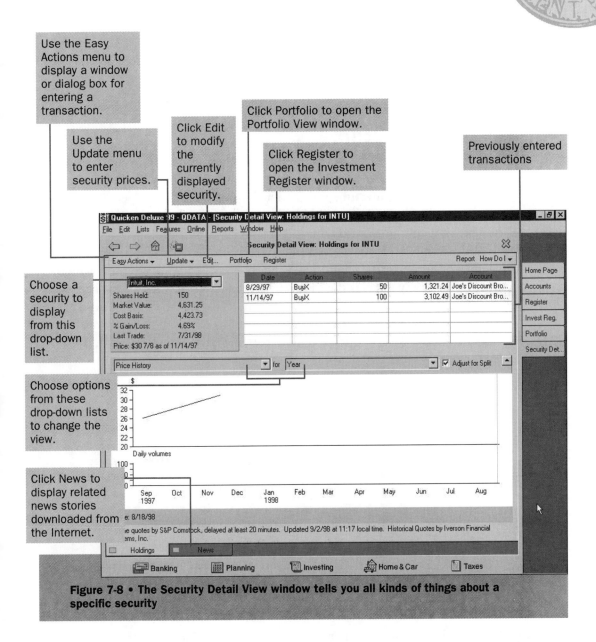

Figure 7-8 • The Security Detail View window tells you all kinds of things about a specific security

Recording Investment Transactions

The most important part of properly tracking investments is recording all investment transactions. This includes purchases, sales, dividends, and other activity affecting your portfolio's value.

In this section, I provide step-by-step instructions for entering the most common investment transactions. I also provide the basic information you need to enter more obscure transactions, such as stock splits, corporate acquisitions, and stock dividends.

Before You Start

Before you enter a transaction, you must have all of its details. In most cases, you can find the information you need on a confirmation form or receipt you receive from your broker or investment firm. The information varies depending on the transaction, but it generally should include the security name, transaction date, number of shares, price per share, and commissions or fees.

You can enter most security transactions within the Investment Register window or the Security Detail View window, so switch to one of those windows when you're ready to enter the transaction. To follow the instructions here, switch to the Investment Register window and click the tab at the bottom of the window to view the account in which you want to record the transaction. You can then choose the appropriate option from the Easy Actions menu in the Button bar.

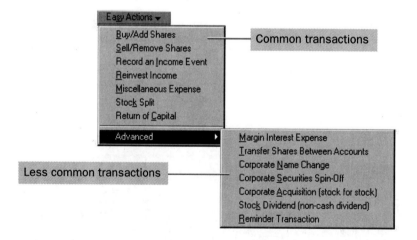

Shortcut Experienced Quicken users may prefer to enter transactions directly into the Investment Register for an account. A drop-down list in the transaction's entry area offers appropriate transaction codes for all kinds of transactions. Explore this feature on your own once you're accustomed to entering investment transactions with Easy Actions.

Purchases

A security purchase normally involves the exchange of cash for security shares. In some cases, you may already own shares of the security or have it listed on your Watch List. In other cases, the security may not already exist in your Quicken data file, so you'll need to set up the security when you make the purchase.

Start by choosing Easy Actions | Buy/Add Shares. The Buy/Add Shares window appears:

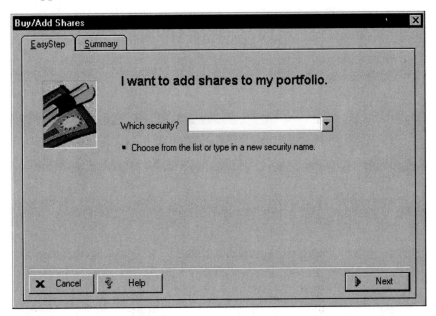

How you proceed depends on whether you already own shares in the security:

- To add shares for a new security, enter the security name in the text box. When you click Next, the Set Up Security dialog box appears. Enter information about the security and click OK to add it to the Security List.
- To add shares for a known security, select its name from the drop-down list and click Next.

Shortcut At this point, you can click the Summary tab to complete entries for the transaction if you don't need the guidance of EasyStep.

The next EasyStep step offers two options for the source of funds for the purchase:

- **Yes, from the following account** enables you to select a Quicken account from which money should be deducted for the purchase of the shares.
- **No, deposit the shares without affecting any cash balance** adds the shares to your Investment Register account without deducting cash from any other account. You might use this option to add shares omitted when you initially set up the account.

Make your selection and click the Next button. You can then enter details about the transaction in the appropriate text boxes of the next window that appears:

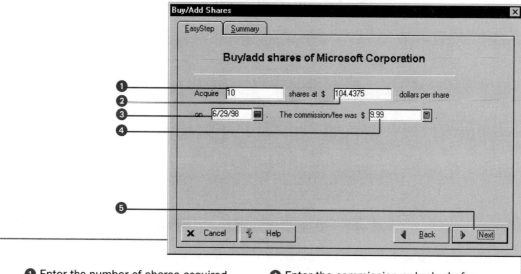

① Enter the number of shares acquired. ④ Enter the commission or broker's fee.
② Enter the price per share. ⑤ Click Next.
③ Enter the transaction date.

Finally, the Summary tab of the Buy/Add Shares window appears:

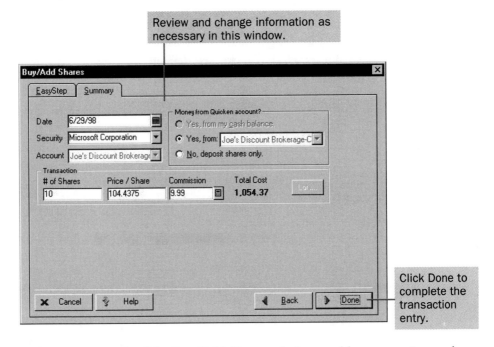

Review and change information as necessary in this window.

Click Done to complete the transaction entry.

The Summary tab of the Buy/Add Shares window enables you to view and change entries for a security acquisition. When the Summary tab displays accurate information for the transaction, click Done. The entry is added to the account register, as shown here:

6/29/98	BuyX	Microsoft Corporation	104 7/16	10	1,054	37	0	00
			[Joe's Discount B	1,054.37	9	99		

Sales

A security sale also involves the exchange of cash for security shares. Normally, you dispose of shares you already own, but in some instances, you may sell shares you don't own. This is called *selling short,* and it is a risky investment technique sometimes used by experienced investors.

Start by choosing Easy Actions | Sell/Remove Shares. The Sell/Remove Shares window, which looks very much like the Buy/Add Shares window, shown previously, appears. How you proceed depends on whether you already own shares in the security:

- To remove shares of a known security, select its name from the drop-down list and click Next.
- To remove shares of a new security, enter the security name in the text box. When you click Next, the Set Up Security dialog box appears. Enter information about the security and click OK to add it to the Security List.

Shortcut   At this point, you can click the Summary tab to complete entries for the transaction if you don't need the guidance of EasyStep.

The next EasyStep step offers two options for recording proceeds from the sale:

- **Yes, transfer to the following account** enables you to select a Quicken account to which money should be added from the sale of the shares.
- **No, withdraw the shares without affecting any cash balance** removes the shares from your Investment Register account without adding cash to any other account. You might use this option to record the disposal of shares given as a gift.

Make your selection and click the Next button. You can then enter details about the transaction in the appropriate text boxes of the next window that appears:

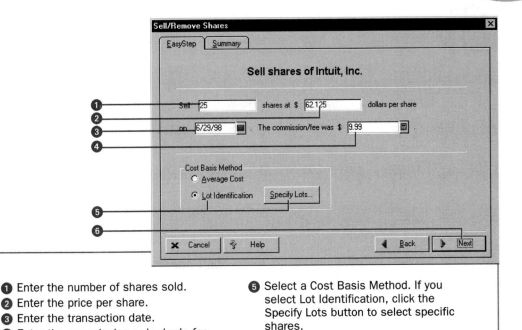

1. Enter the number of shares sold.
2. Enter the price per share.
3. Enter the transaction date.
4. Enter the commission or broker's fee.
5. Select a Cost Basis Method. If you select Lot Identification, click the Specify Lots button to select specific shares.
6. Click Next.

The Lot Identification option in the previous window enables you to specify exactly which shares of stock to sell. You can use this option for additional control over capital gains. For example, if you want to take advantage of long-term capital gains tax breaks, you could sell shares that have been in your possession for more than 12 or 18 months. If you want to record a loss, you could sell shares that cost more than the selling price. Obviously, your options will vary depending on the lots, their acquisition prices, and your selling price.

SAVE MONEY By controlling the term and amount of capital gains, you can minimize your tax bill. Use the Capital Gains Estimator, which I discuss in Chapter 16, to help you select lots before you sell investments.

To use Lot Identification, select its option button, and then click the Specify Lots button beside it. This displays the Specify Lots dialog box. Here you can select the lots you want to sell:

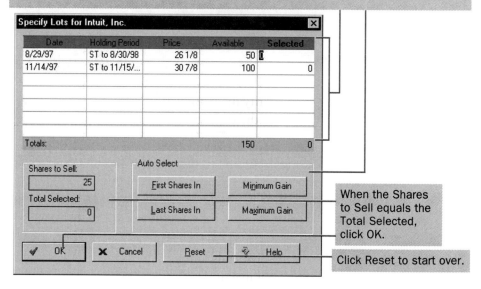

Finally, the Summary tab of the Sell/Remove Shares window appears. Use it to review and, if necessary, change your entry.

Review and change information as necessary in this window.

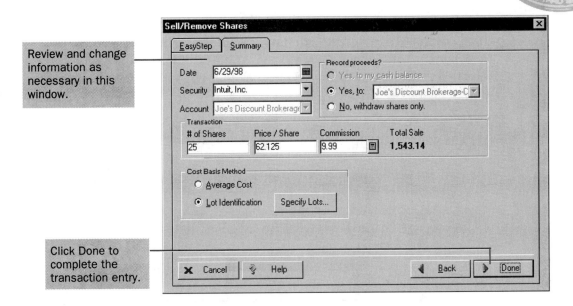

Click Done to complete the transaction entry.

The Summary tab of the Sell/Remove Shares window enables you to view and change entries for a security disposition. When the Summary tab displays accurate information for the transaction, click Done. The entry is added to the account register, as shown here:

6/29/98	SellX	Intuit, Inc.		62 1/8	25		1,543 14		0 00
				[Joe's Discount B		1,543.14	9 99		

Dividend Payments and Other Income

Many investments pay dividends, interest, or other income in cash. (That's why they're so attractive to an investor!) Recording this activity in the appropriate account register enables Quicken to accurately calculate performance, while keeping account balances up-to-date.

Caution   Many mutual funds are set up to reinvest income, rather than pay it in cash. Do not use the steps in this section to record a reinvestment of income. Instead, choose Easy Actions I Reinvest Income and use the Reinvest Income dialog box that appears to enter transaction information.

Choose Easy Actions I Record an Income Event. The Record Income dialog box appears, as shown here:

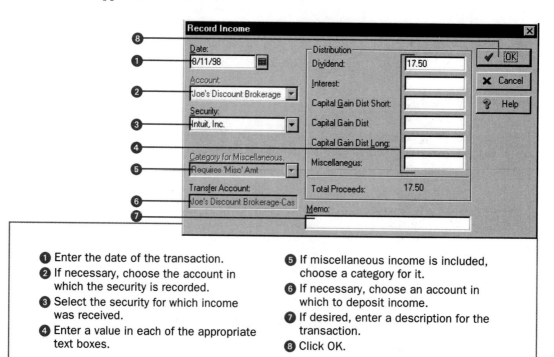

① Enter the date of the transaction.
② If necessary, choose the account in which the security is recorded.
③ Select the security for which income was received.
④ Enter a value in each of the appropriate text boxes.
⑤ If miscellaneous income is included, choose a category for it.
⑥ If necessary, choose an account in which to deposit income.
⑦ If desired, enter a description for the transaction.
⑧ Click OK.

Use the Record Income dialog box to enter information about a cash payment on an investment. When you click OK to record the transaction, it appears in the Investment Register window for the account, as shown here:

| 8/11/98 | DivX | Intuit, Inc. | | | 17 50 | | 0 00 |
| | | | | Joe's Discount B | | | |

Other Transactions

Other transactions are just as easy to enter as purchases, sales, and dividends. Simply choose the appropriate option from the Easy Actions drop-down list, and then enter the transaction information in the window or dialog box that appears. If you have the transaction confirmation or brokerage statement in front of you when you enter the transaction, you have all the information you need to enter it.

Tip   If you need additional guidance while entering a transaction, click the Help button in the transaction window or dialog box to learn more about the options that must be entered.

Adjusting Balances

Occasionally, you may need to adjust the cash balance or number of shares in an investment account. The Investing submenu under the Features menu offers three commands to do this:

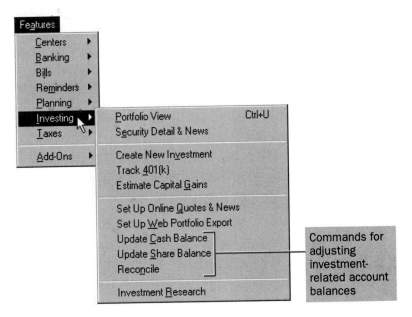

Commands for adjusting investment-related account balances

Update Cash Balance   Use the Update Cash Balance command to adjust the balance in a linked cash account, an investment account with a cash balance, or an asset account used to track investments and cash. Simply enter the adjustment date and correct balance in the dialog box that appears. When you click OK, Quicken creates an adjusting entry.

Update Share Balance   Use the Update Share Balance command to adjust the number of shares in an investment account. Just enter the adjustment date, security, and correct number of shares in the dialog box that appears. When you click OK, Quicken creates an adjusting entry.

Reconcile You can use the Reconcile command to reconcile the transactions and balance in a linked cash account—or an investment account—with a cash balance. This command begins a regular bank account reconciliation, which I discuss in detail in Chapter 4. You should have the account's statement handy before beginning the reconciliation process. At the end of the reconciliation, Quicken can make any necessary adjustments to the account balance.

Adding Watch List Securities

Quicken's Watch List feature enables you to track securities you don't own. You add a security to the Security List (refer to Figure 7-5) and enable its Watch List check box. You can then view the security in the Portfolio View window (refer to Figure 7-7), using the Watch List option on the Group by drop-down list. Because each Watch List security is included on the Security List, it also appears on Security drop-down lists in dialog boxes. This speeds up transaction recording time when you're ready to invest.

Before you can add a security to the Watch List, you must add it to the Security List. Choose Lists | Investment | Security to open the Security List window. Then click the New button in the Button bar. The Set Up Security dialog box appears. Use it to enter basic information about the security and add it to the Watch List.

I discuss most of the options in this dialog box earlier in this chapter, but there are three at the bottom of the dialog box that I saved for now:

- **High End Price** is the high price at which you want Quicken to alert you. For example, if the security is trading at $20 a share and you want to be alerted when it reaches $30, enter **30** in the High End Price text box.
- **Low End Price** is the low price at which you want Quicken to alert you. For example, if the security is trading at $20 a share and you want to be alerted when it reaches $10, enter **10** in the Low End Price text box.

Tip I use the High End Price and Low End Price options to alert myself when it's time to consider selling or buying a security.

- **Show In Watch List**, when turned on, adds the security to the Watch List.

When you are finished setting up the security, click OK. It appears on the Security List and, if the Show in Watch List check box is turned on, in the list of Watch List securities in the Portfolio View window.

Tip   Although the Watch List feature does not require Internet access, it's a heck of a lot more useful if you regularly download stock prices using the Online Quotes feature of Quicken. I tell you about Online Quotes in Chapter 14.

Tracking Security Values

Quicken can automatically do all the math to tell you what your investments are worth—if you take the time to enter the per share prices of each of your securities. When you record types of transactions, Quicken automatically records the security price. It uses the most recently entered price as an estimate to calculate the current value of the investment. You can see this in the Portfolio View window—those black e characters indicate that the price is an estimate. The e characters appear if the current date is on a weekend or holiday or you haven't entered or downloaded the current day's prices.

Of course, Portfolio View is a lot more valuable with up-to-date security price information and a history of prices, as you can see here:

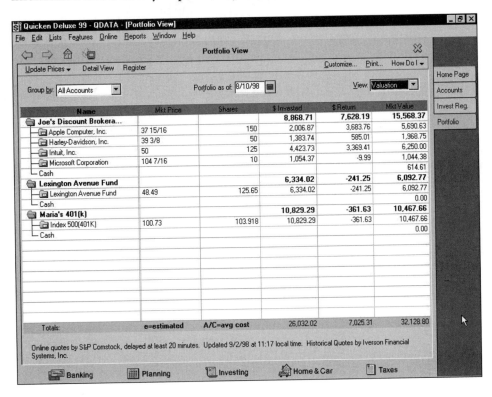

You can enter price information two ways: manually (the hard way) and automatically (the easy way). I show you how to manually enter security prices in this chapter; to learn how to automatically enter prices via Internet download, skip ahead to Chapter 14.

SAVE TIME If you track more than one or two securities and want to update price information more often than once a week, stop reading now. You don't want to enter security prices manually. Trust me. It's an extremely tedious task. Quicken's ability to download stock prices directly from the Internet—even five-year price histories—can save you tons of time and prevent data entry errors. And best of all, it's free. All you need is an Internet connection. Learn about setting up an Internet connection in Chapter 3, and about downloading quotes in Chapter 14.

Entering Security Prices

Manually entering security prices isn't really hard. It's just time-consuming. And the more securities you track, the more time-consuming it is. But without an Internet connection, this may be the only way you can enter prices into Quicken.

Start by choosing Features | Investing | Security Detail & News to display the Security Detail View window (refer to Figure 7-8). Use the drop-down list within the window to display the security for which you want to enter price information. Then choose Update | Edit Price History (on the Button bar). The Price History window for the security appears. It shows all the price information stored within the Quicken data file for the security. You can use buttons on the window's Button bar to add, edit, delete, and print the price history, as shown here:

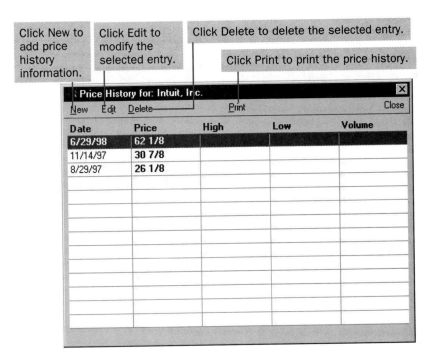

When you click the New button, the New Price dialog box appears, as shown here:

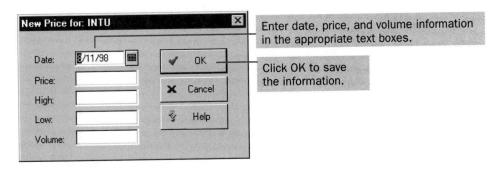

The Edit Price dialog box looks and works much the same way.

Viewing Market Values and Performance

Once you've entered price information for your securities, you can view their market value and performance information in the Portfolio View window and Security Detail View window (see Figure 7-9). Use options within the windows to modify the information that is displayed. I tell you how earlier in this chapter.

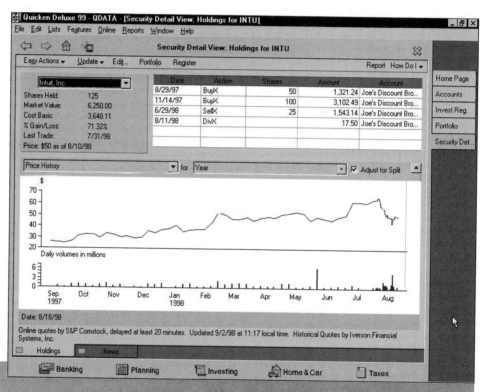

Figure 7-9 • Here's the Security Detail View window with a full year's worth of price information. Do you think I entered all those security prices manually?

Reports and Graphs

Chapter 8

In This Chapter:

- *Financial Activity Centers*

- *Customizing a Center Window*

- *Creating Reports*

- *Creating Graphs*

- *Customizing Reports and Graphs*

- *Printing Reports and Graphs*

181

At this point, you'll probably agree that entering financial information into Quicken is a great way to organize it. But sometimes organizing information isn't enough. Sometimes you need to see concise summaries of the information you entered, in the form of balances, activity reports, and graphs.

Quicken's Financial Activity Centers, reports, and graphs are three highly customizable features you can use to view and analyze your financial information. As you'll see in this chapter, they quickly and easily provide the information you need about your accounts and categories.

Financial Activity Centers

Quicken's Financial Activity Centers (or Centers) provide snapshots of your financial information, complete with balances and graphs. They also provide useful links for accessing Quicken features and, if you have Internet access, Web pages on Quicken.com and other Internet destinations.

To open a Center window, choose Features | Centers, and then choose the name of the Center you want from the submenu that appears. Or, if a Center window is already displayed, click the name of the Center you want on the navigation bar at the top of the window. You'll see a window like the one shown in Figure 8-1.

Tip   You can act on many items or snapshots listed in a Financial Center Window by pointing to the item, clicking the right mouse button, and choosing a command from the menu that appears.

The Financial Activity Centers

Quicken Deluxe offers six customizable Financial Activity Center windows:

- The **Quicken Home Page**, which is shown in Figure 8-1, is the main Center window. It provides an overview of the most important information about your finances, including scheduled transactions, alerts, reminders, account balances, Watch List items, credit card analysis, and income vs. expenses graphs.

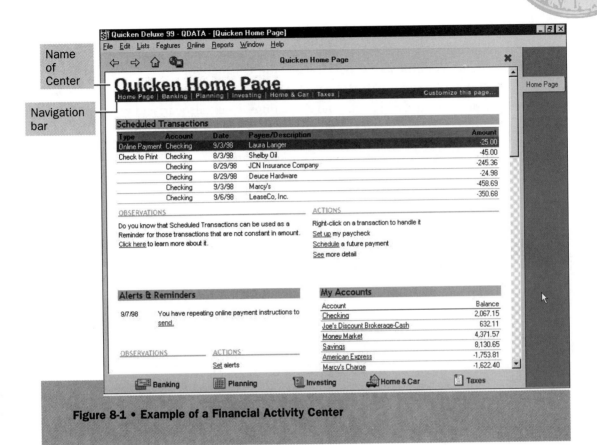

Name of Center

Navigation bar

Figure 8-1 • Example of a Financial Activity Center

- **Banking Center** displays banking-related information, including extended account lists, account overviews, and credit card analysis. You learn more about the Banking Center in Chapter 18.

- **Planning Center** displays information useful for financial planning, such as savings, expenses, budgets, and net worth. I provide more information about the Planning Center in Chapter 21.

- **Investing Center** displays investing-related information, including your Watch List, portfolio, asset allocation chart, and investment return graph. I discuss the Investing Center in Chapter 19.

- **Home & Car Center** displays information about your assets and liabilities, including an asset account list, a loan summary, and auto expenses. You learn more about the Home & Car Center in Chapter 18.
- **Taxes Center** provides information related to your income taxes, including your year-to-date income and deductions, a tax calendar, and your projected tax. I discuss the Taxes Center in Chapter 16.

In each Center window except Quicken Home Page, clickable links along the right-hand window enable you to access related Quicken commands, Web pages on the Internet, and instructions for a number of related Quicken features.

Quicken Quote

"The Home Page and Investing Center make it easy to keep track of my investments, budgets, and income. They are a great improvement."

Joyce Speelman, Winchester, VA

Customizing the Quicken Home Page

You can customize the Quicken Home Page by creating or modifying views. This makes it possible to include only the information you think is important in the Home Page window.

Modifying the Current View

In the Home Page window, choose "Customize this view" from the "Customize this page" menu at the far right end of the navigation bar. The Customize View dialog box appears:

To add a snapshot to the view, select it in the Available Items list and then click Add.

To change the view's name, enter a new name in the View Name text box.

To remove a snapshot from the view, select it in the Chosen Items list and then click Remove.

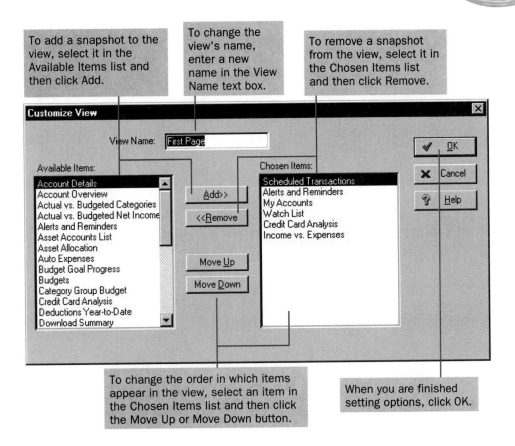

To change the order in which items appear in the view, select an item in the Chosen Items list and then click the Move Up or Move Down button.

When you are finished setting options, click OK.

You can include up to fifteen items in the Home Page. To add an item, select it in the Available Items list and click Add. Its name appears in the Chosen Items list. You can rearrange the order of items in the Chosen Items list by selecting an item and clicking the Move Up or Move Down button. To remove an item from the Home Page, select it in the Chosen Items list and click Remove. When you're finished making changes, click OK. The Home Page is redrawn to reflect your changes.

Creating a New View

In the Home Page window, choose "Create a New View" from the "Customize this page" menu at the far right end of the navigation bar. The Customize View dialog box, previously illustrated, appears. This time, the Chosen Items list is empty.

Enter a name for the view in the View Name text box. Then add items to the Chosen Items list as previously instructed. When you're finished, click OK. The new Home Page view is created to your specifications and appears on screen.

Switching from One View to Another

If you have created more than one view for the Home Page, each view is listed at the bottom of the "Customize this page" menu, as shown next. To switch from one view to another, simply select it from the menu.

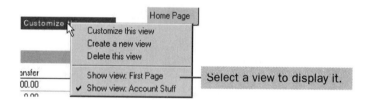

Deleting a View

To delete a view, begin by switching to the view you want to delete. Then choose "Delete this view" from the "Customize this page" menu. Click OK in the confirmation dialog box that appears. The view is deleted and another view takes its place.

 Tip You cannot delete a view if only one view exists for the Home Page.

Customizing Other Center Windows

Customization options for other views vary based on the snapshots they display. Some snapshots offer customization options; others don't.

For example, you can customize the Investment Return graph that appears in the Investing Center window by pointing to it, clicking the right mouse button, and choosing the "Customize this graph" command. The Customize Snapshot dialog box appears, as shown here. Use this dialog box to set customization options for the snapshot:

Click a tab to set
its options.

Set date options in
the Graph Dates area.

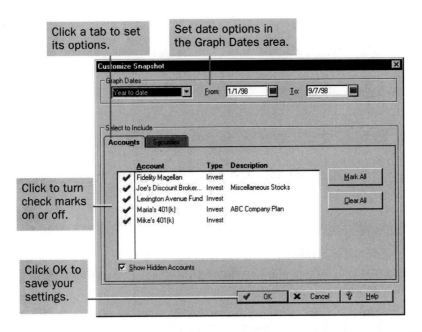

Click to turn
check marks
on or off.

Click OK to
save your
settings.

The Customize Snapshot dialog box varies from snapshot to snapshot. It's impossible to show all options here. In most cases, the dialog box includes tabs for different categories of options. You can click to toggle check marks beside items in lists; only those items that are checked will be included in the snapshot. When you are finished setting options, click OK to save them. The snapshot is redrawn to your specifications.

Types of Reports and Graphs

Quicken offers a variety of reports and graphs, each of which can be customized to meet your needs. In this section, I tell you about the different types of reports and graphs and explain how you can create, customize, and print a report or graph based on the financial information in your Quicken data file.

Within Quicken are essentially three kinds of reports and graphs: EasyAnswer, predefined, and customized. Here's an overview of each one.

EasyAnswer

EasyAnswer reports and graphs answer specific predefined questions such as

- Where did I spend my money?
- How much did I pay to...?
- Did I meet my budget?
- How is my investment performing?

You select a question, and then provide optional detail information such as a date range, payee, or account. Quicken gathers the information and generates the report or graph.

Predefined

Quicken's Report menu includes a number of predefined reports and graphs. Reports are organized by category: banking, planning, investment, taxes, and business. Each report or graph includes the kind of information you'd logically expect to find in that particular kind of report or graph. For example, the Transaction Report shows a list of all transactions made during a period you specify. For each transaction, the report displays the date, number, description, memo, category, clear status, and amount. The Net Worth Graph uses bars to chart your assets and liabilities, and a line to show your net worth. You can also create predefined reports using the Report button in the Button bar or contextual menus that you can display for items in some windows.

Custom

You can create custom reports and graphs by customizing the predefined reports and graphs. This multiplies your reporting capabilities, enabling you to create reports or graphs that show exactly what you need to show.

Creating Reports and Graphs

With Quicken, creating a report or graph is as simple as choosing a menu command or clicking a Button bar button. In this section, I show you how to create reports and graphs using a variety of different methods.

Using the Report Menu

The Report menu is your main tool for creating reports. Use it to create EasyAnswer and predefined reports, either of which can be customized.

Creating an EasyAnswer Report or Graph

Choose Reports | EasyAnswer Reports. The EasyAnswer Reports & Graphs dialog box appears:

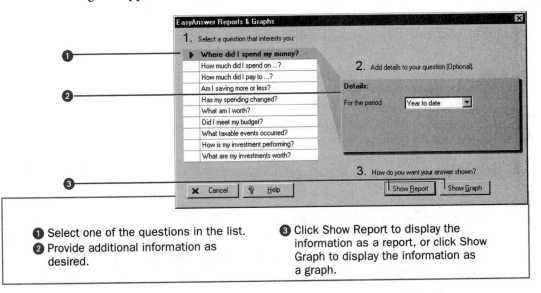

❶ Select one of the questions in the list.
❷ Provide additional information as desired.

❸ Click Show Report to display the information as a report, or click Show Graph to display the information as a graph.

Select a question for the report or graph you want to produce. If desired, provide additional information in the Details area. The options that appear here vary depending on the question you select. Then click the Show Report or Show Graph button. Figure 8-2 is an example of a report produced by the settings shown in the preceding illustration.

Click Customize to modify report settings.

Click Memorize to memorize the report's settings.

Click Copy to copy the report to the clipboard so it can be pasted into other documents.

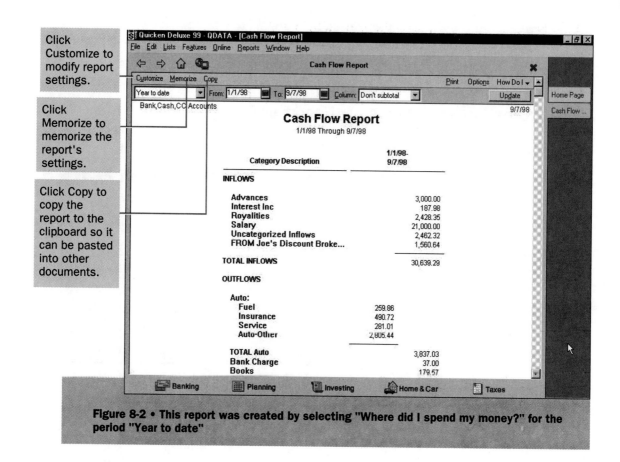

Figure 8-2 • This report was created by selecting "Where did I spend my money?" for the period "Year to date"

> **Tip** Double-clicking on a number in some reports produces a QuickZoom report showing the detail for that number.

Creating a Report

From the Reports menu, choose the category for the report you want to produce to display a submenu of reports. Choose the report you want to produce from the submenu. The Create Report window opens as shown at the top of the next page. This window gives you access to all of the predefined reports available on the Reports menu. To change to a different report category, simply click the tab for that category. The window lists all the reports available for the current category. Select the report you want to create, enter date information in the Report Dates area, and click Create. The report appears in its own window.

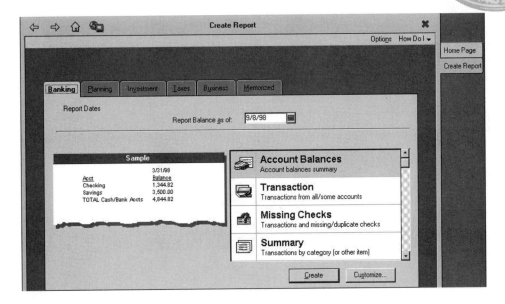

Creating a Graph

You can also use the Reports menu to create a graph. Choose Reports | Graphs to display a submenu of graphs. Choose the one you want to create. The Create Graph dialog box appears. This dialog box lists all the graphs you can create. Select one, enter date information in the Graph Dates area, and click Create. The graph appears in its own window. Figure 8-3 shows what the Income and Expense Graph looks like.

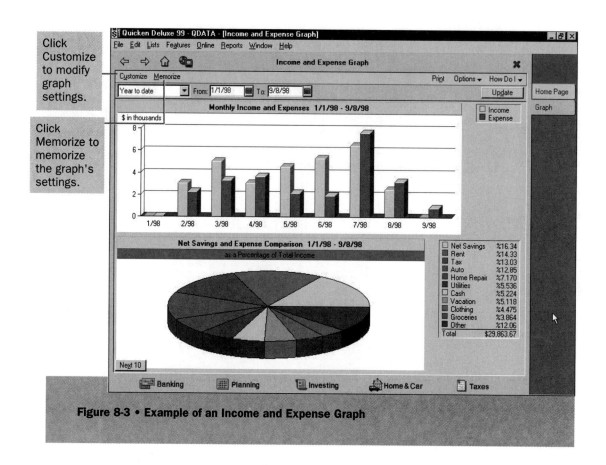

Figure 8-3 • Example of an Income and Expense Graph

Using the Report Button

You can also create a report by using the Report button or menu on the Button bar in some windows. This normally creates a report based on information selected within the window.

In a window that includes a Report button on the Button bar, select one of the items in the window. Then click the Report button. A report appears in its own window. For example, you could create a Category Report by selecting a category in the Category & Transfer List window and then clicking the Report button.

Using Contextual Menus

The contextual menu that appears when you click the right mouse button while pointing to an item sometimes includes a command that will create a report for the item. For example, right-clicking on the name of a payee in the account register window displays a menu that includes the "Payments made to" command, as shown here:

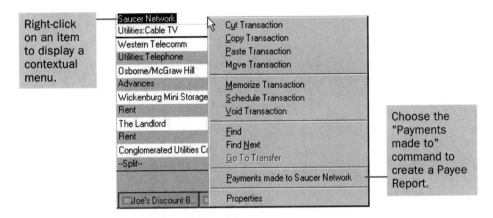

Figure 8-4 shows a Payee Report that was created by right-clicking on the name of a payee and choosing the "Payments made to" command.

Working with Reports and Graphs

Once you've created a report or graph, there are a few things you can do with it:

- Customize it so it shows only the information you want to display.
- Memorize it so you can create it again quickly.
- Print it so you have hard copy for your paper files.

In this section, I show you how to do all of these things.

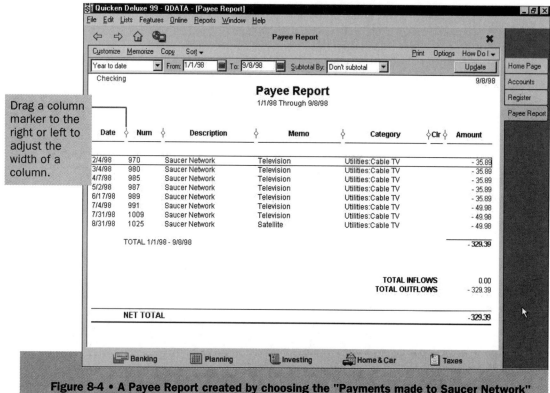

Figure 8-4 • A Payee Report created by choosing the "Payments made to Saucer Network" command from the shortcut menu

Customizing Reports and Graphs

You can customize just about any report or graph you create. When you can customize it, however, depends on how you create it:

- When you create a report or graph using the Reports menu, you can customize it before or after you create it.
- When you create a report using the Report button in the Button bar or a command on a contextual menu, you can only customize it after you create it.

Customization options vary from one type of report or graph to another. It's impossible to cover all variables in this chapter. I will, however, tell you about the most common options so you know what to expect. I'm sure you'll agree that Quicken's reporting feature is very flexible when you go beyond the basics.

Customizing a Report

To customize a report, click the Customize button in the Create Report window or the Customize button on the Button bar in the report window. The Customize Report dialog box appears. Here's what it looks like for a Cash Flow report:

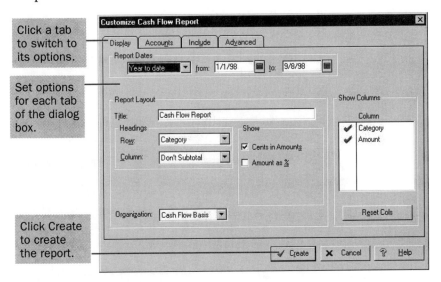

Click a tab to switch to its options.

Set options for each tab of the dialog box.

Click Create to create the report.

The Customize Report dialog box normally includes four tabs of options that you can set to customize the report:

- **Display** (shown in the previous illustration) enables you to set display options for the report, such as the title, row and column headings, organization, number formatting, and columns.
- **Accounts** enables you to select the accounts that should be included in the report.
- **Include** enables you to select the categories, classes, or category groups to include in the report. If desired, you can use this tab to include only transactions for which the payee, category, class, or memo contains certain text. If you use Quicken's Class feature, this tab makes it possible to generate reports by class.
- **Advanced** enables you to set additional criteria for transactions to be included in the report, such as amount, status, and transaction type.

On each tab, you also have access to the Report Dates area, which you can use to specify a date or range of dates for the report.

Once you have set options as desired, click the Create tab. Quicken creates the report to your specifications. If it isn't exactly what you want, that's okay. Just click the Customize button again and change settings in the dialog box to fine-tune the report. You can repeat this process until the report is exactly the way you want it.

Customizing a Graph

To customize a graph, click the Customize button in the Create Graph dialog box. The Customize Graph dialog box appears. Here's what it looks like for an Income and Expense Graph:

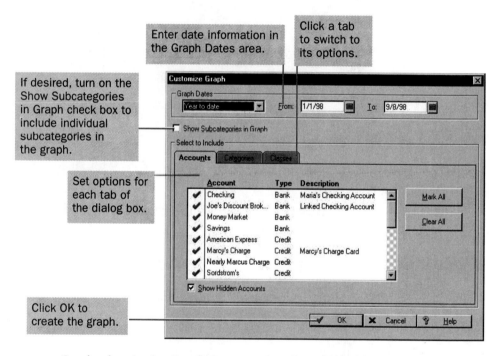

Set the date in the Graph Dates area at the top of the dialog box. Then set options in each of the dialog box's three tabs:

- **Accounts** (shown in the previous illustration) enables you to select the accounts that should be included in the graph.

- **Categories** enables you to select the categories that should be included in the graph.
- **Classes** enables you to select the classes that should be included in the graph.

When you're finished setting options, click the OK button. Quicken creates the graph to your specifications. If it isn't exactly what you want, click the Customize button in the graph window and change settings in the dialog box to fine-tune the graph. You can repeat this process until the graph is the way you want it.

Using the Customize Bar

The Customize bar at the top of a report or graph window (right beneath the Button bar) offers another way to customize a report or graph. Use it to change date ranges or modify subtotal settings for the report. When you make a change in the Customize bar, be sure to click the Update button to update the report or graph to reflect your change.

Setting Report Options

The Options button on the Button bar of the report window displays the Report Options dialog box, which enables you to set default options for creating reports:

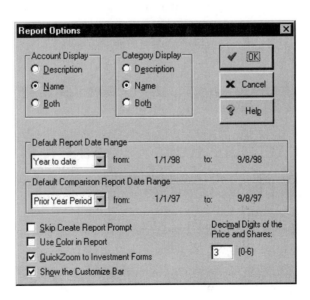

You can set the following options in this dialog box:

- **Account Display** and **Category Display** enable you to set what you want to display for each account or category listed in the report: description, name, or both.
- **Default Report Date Range** and **Default Comparison Report Date Range** enable you to specify a default range for regular and comparison reports. Choose an option from the drop-down list. If you choose Custom, you can enter exact dates.
- **Skip Create Report Prompt** tells Quicken to create the report without showing the Create Report window. Simply select the report from a submenu under the Reports menu and the report appears.
- **Use Color in Report** tells Quicken to use color when displaying report titles and negative numbers.
- **QuickZoom to Investment Forms** tells Quicken to display the investment form for a specific investment when you double-click it in an investment report. With this check box turned off, Quicken displays the investment register transaction entry instead.
- **Show the Customize Bar** tells Quicken to display the Customize bar in the report window, right beneath the Button bar.
- **Decimal Digits of the Price and Shares** enables you to specify the number of decimal places to display for per share security prices and number of shares in investment reports.

Set options as desired and click OK. Your settings are saved for use with all the reports you create.

Memorizing Reports and Graphs

Often, you'll create a predefined report and customize it to create a report you want to be able to see again and again. Rather than creating and customizing the report from scratch each time you want to see it, you can memorize its settings. Then, when you want to view the report again, just select it from a list and it appears. You can do the same for graphs.

Memorizing a Report

To memorize a report, start by creating and customizing a report. When it looks just the way you want it, click the Memorize button on the Button bar. The Memorize Report dialog box appears:

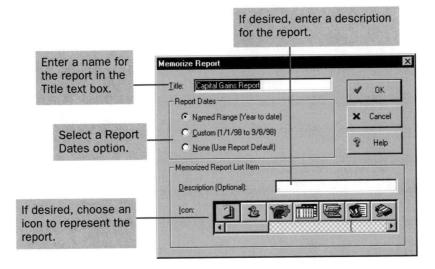

If desired, enter a description for the report.

Enter a name for the report in the Title text box.

Select a Report Dates option.

If desired, choose an icon to represent the report.

Enter a name for the report in the Title text box. Then select one of the three Report Dates options:

- **Named Range** applies the named range currently in use in the report. Named date ranges, such as Year to Date, Last Quarter, or Last Year, use dates relative to the current date. When you use this option, the dates change as necessary each time you create the report.
- **Custom** applies the exact dates currently in use in the report. When you use this option, the dates are always exactly the same when you display the report.
- **None** instructs Quicken to use the Default Report Date setting in the Report Options dialog box, which I tell you about earlier in this chapter.

If you like, you can enter a description for the report and select a report icon. This information appears with the report name in the Memorized Reports list.

When you're finished setting options in the dialog box, click OK to save them. The report is memorized.

Memorizing a Graph

Memorizing a graph works almost the same way as memorizing a report. There are just less options to set.

Create and customize a graph. When it looks just the way you want it to, click the Memorize button in the Button bar. The Memorize Graph dialog box appears:

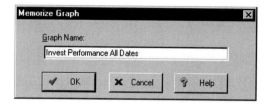

Enter a name for the graph in the Graph Name text box and click OK. The graph is memorized.

Viewing a Memorized Report

After memorizing a report, a new option appears on the Reports menu, right under the EasyAnswer Reports command: Memorized Reports. Choose this command. The Memorized tab of the Create Report dialog box appears:

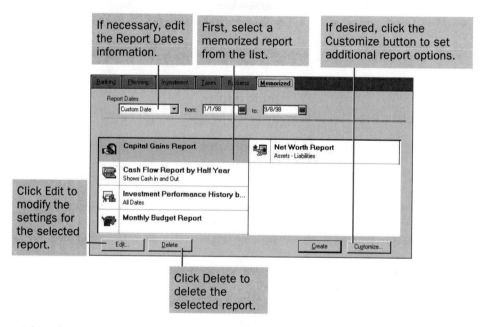

Select the memorized report you want to view and then click the Create button to display it.

Viewing a Memorized Graph

To view a memorized graph, choose Reports | Graphs | Memorized Graphs. The Memorized Graphs window appears:

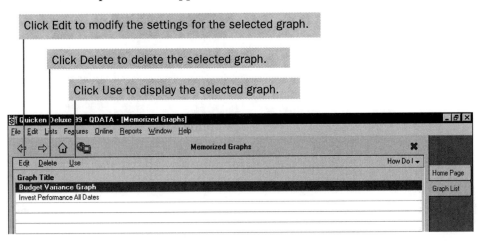

Click Edit to modify the settings for the selected graph.

Click Delete to delete the selected graph.

Click Use to display the selected graph.

Select the graph you want to display. When you click the Use button on the Button bar, the Recall Memorized Graph dialog box appears. It works just like the Customize Graph dialog box explained earlier in this chapter. Use it to set options for the graph. When you click OK, the graph appears.

Printing Reports and Graphs

You can also print reports and graphs. This enables you to create hard copies for your paper files or for use when applying for loans or completing your tax returns.

Tip   When I applied for my mortgage, I was able to create and print all kinds of useful reports to include with my mortgage application forms. I don't know if it helped me get the mortgage, but it saved the time I would have spent manually duplicating needed information.

Printing a Report

There are three ways to begin printing a report:

- Click the Print button in the Button bar of the report window.
- Choose File | Print Report.
- Press CTRL-P.

All three actions call up the Print dialog box, shown here:

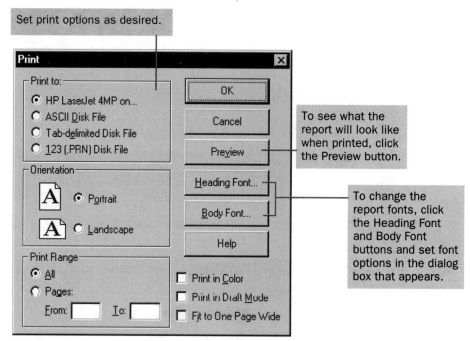

Set print options as desired.

To see what the report will look like when printed, click the Preview button.

To change the report fonts, click the Heading Font and Body Font buttons and set font options in the dialog box that appears.

Begin by selecting a Print to option. You have four choices:

- **[Your Printer]** (the first option) prints to your printer. The wording of this option varies depending on the name of your default printer. This is the option you'll probably select most often.
- **ASCII Disk File** enables you to create a text file that includes all the information in the report. You can import the resulting file into a word processing program.
- **Tab-delimited Disk File** enables you to create a tab-delimited text file that includes all the information in the report. In a tab-delimited text file, each column is separated by a tab character, making it easier to import the file into spreadsheet or database programs.
- **123 (.PRN) Disk File** enables you to create a comma-delimited text file that is easily recognized by Lotus 1-2-3 and other spreadsheet programs.

Next, select an orientation: Portrait or Landscape. These are standard options offered by all programs. The icon beside each orientation illustrates the positioning of the paper.

Set a print range: All or Pages. All prints all the pages of the report; this is the default setting. Pages enables you to enter the first and last page number you want to print.

Set additional print options as desired:

- **Print in Color** enables you to print in color—if you have a color printer.
- **Print in Draft Mode** substitutes a printer font for the fonts you may have selected for the report. This can speed up printing. With this option turned on, the Print in Color and Fit to One Page Wide options are not available.
- **Fit to One Page Wide** scales the report so that it fits widthwise on the page. This sometimes involves changing the font size.

You can change the fonts used for the report by clicking the Heading Font and Body Font buttons. Each one displays a Select Font dialog box that you can use to specify a font, font style, and font size, as shown here:

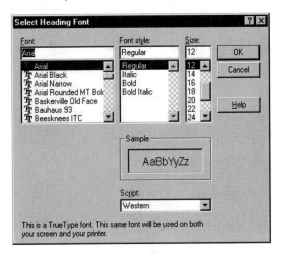

When you're finished setting options, you can click the Preview button to see what the report will look like when printed. This gives you one last chance to check the appearance of the report before committing it to paper. Figure 8-5 shows what one of my memorized reports looks like in the Print Preview window.

Click Next Page to view the next page of the report.

Click Prev Page to view the previous page of the report.

Click Zoom In to magnify the report.

Click Print to print the report.

Click Close to close the Print Preview window without printing the report.

Click on the report to magnify it.

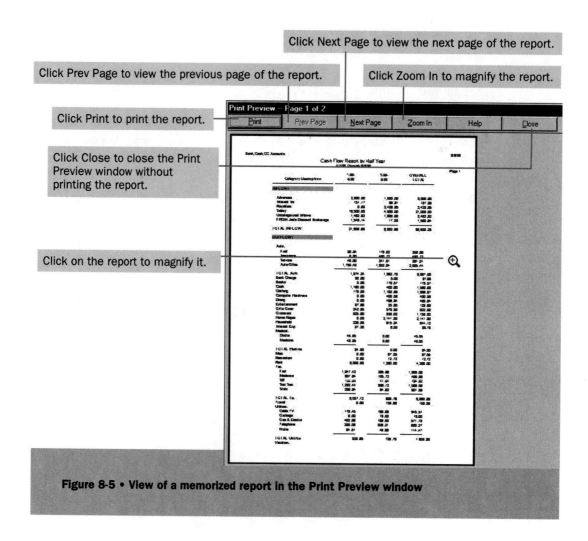

Figure 8-5 • View of a memorized report in the Print Preview window

When you're finished setting options in the Print dialog box, click the OK button to print the report.

Printing a Graph

Printing a graph is easy. Just click the Print button in the Button bar of the graph window, choose File | Print Graph, or press CTRL-P. Quicken doesn't ask any questions with a dialog box. It simply sends the graph to the printer and prints it.

Budgeting and Forecasting

In This Chapter:

Chapter 9

207

When money is tight or you're interested in meeting financial goals, it's time to create a budget and monitor your spending. But if you're serious about managing your money, you might want to create a budget before you need one. While Quicken's categories give you a clear understanding of where money comes from and where it goes, budgets enable you to set up predefined amounts for each category, thus helping you to control spending.

Budgets also make it easier to create forecasts of your future financial position. This makes it possible to see how much cash will be available at a future date—before the holidays, for summer vacation, or for the day you plan to put down a deposit on a new car.

In this chapter, I tell you how to create a budget and use it to monitor your spending habits. I also explain how to create a forecast so you can glimpse your financial future.

Budgeting

The idea behind a budget is to determine expected income amounts and specify maximum amounts for expenditures. This helps prevent you from spending more than you earn. It also enables you to control your spending in certain categories. For example, say you realize that you go out for dinner a lot more often than you should. You can set a budget for the Dining category and track your spending to make sure you don't exceed the budget. You'll eat at home more often and save money.

In this section, I explain how to set up a budget and use it to keep track of your spending. I think you'll agree that budgeting is a great way to keep spending under control.

Organizing Categories into Groups

Budgets are based on transactions recorded for categories and subcategories. (That's why it's important to categorize all your transactions—and not to the Misc category!) Quicken also enables you to organize categories by category groups. Grouping similar categories together can simplify your budget.

You can see the group to which each category is assigned in the Category & Transfer List window (see Figure 9-1). Choose Lists | Category/Transfer, or press CTRL-C, to display it.

The group to which a category is assigned appears in this column.

Click Delete to delete the selected category.

Click Edit to modify the selected category.

Categories that have not been assigned to groups.

Click New to create a new category.

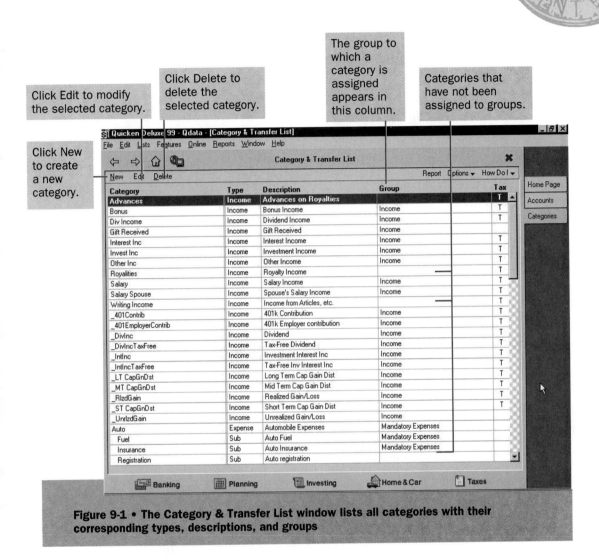

Figure 9-1 • The Category & Transfer List window lists all categories with their corresponding types, descriptions, and groups

Tip You don't have to take advantage of the Groups feature when creating your budget. It's entirely optional.

The Default Groups

By default, Quicken includes four category groups that it assigns to the categories it creates when you first set up your Quicken data file:

- **Salary Income** is for earned income such as your salary.
- **Income** is for miscellaneous income items, such as interest, dividends, and gifts received.
- **Mandatory Expenses** are expenses you can't avoid, such as fuel for your car, groceries, rent, and insurance.
- **Discretionary** is for expenses you can avoid (or at least minimize), such as entertainment, subscriptions, and vacation.

You're not stuck with these groups. You can change them as desired to meet your needs.

Assigning Categories to Groups

You can assign a category to a group when you create or edit the category. In the Category & Transfer List window, either click the New button or select an existing category and click the Edit button. The Set Up Category or Edit Category dialog box appears. Click the arrow next to the Group text box to display the Group drop-down list, which looks like this:

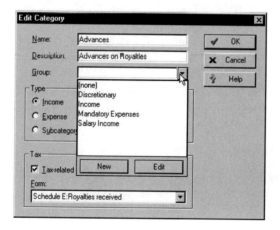

You have three options:

- Click the name of an existing group to assign it to a category.
- Click the New button to display a dialog box for creating a new group. When you enter a group name and click the OK button in the dialog box to save it, the new group is assigned to the category and appears in all group lists.
- Click the Edit button to display the Manage Category Groups dialog box, which you can use to create, edit, or delete groups.

Creating a Budget

Quicken can automatically generate a budget for you based on past transactions. You can edit the budget it creates to meet your needs. Or you can create a budget from scratch.

Creating a Budget Automatically

The quickest and easiest way to create a budget is to let Quicken do it for you based on your income and expenditures. For Quicken to create an accurate budget, however, you must have several months of transactions in your Quicken data file. Otherwise, the budget may not reflect all regular income and expenses.

Choose Features | Planning | Budgets to display the Budget window. Then choose Edit | AutoCreate (on the Button bar) to display the Automatically Create Budget dialog box (see Figure 9-2), which you can use to set options for the budget.

Tip If you have never created a budget, Quicken may display a dialog box offering to create a budget for you based on the past year's information. You can click OK to generate the budget and display it in the Budget window.

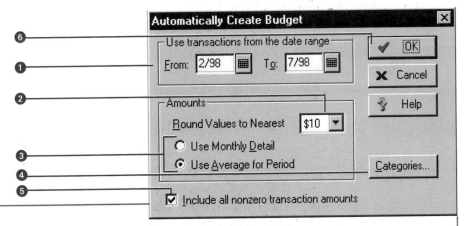

❶ Enter the starting and ending months for the transactions on which you want to base the budget.

❷ Enter the value to which you want to round numbers.

❸ Select an Amount option.

❹ If desired, click Categories to select the categories to include in the budget.

❺ To include transactions with values less than $100, turn on the Include all nonzero transaction amounts check box.

❻ Click OK.

Figure 9-2 • The Automatically Create Budget dialog box enables you to set options for auto-creating a budget

The Amounts option you select will affect the budget as follows:

- **Use Monthly Detail** copies the values for each month to the corresponding month in the budget.
- **Use Average for Period** enters monthly averages based on the period in the date range.

Tip   Select Use Monthly Detail if you have a full year's worth of transactions (or close to it) and you have seasonal income (such as a teaching job) or expenses (such as a vacation home). Select Use Average for Period if you have less than six months of transactions or don't have seasonal income or expenses.

The Categories button displays the Select Categories to Include dialog box, shown in Figure 9-3. You can use this dialog box to select specific categories to budget. You may find this useful if you only want to budget certain categories, such as dining, clothing, and entertainment. Click to toggle the check boxes beside each category name. The categories with check marks will be included in the budget when you click OK.

When you click OK in the Automatically Create Budget dialog box, Quicken creates a budget and displays it in the Budget window (see Figure 9-4).

Changing the View of a Budget

You can modify your view of the budget with commands under the Options menu on the Button bar, as shown here:

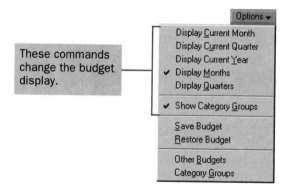

These commands change the budget display.

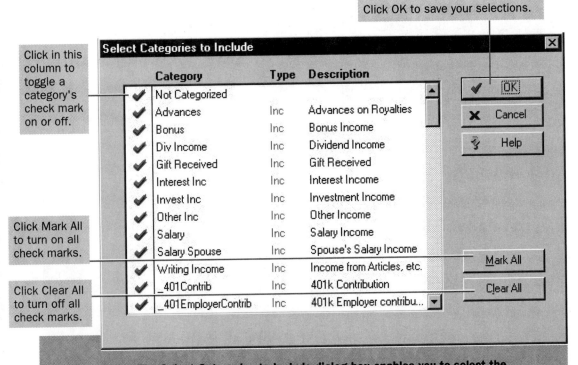

Figure 9-3 • The Select Categories to Include dialog box enables you to select the categories included in your budget

The commands under the Options menu are as follows:

- **Display Current Month** displays the budget for just the current month.
- **Display Current Quarter** displays the budget for just the current quarter. Quicken automatically adds monthly values to display a quarterly budget.
- **Display Current Year** displays the budget for just the current year. Quicken automatically adds monthly values to display an annual budget.
- **Display Months** displays the budget for all months in the year. This option is selected by default.
- **Display Quarters** displays the budget for all quarters in the year. Quicken automatically adds monthly values to display a quarterly budget.
- **Show Category Groups** organizes categories by groups. This option is selected by default. If you do not want to organize categories by groups, select this option again to turn it off.

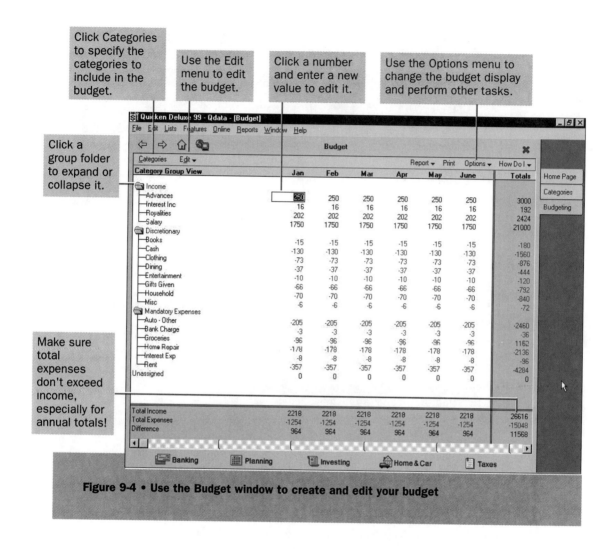

Click Categories to specify the categories to include in the budget.

Use the Edit menu to edit the budget.

Click a number and enter a new value to edit it.

Use the Options menu to change the budget display and perform other tasks.

Click a group folder to expand or collapse it.

Make sure total expenses don't exceed income, especially for annual totals!

Figure 9-4 • Use the Budget window to create and edit your budget

Modifying a Budget

You can modify a budget in a number of ways:

- To change a specific budget value, click the value you want to change and enter a new value.
- To copy a selected category value to all budget periods after the selected value's period, choose Edit | Fill Row Right (on the Button bar). Click Yes in the confirmation dialog box that appears.

- To copy a selected column's budget to all budget periods after the selected period, select any value in the column and choose Edit | Fill Columns (on the Button bar). Click Yes in the confirmation dialog box that appears.

- To accurately enter biweekly budget amounts (such as a biweekly pay check), click a value for the category and choose Edit | 2-Week (on the Button bar). This displays the Set Up Two-Week Budget dialog box, shown here, which you can use to enter an expected budget value and exact starting date:

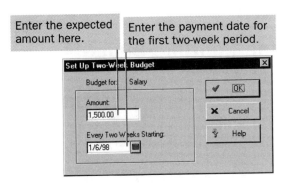

Enter the expected amount here.

Enter the payment date for the first two-week period.

When you're done, click OK.

- To clear all entries for a category, select any entry in the category and choose Edit | Clear Row (on the Button bar). Click Yes in the confirmation dialog box that appears.

- To clear all entries for a budget, choose Edit | Clear All (on the Button bar). Click Yes in the confirmation dialog box that appears.

Whenever you make a budget change, Quicken automatically recalculates the totals for you.

Creating a Budget from Scratch

If you prefer, you can create a budget from scratch. This is more time-consuming, but it forces you to look at each category carefully to estimate future expenses.

The previous sections in this chapter provide most of the information you need to do this. Here are the steps to follow; not all steps may be necessary, depending on your situation:

1. Choose Features | Planning | Budgets to open the Budget window (refer to Figure 9-4).

2. Choose Edit | Clear All (on the Button bar) to clear all values out of an existing budget.

3. Change the budget view by selecting a command from the Options menu on the Button bar.

4. Click the Categories button on the Button bar to choose budget categories with the Select Categories to Include dialog box (refer to Figure 9-3).

5. Enter values for categories. You don't have to enter a minus sign for expenditures; Quicken enters it automatically for you.

6. Use commands under the Edit menu on the Button bar to copy category or column values.

Managing Multiple Budgets

Quicken enables you to have more than one budget. Simply save one budget and create another.

Saving a Budget

Quicken automatically saves budget information. But if you have more than one budget, you must save each one separately.

To save a budget, choose Options | Save Budget (on the Button bar). The budget is saved as *Budget*.

Creating a New Budget

To create additional budgets, first choose Options | Other Budgets (on the Button bar). The Manage Budgets dialog box appears, as shown here:

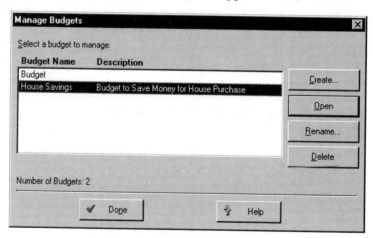

Then click the Create button to display the Create Budget dialog box, which you can use to set options for a budget:

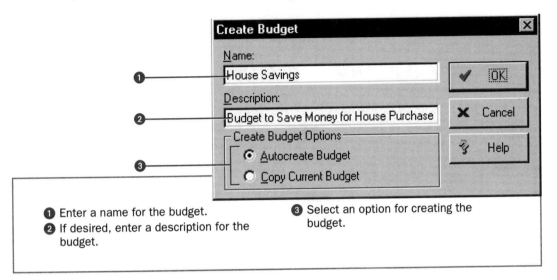

① Enter a name for the budget.
② If desired, enter a description for the budget.

③ Select an option for creating the budget.

When you're done setting these options, click OK.

If you select the Autocreate Budget option in the Create Budget dialog box, when you click OK, the Automatically Create Budget dialog box appears (refer to Figure 9-2). Use it to set options as explained earlier in this chapter. When you're done adjusting these settings, the new budget will appear in the Budget window (refer to Figure 9-4).

Managing Budgets

As you've probably guessed, you use the Manage Budgets dialog box to work with budgets when you have more than one. Select the budget with which you want to work and click one of the buttons to work with it:

- **Open** opens the selected budget.
- **Rename** displays a dialog box you can use to change the name and description of the selected budget.
- **Delete** deletes the selected budget.

Tip Neither the Rename nor Delete button in the Manage Budgets dialog box is available if the selected budget is currently open.

Comparing a Budget to Actual Transactions

Once you have created a budget you can live with, it's a good idea to periodically compare your actual income and expenditures to budgeted amounts. Quicken lets you do this a number of different ways.

Tip When you first start to use Quicken, make sure you compare budgeted amounts to actual results for the period for which you have recorded data. For example, don't view a year-to-date Budget Report if you began entering data into Quicken in March. Instead, customize the report to show actual transactions beginning in March.

Budget Reports

The Reports menu on the Button bar in the Budget window offers two different reports for comparing budgeted amounts to actual results:

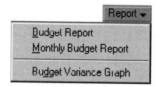

- **Budget Report** (see Figure 9-5) displays the year-to-date actual and budgeted transactions.
- **Monthly Budget Report** displays the actual and budgeted transactions by month.

In both reports, favorable differences appear as black, positive numbers; unfavorable differences appear as red, negative numbers.

Tip You learn more about reports, including how to customize them, in Chapter 8.

Budget Variance Graph

The Budget Variance Graph option on the Reports menu on the Budget window's Button bar creates two charts in the Budget Variance Graph window:

- **Actual vs. Budgeted Net Income** shows the favorable and unfavorable differences between actual and budgeted income amounts.
- **Actual vs. Budgeted Category Groups** shows the budgeted, actual, and over budget values for each of the category groups.

Use Button bar commands or change the reporting dates to customize the report.

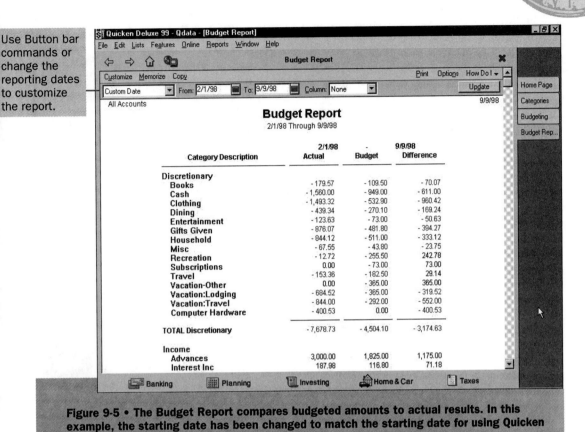

Figure 9-5 • The Budget Report compares budgeted amounts to actual results. In this example, the starting date has been changed to match the starting date for using Quicken

Figure 9-6 shows an example of a Budget Variance Graph window.

Tip You learn more about graphs, including how to customize them, in Chapter 8.

Progress Bars

Progress bars graphically display two separate comparisons of actual to budgeted amounts. You can toggle the display of the progress bars by choosing Window |

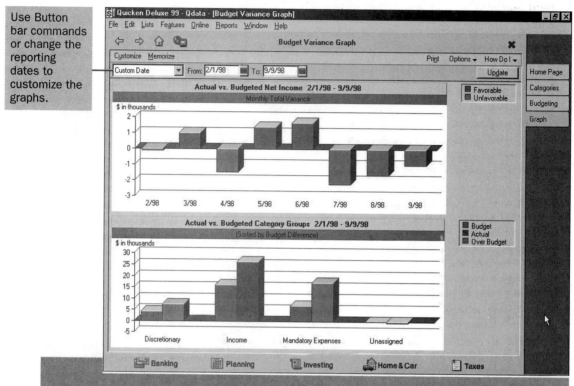

Use Button bar commands or change the reporting dates to customize the graphs.

Figure 9-6 • The Budget Variance Graph graphically represents budgeted amounts and actual results. This example also uses a custom starting date to report only the period for which transactions have been entered

Show Progress Bar. The two color-coded bars appear at the bottom of the screen, below the Activity bar. Here's an example:

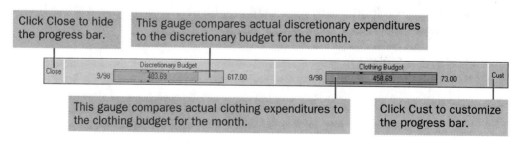

Click Close to hide the progress bar.

This gauge compares actual discretionary expenditures to the discretionary budget for the month.

This gauge compares actual clothing expenditures to the clothing budget for the month.

Click Cust to customize the progress bar.

You can set the progress bar's display by clicking its Cust button. This displays the Customize Progress Bar dialog box, which you can use to set the left and right gauges' options.

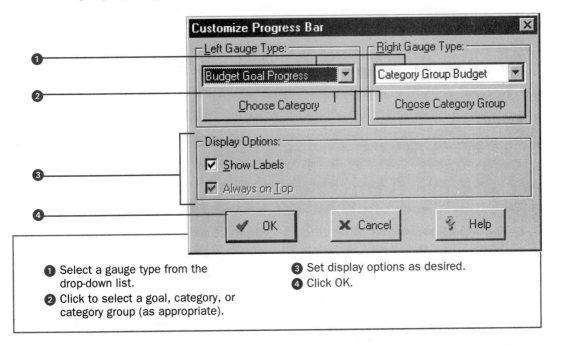

① Select a gauge type from the drop-down list.
② Click to select a goal, category, or category group (as appropriate).
③ Set display options as desired.
④ Click OK.

There are three types of gauges: Savings Goal Progress (available in Quicken Deluxe only), Budget Goal Progress, and Category Group Budget. Only the second and third types apply to budgeting; I tell you about savings goals in Chapter 21.

Using Alerts

If you're not interested in fancy reports and charts but want to be alerted when you spend too much, you can use Quicken's Alert feature. Just set up spending limits for each expense category or subcategory you want to be alerted about. Quicken displays a dialog box when you exceed the amount.

Choose Features | Reminders | Alerts to display the Set Up Alerts window. In the Accounts tab, click Monthly Expenses to display and set its options (see Figure 9-7).

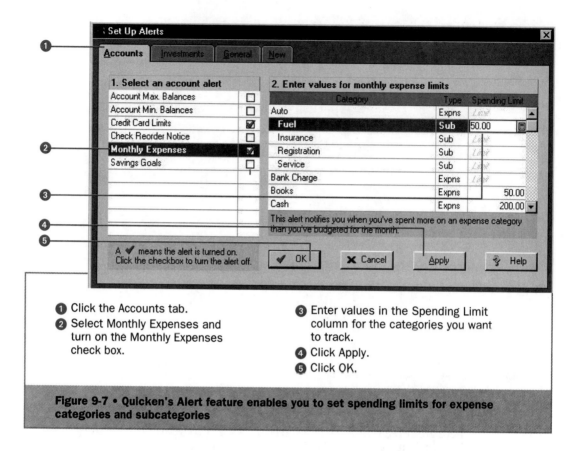

① Click the Accounts tab.
② Select Monthly Expenses and turn on the Monthly Expenses check box.
③ Enter values in the Spending Limit column for the categories you want to track.
④ Click Apply.
⑤ Click OK.

Figure 9-7 • Quicken's Alert feature enables you to set spending limits for expense categories and subcategories

Once set up, Quicken monitors spending in the background. When you enter a transaction that causes a category to exceed its spending limit, a dialog box appears to scold you.

Forecasting

Forecasting uses known and estimated transactions to provide a general overview of your future financial situation. This "crystal ball" can help you spot potential cash flow problems (or surpluses) so you can prepare for them.

Opening the Forecasting Window

Your financial forecast appears in the Forecasting window, which also offers commands and options to modify the forecast. To open this window, choose Features | Planning | Forecasting. Before you enter forecasting data, the forecast will probably look like a straight line. You can see a completed forecast (which is much more interesting) in the section entitled "Creating a Forecast with Budget Data," below.

Entering Forecasting Data

A forecast without data is like a crystal ball that's been dipped in ink—it doesn't show you much. To get a clear picture, you need to enter data about future transactions. Quicken lets you do this in two ways:

- Automatically create a forecast based on existing scheduled and register transactions or a budget.
- Manually enter known and estimated income and expense items for the forecast period.

Tip   In my opinion, the best way to create a forecast is to let Quicken automatically create it for you, and then fine-tune it by entering additional items that do not appear in your budget or register.

Automatically Creating a Forecast

On the Forecasting window's Button bar, select Options | Update Forecast to display the Automatically Create Forecast dialog box:

How you proceed depends on the kind of data you use—budget data or register data.

Creating a Forecast with Budget Data   Enter beginning and ending dates for which you have a budget. This will normally be the current year. Click the

Advanced button to display the Advanced AutoCreate dialog box (see Figure 9-8). Select Create Both in the top part of the dialog box, and From Budget Data in the bottom part of the dialog box. Click Done to save your settings, and then click OK in the Automatically Create Forecast dialog box to create the forecast.

Creating a Forecast with Register Data Enter beginning and ending dates for which you have register data. The time span should cover at least six months, but for best results, they should cover a full year. Click the Advanced button to display the Advanced AutoCreate dialog box (see Figure 9-8). Select Create Both in the top part of the dialog box and From Register Data in the bottom part of the dialog box. Click Done to save your settings, and then click OK in the Automatically Create Forecast dialog box to create the forecast. Figure 9-9 shows an example of a forecast based on register entries.

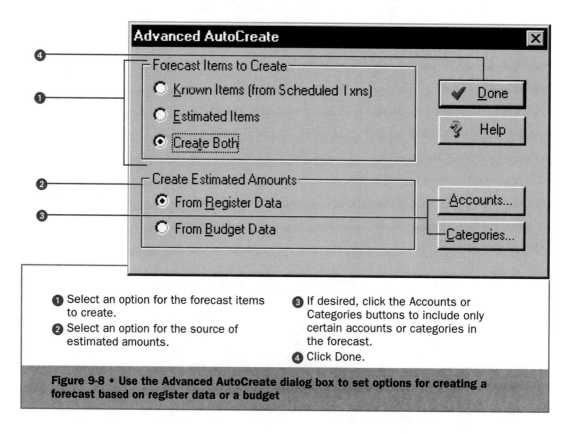

1 Select an option for the forecast items to create.
2 Select an option for the source of estimated amounts.
3 If desired, click the Accounts or Categories buttons to include only certain accounts or categories in the forecast.
4 Click Done.

Figure 9-8 • Use the Advanced AutoCreate dialog box to set options for creating a forecast based on register data or a budget

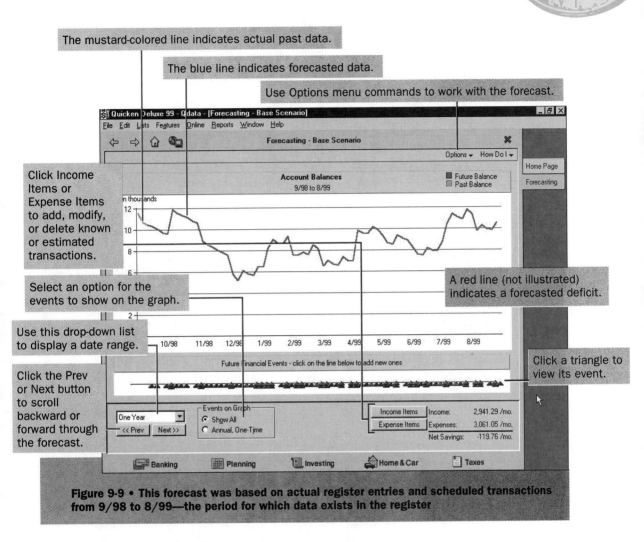

The mustard-colored line indicates actual past data.

The blue line indicates forecasted data.

Use Options menu commands to work with the forecast.

Click Income Items or Expense Items to add, modify, or delete known or estimated transactions.

Select an option for the events to show on the graph.

Use this drop-down list to display a date range.

Click the Prev or Next button to scroll backward or forward through the forecast.

A red line (not illustrated) indicates a forecasted deficit.

Click a triangle to view its event.

Figure 9-9 • This forecast was based on actual register entries and scheduled transactions from 9/98 to 8/99—the period for which data exists in the register

Entering Income and Expense Items

Once you've created a forecast, you can fine-tune it by entering or modifying known or estimated events. Click the Income Items or Expense Items button in the Forecasting window (see Figure 9-9). The Forecast Income Items or Forecast Expense Items window appears, as shown here; use this window to add, modify, or delete items:

Forecast Expense Items				
Expense Item	Amount	Frequency	Date	
📁 **Known Items**				
├─LeaseCo, Inc.	350.68	Monthly	9/6/98	
├─Saucer Network	49.98	Monthly	11/30/98	
└─Wickenburg ...	80.00	Monthly	9/1/98	
📁 **Estimated It...**				
├─Auto:Fuel	13.47	Monthly	Average	
├─Auto:Service	6.66	Monthly	Average	
├─Cash	193.33	Monthly	Average	
├─Clothing	28.89	Monthly	Average	
├─Entertainment	10.99	Monthly	Average	
├─Gifts Given	40.47	Monthly	Average	
├─Groceries	137.65	Monthly	Average	
├─Household	38.14	Monthly	Average	
├─Medical:Doctor	7.65	Monthly	Average	
├─Medical:Medi...	8.15	Monthly	Average	
├─Utilities:Garb...	2.16	Monthly	Average	
├─Utilities:Gas ...	67.10	Monthly	Average	
└─Utilities:Water	10.75	Monthly	Average	

Buttons: ✓ Done, ✎ Help

Show:
○ Income Items
● Expense Items

New   Edit   Delete

Average Monthly Expense: -1,288.19

When you click the New or Edit button, the Create New Income/Expense Item or Edit Income/Expense Item dialog box appears. Use this dialog box to enter or edit information for a forecast item. The exact name of the dialog box varies, depending on how you're using it, but the options are the same.

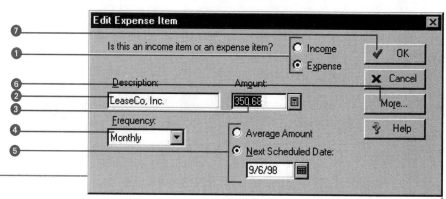

Edit Expense Item

❼
❶ Is this an income item or an expense item?   ○ Income   ✓ OK
                                                 ● Expense

❻ Description: Amount: ✗ Cancel
❷ LeaseCo, Inc.   350.68   🖩   More...
❸

❹ Frequency: ✎ Help
   Monthly ▼   ○ Average Amount
❺   ● Next Scheduled Date:
                      9/6/98 🖩

❶ Select the option button for the type of item.
❷ Enter or edit the item description.
❸ Enter or edit the item amount.
❹ Select an option from the Frequency drop-down list.
❺ If the amount is a regular average, select the Average Amount option; or if

the item is an exact amount on a scheduled date, select the Next Scheduled Date option and enter a date.
❻ If desired, click More to select a category for tracking the item and the number of entries.
❼ Click OK to save the item.

Working with Scenarios

When you create a single forecast, you create a forecast for the *base scenario*. Just as you can have multiple budgets, you can also have multiple forecast scenarios.

Creating a New Scenario

To create a new scenario, choose Options | Manage Scenarios on the Forecast window's Button bar. The Manage Forecast Scenarios dialog box appears, as shown here:

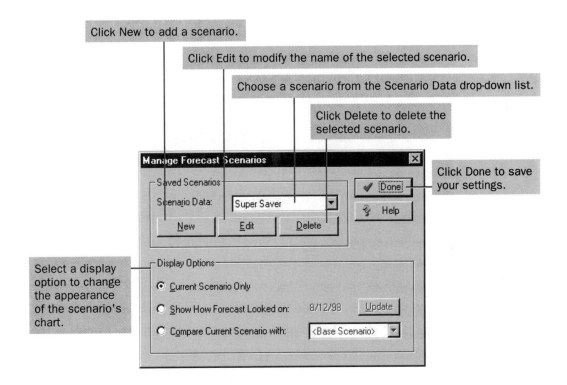

Click New to add a scenario.

Click Edit to modify the name of the selected scenario.

Choose a scenario from the Scenario Data drop-down list.

Click Delete to delete the selected scenario.

Click Done to save your settings.

Select a display option to change the appearance of the scenario's chart.

Click the New button to display a dialog box in which you can enter a scenario name and choose to copy the existing scenario. When you click OK, the new scenario's name appears as the selected scenario on the Scenario Data drop-down list.

Changing a Scenario's Display

The Display Options in the Manage Forecast Scenarios dialog box lets you change the display of a selected scenario:

- **Current Scenario Only**, which is the default option, displays only one scenario in the Forecasting window.
- **Show How Forecast Looked on** enables you to update the scenario for the current date. Select this option, and then click the Update button.
- **Compare Current Scenario with** enables you to include two scenarios in the Forecasting window (see Figure 9-10). This makes it easy to see which is better.

Select the option you want and click Done to apply it.

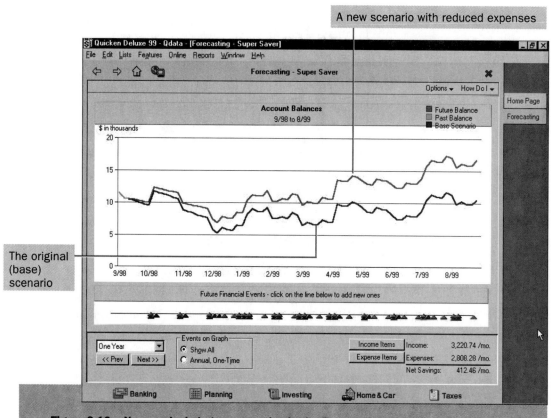

Figure 9-10 • You can include two scenarios in the Forecasting window. This makes it easy to see which scenario is better

Preparing for Emergencies

In This Chapter:

- *Emergency Records Organizer*

- *Quicken Home Inventory*

- *Financial Address Book*

Chapter 10

When the unexpected happens, some information is more important than other information. For example, if a burglar makes off with your stamp collection and fax machine, do you have details about the missing objects for the police report and insurance agent? If your daughter breaks her arm at summer camp 500 miles away, do the counselors have all your contact information and know about her allergy to Ibuprofen? If your wallet falls out of your pocket and into the lake while sailing with some friends, do you know who to call to report the lost credit cards?

Quicken Deluxe includes three features to help you track the kind of information you or someone else may need in an emergency. In this chapter, I give you a brief overview of each and encourage you to explore them on your own *before* you need the information they can track for you.

Emergency Records Organizer

The Emergency Records Organizer (ERO) enables you to track personal, financial, and legal information that may come in handy in the event of an emergency. It consists of a number of forms you can fill in with information. You can enter as much or as little information as you like. You can go into great detail on subjects that are important to you and completely ignore others. You can update and print the information at any time. It's this flexibility—and the fact that all information can be stored in one place—that makes the ERO a useful tool.

To open the ERO, choose Features | Planning | Emergency Records Organizer. Its main window, which provides an introduction to its features, appears (see Figure 10-1). Read what's in the window or click the Getting Started link to learn more.

Creating and Updating Records

To create or modify ERO records, click the ERO's Create/Update Records tab to display the entry window, as shown in Figure 10-2. The window has three parts: the area drop-down list, the topic list, and the entry form. To enter the information you want to organize, follow the steps as they appear in the window:

1. Select an area.
2. Select a topic.
3. Enter Contact List records.

Quicken Quote

"This feature is particularly important to my wife. I travel so much that in the event of a tragedy, she would not know where to start with our finances. Now with this feature, she has comfort in knowing the necessary information is there."

Tom Mitchell, Carrollton, TX

Click Create/Update Records to add or modify ERO records.

Click Report to generate printed reports from ERO data.

Click Getting Started to learn more about the ERO.

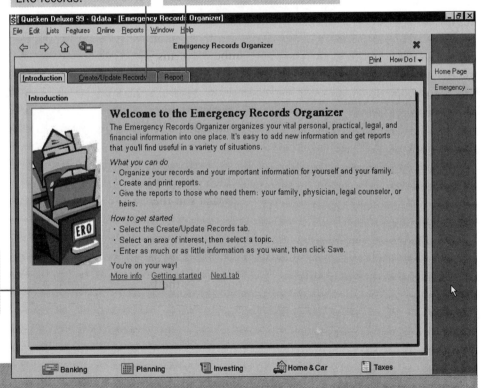

Figure 10-1 • The main window of the Emergency Records Organizer, or ERO, provides general information about its features and use

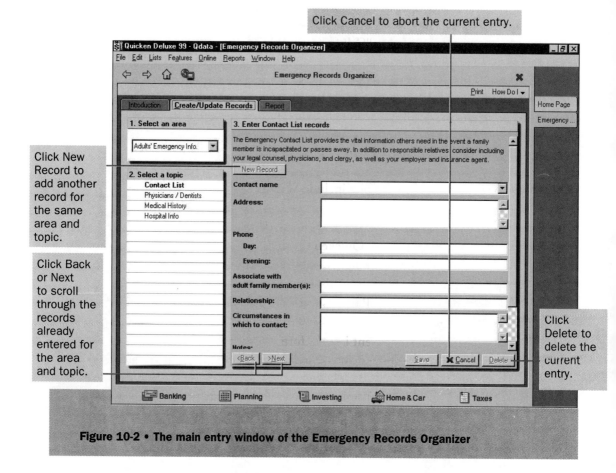

Figure 10-2 • The main entry window of the Emergency Records Organizer

Then click Save to save the record. You can click New Record to add another record for the same area and topic, or repeat Steps 1 through 3 to add records for other areas or topics.

Areas and Topics

The ERO offers eleven different areas of information, each with its own set of topics:

- **Adults' Emergency Info** is information you may need in the event of an adult's health-related emergency. Topics include Contact List (refer to Figure 10-2), Physicians/Dentists, Medical History, and Hospital Information.

- **Children's Emergency Info** is information you may need in the event of a child's health-related emergency. Topics include Contact List, Physicians/Dentists, Medical History, and Hospital Information.

- **Adults' Important Info** is important information about the adults in your home or family. Topics include Summary (for birth date, social security number, driver's license number, etc.), Residence, Employment/Business, Business Partners, Education, Marriage Info, and Military Record.

- **Children's Important Info** is important information about the children in your home or family. Topics include Child's Summary (for birth date, school, grade, and social security number), School, Caretaker, Schedules, and Guardian.

- **Personal & Legal Docs** is for information about important personal and legal documents. Topics include Will, Living Will, Funeral Arrangements, Powers of Attorney, Birth Certificate, Passport, and Tax Records.

- **Accounts** is for bank and other account information. Topics include Quicken Bank Acct., Quicken Credit Acct., Quicken Asset Acct., Quicken Liability Acct., Checking, Savings, Credit/Debit, and Other Accounts.

- **Income** is for information about sources of income. Topics include Salary, Dividends, Interest, Rental Income, Annuity, Trust Fund, Alimony, Child Support, and Other.

- **Invest. and Retirement** is for information about regular and retirement investments. Topics include Quicken Invest. Acct., IRA Account, 401(k) Account, Money Market, Cert. of Deposit, Stocks, Bonds, Mutual Funds, Keogh/SEP Plan, Pension, and Social Security.

- **Auto/Home/Property** is for general information about your property and vehicles. Topics include Property, Prev Residence, Safe Deposit Box, Post Office Box, Safe, Alarm Information, Storage, Pets, Automobile, Motorcycle, and Recreational.

- **Insurance** is for insurance information. Topics include Life Insurance, Medical Insurance, Dental Insurance, Auto Insurance, Property Insurance, Disability Insurance, and Other Insurance.

- **Mortgage/Loans** is for information about loans. Topics include Mortgage, Personal Loans, Auto Loans, and School Loans.

Tip   At this point, you might be wondering about the wisdom of keeping all kinds of important—and often private—information in one place. After all, the burglar who took your stamp collection and fax machine could also take your computer. Fortunately, you can back up and password-protect your Quicken data file. I show you how in Appendix A.

Entry Form

The entry form that appears when you choose an area and select a topic varies with the area and topic. Each form offers labeled text boxes for entering appropriate information. You can enter as much information as you like and skip over as many fields as you like. You won't get an error message for entering "wrong" information.

When you're finished filling in a form for a topic, click the Save button in the entry form part of the window. Then, to create a new record in the same area, click the New Record button and fill in a fresh form. You can view and edit other records at any time by clicking the Prev or Next button.

Printing Reports

The ERO includes its own reporting feature, which makes it easy to generate reports for a variety of purposes based on the information you entered. You can then give printed reports to people who may need them and lock others up in a secure place for when you need them.

Click the Report tab on the ERO window to display the report options (see Figure 10-3). You can select a report from the drop-down list at the top of the window and preview it in the area below. Then click Print to print the currently selected report. It's as simple as that.

Here's a quick list of the reports so you know what's available:

- The **Emergency Report** (shown in Figure 10-3) is for someone in case of a family emergency.
- The **Caretaker Report** is for someone taking care of your home or pet while you are away.
- The **Survivor's Report** is for your lawyer or heirs in the event of your death.
- The **Summary of Records Entered Report** lists the areas, topics, and record names you've entered in the ERO. It does not provide any detailed information.
- The **Detail Report** lists everything you've entered into the ERO. As the name implies, it provides detail and can be used as a kind of master list.

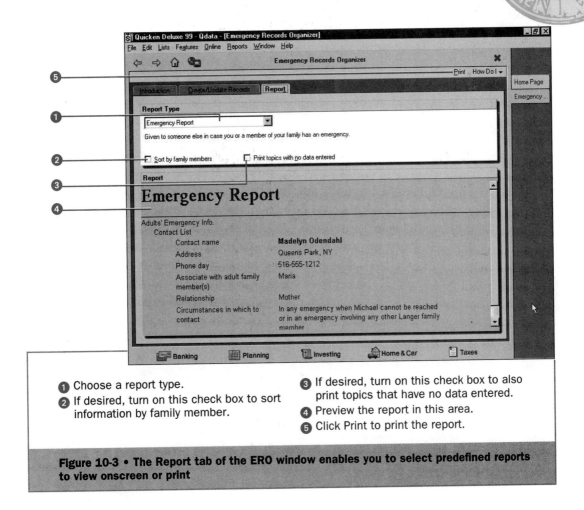

① Choose a report type.

② If desired, turn on this check box to sort information by family member.

③ If desired, turn on this check box to also print topics that have no data entered.

④ Preview the report in this area.

⑤ Click Print to print the report.

Figure 10-3 • The Report tab of the ERO window enables you to select predefined reports to view onscreen or print

Quicken Home Inventory

Quicken Home Inventory is a separate program that comes with Quicken Deluxe. You can open it from within Quicken, enter or edit information about the things in your home, and then update your Quicken data file with item valuations.

Quicken Home Inventory is excellent for providing detailed information about your possessions. This information is extremely valuable in the event of a burglary, fire, or other loss when you need to provide details to the police and/or insurance company. Enter this information and print reports to keep in a safe place. Then, once a year or so, update the entries and prepare a fresh report so your printed files are up-to-date.

Entering and Updating Information

To start, choose Features | Planning | Quicken Home Inventory. The Quicken Home Inventory program starts and appears onscreen, over your Quicken program window (see Figure 10-4). You can use this List View window to add or modify summary information about each inventory item.

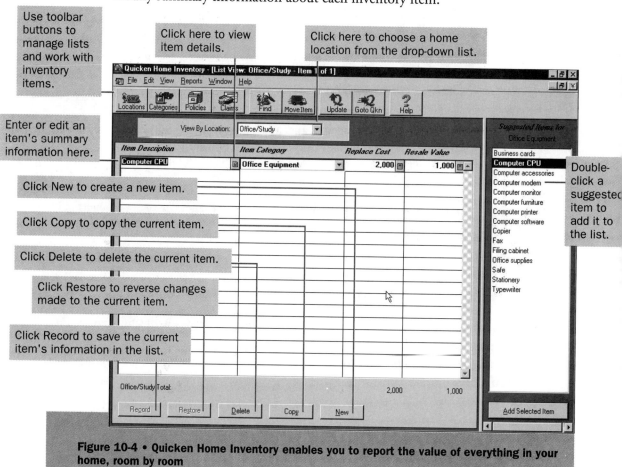

Use toolbar buttons to manage lists and work with inventory items.

Click here to view item details.

Click here to choose a home location from the drop-down list.

Enter or edit an item's summary information here.

Click New to create a new item.

Click Copy to copy the current item.

Click Delete to delete the current item.

Click Restore to reverse changes made to the current item.

Click Record to save the current item's information in the list.

Double-click a suggested item to add it to the list.

Figure 10-4 • Quicken Home Inventory enables you to report the value of everything in your home, room by room

Here are the steps for adding a home inventory:

1. Click New to create an item.
2. Select a home location from the drop-down list.
3. Double-click the suggested item to add it to the list.
4. Edit the item's summary information.
5. Click Record to save the item's information in the list.

Tip   Although you can use Quicken Home Inventory to track every possession in every room, from the ceiling lamp to the carpeting, entering that kind of detail isn't really necessary. Instead, enter the most valuable items, the ones that would be most difficult or costly to replace. This will save you time while enabling you to record your most important belongings.

To add details about an item, click to select it, and then click the icon beside the item description. Use the Detail View window (see Figure 10-5) to enter detailed information about the item, such as its make and model, its serial number, and its purchase date. You can also click buttons in this window to enter information about the receipts and other records you have on hand for the item and changes in its resale value.

Customizing Options

You can customize the drop-down and scrolling lists that appear in Quicken Home Inventory by clicking buttons on the toolbar at the top of the window (refer to Figure 10-4).

- **Locations** enables you to add, modify, or remove names for rooms in your home. It also displays a list of entered items by location.
- **Categories** enables you to add, modify, or remove item categories. It also displays a list of entered items by category.
- **Policies** enables you to add, modify, or remove insurance policy names. It also displays a list of entered items by insurance policy.
- **Claims** enables you to add, modify, or remove insurance claims. It also displays a list of entered items by claim.

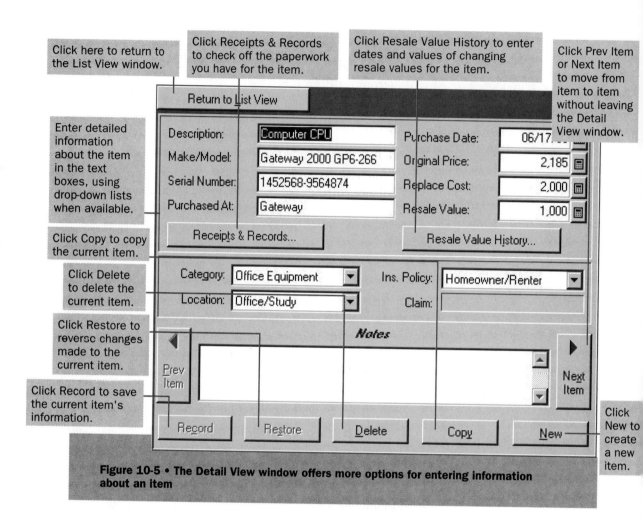

Click here to return to the List View window.

Click Receipts & Records to check off the paperwork you have for the item.

Click Resale Value History to enter dates and values of changing resale values for the item.

Click Prev Item or Next Item to move from item to item without leaving the Detail View window.

Enter detailed information about the item in the text boxes, using drop-down lists when available.

Click Copy to copy the current item.

Click Delete to delete the current item.

Click Restore to reverse changes made to the current item.

Click Record to save the current item's information.

Click New to create a new item.

Figure 10-5 • The Detail View window offers more options for entering information about an item

Caution Don't confuse Categories in Quicken Home Inventory with Categories in Quicken. The two terms are used differently. Quicken Home Inventory categories have nothing to do with Quicken categories.

Printing Home Inventory Reports

The Reports menu in the Quicken Home Inventory program window (shown in Figure 10-4) offers a number of basic reports you can use to print inventory information. This is extremely useful when applying for homeowner or home office insurance, when the insurance company requires detailed information about certain types of belongings.

Updating Quicken Information

When you're finished adding or updating Quicken Inventory information, you can update corresponding accounts in Quicken with the new asset values. Click the Update button on the toolbar. A small dialog box appears, asking you if you want to send inventory data to the Home Inventory account in your Quicken data file. Click Yes.

When you switch back to Quicken by clicking the Goto Qkn button in Quicken Home Inventory, you'll see a Home Inventory account—even if you didn't create one—with a balance corresponding to the resale value of home inventory items. When you open the account from the Account List window, Quicken Home Inventory automatically launches, enabling you to add or update information.

Financial Address Book

Quicken's Financial Address Book feature is another program accessible from within Quicken Deluxe. The Financial Address Book automatically stores the address information you enter when using the Write Checks window. You can also use this feature to modify or delete existing information or add new entries.

Entering and Modifying Entries

Choose Lists | Track Important Addresses. The Financial Address Book for your Quicken data file appears (see Figure 10-6). Use this window to add, modify, and delete contact entries.

To add a new contact, follow these steps:

1. Click New to create a contact entry.
2. Enter the name and address information in the bottom half of the window.
3. Choose a group from the drop-down list.
4. If desired, click Notes to enter notes about the contact.
5. Click Record to save your entry.

To modify an existing contact, select it, click the Edit button, make your changes, and then click Record to save the entry.

Enter a name in the Find text box or choose an option from the Group drop-down list to display existing entries.

Use toolbar buttons to work with address book entries.

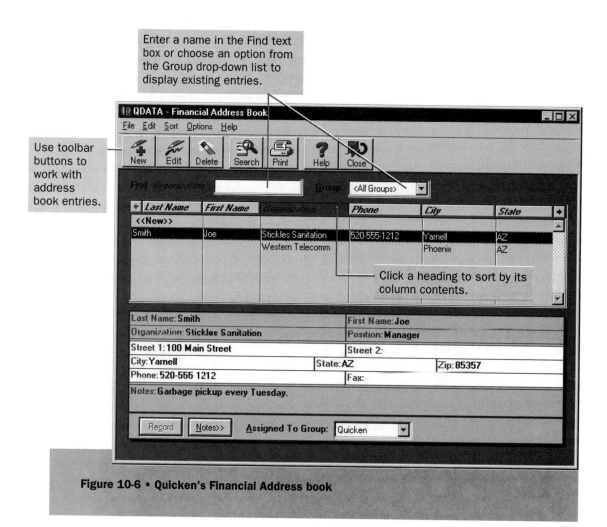

Click a heading to sort by its column contents.

Figure 10-6 • Quicken's Financial Address book

Printing Entry Information

You can print the information in the list in a variety of formats. First, click an entry to select it or use the Find text box or Group drop-down list at the top of the Financial Address Book window to display the entries you want to print. Then click the Print button to display a simple Print dialog box (see Figure 10-7). Set options in the dialog box and click OK to print.

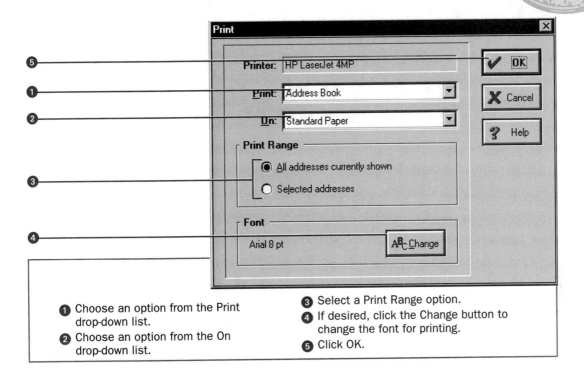

① Choose an option from the Print drop-down list.

② Choose an option from the On drop-down list.

③ Select a Print Range option.

④ If desired, click the Change button to change the font for printing.

⑤ Click OK.

The Print drop-down list offers four options: address book, phone book, labels, or Rolodex cards. The On drop-down list also offers four options, each of which is appropriate for a different type of printout: Standard Paper and three different Avery label/card products.

Saving Time with Online Features

This part of the book explains how you can save time by taking advantage of Quicken's online features for banking, tracking credit cards, and monitoring your investments. It shows you how you can access some of your Quicken data via the Web—from anywhere in the world. It also gives you a formal introduction to Quicken.com and other Quicken features accessible via the Internet.

This part of the book has five chapters:

Part Three

Exploring Quicken.com

In This Chapter:

- *An Introduction to Web Surfing*

- *Accessing Quicken on the Web*

- *Quicken.com Departments*

- *Other Quicken.com Features*

- *Quicken Financial Partners*

- *Applying for Online Financial Services*

Chapter 11

247

The World Wide Web has had a greater impact on the distribution of information than any innovation since the invention of moveable type hundreds of years ago. The Web makes it possible to publish information almost instantly, as it becomes available. Accessible by anyone with a computer, an Internet connection, and Web browsing software, it gives individuals and organizations the power to reach millions of people worldwide without the delays and costs of traditional print and broadcast media.

While this power to publish has flooded the Internet with plenty of useless and trivial information, it has also given birth to exceptional Web sites, full of useful, timely, and accurate information that can make a difference in your life. Quicken.com, Intuit's site, is one of the best financial information sites around.

In this chapter, I'll lead you on a short tour of Quicken.com and other Quicken features on the Web. My goal is to introduce you to what's out there so you can explore the areas that interest you most.

Tip   Chapter 3 explains what an Internet connection is and what it requires. It also shows you how to set up and test Quicken for accessing its online features, including the Web. If you haven't already read that chapter and completed Quicken's online setup process, go back and do that now.

Keep one thing in mind as you read through this chapter: Quicken.com is an incredibly dynamic Web site that changes frequently. The screen illustrations and features I tell you about will probably appear differently when you connect. In addition, brand-new features might be added after the publication of this book. That's why I won't go into too much detail in this chapter. The best way to learn about all the features of Quicken.com when you're ready for them is to check them out for yourself.

Tip   This chapter assumes you have set up Internet Explorer 4.0 or later as the Web browser for use with Quicken. If you are using another browser, Quicken will launch that browser and display Web pages in its windows, rather than the Quicken Internet window.

An Introduction to Web Surfing

Before I start my overview of Quicken on the Web, let me take a moment to explain exactly what you're doing when you connect to Quicken.com and the other Quicken features on the Web. If you're brand-new to Web surfing—that is, exploring Web sites—be sure to read this section. But if you're a seasoned surfer, you probably already know all this stuff and can skip it.

One more thing: This section is not designed to explain everything you'll ever need to know about browsing the World Wide Web. It provides the basic information you need to use the Web to get the information you need.

Going Online

When you access Quicken's online features, you do so by connecting to the Internet through your ISP. It doesn't matter whether you connect via a modem or a network, or whether your ISP is America Online or Joe's Dial-up Internet Service. The main thing is having a connection or a conduit for information.

Think of an Internet connection as some PVC piping running from your computer to your ISP's, with a valve to control the flow of information. Once the valve is open (you're connected), any information can flow through the pipe in either direction. You can even exchange information through that pipe in both directions at the same time. This makes it possible to download (or retrieve) a Web page with your Web browser while you upload (or send) e-mail with your e-mail program.

Quicken's online features use the pipe (or connection) in two ways:

- The integrated Web browser enables you to request and receive the information you want. It's live and interactive—click a link and a moment later your information starts to appear. Quicken displays Web pages in its Internet window (see Figure 11-1).
- The online account access and payment features work in the background to communicate with financial institutions with which you have accounts. Quicken sends information you prepared in advance and retrieves the information the financial institution has waiting for you.

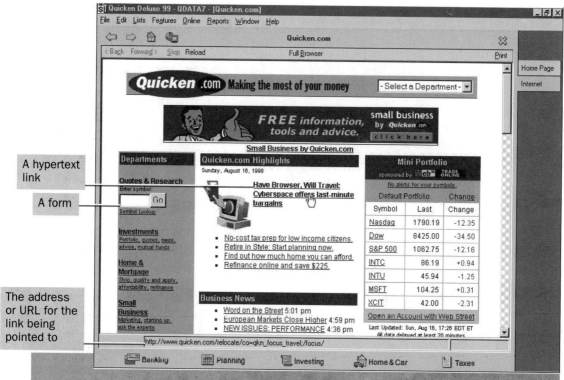

Figure 11-1 • Quicken's Internet window displaying the home page for Quicken.com. The page is full of information, with links to even more information.

This chapter concentrates on Web browsing—the interactive features of Quicken.com. But it also provides some information to help you find financial institutions that work with Quicken for the online access and payment features.

Navigating

The main thing to remember about the Web is that it's interactive. Every time a Web page appears on your screen, it'll offer a number of options for viewing other information. This is known as navigating the Web.

Hyperlinks and Forms

You can move from page to page on the Web in two ways, both of which are illustrated in Figure 11-1:

- Hyperlinks (or links) are text or graphics that, when clicked, display another page. Hypertext links are usually underlined, colored text. Graphic links sometimes have a colored border around them. You can always identify a link by pointing to it—your mouse pointer will turn into a hand with a pointing finger.
- Forms offer options for going to another page or searching for information. Options can appear in pop-up menus, text boxes that you fill in, check boxes that you turn on, or option buttons that you select. Often times, there are multiple options. You enter or select the options you want and click a button to send your request to the Web site. The information you requested appears a moment later.

Other Navigation Techniques

Quicken's Internet window (refer to Figure 11-1) also includes a number of navigation buttons:

- **<Back** displays the previously viewed page.
- **Forward>** displays the page you viewed after the current page. This button is only available after you have used the <Back button.
- **Stop** stops the loading of the current page. This may result in incomplete pages or error messages on the page. You might use this button if you click a link and then realize that you don't really want to view the information you requested.
- **Reload** refreshes the information on the page by loading a new copy from the Web site's server. This button is handy for updating stock quotes or news that appears on a page.
- **Full Browser** starts and switches to your default Web browser. Quicken continues to run in the background and you can switch back to it at any time by clicking its icon on the task bar.

Working Offline

When you're finished working with online features, if you have a dial-up connection you may want to disconnect. This frees up your telephone line for incoming calls. You can continue working offline with features that don't require Internet access.

To work offline, choose Online | Disconnect. Quicken displays a dialog box offering to disconnect you from the Internet. Click Yes.

Tip If you're connected via a direct network connection, there's no reason to disconnect.

Accessing Quicken on the Web

You can access Quicken's online features using commands on its Online menu. One of these commands, Quicken on the Web, is really a submenu full of options for Quicken Web features:

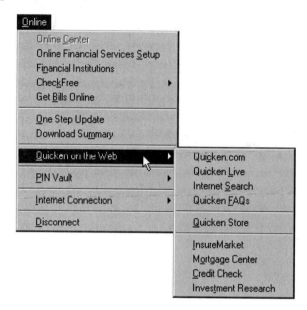

I tell you more about some of these options next.

Quicken.com

Quicken.com is Intuit's financial Web site. Although designed to be of most use to Quicken users, most of its features are accessible to anyone. (Tell your friends about it. Then tell them to buy Quicken Deluxe and this book!)

Quicken.com is divided into different departments. You can go to a department by choosing it from the drop-down list near the top of any Quicken.com page (refer to Figure 11-1). Here's a brief look at what each department offers.

Quicken.com Home

Quicken.com Home (shown in Figure 11-1) is the home page, or main page, for Quicken.com. It's a starting place for accessing Quicken.com's information. It also offers tidbits about new information you can find at the site.

Investments

The Investments department has information of interest to investors, including news, quotes, and research tools. There's specific information about stocks, mutual funds, and bonds, as well as a retirement link. If you're new to investing, be sure to check out the Investing Basics section for the concepts and terms you'll need to know to get started as an investor. I tell you more about Investments department options in Chapters 14 and 19.

Taxes

The Taxes department provides information you can use to prepare and file your tax returns, including federal tax forms, IRS publications, and state tax forms. News, articles, and advice offer additional insight into the world of taxation, to help you understand and minimize your tax burden. There are even links to the TurboTax home page, where you can learn about and download Intuit's TurboTax package. You learn more about the Taxes department options in Chapter 16.

Small Business

The Small Business department is a great Web destination for small business owners and self-employed individuals. You'll find links to information about taxes, accounting, payroll, benefits, retirement, legal issues, and your industry. Research tools help you shop for the best deals in office supplies, hardware, and software. And, of course, there are timely articles about the issues facing small business owners today.

Insurance

The Insurance department provides a wide range of tools for evaluating your insurance needs. A number of links offer information about insurance basics so you know what your agent is talking about when he or she throws around words like *annuity* and *rider*. You can even shop for insurance online. I cover some of the Insurance department options in Chapter 17.

Home & Mortgage

The Home & Mortgage department should be your first stop if you're looking for a home or shopping for the right mortgage. In addition to current information about national mortgage rates, you'll find interactive tools to help you find out what kinds of loans you qualify for and how much you can afford. Other links cover all stages of home ownership, from planning to owning. Even if you're not shopping for a home, this department might help you decide whether now is the right time to refinance your current home. You learn more about Home & Mortgage department options in Chapter 18.

Banking & Borrowing

The Banking & Borrowing department offers a wealth of up-to-date information about current interest rates on savings and loans, as well as banking-related news stories. This is where you can follow links to find a bank account, get your credit report, and shop for a credit card. If you don't know much about banking or credit, this is the place to come to learn. I cover Banking and Borrowing department options in Chapters 18 and 21.

People & Chat

If you like to communicate one-on-one with other people just like you—either via message boards or live chat rooms—the People & Chat department has you covered. Stop in to browse the message boards or join in on a live chat. There's always something interesting going on and always someone who has something to say about it.

Retirement

It's never too early to plan for your retirement. (In fact, the earlier you start planning, the better off you'll be.) The Retirement department is a great place to research options for funding your retirement years. Learn about 401(k) and 403(b) plans, and all kinds of IRAs. There's even information about social security, pension plans, mutual funds, and stocks. News, articles, and advice provide expert insight to put you on the right path. I cover some of the Retirement department's options in Chapter 20.

Saving & Spending

Spending is easy. It's saving that's difficult. The Saving & Spending department covers both of these topics. That's where you'll find tools to check your financial health and fitness, reduce your debt, and plan for college or the major events in your life. The Savers toolbox is especially useful for folks who want to save smarter. I tell you more about saving money in Chapter 21.

Site Index and Site Map

The Site Index and Site Map aren't really departments, even though you can select them from any Quicken.com department drop-down list. Instead, they offer tools and links for navigating the pages of Quicken.com. Try one of these options if you're searching for specific information and can't find it any other way.

Quicken Live

Quicken Live is part of Quicken.com. It offers links to Quicken.com's departments and many of its other pages, as well as other informative sites on the Web. The Quicken Tips & Tricks links can help you get more out of using Quicken.

Internet Search

Internet Search brings you to the Excite.com search page. You can use Excite's powerful Internet searching features to find information on the Web. There are dozens of links on this page, too—making it a perfect starting point for browsing the Web for a wide variety of topics that interest you.

Quicken FAQs

The Quicken FAQs command take you to Quicken's Technical Support page. This is where you can find answers to frequently asked questions, information about solving problems with Quicken, and program updates. Use this command when you can't find the information you need in this book or with Quicken's Online Help feature.

Tip   The Technical Support page covers all Intuit products, not just Quicken.

Quicken Store

I live in a remote area and do most of my shopping on the Internet or through mail-order catalogs. Not only does it save me time—I don't have to make the 60-mile drive to Phoenix—but it usually saves me money, too. And I can do it from the comfort of my own home or office. No dealing with crowds, trudging through hot parking lots, or carrying heavy packages.

The Quicken Store is Intuit's online shopping center, where you can buy Quicken software and supplies for personal finance, tax preparation, and small business. Stop by once in a while to check out its special offers and new products.

Quicken Financial Partners

If you're interested in keeping track of your finances with the least amount of data entry, you should be considering Quicken's online features for account access and payment, credit card account access, and investment tracking. Back in Chapter 3, I tell you about the benefits of these features. The next three chapters tell you how to use them. But you can't use them until you've set up an account with a Quicken financial partner and have applied for the online financial services you want to use.

Finding a Quicken Partner

Finding a Quicken financial partner is easy. Choose Online | Financial Institutions. The Apply for Online Financial Services window appears (see Figure 11-2). This page, which is updated each time a new partner comes on board, offers links with information about each of the partner institutions.

If your bank, credit card company, or brokerage firm is not on the list, you have two options: either open an account with one of the institutions on the list or forgo online financial services.

Tip If all you're interested in is paying bills online, you can use Intuit Online Payment. You learn all about that in Chapter 12.

Applying for Online Financial Services

The information pane of the window for the financial institution you selected provides information about how you can apply for online account access. In most cases, you'll either click the Apply Now button to apply or learn more, or call the toll-free number onscreen and speak to a company representative. This gets the wheels turning to put you online. It may take a few days to get the necessary access information, so apply as soon as you're sure you want to take advantage of the online financial services features.

Click an Online Financial Services link to narrow down the list of institutions by the type of services it offers.

Then click a Financial Institution Directory link to learn more about that institution.

Information about an institution appears here when you click its link.

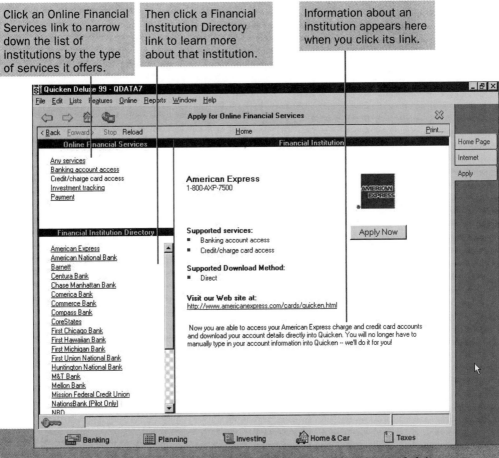

Figure 11-2 • Use the Apply for Online Financial Services window to locate Quicken partners and apply for online financial services

Using Online
Account Access
and Payment

In This Chapter:

259

Quicken's online account access and payment features enable you to do most (if not all) of your banking from the comfort of your own home. These two individual features can be used separately or together:

- **Online account access** enables you to download bank account activity and transfer money online between accounts.
- **Online payment** enables you to pay bills online, without manually writing or mailing a single check.

In this chapter, I explain how these two features work and how you can use them to save time and money.

Note The instructions in this chapter assume that you have already configured your computer for an Internet connection. If you have not done so, do it now. Chapter 3 provides the instructions you need to set up and test an Internet connection. This chapter also assumes that you understand the topics and procedures discussed in Chapters 2, 4, and 5. This chapter builds on many of the basic concepts discussed in those chapters.

Why Do Your Banking Online?

Consider the following scenario: Every week (or two), you go to the bank to deposit your paycheck. (If you're lucky, you can use an ATM or drive-up window where you don't have to wait in line.) Throughout the month, you stop at ATMs and withdraw cash. You use your debit card at the pharmacy. You write checks for groceries, dentist visits, and car repairs. Periodically, you sit down to pay your bills. You write checks, insert them with statement stubs in window envelopes, put your return address on the envelopes, and stick on stamps. (Forgot the stamps? Remember to wait in line at the post office to get them!) Once in a while, you call your bank to transfer money from one account to another. At month-end, you get a bank statement full of surprises: ATM withdrawals, debit card transactions, and checks you neglected to enter. Your bank balance may be dangerously close to zero because of these omissions. Or maybe you even bounced a few checks. And what about late payments (and fees) for the bills that sat on a table by the door, waiting for days to be mailed?

Sound familiar? At least some of it should. Life can be pretty hectic sometimes—too hectic to keep track of your bank accounts, pay bills before they're overdue, and buy stamps. But with online account access and payment, banking can be a lot less of a chore.

Benefits

The benefits of online financial services vary depending on the services you use. I've been doing my banking online for years. Here are some of the benefits I've seen.

Online Account Access

Online account access performs three primary tasks:

Download Transactions That Have Cleared Your Bank Account

Transaction downloads include all deposits, checks, interest payments, bank fees, transfers, ATM transactions, and debit card transactions. Quicken displays all the transactions, including the ones you have not yet entered in your account register, as well as the current balance of the account. A few clicks and keystrokes is all it takes to enter the transactions you missed. This feature makes it virtually impossible to omit entries, while telling you exactly how much money is available in the account. No more monthly surprises in that bank statement.

Transfer Money Between Accounts

If you have more than one bank account at the same financial institution, you can use online account access to transfer money between accounts. Although many banks offer this feature by phone, it usually requires dialing a phone number and entering an account number and PIN while navigating through voice prompts. Even if you get a real person on the phone, you still have to provide the same information every time you call. With online account access, you merely enter a transfer transaction and let Quicken do the rest.

 SAVE MONEY   I use this feature to transfer money between my low interest-bearing checking account and high interest-bearing money market account. Because I always know the exact balance of these two accounts, as well as the checks that will probably clear within the next few days, I can keep my money where it will earn the most interest until the money is needed to cover checks.

Send E-mail Messages to Your Bank   Ever call the customer service center at your bank to ask a question? If you're lucky, your bank is responsible and has real people waiting to answer the phone. But if you're like most people, your bank uses a call routing system that requires you to listen to voice prompts and press telephone keypad keys to communicate with a machine. Either way, when a real person gets on the line, you have to provide all kinds of information about yourself just to prove that you are who you say you are. Then you can ask your question.

The e-mail feature that's part of online account access enables you to exchange e-mail messages with your bank's customer service department. You normally get a response within one business day.

SAVE TIME   Don't like being on hold? You're not alone. Use this feature to ask questions for which you don't need answers right away. It only takes a moment to fire off an e-mail message. And you don't have to wait on hold.

Online Payment

Online payment enables you to send a check to anyone without physically writing, printing, or mailing a check. You enter and store information about the payee within Quicken. You then create a transaction for the payee that includes the payment date and amount. You can enter the transaction weeks or months in advance if desired—the payee receives payment on the date you specify.

Online payment is one of the least understood Quicken features. Many folks think it can only be used to pay big companies like the phone company or credit card companies. That just isn't true. You can use online payment to pay any bill, fund your IRA, donate money to a charity, or send your niece a graduation gift.

How It Works   Suppose you use Quicken to send online payment instructions to pay your monthly bill at Joe's Hardware Store. You've already set up Joe as a payee by entering the name, address, and phone number of his store, as well as your account number there. Quicken sends your payment instructions to your bank, which stores it in its computer with a bunch of other online payment instructions. When the payment date nears, the bank's computer looks through its big database of payees that it can pay by wire transfer. It sees phone companies and credit card companies and other banks. But because Joe's store is small, it's probably not one of the wire transfer payees. So the bank's computer prepares a check using all the information you provided. It mails the check along with thousands of others due to be paid that day.

Joe's wife, who does the accounting for the store (with QuickBooks, in case you're wondering), gets the check a few days later. It looks a little weird, but when she deposits it with the other checks she gets that day, it clears just like any other check. The amount of the check is deducted from your bank account and your account balance at Joe's. If you use online account access, the check appears as a transaction. It also appears on your bank statement. If your bank returns canceled checks to you, you'll get the check along with all your others.

Tip   If your bank doesn't return canceled checks, you can see for yourself what an online payment check looks like. Just use the online payment feature to write a check to yourself. It'll arrive in the mail on or before the date you specified. Although the check looks different, it works like any other check.

When the Money Leaves Your Account   The date the money is actually withdrawn from your account to cover the payment varies depending on your bank. There are four possibilities:

- One to four days before the payment is processed for delivery
- The day the payment is processed for delivery
- The day the payment is delivered
- The day the paper check or electronic funds transfer clears your bank

You can find out when funds are withdrawn from your account for online payments by contacting your bank.

The Benefits of Online Payment   Online payment can benefit you in several ways. You can pay your bills as they arrive, without paying them early—the payee never receives payment before the payment date you specify. You don't have to buy stamps and the bank never forgets to mail the checks.

SAVE MONEY   If you usually wait until month-end to pay all your bills at once, you probably pay some of them late and some of them early—not all bills are due the same day. By using online payment to make future transactions automatically, you can enter your bills as you receive them and pay them all right on time. This prevents you from paying bills late, thus avoiding late fees and damage to your credit. It also enables you to keep your money in an interest bearing account as long as possible—so you can increase your interest earnings.

Quicken Quote

"Since using this feature, my financial records are much more complete. The ability to enter a payment the day I receive the bill eliminates my need for a tickler file and gives me confidence that I have not forgotten to pay a bill."

John Harris, Atlanta, GA

Costs

The cost of online account access and online payment varies from bank to bank. Check with your bank to see what the exact fees are. Here's what you can expect:

- Online account access is often free to all customers or to customers who maintain a certain minimum account balance. Otherwise, you could pay up to $5 for this service. My bank claims it charges $3, but I haven't been billed once. (Don't tell anyone.)

- Online payment is sometimes free, but more often it costs from $5 to $10 per month for 20 to 25 payments per month. Each additional payment usually costs 40¢ to 60¢. Again, some banks waive this fee if you maintain a certain minimum balance. My bank, for example, requires $5,000 to waive the fee.

If you think this sounds expensive, do the math for your bank's deal. Here's an example. I get 25 payments per month for $5. If I had to mail 25 checks, it would cost me $8. So I'd actually save $3 per month if I made 25 online payments. Although I don't make 25 payments a month—it's more like 15 for me—I also don't have to stuff envelopes, apply return address labels, or stick on stamps. Or wait in line at the post office. My bills get paid right on time, I earn more interest income, and I haven't bounced a check in over three years.

Does it sound like I'm sold on this feature? You bet I am!

Security

If you're worried about security, you must have skipped over the security information in Chapter 3. Go back and read that now. It explains how Quicken and financial institution security works to make online account access and online payment safe.

Setting Up Online Financial Services

To use either online account access or online payment, you must configure the appropriate Quicken accounts. This requires that you enter information about your bank and the account with which you want to use these online financial services features.

Applying for Online Account Access and Payment

Before you can use online account access or payment, you must apply for it. I tell you how at the end of Chapter 11. Normally, all it takes is a phone call, although some banks do allow you to apply online. The process usually takes a week, but may take less. You'll know that you're ready to go online when your bank sends you a letter with setup information.

The Setup Information

The setup information your bank sends usually consists of the following information:

- **A PIN (or Personal Identification Number).** You'll have to enter this code into Quicken when you access your account online. This is a security feature, so don't write down your PIN on a sticky note and attach it to your computer screen. There is a chance that your bank may send this information separately for additional security.
- **A customer ID number.** This is often your social security number or taxpayer identification number.

- **The bank routing number.** This information tells Quicken which bank your account is with.

- **Account number for each online-access-enabled account.** This tells your bank which account you want to work with.

If Your Bank Is Not a Partner

If your bank is not one of those listed in the Apply window described in Chapter 11, you have three options:

- *Change banks.* I know it sounds harsh, but if your bank doesn't support online account access with Quicken and you really want to use this feature, you can find a bank that does support it and open an account there.

- *Wait until your bank appears on the list.* The list of partner institutions is updated quite often. If your bank doesn't appear there today, it may appear next month. Or next year. You can hurry things along by asking your bank to become a Quicken partner institution. If enough customers ask for it, your bank might add this feature for you.

- *Use Intuit Online Payment or CheckFree.* If all you're interested in is the online payment feature, you can use Intuit Online Payment. This enables you to process online payments via CheckFree Corporation, which can prepare checks from your existing bank accounts. There's no need to change banks or wait until your bank signs on as a Quicken partner. You can learn more about Intuit Online Payment in the Apply window, where the other financial institutions are listed.

Setting Up

With a PIN, a routing number, and account numbers in hand, you're ready to set up your bank account(s) for online financial services features.

Adding and Selecting Your Financial Institution

Choose Online | Online Financial Services Setup to display the Get Started with Online Financial Services dialog box. Click the Enable Accounts button. The Select Financial Institution dialog box appears, as shown here:

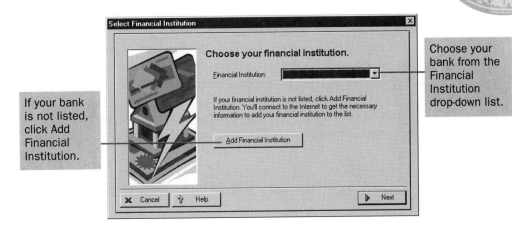

If your bank is not listed, click Add Financial Institution.

Choose your bank from the Financial Institution drop-down list.

If your bank's name appears on the drop-down list, choose it. Then click Next and skip ahead to the next section, "Setting Up Your Accounts."

If not, click the Add Financial Institution button. Quicken connects to the Internet and displays a list of financial institutions in the Apply window. Click the name of your bank. Quicken has a "conversation" with your bank, obtaining the information it needs to communicate with it. You can see its status in the Updating Financial Institution Information dialog box, which looks like this:

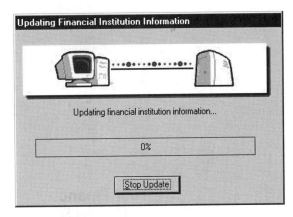

When Quicken has the information it needs, the dialog box disappears. Your bank's name should appear in the drop-down list in the Select Financial Institution window. Click Next.

Setting Up Your Accounts

The Online Account Setup dialog box appears next. Select the appropriate option button to either create a new account or edit an existing account for online financial services. If you want to edit an existing account, be sure to select the account you want to edit from the scrolling list of accounts. Click Next.

If you are creating a new account, the Create New Account window appears. I tell you about this window in Chapter 2. Use this window to set up the appropriate type of account.

The EasyStep tab of the Edit Bank Account window appears next. The first EasyStep window offers option buttons for enabling online account access and online payment. Select the Yes option button for the feature(s) you want to enable. Then click Next.

Tip If you're using Intuit Online Payment, the Online Account Access option will not be available.

The next window displays the name of your financial institution and prompts you to enter its routing number, as shown in the following illustration. Consult that piece of paper you've been holding and enter the appropriate number in the text box. Then click Next.

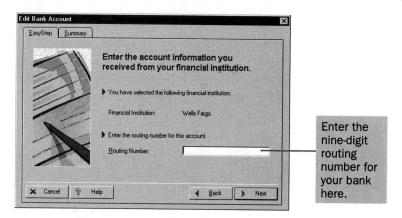

Next, you're prompted to enter the account number and type of account. Enter the account number in the Account Number text box. Then choose an account type from the drop-down list. Click Next to continue.

The next window requests your customer ID number. Enter this number in the text box and click Next.

The Summary tab of the Edit Bank Account window appears. It summarizes account information. This is the same dialog box that appears when you edit an

account. But as you can see in the following illustration, the Enable Online
Account Access and/or Enable Online Payment check boxes are turned on.
Edit the information as necessary.

> **Tip**   You can also set up an account for online account access or online
> payment by selecting the account in the Account List window and clicking
> the Edit button to display the Summary tab of the Edit Bank Account
> window. Turn on the appropriate check boxes and follow the prompts to
> enter online financial services information.

When you click Next, all online financial services information—bank name,
routing number, account number, account type, and customer ID—appear in a
Summary tab window. Check this information against the information provided
by your bank and make changes as necessary. Then click Done.

A little Service Agreement Information dialog box appears next. It tells you
that online financial services are provided by your financial institution and not
Intuit. (I think the lawyers at Intuit whipped this one up.) Read the contents of
the dialog box and click OK.

Setting Up More Accounts or Finishing Up

If you've followed all these instructions to the letter, the Online Account Access
dialog box should appear again, asking if you want to set up more accounts.
Select the Yes or No option button and click Next.

- If you select Yes, the whole setup process begins all over again.
- If you select No, the Online Setup Complete dialog box appears, congratulating
  you on successfully completing the setup process and reminding you about the
  features you can use. Click OK, and then close the Get Started with Online
  Financial Services window to try out your new online features.

Using the Online Financial Services Center

When you enable online account access and/or online payment, you can use the Online Financial Services Center to work with Quicken's online financial services features. This window gives you access to all the lists and commands you need to download transactions, create payments, transfer money, and exchange e-mail with your bank.

To open the Online Financial Services Center window, choose Online | Online Center. Figure 12-1 shows what this window looks like for my setup.

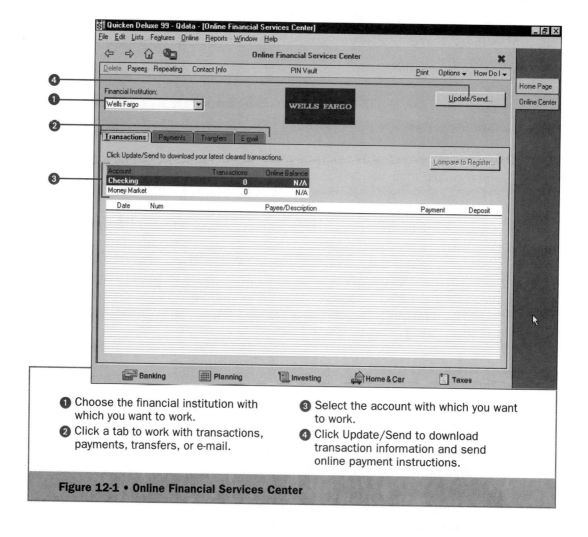

❶ Choose the financial institution with which you want to work.

❷ Click a tab to work with transactions, payments, transfers, or e-mail.

❸ Select the account with which you want to work.

❹ Click Update/Send to download transaction information and send online payment instructions.

Figure 12-1 • Online Financial Services Center

Downloading Transactions

One of the main features of online account access is the ability to download transactions directly from your bank into Quicken. Here's how you can take advantage of this feature.

Connecting to the Bank

Start by opening the Online Financial Services Center window. Choose the name of your bank from the Financial Institution drop-down list. If necessary, click the Transactions tab. Then click the Update/Send button. The Instructions to Send dialog box appears. Enter your PIN and click Send.

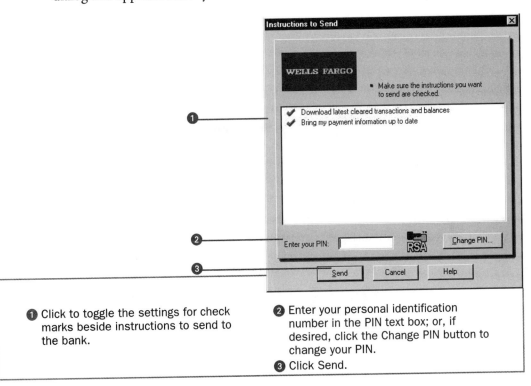

❶ Click to toggle the settings for check marks beside instructions to send to the bank.

❷ Enter your personal identification number in the PIN text box; or, if desired, click the Change PIN button to change your PIN.

❸ Click Send.

The first time you communicate with your bank, the Instructions to Send dialog box may not include a text box for your PIN, as shown in the preceding illustration. Instead, when you click Send, a Change Assigned PIN dialog box like the one shown next may appear. Enter the PIN the bank assigned to you in the top text box. Then enter a preferred PIN code in the bottom two text boxes. None of the characters you enter will appear onscreen. Instead, you'll just see asterisks (*). Click OK.

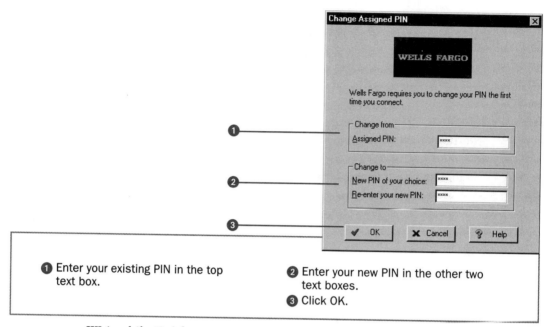

① Enter your existing PIN in the top text box.

② Enter your new PIN in the other two text boxes.

③ Click OK.

Wait while Quicken connects to your bank. A status dialog box like the one illustrated earlier in this chapter appears while it works. When it's finished exchanging information, the dialog box disappears.

Reviewing Transactions

When the connection is complete, an Online Transmission Summary window appears to summarize the activity that took place while you waited.

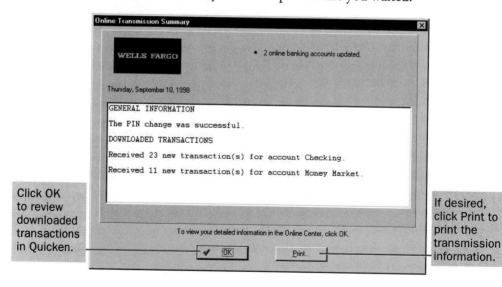

Click OK to review downloaded transactions in Quicken.

If desired, click Print to print the transmission information.

The transactions you downloaded appear in the Transactions tab of the Online Financial Services Center window, as shown in the following illustration. You can scroll through the Transaction List to view the transactions that were downloaded. As you can see, not much information is provided for the checks because the bank's computer doesn't record payee names or Quicken categories.

1 Select an account.
2 Review downloaded transactions here.

3 Click Compare to Register to compare downloaded transactions to transactions in your account register.

> **Note**   The first time you connect, the bank sends all transactions from the past 60 days. After that, only new transactions will be downloaded.

Comparing Downloaded Transactions to Register Transactions

Once the information has been downloaded, you can compare the transactions to the transactions already entered in your account register. This enables you to identify transactions that you neglected to enter or that you entered incorrectly.

Click the Compare to Register button. The Register window opens, with the downloaded transaction list in the bottom half of its window. Figure 12-2 shows what the window might look like with a few transactions already accepted.

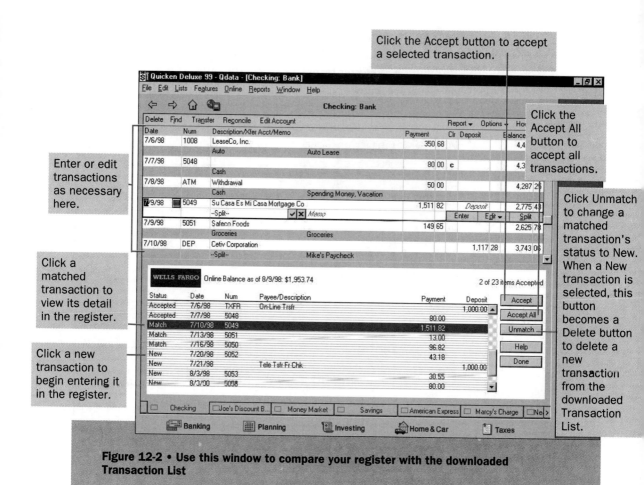

Click the Accept button to accept a selected transaction.

Click the Accept All button to accept all transactions.

Enter or edit transactions as necessary here.

Click a matched transaction to view its detail in the register.

Click a new transaction to begin entering it in the register.

Click Unmatch to change a matched transaction's status to New. When a New transaction is selected, this button becomes a Delete button to delete a new transaction from the downloaded Transaction List.

Figure 12-2 • Use this window to compare your register with the downloaded Transaction List

The Status column in the bottom half of the window identifies three types of transactions:

- **Match** identifies downloaded transactions that match those in the register.
- **New** identifies transactions that do not appear to be in the register.
- **Accepted** identifies matched transactions that you have accepted.

Accepting a Matched Transaction   If a transaction matches one in the register, you can accept it by selecting it in the list at the bottom of the window and clicking the Accept button. A small *c* appears in the Clr column to indicate that the item has cleared the bank but has not yet been reconciled.

Entering and Accepting a New Transaction   To enter and accept a new transaction, select the new transaction in the bottom half of the window. Quicken begins preparing a register transaction entry for it. Fill in the missing details, including the payee, category, and memo. Then click Enter. Quicken enters and accepts the transaction. Note: When you click the Accept or Accept All button, you may be prompted to enter additional information, such as the transaction category, for transactions identified as New.

SAVE TIME   Because Quicken will automatically enter a date, transaction number, and amount—and, in the case of a debit card transaction, the payee and category (based on previous memorized transactions)—using this method to enter a transaction can be much faster than entering it manually in the account register window.

Matching a New Transaction   If a downloaded transaction identified as New should match one in the register, you can modify the information in the register to match the information in the downloaded transaction. When you click the Enter button for the register transaction, the word Match should appear beside the downloaded transaction. You can then accept it.

Unmatching a Matched Transaction   If a matched transaction really shouldn't be matched, select it in the bottom half of the window and click the Unmatch button. You can then treat it as a new transaction.

Deleting a New Transaction   To delete a new transaction, select the transaction in the bottom half of the window and click the Delete button. The transaction is removed from the downloaded Transaction List.

Tip   This option is especially useful the first time you download transactions. You may download transactions that have already been reconciled. Use the Unmatch button to unmatch them as necessary, and then use the Delete button to delete them from the downloaded Transaction List.

Resolving Duplicate Check Numbers   If you attempt to accept a transaction with the same check number but a different amount, Quicken displays a dialog box like the one shown here:

This dialog box usually appears when you enter an incorrect check number for one of two transactions or an incorrect check amount for the same transaction. Correct the entry in the register part of the window.

Finishing Up   When you're finished comparing downloaded transactions to register transactions, click the Done button. If you failed to accept all of the transactions, Quicken displays a dialog box offering to finish now or later. If you click the Finish Later button, the unaccepted transactions are saved in the downloaded Transaction List for the next time you compare transactions.

Caution   Downloaded transactions that have not been accepted may not be entered in your account register. Thus, your register balance may be misstated until you accept all downloaded transactions.

Making Payments

The Payments tab of the Online Financial Services Center window enables you to enter payment instructions for accounts for which you have enabled the online payment feature. Figure 12-3 shows what it looks like.

In the rest of this section, I explain how to set up online payees, enter payment information for one-time and repeating payments, and work with payment instructions.

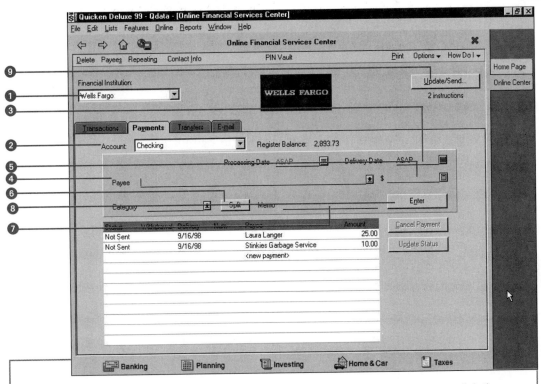

❶ Choose a financial institution with which you want to work.

❷ Select an account from which you want to send a payment.

❸ Enter the date you want the payment delivered.

❹ Enter or choose a payee name.

❺ Enter the payment amount.

❻ Enter or choose a category, or click the Split button to enter multiple categories.

❼ If desired, enter a note for the transaction.

❽ Click Enter to complete the entry.

❾ When you're finished entering instructions, click Update/Send to send them to the financial institution.

Figure 12-3 • Payments tab of the Online Financial Services Center

Entering Online Payee Information

To send payments from your account, your bank must know who and where each payee is. To ensure that your account with the payee is properly credited, you must also provide account information. You do this by setting up online payees.

Click the Payees button in the Online Financial Services Center window or choose Lists | Online Payees. The Online Payee List window shown here lists all the individuals and organizations you pay using Quicken's Online Payment feature:

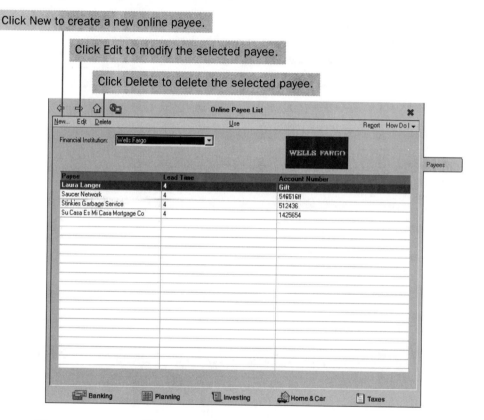

To create a new online payee, click the New button. Then fill in the text boxes in the Set Up Online Payee dialog box, shown here:

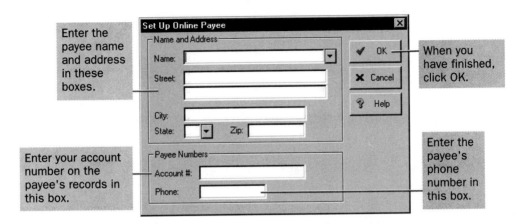

Enter the payee name and address in these boxes.

When you have finished, click OK.

Enter your account number on the payee's records in this box.

Enter the payee's phone number in this box.

When you click OK, a dialog box containing the information you just entered appears. Check the information in this box and click OK. A message tells you that the Financial Address Book (which I discuss in Chapter 10) has been updated. Click OK again. The payee is added to the list with a default lead time of four days. You learn more about the lead time later.

Caution   Check the payee information carefully! If there is an error, your payment might not reach the payee or it might not be properly credited to your account. Remember, your bank will not be sending a billing stub with the payment—just the check.

You can also use the Online Payee List window to modify or delete an existing payee:

- To modify a payee, select it in the list and click the Edit button on the Button bar. The Edit Online Payee dialog box, which looks just like the Set Up Online Payee dialog box, appears. Modify the information and click OK. Confirm that the information is correct when prompted.
- To delete a payee, select it in the list and click the Delete button on the Button bar. Then click the OK button in the confirmation dialog box that appears to remove the payee from the list.

Tip Deleting a payee simply deletes the payee's information from the Online Payee List. It does not change any transactions for a payee. You cannot delete a payee for which unsent payment instructions exist in the Online Financial Services Center window.

Entering Payment Instructions

If necessary, switch back to the Payments tab of the Online Financial Services Center window. Then fill in the fields in the middle of the window with the payment information:

- **Delivery Date** is the date you want the payee to receive payment. This is the date the bank will either write on the check or make the electronic funds transfer. The check may be received before that date, depending on the mail. The date you enter, however, must be at least the same number of business days in advance as the lead time for the payee—usually four days. That means if you want to pay a bill on Wednesday, October 21, you must enter and send its instructions to your bank on or before Friday, October 16. Quicken will adjust the date for you if necessary. To process payment as soon as possible, just enter **ASAP**. Quicken will enter the date for you.

Tip Whenever possible, I give the bank an extra two days. So, in the previous example, if the bill is due on October 21, I'd instruct the bank to pay on October 19. This isn't because I don't have confidence in Quicken or my bank. It's because I have less confidence in the postal service.

- **Payee** is the online payee to receive payment. Quicken's QuickFill feature fills in the payee's name as you type it. If desired, you can choose it from the drop-down list of online payees. If you enter a payee that is not in the Online Payee List, Quicken displays the Set Up Online Payee dialog box so you can add the new payee's information. This enables you to create online payees as you enter payment instructions.
- **$** is the amount of the payment.

- **Category** is the category to which the payment should be associated. You can either enter a category, choose one from the drop-down list, or click the Split button to enter multiple categories.
- **Memo**, which is optional, is for entering a note about the transaction.

When you're finished entering information for the transaction, click Enter. The transaction appears in the list in the bottom half of the window. You can repeat this process for as many payments as you want to make.

Scheduling Repeating Online Payments

Some payments are exactly the same every month, such as your rent, a car loan, or your monthly cable television bill. You can set these payments up as repeating online payments.

Here's how it works. You schedule the online payment once, indicating the payee, amount, and frequency. Quicken sends the instructions to your bank. Thirty days before the payment is due, your bank creates a new postdated payment based on your instructions. It notifies you that it has created the payment. Quicken automatically enters the payment information in your account register with the appropriate payment date. The payment is delivered on the payment date. This happens regularly, at the interval you specify, until you tell it to stop.

Tip   Using this feature to pay an amortized loan such as a mortgage works a little differently. I tell you about it in Chapter 18.

In the Online Financial Services Center window, click the Repeating button. The Repeating Online tab of the Scheduled Transaction List window appears. The Create Repeating Online Payment dialog box may appear automatically; if it does not, click the New button on the Button bar. Use this dialog box to enter information about the repeating payment.

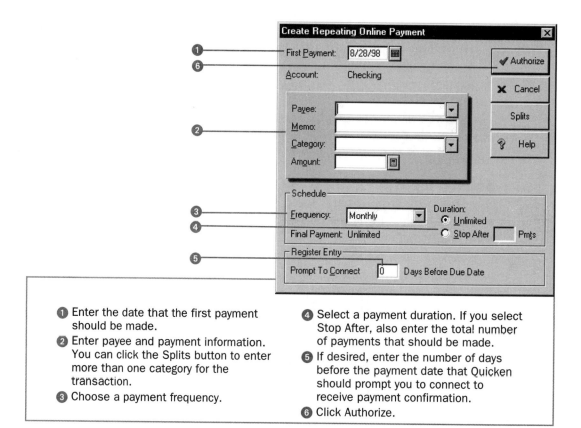

① Enter the date that the first payment should be made.

② Enter payee and payment information. You can click the Splits button to enter more than one category for the transaction.

③ Choose a payment frequency.

④ Select a payment duration. If you select Stop After, also enter the total number of payments that should be made.

⑤ If desired, enter the number of days before the payment date that Quicken should prompt you to connect to receive payment confirmation.

⑥ Click Authorize.

When you click Authorize, the payment appears in the Scheduled Transaction List window (see Figure 12-4). You can use buttons in the Button bar to add, modify, or delete repeating online payments in this window.

 SAVE TIME   The best part of the repeating online payment feature is that once a payment instruction is sent, you don't have to do a thing to continue paying regularly. The more payments you make with this feature, the more time you save.

Click New to create a new repeating online payment.

Click Edit to modify the selected repeating online payment.

Click Delete to delete the selected repeating online payment.

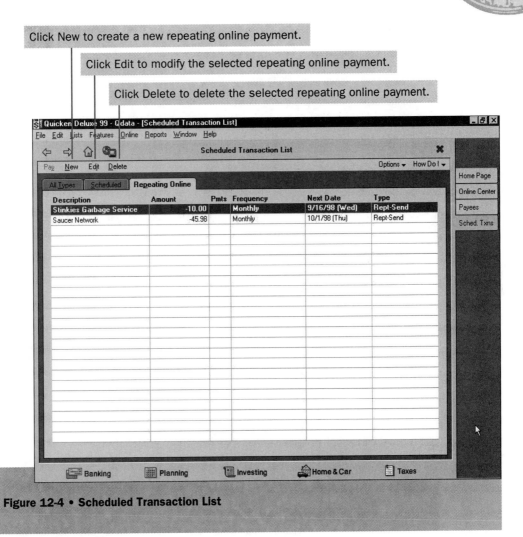

Figure 12-4 • Scheduled Transaction List

Sending Payment Instructions

Remember the bills I told you about? The ones waiting on a table by the door to be mailed? Payment instructions that have not yet been sent to the bank are just like those stamped envelopes. They're ready to go, but they won't get where they're going without your help.

Once your payment instructions have been completed, you must connect to your bank to send the instructions. In the Online Financial Services Center window, click the Update/Send button. Quicken displays the Instructions to Send window, shown here. This window includes all the payment instructions, including any repeating payment instructions. Enter your PIN and click the Send button.

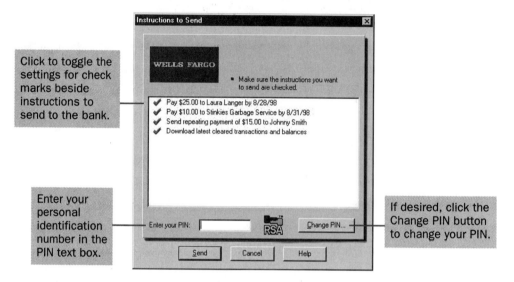

Click to toggle the settings for check marks beside instructions to send to the bank.

Enter your personal identification number in the PIN text box.

If desired, click the Change PIN button to change your PIN.

Wait while Quicken establishes an Internet connection with your bank and sends your payment (or payment cancellation) instructions. When it's finished, it displays the Online Transmission Summary window. Review the information in this window to make sure all instructions were sent and no errors occurred.

When you're finished, click OK to return to the Payments tab of the Online Financial Services window. As you can see in the following illustration, the word Sent appears in the Status column beside the payment instructions that have been sent to your bank.

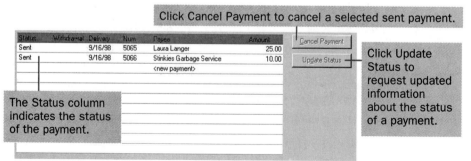

Click Cancel Payment to cancel a selected sent payment.

Click Update Status to request updated information about the status of a payment.

The Status column indicates the status of the payment.

Canceling a Payment

Occasionally, you may change your mind about making a payment. Perhaps you found out that your spouse already sent a check. Or that you set up the payment for the wrong amount. For whatever reason, you can cancel an online payment that you have sent to your bank—as long as there's enough time to cancel it.

Here's how it works. When you send a payment instruction to your bank, it waits in the bank's computer. When the processing date (determined by the number of days in the payee's lead time and the payment date) arrives, the bank makes the payment. Before the processing date, however, the payment instructions can be canceled. If you send a cancel payment instruction to the bank before the processing date, the bank removes the instruction from its computer without sending payment to the payee. Quicken won't let you cancel a payment if the processing date has already passed. If you wait too long, the only way to cancel the payment is to call the bank directly and stop the check.

Tip Canceling a payment instruction isn't the same as stopping a check. If you send the cancel payment instruction in time, there should be no bank fee for stopping the payment.

Canceling a Regular Online Payment In the Online Financial Services Center window, select the payment that you want to cancel and click the Cancel Payment button. Click Yes in the confirmation dialog box that appears. The word Cancel appears in the Status column beside the payment. Use the Send/Update button to send the cancel payment instruction.

Stopping a Single Repeating Online Payment In the Online Financial Services Center window, select the payment you want to stop, and click the Cancel Payment button. Click Yes in the confirmation dialog box that appears. The word Cancel appears in the Status column beside the payment. Use the Send/Update button to send the cancel payment instruction.

Stopping All Future Payments for a Repeating Online Payment In the Scheduled Transaction List window, select the payment you want to stop and click Delete. Click Yes in the confirmation dialog box that appears. The transaction is removed from the list. Then use the Send/Update button in the Online Financial Services Center window to send the cancel payment instruction.

Caution You must *send the cancel payment instruction to your bank to cancel a payment. Be sure to click the Send/Update button in the Online Financial Services Center window after canceling any payment. If you fail to do this, the cancel payment instruction may not reach your bank in time to cancel the payment.*

Transferring Money Between Accounts

If you have more than one account enabled for online account access at the same financial institution, you can use the Transfers tab of the Online Financial Services Center window, shown here, to transfer money from one account to another:

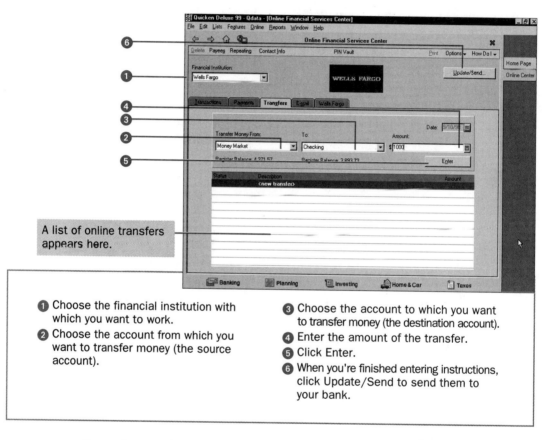

A list of online transfers appears here.

① Choose the financial institution with which you want to work.

② Choose the account from which you want to transfer money (the source account).

③ Choose the account to which you want to transfer money (the destination account).

④ Enter the amount of the transfer.

⑤ Click Enter.

⑥ When you're finished entering instructions, click Update/Send to send them to your bank.

Enter the transfer information in the fields in the middle of the window. When you click Enter, the information is added to the list of transfers at the bottom of the window.

Like payment instructions, you must send transfer instructions to your bank in order for the transaction to take place. Click the Send/Update button to display the Instructions to Send window, which includes the transfer instructions to be sent. Enter your PIN and click the Send button. Then wait while Quicken establishes an Internet connection with your bank and sends the instructions.

When Quicken is finished, it displays the Online Transmission Summary window. Review the information in this window and click OK. The word Sent appears in the Status column beside the transfer instructions that have been sent to your bank.

Exchanging E-mail with Your Bank

You can use the E-mail tab of the Online Financial Services Center window, shown next, to exchange e-mail messages with financial institutions for which you have enabled online account access:

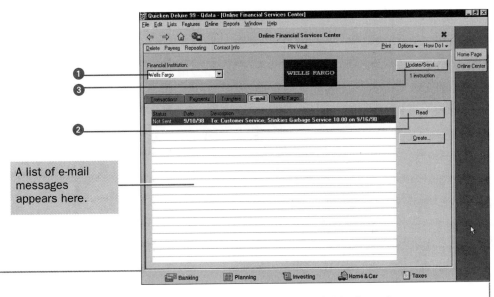

A list of e-mail messages appears here.

1. Choose the financial institution with which you want to exchange e-mail.
2. Click Read to read a selected message, or click Create to create a new message.
3. When you're finished creating messages, click Update/Send to send them to your bank.

Creating an E-mail Message

In the Online Financial Services Center window, click Create. The Create dialog box appears, as shown next. Use it to set general options for your e-mail message. If your message is about an online payment, choose the account from the Account drop-down list and select the payment from the Payments scrolling list.

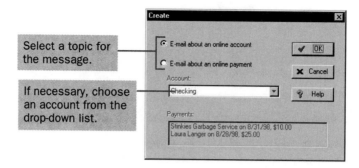

Select a topic for
the message.

If necessary, choose
an account from the
drop-down list.

When you click OK, a message window appears. Use it to compose your
e-mail message. Here's what the Message window looks like for a message about
an account; it appears differently for a message about a payment:

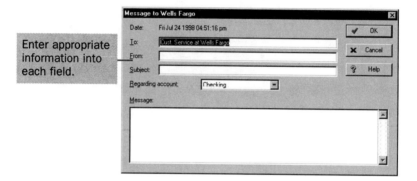

Enter appropriate
information into
each field.

When you click OK, the message is saved. It appears in the bottom half of the
E-mail tab of the Online Financial Services Center window, ready to be sent to
your bank.

Exchanging E-mail Messages

Using e-mail is a lot like having a box at the post office. When you write a letter,
you have to get it to the post office to send it to the recipient. When you receive
a letter, you have to go to the post office and check your box to retrieve it. E-mail
works the same way. Connecting is a lot like going to the post office to send and
retrieve messages.

In the Online Financial Services Center window, click the Send/Update
button. Quicken displays the Instructions to Send window, which includes any
e-mail messages you may have created that need to be sent. Enter your PIN and
click the Send button. Then wait while Quicken establishes an Internet
connection with your bank and exchanges e-mail.

When Quicken is finished, it displays the Online Transmission Summary window. Review the information in this window and click OK. The word Sent appears in the Status column beside the e-mail messages that have been sent to your bank.

Reading an E-mail Message

When your bank sends you an e-mail message, it appears in the E-mail tab of the Online Financial Services Center window. To read the message, select it and click Read. The message appears in a Message window like this:

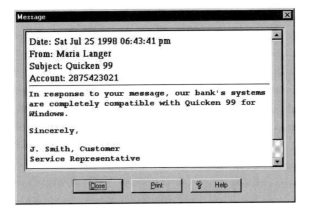

Although there's no reply button in this window, you can reply to a message by sending another message as instructed earlier.

Tracking Credit Cards Online

In This Chapter:

- *Benefits and Costs of Tracking Credit Cards Online*

- *Downloading Transactions*

- *Comparing Downloaded Transactions to Register Transactions*

- *Paying Bills*

- *Exchanging E-mail with Your Financial Institution*

Chapter 13

Quicken's online account access feature enables you to download credit card account activity and pay your credit card bills. In this chapter, I explain how to set up and use this feature. As you'll see, it can save you a lot of time and effort by automating the entry of credit card transactions, including charges, fees, and payments.

Tip The instructions in this chapter assume you have already configured your computer for an Internet connection. If you have not done so, do it now. Chapter 3 provides the instructions you need to set up and test an Internet connection. This chapter also assumes you understand the topics and procedures discussed in Chapters 2 and 6, and builds on many of the basic concepts discussed in those chapters.

Why Track Credit Cards Online?

Consider the following scenario: You just returned from a lengthy, well-deserved vacation. While you were away, you used your credit cards to pay for everything, from meals and hotels to cab rides and sightseeing tours. (You would have used it to tip the bellman for carrying your luggage, but he wasn't too receptive to the idea.) Now you're home, sitting in front of your computer with a huge stack of credit card receipts.

With online account access for your credit card accounts, you could simply file those receipts and let Quicken download the transactions for you. All transactions are included—charges, cash advances, interest or finance fees, and payments. Once the transactions are on your computer, all it takes is a few keystrokes and mouse clicks to enter them into your Quicken account registers. If a payment is due, Quicken tells you and offers to prepare a payment transaction for you.

The cost of this time-saving feature? Most financial institutions don't charge a penny.

Setting Up Online Account Access

To use online account access to track credit card transactions, you must configure the appropriate Quicken accounts. This requires that you enter information about your financial institution and the account(s) you want to track.

Setting up online account access is virtually identical to setting it up for a bank account. You can find step-by-step instructions for that in Chapter 12, so I won't repeat them here.

Using the Online Financial Services Center

When you enable online account access, you can use the Online Financial Services Center to download transactions, compare them to transactions in your account register, enter new transactions, and pay your bill. To get started, choose Online | Online Center. Here's what this window looks like for my American Express card:

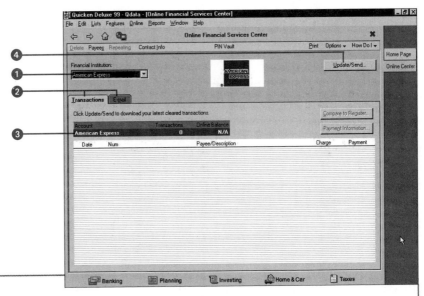

① Choose the financial institution with which you want to work.

② Click a tab to work with transactions or e-mail.

③ Select the account with which you want to work.

④ Click Update/Send to download transaction information.

Tip When you choose your credit card company's name from the Financial Institution drop-down list, Quicken may display a message telling you that Intuit Online Payment is available for the account(s). Click OK to dismiss the dialog box. I tell you about online payments in Chapter 12, and about paying your bill later in this chapter.

Downloading Transactions

The main feature of online account access for a credit card account is the ability to download transactions directly from your financial institution. The following sections show you how you can take advantage of this feature.

Connecting to the Financial Institution

To download transactions, you must connect to your financial institution. Make sure the financial institution is selected in the Online Financial Services Center window and click the Update/Send button. The Instructions to Send dialog box appears. Enter your PIN and click Send, as shown here:

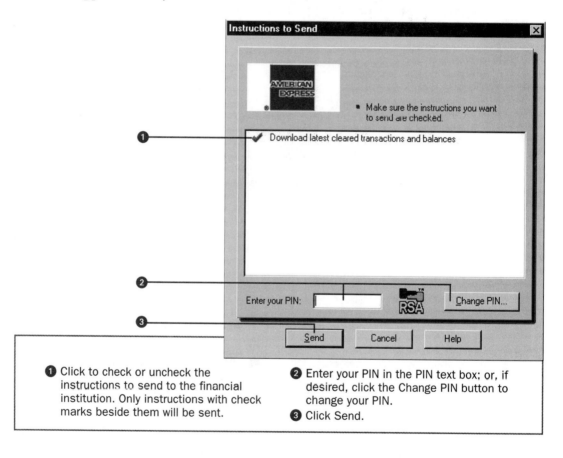

❶ Click to check or uncheck the instructions to send to the financial institution. Only instructions with check marks beside them will be sent.

❷ Enter your PIN in the PIN text box; or, if desired, click the Change PIN button to change your PIN.

❸ Click Send.

● **Tip**   The first time you communicate with your financial institution, the Instructions to Send dialog box may not include a text box for your PIN as just shown. Instead, when you click Send, a Change Assigned PIN dialog box may appear. Enter the PIN the financial institution assigned to you in the top text box. Then enter a preferred PIN code in the bottom two text boxes. None of the characters you enter will appear onscreen. Instead, you'll just see asterisks (*). Click OK.

Wait while Quicken connects to your financial institution. A connection status window appears while it works.

Reviewing Transactions

When the update is complete, the status window disappears and an Online Transmission Summary window appears to summarize the activity that took place while you waited:

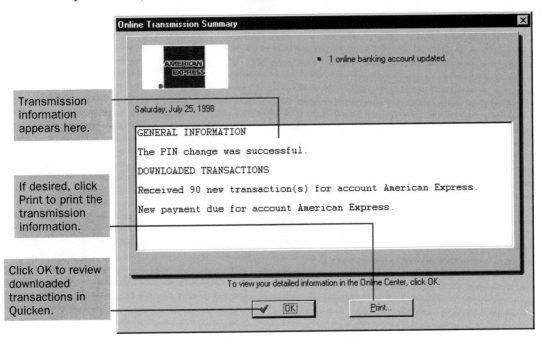

Transmission information appears here.

If desired, click Print to print the transmission information.

Click OK to review downloaded transactions in Quicken.

The transactions you download appear in the Transactions tab of the Online Financial Services Center window. You can scroll through the Transaction List to view the downloaded transactions. Because your credit card company knows exactly who it paid, payee information appears along with the transaction date and amount.

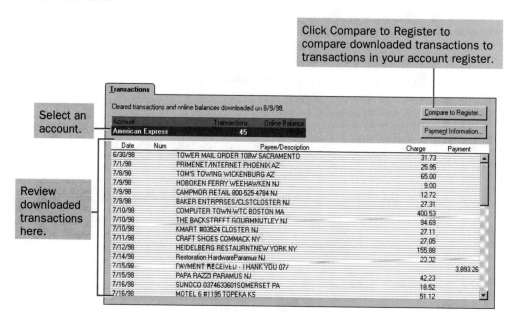

Click Compare to Register to compare downloaded transactions to transactions in your account register.

Select an account.

Review downloaded transactions here.

Date	Num	Payee/Description	Charge	Payment
6/30/98		TOWER MAIL ORDER 108W SACRAMENTO	31.73	
7/1/98		PRIMENET/INTERNET PHOENIX AZ	25.95	
7/8/98		TOM'S TOWING WICKENBURG AZ	65.00	
7/9/98		HOBOKEN FERRY WEEHAWKEN NJ	9.00	
7/9/98		CAMPMOR RETAIL 800-525-4784 NJ	12.72	
7/9/98		BAKER ENTRPRSES/CLSTCLOSTER NJ	27.31	
7/10/98		COMPUTER TOWN WTC BOSTON MA	400.53	
7/10/98		THE BACKSTREET GOURMNUTLEY NJ	94.68	
7/10/98		KMART #03524 CLOSTER NJ	27.11	
7/11/98		CRAFT SHOES COMMACK NY	27.05	
7/12/98		HEIDELBERG RESTAURNTNEW YORK NY	155.88	
7/14/98		Restoration HardwareParamus NJ	20.32	
7/15/98		PAYMENT RECEIVED - THANK YOU 07/		3,893.26
7/15/98		PAPA RAZZI PARAMUS NJ	42.23	
7/16/98		SUNOCO 0374633601SOMERSET PA	18.52	
7/16/98		MOTEL 6 #1195 TOPEKA KS	51.12	

Tip   The first time you connect, your financial institution sends all transactions from the past 60 days. After that, only new transactions will be downloaded.

Comparing Downloaded Transactions to Register Transactions

Once the information has been downloaded, you can compare the transactions to the transactions already entered in your account register. This enables you to identify transactions you neglected to enter or entered incorrectly.

Click the Compare to Register button. The Register window opens with the downloaded transaction list in the bottom half of its window. Here's what the window might look like with a few transactions already accepted:

Click the Accept
button to accept a
selected transaction.

Click the Accept
All button to
accept all
transactions.

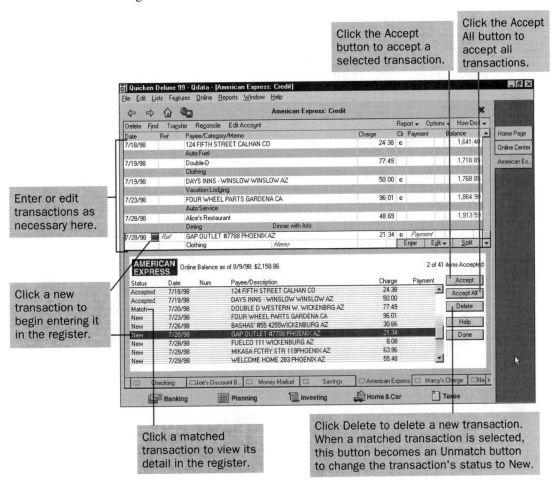

Enter or edit
transactions as
necessary here.

Click a new
transaction to
begin entering it
in the register.

Click a matched
transaction to view its
detail in the register.

Click Delete to delete a new transaction.
When a matched transaction is selected,
this button becomes an Unmatch button
to change the transaction's status to New.

A *c* in the Clr column indicates a transaction that has been processed by your financial institution.

Tip When you click the Accept or Accept All button, you may be prompted to enter additional information, such as the transaction category, for transactions identified as New.

The Status column in the bottom half of the window identifies three types of transactions:

- **Match** identifies downloaded transactions that match those in the register.
- **New** identifies transactions that do not appear to be in the register.
- **Accepted** identifies matched transactions that you have accepted.

Accepting a Matched Transaction   If a transaction matches one in the register, you can accept it by selecting it in the list at the bottom of the window and clicking the Accept button. A small *c* appears in the Clr column to indicate that the item has been processed by your financial institution but has not yet been reconciled.

Entering and Accepting a New Transaction   Select the new transaction in the bottom half of the window. Quicken begins preparing a register transaction entry for it. Fill in the missing details, including the category and memo. Then click Enter. Quicken enters and accepts the transaction.

SAVE TIME   Because Quicken automatically enters a date, transaction number, payee, and amount, using this method to enter a transaction can be much faster than entering it manually in the account register window.

Matching a New Transaction   If a downloaded transaction identified as New should match one in the register, you can modify the information in the register to match the information in the downloaded transaction. When you click the Enter button for the register transaction, the word Match should appear beside the downloaded transaction. You can then accept it.

Unmatching a Matched Transaction   If a matched transaction really shouldn't be matched, select it in the bottom half of the window and click the Unmatch button. You can then treat it as a new transaction.

Deleting a New Transaction   To delete a new transaction, select the transaction in the bottom half of the window and click the Delete button. The transaction is removed from the downloaded Transaction List.

Tip   This option is especially useful the first time you download transactions. You may download transactions that have already been reconciled. Use the Unmatch button to unmatch them as necessary, and then use the Delete button to delete them from the downloaded Transaction List.

Finishing Up   When you're finished comparing downloaded transactions to register transactions, click the Done button. If you failed to accept all of the transactions, Quicken displays a dialog box offering to finish now or later. If you click the Finish Later button, the unaccepted transactions are saved in the downloaded Transaction List for the next time you compare transactions.

Caution   Downloaded transactions that have not been accepted may not be entered in your account register. Thus, your register balance may be misstated until you accept all downloaded transactions.

Paying Your Bill

If payment on your credit card bill is due, you're notified in the Online Transmission Summary window when you successfully download transactions. When you're finished reviewing, comparing, and accepting downloaded transactions, you can use Quicken to review your bill and enter a payment transaction.

Click the Payment Information button in the Online Financial Services Center window. A dialog box like the following appears, providing information about the statement date, minimum payment due, and account balance:

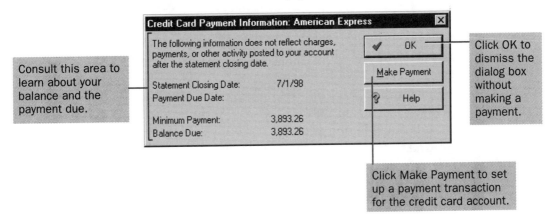

Consult this area to learn about your balance and the payment due.

Credit Card Payment Information: American Express

The following information does not reflect charges, payments, or other activity posted to your account after the statement closing date.

Statement Closing Date: 7/1/98
Payment Due Date:

Minimum Payment: 3,893.26
Balance Due: 3,893.26

Click OK to dismiss the dialog box without making a payment.

Click Make Payment to set up a payment transaction for the credit card account.

If you click the Make Payment button, the Make Credit Card Payment dialog box appears; use this dialog box to set up a payment transaction for the credit card account:

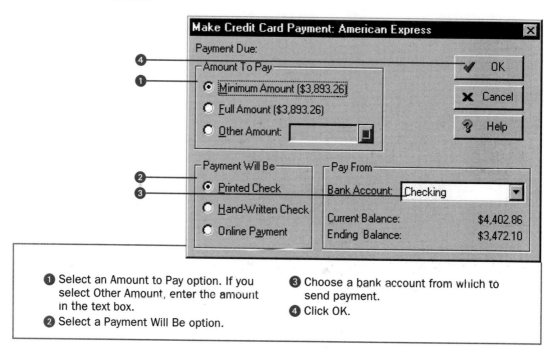

❶ Select an Amount to Pay option. If you select Other Amount, enter the amount in the text box.

❷ Select a Payment Will Be option.

❸ Choose a bank account from which to send payment.

❹ Click OK.

The option you select in the Payment Will Be area determines what happens when you click OK:

- **Printed Check** displays the Write Checks window, with the payment transaction already filled in. Edit the transaction as necessary and click the Record Check button to complete it. The check can be printed the next time you use the Print Checks command.

- **Hand-Written Check** displays the account register window, with the payment transaction already filled in. Edit the transaction as necessary and click the Enter button to complete it. You must then write the check by hand.

- **Online Payment** displays the Payments tab of the Online Financial Services Center window with the payment transaction already filled in. Edit the transaction as necessary and click the Enter button to complete it. The payment instruction will be sent to your bank the next time you click the Update/Send button.

Tip   To use the Online Payment option, one of your bank accounts must be set up for online payment through your bank or Intuit Online Payments. In addition, the credit card company must be set up as an online payee. I explain how to do these things in Chapter 12.

Exchanging E-Mail with Your Financial Institution

You can use the E-mail tab of the Online Financial Services Center window to exchange e-mail messages with financial institutions for which you have enabled online account access. I tell you how to do this for bank accounts in Chapter 12. E-mail works almost exactly the same way for credit card accounts so I won't repeat the instructions here. See Chapter 12 for details.

Tracking
Investments Online

Chapter 14

In This Chapter:

- Benefits and Costs of Online Investment Tracking

- Downloading Transactions

- Comparing Downloaded Transactions to Register Transactions

- Reviewing Account Balance Details

- Comparing Downloaded Holdings to Recorded Holdings

- Downloading Stock Quotes and News

Quicken offers two individual features for tracking investments online:

- **Online investment tracking** enables you to download transactions and balances for your investment accounts. This helps automate the entry of investment transactions and keep your Quicken records in sync with your brokerage firm's records.
- **Online quotes and news** enables you to obtain current and historical quotes and news stories about individual stocks, mutual funds, and other investments. This automates the tracking of market values and provides valuable information you can use to make better investment decisions.

In this chapter, I tell you about each of these features and explain how they can help you save time and stay informed.

Tip   The instructions in this chapter assume that you have already configured your computer for an Internet connection. If you have not done so, do it now. Chapter 3 provides the instructions you need to set up and test an Internet connection. The present chapter also assumes that you understand the topics and procedures discussed in Chapters 2 and 7, and builds on many of the basic concepts discussed in those chapters.

Benefits and Costs of Online Investment Tracking

Consider the following scenario: You wake up one morning and realize that your future financial security is very important to you. (This happened to me about four years ago.) You make a conscious effort to save and invest money. After a few years, you own shares of a few stocks and mutual funds, which you track in your Quicken data file. With your growing portfolio, you find that half the time you spend with Quicken is spent entering up-to-date stock quotes and transaction details. You like keeping the market value information current, but you'd like to spend more of your time researching new investments and following news stories about the investments you already have.

With online investment tracking, you can let Quicken download and enter the transactions for you. All transactions are included—additional investments, dividends, income and capital gain reinvestments, management fees, disbursements, and stock splits.

As for the tedious chore of entering stock quotes, Quicken can do that, too. You can download quotes throughout the day or at the day's end. If you miss a few days, don't worry. You can get up to five years of stock quotes for any company with the click of a mouse. And as an added bonus, Quicken can even download links to news stories about the investments you own or watch.

The cost? Most financial institutions that make online investment tracking available provide it free of charge to account holders. Stock quotes and news are free to Quicken Deluxe users, courtesy of Intuit.

Online Investment Tracking

Online investment tracking enables you to download transactions, balance details, and holding information directly from the financial institutions with which you maintain investment accounts. Each transaction can then be entered into your Quicken investment account with the click of a mouse button. You can also review downloaded account balance details and compare downloaded holdings information to the information recorded in your portfolio.

Setting Up Online Investment Tracking

To use online investment tracking, you must configure the appropriate Quicken accounts. This requires that you enter information about your financial institution and the account(s) you want to track.

Setting up online investment tracking is virtually identical to setting up online account access for a bank account or credit card account. I provide step-by-step instructions in Chapter 12, so I won't repeat them here. Consult that chapter for details.

Downloading Account Information

When you enable online investment tracking, you can use the Online Financial Services Center to download account information, compare it to data in your Quicken file, and enter new transactions and adjustments. Choose Online | Online Center. Here's what this window looks like for an Accutrade investments account:

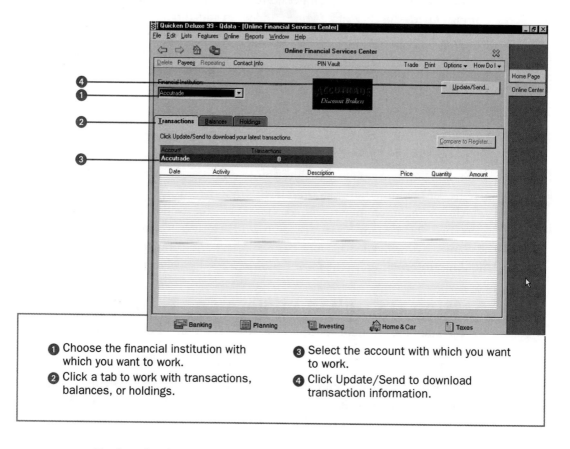

➊ Choose the financial institution with which you want to work.

➋ Click a tab to work with transactions, balances, or holdings.

➌ Select the account with which you want to work.

➍ Click Update/Send to download transaction information.

To download transactions, you must connect to your financial institution. Make sure the financial institution is selected on the Online Financial Services

Center window and click the Update/Send button. The Instructions to Send dialog box appears.

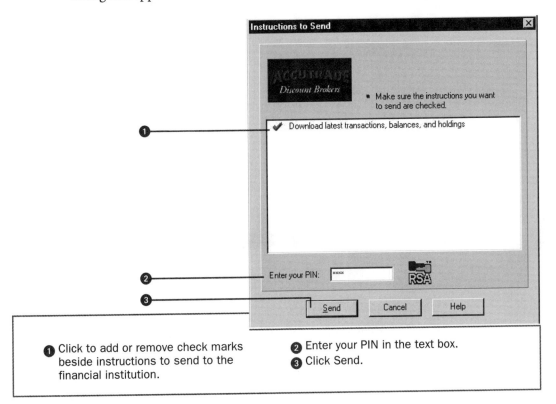

1 Click to add or remove check marks beside instructions to send to the financial institution.

2 Enter your PIN in the text box.
3 Click Send.

Select the instructions to send, enter your PIN, and then click Send. Wait while Quicken connects to your financial institution. A status window appears during the connection.

Reviewing Transactions

When Quicken is finished exchanging information, the status window disappears and an Online Transmission Summary window appears to summarize the activity that took place while you waited:

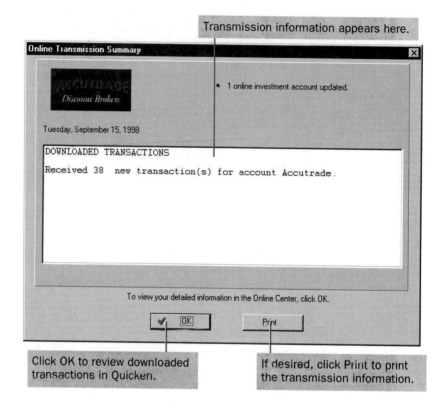

Transmission information appears here.

Online Transmission Summary

Tuesday, September 15, 1998

1 online investment account updated.

DOWNLOADED TRANSACTIONS

Received 38 new transaction(s) for account Accutrade.

To view your detailed information in the Online Center, click OK.

OK   Print

Click OK to review downloaded transactions in Quicken.

If desired, click Print to print the transmission information.

Reviewing a List of Downloaded Transactions

The transactions you download appear in the Transactions tab of the Online Financial Services Center window. You can scroll through the Transaction List to view the transactions that were downloaded. Because your investment firm knows exactly what you bought and sold, all transaction details appear in the window.

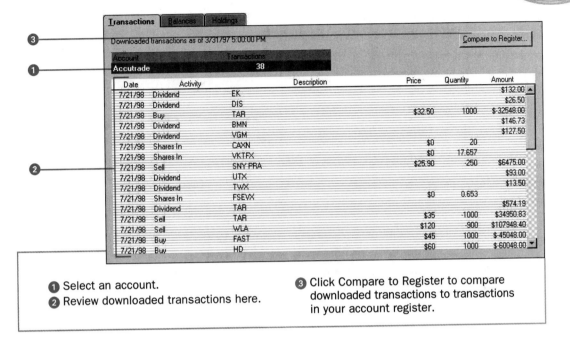

1 Select an account.

2 Review downloaded transactions here.

3 Click Compare to Register to compare downloaded transactions to transactions in your account register.

Tip The first time you connect, your financial institution sends all transactions from the past 60 days. After that, only new transactions will be downloaded.

Comparing Downloaded Transactions to Register Transactions

You can also compare downloaded transactions to the transactions already entered in your account register. This enables you to identify transactions you neglected to enter or entered incorrectly.

Click the Compare to Register button in the Transactions tab of the Online Financial Services Center window. Quicken attempts to match securities in the downloaded Transaction List to securities in the Security List within Quicken. It displays the Matching Security dialog box shown here for each security it doesn't recognize:

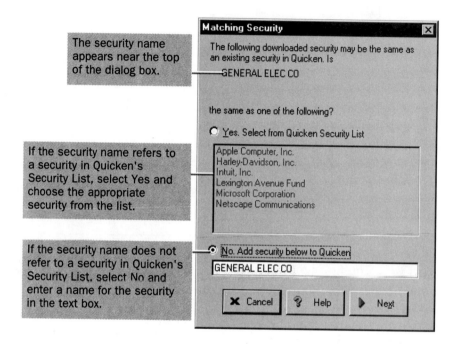

The security name appears near the top of the dialog box.

If the security name refers to a security in Quicken's Security List, select Yes and choose the appropriate security from the list.

If the security name does not refer to a security in Quicken's Security List, select No and enter a name for the security in the text box.

Click Next to move to the next security. When you're finished matching or entering securities, the account register window opens with the downloaded Transaction List in the bottom half of its window. Here's what the window might look like with a few transactions already accepted:

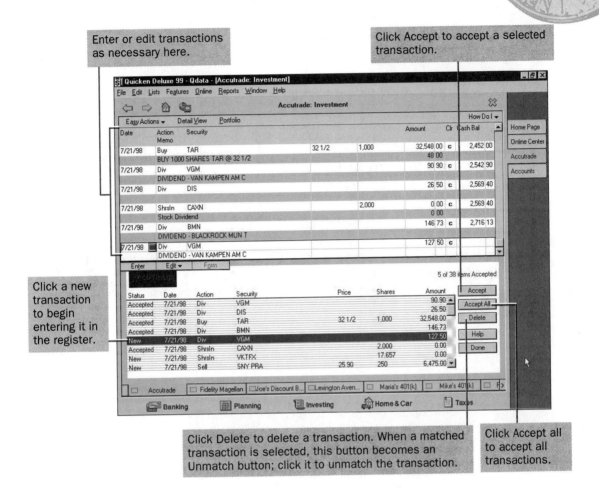

Enter or edit transactions as necessary here.

Click Accept to accept a selected transaction.

Click a new transaction to begin entering it in the register.

Click Delete to delete a transaction. When a matched transaction is selected, this button becomes an Unmatch button; click it to unmatch the transaction.

Click Accept all to accept all transactions.

The Status column on the bottom half of the window identifies three types of transactions:

- **Match** identifies downloaded transactions that match those in the register.
- **New** identifies transactions that do not appear to be in the register.
- **Accepted** identifies matched transactions that you have accepted.

Accepting a Matched Transaction   If a transaction matches one in the register, you can accept it by selecting it in the list at the bottom of the window and clicking the Accept button. A small *c* appears in the Clr column to indicate that the item has cleared the bank but has not yet been reconciled.

Entering and Accepting a New Transaction   To enter and accept a new transaction, select the new transaction in the bottom half of the window. Quicken begins preparing a register transaction entry for it. If necessary, fill in any missing details. Then click the Enter button for the register entry. Quicken enters and accepts the transaction.

SAVE TIME   Because Quicken will automatically enter most transaction information, using this method to enter an investment transaction can be much faster than entering it manually in the account register window.

Matching a New Transaction   If a downloaded transaction identified as New should match one in the register, you can modify the information in the register to match the information in the downloaded transaction. When you click the Enter button for the register transaction, the word Match should appear beside the downloaded transaction. You can then accept it.

Unmatching a Matched Transaction   If a matched transaction really shouldn't be matched, select it in the bottom half of the window and click the Unmatch button. You can then treat it as a new transaction.

Deleting a New Transaction   To delete a new transaction, select the transaction in the bottom half of the window and click the Delete button. The transaction is removed from the downloaded Transaction List.

Tip   This option is especially useful the first time you download transactions. You may download transactions that have already been reconciled. Use the Unmatch button to unmatch them as necessary, and then use the Delete button to delete them from the downloaded Transaction List.

Finishing Up   When you're finished comparing downloaded transactions to register transactions, click the Done button. If you didn't accept all of the transactions, Quicken displays a dialog box offering to finish now or later. If you click the Finish Later button, the unaccepted transactions are saved in the downloaded Transaction List for the next time you compare transactions.

Caution   Downloaded transactions that have not been accepted may not be entered in your investment register. Thus, your register and portfolio balances may be misstated until you accept all downloaded transactions.

Reviewing Balances

When you download transactions from your financial institution, you also receive detailed account balance information. To review this information, click the Balances tab in the Online Financial Services Center window. Here's what it might look like for a mutual fund account:

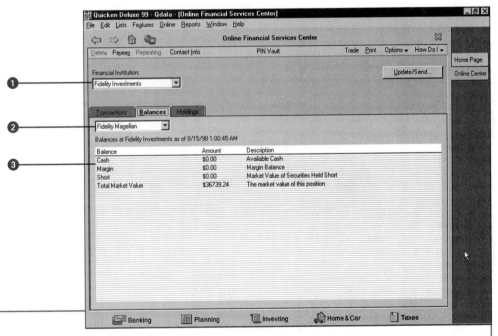

❶ Choose a financial institution.
❷ Choose an account.

❸ Review account balance information here.

Reviewing Holdings

The financial institution also sends you information about your holdings. You can review this information in the Online Financial Services Center window and compare it to the information in your portfolio.

To review holdings, click the Holdings tab in the Online Financial Services Center window. Here's what it looks like for the same account shown in the previous illustration:

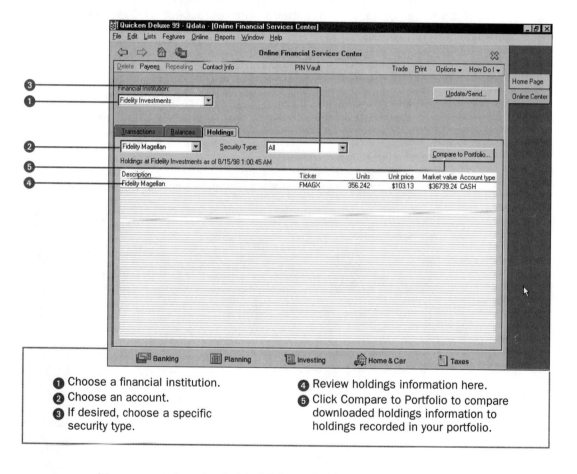

1 Choose a financial institution.
2 Choose an account.
3 If desired, choose a specific security type.

4 Review holdings information here.
5 Click Compare to Portfolio to compare downloaded holdings information to holdings recorded in your portfolio.

To compare downloaded holdings to holdings in your portfolio, click the Compare to Portfolio button. Quicken compares the holdings information. What happens next depends on whether the holdings information matches.

When Holdings Match

When downloaded holdings match the holdings recorded in your portfolio, Quicken displays a dialog box like this one:

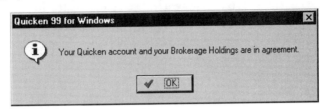

Click OK to dismiss it and continue working with Quicken.

When Holdings Don't Match

When downloaded holdings don't match the holdings recorded in your portfolio, the investment register window for the account appears. A list of discrepancies between the downloaded and recorded holdings is included in the bottom half of the window:

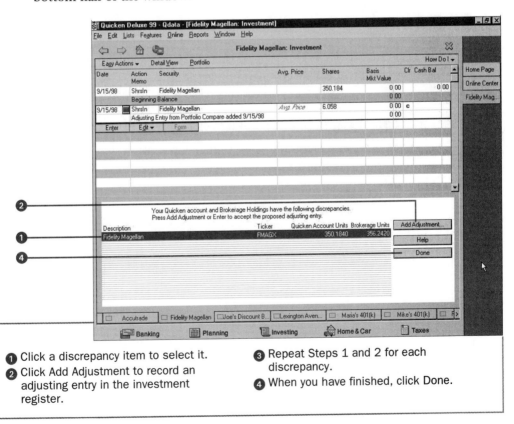

❶ Click a discrepancy item to select it.

❷ Click Add Adjustment to record an adjusting entry in the investment register.

❸ Repeat Steps 1 and 2 for each discrepancy.

❹ When you have finished, click Done.

When you select a discrepancy item and click the Add Adjustment button, the Buy/Add Shares or Sell/Remove Shares dialog box appears. I tell you how to use these dialog boxes in Chapter 7. Use the dialog box to provide details for the adjusting entry. Do this for each discrepancy listed in the bottom half of the investment account register. When you are finished, Quicken displays a dialog box confirming that the information matches. Click OK to dismiss the dialog box and continue working with Quicken.

Online Quotes and News

Quicken's Online Quotes & News feature enables you to download up-to-date stock quotes and links to news articles about the securities that interest you. You set it up once, and then update the information as often as desired. You can even download historical price information so you can review price trends for a security that only recently caught your eye. I tell you about all these features next.

Tip   Because Online Quotes & News is a built-in Quicken Deluxe feature, it doesn't rely on your brokerage firm for information. That means you can take advantage of online quotes and news even if your brokerage firm doesn't offer online investment tracking.

Setting Up Online Quotes and News

Before you can get quotes and news online, you must set it up. Choose Features | Investing | Set Up Online Quotes & News. The Customize Investment Download dialog box appears:

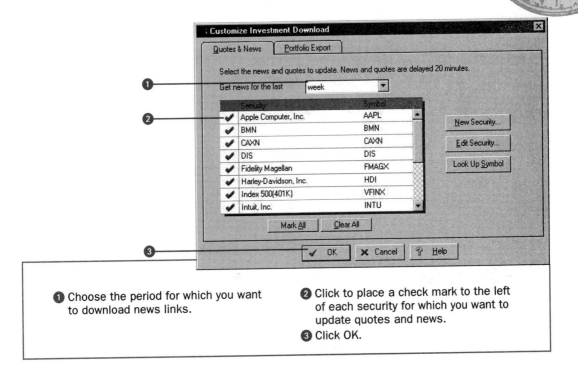

❶ Choose the period for which you want to download news links.

❷ Click to place a check mark to the left of each security for which you want to update quotes and news.

❸ Click OK.

First, choose the period for which you want to download news links. Turn on check marks for the securities for which you want to update quotes and news. Then click OK to save your settings.

Updating Quotes and News

Begin by choosing Features | Investing | Security Detail & News to display the Security Detail View window, which I discuss in detail in Chapter 7. Then choose Update | Get Online Quotes & News on the Button bar in the window. The Download Selection dialog box appears:

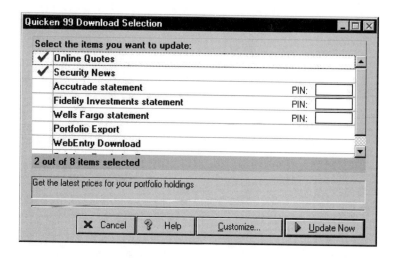

Shortcut   Clicking the One Step Update button on the navigation bar in any window also displays this dialog box. Use it to update all your online information at once. I tell you more about One Step Update in Chapter 15.

Make sure check marks appear beside Online Quotes and Security News in the list. Then click the Update Now button. Quicken connects to the Internet and begins downloading information. While it works, a Download Status dialog box shows you what's going on:

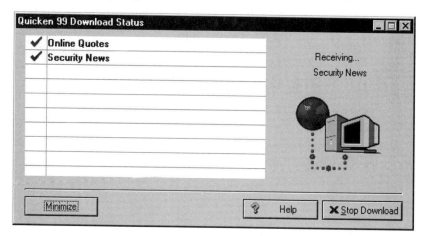

When Quicken is finished downloading information, it displays the Download Summary dialog box, which tells you how many securities were updated and how many headlines were received:

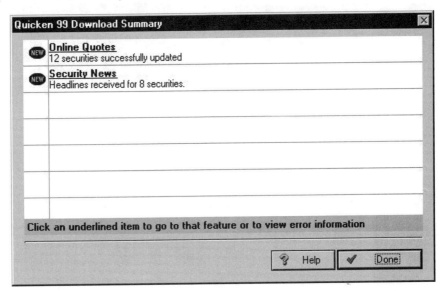

Viewing Downloaded Quotes and News

You can view quotes and news headlines for a security in the Security Detail View window. Choose Features | Investing | Security Detail & News to display the window. Then choose the security that interests you from the drop-down list near the top of the window.

Viewing Stock Quotes

To view stock quotes for a security, click the Holdings tab at the bottom of the window. Then, if necessary, choose Price History from the drop-down list in the middle of the window. The window should look something like this:

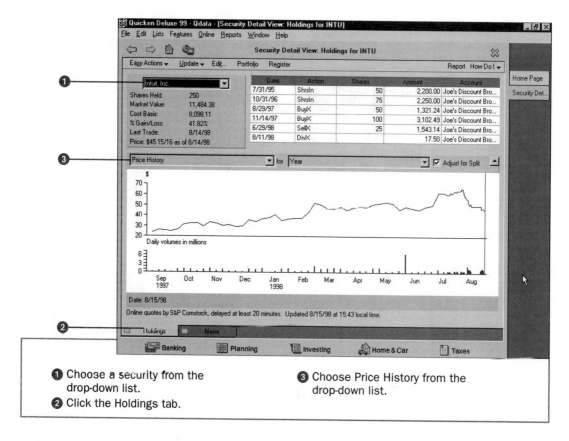

❶ Choose a security from the drop-down list.

❷ Click the Holdings tab.

❸ Choose Price History from the drop-down list.

You can also view stock quotes by choosing Update | Edit Price History on the Button bar. This displays the Price History window, which displays all the recorded stock quotes for the security:

Price History for: Intuit, Inc.

New   Edit   Delete   Print   Close

Date	Price	High	Low	Volume
8/14/98	45 15/16	48 1/8	45 1/4	424,900
8/13/98	47 3/16	49 1/8	47	1,191,100
8/12/98	47 7/8	48 7/16	45 7/8	1,617,200
8/11/98	47 1/4	49 3/8	46 3/8	1,312,500
8/10/98	50	51 1/8	48 9/16	766,200
7/31/98	49 3/4	53 1/8	49 3/4	787,700
7/30/98	51 15/16	53 3/8	51 3/4	1,203,600
7/29/98	51 1/8	54 7/16	50 15/16	1,361,300
7/28/98	53 1/16	56 3/4	52 1/4	1,477,900
7/27/98	56 1/2	58 3/4	52 7/8	2,457,700
7/24/98	58 13/16	63 1/2	58 1/4	678,600
7/23/98	61 11/16	66	61 1/4	678,400
7/22/98	65 3/4	66 7/8	64 3/4	402,300
7/21/98	66 1/2	67 15/16	65	762,400

Viewing News Headlines

To view news headlines for a security, click the News tab at the bottom of the
Security Detail View window. The headlines appear in chronological order, with
the most recent headline at the top of the list:

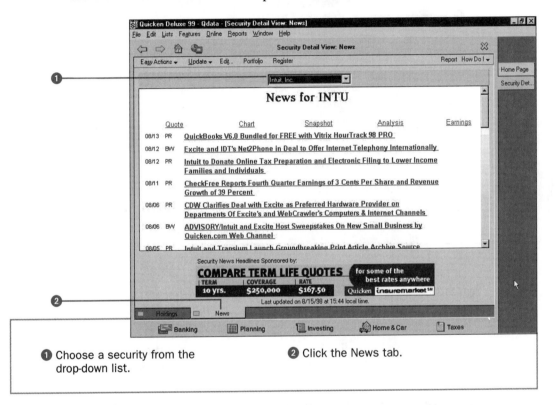

❶ Choose a security from the
drop-down list.

❷ Click the News tab.

To view a news story, click its underlined link. Quicken connects to the
Internet and displays the story in an Internet window.

Downloading Historical Quote Information

You can also download historical price information from within the Security
Detail View window. Choose Update | Get Historical Prices on the Button bar.
Quicken displays the Get Historical Prices dialog box:

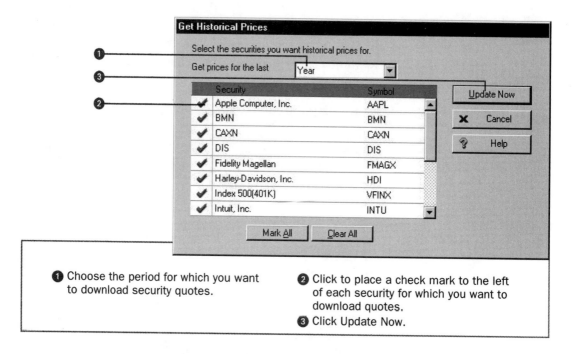

① Choose the period for which you want to download security quotes.

② Click to place a check mark to the left of each security for which you want to download quotes.

③ Click Update Now.

Choose a time period from the "Get prices for the last" drop-down list. Make sure check marks appear beside all securities for which you want to get historical quotes. Then click the Update Now button. Quicken connects to the Internet and retrieves the information you requested. When it is done, it displays the Download Summary dialog box. Click OK to dismiss the dialog box. You can review the quotes that were downloaded in the Security Detail View window.

Downloading Asset Class Information

For each security you own or watch, you can include asset class information. This enables you to create accurate asset allocation reports and graphs. I explain how to manually enter asset class information in Chapter 7.

The trouble is, most mutual funds consist of many investments in a variety of asset classes. Manually looking up and entering this information is time-consuming and tedious. Fortunately, Quicken can download this information from the Internet and enter it for you.

Choose Update | Get Asset Classes on the Button bar of the Security Detail View window. Quicken displays the Download Security Asset Classes dialog box, which looks and works very much like the Get Historical Prices dialog box shown in the previous illustration. Make sure check marks appear beside all securities for which you want to download asset class information, and then click the Update Now button. Quicken connects to the Internet and retrieves the information you requested. When it is done, it displays the Download Summary dialog box. Click OK to dismiss the dialog box. The asset classes are automatically entered for each security.

Accessing Quicken Data on the Web

In This Chapter:

- *Entering Quicken Transactions on the Web*

- *Viewing Your Portfolio on the Web*

- *Using One Step Update*

- *Using the PIN Vault*

Chapter 15

325

Chapters 12, 13, and 14 provided the basic instructions you need to take advantage of Quicken's online financial services features. In this chapter, you learn how you can use an Internet connection to update Quicken information and keep an eye on your portfolio when you're away from home. I also tell you about One Step Update and the PIN Vault, two related features that can make updating Quicken data fast and easy.

Tip This chapter builds on the information covered in Chapters 12, 13, and 14. If you are unfamiliar with the concepts and techniques discussed in those chapters, go back and read them now.

Accessing Quicken Data via the Web

Quicken Deluxe includes a number of features you can use to, in effect, take a piece of Quicken with you when you're away from home:

- **Portfolio Export** enables you to track your Quicken portfolio on the Web.
- **WebEntry** enables you to enter transactions into account registers via a form on a Web page.
- **Quicken Reminders Export** enables you to export Quicken alerts and reminders to the Web.

All of these features work with the Quicken.com Web site, enabling you to use them from anywhere in the world.

Registering with Quicken.com

To take advantage of these features, you must register with Quicken.com. This requires you to visit a Web page where you enter some information about yourself and choose a username and password. If you've already done this, you can skip this section. Otherwise, use the following steps.

Choose Online | Quicken on the Web | Quicken.com to display the Quicken.com home page. Scroll down the page and click the Where's My Portfolio link under the Mini Portfolio. The Login page shown in Figure 15-1 should appear. Click the Create New Account link to display the Registration page shown in Figure 15-2.

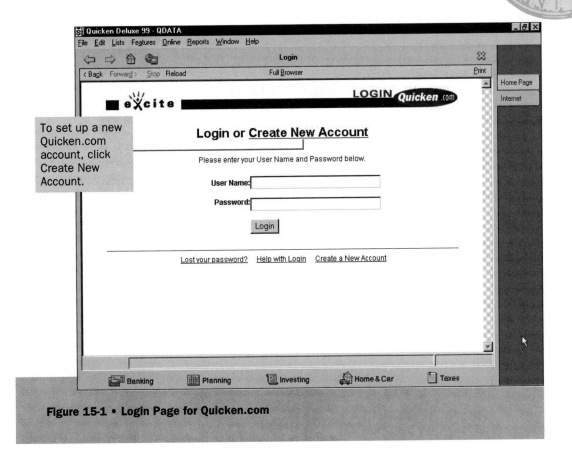

Figure 15-1 • Login Page for Quicken.com

Follow the instructions on this page to fill out the form. Make sure you enter information into each required (bold) field. When you're finished, click the Continue button at the bottom of the page. If you have correctly entered all the required information, a "Thanks!" page appears. Click the Continue button on that page.

The default portfolio page for new Quicken.com users appears. This is the same portfolio that appears on Quicken's home page. You can use Web Portfolio Export to set up and display your portfolio on Quicken.com; I explain how next.

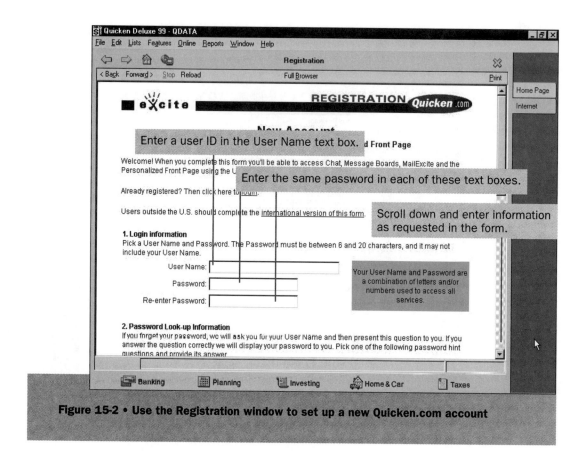

Figure 15-2 • Use the Registration window to set up a new Quicken.com account

Web Portfolio Export

The Web Portfolio Export feature enables you to track your portfolio's value on the Web. Although you can do this without Quicken by manually customizing and updating the default portfolio Web page at Quicken.com, it's a lot easier to have Quicken automatically send updated portfolio information to Quicken.com for you.

Setting Up Your Portfolio

In Quicken, choose Features | Investing | Set Up Web Portfolio Export. The Portfolio Export tab of the Customize Investment Download dialog box appears:

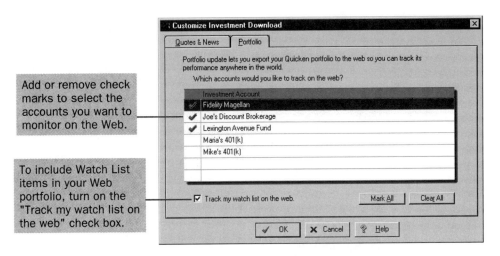

Add or remove check marks to select the accounts you want to monitor on the Web.

To include Watch List items in your Web portfolio, turn on the "Track my watch list on the web" check box.

Set options as desired in this dialog box and click OK.

Choose Online | One Step Update or click the One Step Update button at the top of the window to display the Download Selection dialog box for the One Step Update feature. (I tell you more about this feature later in this chapter). Turn off all check marks except the one beside Portfolio Export. Then click Update Now. A Quicken.com Login dialog box appears. Enter your user ID and password and click Update Now.

Tip If the Quicken.com Login dialog box did not appear, you probably have the "Show me the Quicken.com login when updating" check box turned off in the Internet Connection Options dialog box. I explain the options in this dialog box in Chapter 3.

Quicken establishes a connection to the Internet, and displays a status dialog box while it updates information. When it's finished, it displays the Download Summary dialog box, which informs you that your Portfolio has been updated.

Checking Your Portfolio on the Web

Once your portfolio has been updated, you can view it at any time from any computer with Web access. Use a Web browser to navigate to *http://www.quicken.com/investments/portfolio/*. The contents of your portfolio appear on the page. Here's mine, scrolled down so you can see it:

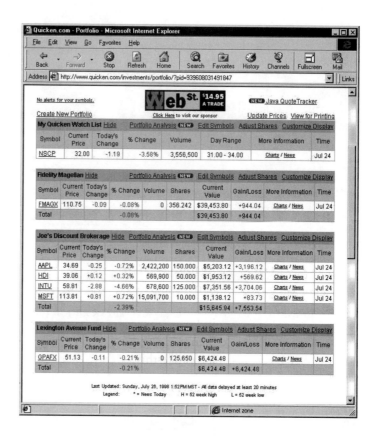

Tip If your computer is set to save your Quicken.com login information or you have manually logged on to Quicken.com, an abbreviated version of your portfolio appears right on the Quicken.com home page, in place of the default portfolio.

WebEntry

Quicken's WebEntry feature enables you to enter transactions for your Quicken accounts via the Web. You use a Web browser to navigate to a specific Web page on the Quicken.com site, enter your user ID and password if prompted, and enter transactions. Then, when you're back at your desk with Quicken running, you can use the One Step Update command to download transactions stored on the Web into your Quicken data file.

Tip This feature is especially useful if you're away for an extended period of time. By entering transactions periodically via the Web, you won't have to enter them all at once when you return.

Quicken Quote

"I just tried out WebEntry. It is so cool! This alone makes the new version better for me. Now I don't have to carry backup floppies around with me if I want to update my register away from my computer."

Suzanne Hardie, Austin, TX

Entering Transactions

Use a Web browser to navigate to the Quicken.com home page at *http://www.quicken.com*. Scroll down in the window and click the Quicken 99 Web Entry link—you'll find it under the Quicken Support link on the left side of the window. A login window may appear; if it does, enter your username and password as prompted. When you click OK, the WebEntry page appears. The first time you access it, it looks like this:

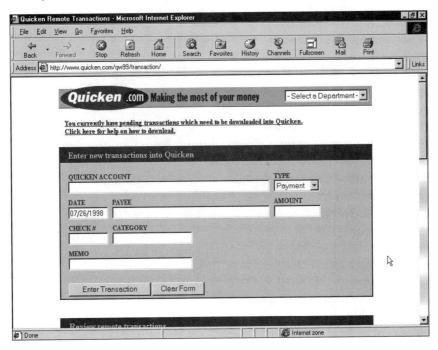

Enter transaction information into the form. Be sure to click the Enter Transaction button after each entry to enter the transaction into the Web database. You can enter as many transactions as you like this way. Don't worry if you don't know the exact name of an account or category; you can correct any errors when you download the transactions into Quicken.

Reviewing Transactions

You can review the transactions you enter by scrolling down in the window after entering any transaction. The Review remote transactions area lists each transaction:

Review entered transactions here.

Review remote transactions				
07/28/1998	American Express	Alice's Restaurant		$48.69
		Dining	Dinner with Arlo	Payment
STATUS: Not Downloaded	Delete Edit			
07/26/1998	Checking	Helicopter Souvenirs		$25.24
	1252	Misc	Spark Plug Helicopter	Payment
STATUS: Not Downloaded	Delete Edit			
07/26/1998	Checking	Sheramada Hotels		$150.00
	1251	Cash	Cashed a Check	Payment
STATUS: Not Downloaded	Delete Edit			

Click Delete to delete a transaction.

Click Edit to modify a transaction.

Downloading Transactions into Quicken

When you enter transactions into the Web transaction entry form, the transactions remain on a database at the Quicken.com Web site until you download them into Quicken. You can use the One Step Update command to download these transactions.

In Quicken, choose Online | One Step Update or click the One Step Update button at the top of the window. The Download Selection dialog box, which I tell you more about later in this chapter, appears. Turn off all check marks except the one beside Web Transaction Download. Then click Update Now. If a Quicken.com Login dialog box appears, enter your username and password in the appropriate text boxes and click OK.

Quicken establishes a connection to the Internet and displays a status dialog box while it updates information. When it's finished, it displays the Download Summary dialog box, which informs you that your Web transactions were downloaded.

Accepting Transactions

You're not done yet. The downloaded transactions must be accepted into the Quicken accounts. Choose Features | Banking | Accept Transactions. The Accept Transactions dialog box appears, as shown here:

If you've used the QuickEntry feature of Quicken Deluxe, this dialog box should look pretty familiar to you. It's the same dialog box you use to review, modify, and accept QuickEntry transactions, which I tell you about in Chapter 4. Here, you use it to work with and accept the transactions you entered on the Web. If you need help using this dialog box, consult Chapter 4.

Using WebEntry Again

The next time you use WebEntry, you should notice two things:

- The transactions you entered on the Web and then imported into Quicken have the status *Sent to Quicken*. These transactions will not be sent again.
- Drop-down lists appear for the Quicken Account, Category, and Class fields. These drop-down lists are updated each time you download WebEntry transactions. This makes it easier to accurately enter transactions in the future.

You can see both of these things in the following illustration:

Enter new transactions into Quicken

Drop-down lists appear for the Quicken Account, Category, and Class fields.

QUICKEN ACCOUNT
Checking

TYPE
Payment

DATE
08/02/1998

PAYEE

AMOUNT

CHECK #

CATEGORY
Advances (Income)

CLASS

MEMO

Enter Transaction   Clear Form

Review remote transactions

07/28/1998	American Express	Alice's Restaurant		$48.69
		Dining	Dinner with Arlo	Payment
STATUS: Sent to Quicken	Remove from web			
07/26/1998	Checking	Helicopter Souvenirs		$25.24
	1252	Misc	Spark Plug Helicopter	Payment
STATUS: Sent to Quicken	Remove from web			
07/26/1998	Checking	Sheramada Hotels		$150.00
	1251	Cash	Cashed a Check	Payment
STATUS: Sent to Quicken	Remove from web			

Downloaded transactions have the status *Sent to Quicken*.

Click the "Remove from web" link to remove a downloaded transaction from the Web.

One Step Update

The Portfolio Export and WebEntry features use One Step Update to update information on the Web and download transactions entered on the Web. But that's not all One Step Update does. This new Quicken Deluxe feature makes it possible to handle many of your connection chores at once. When used in conjunction with the PIN Vault feature, you can click a few buttons, enter a single password, and take a break while Quicken updates portfolio and account information for you.

Using One Step Update

The idea behind One Step Update is to use one command to handle multiple online activities. This eliminates the need to use update commands in a variety of locations throughout Quicken. One command and dialog box does it all.

> **Tip**   One Step Update does not upload payment instructions for online payments.

Setting Up the Update

Choose Online | One Step Update. The Download Selection dialog box appears. It lists all the items that can be updated. Red check marks appear to the left of each item that will be updated when you connect.

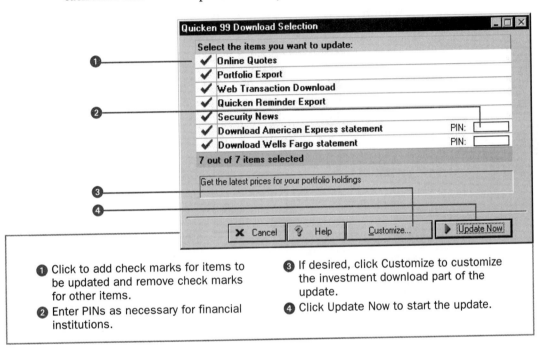

1 Click to add check marks for items to be updated and remove check marks for other items.

2 Enter PINs as necessary for financial institutions.

3 If desired, click Customize to customize the investment download part of the update.

4 Click Update Now to start the update.

The following options appear in the dialog box:

- **Online Quotes** updates the market values of investments you track with Quicken. This option, which I discuss in Chapter 14, can be customized by clicking the Customize button.
- **Portfolio Export** copies information from your portfolio to the Web so you can view it on Quicken.com. This option can also be customized by clicking the Customize button.
- **Web Transaction Download** obtains information entered on the Quicken.com Web site using the WebEntry feature.

- **Quicken Reminder Export** copies your Quicken reminders to the Web so you can view them at Quicken.com. Reminders appear on the Quicken.com home page.
- **Security News** downloads news articles about the securities you track with Quicken. This option, which I discuss in Chapter 14, can be customized by clicking the Customize button.
- **Download Statements** downloads transactions for the financial institutions and accounts for which you have enabled online account access. I tell you about online access in Chapters 12, 13, and 14.

Updating Information

Make sure check marks appear beside the items you want to update in the Download Selection dialog box. If necessary, enter PINs in the text boxes beside financial institutions for which you want to update data. Then click Update Now.

Quicken establishes a connection to the Internet and begins transferring data. A Download Status dialog box appears as it works. When the update is complete, the Download Summary dialog box appears. It summarizes the activity for the update.

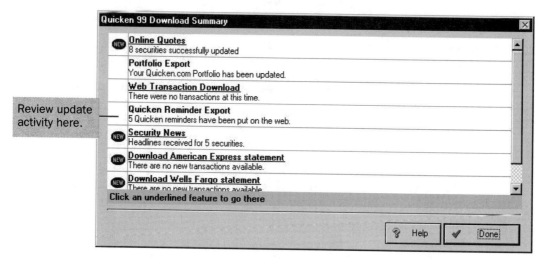

Click Done when you're finished reviewing the summary.

Tip   You can display the Download Summary dialog box for the last update by choosing Online | Download Summary.

The PIN Vault

You might find it a nuisance to have to type in each PIN when you use the One Step Update feature. This is where the PIN Vault can help.

Quicken's PIN Vault feature enables you to store all your Quicken PINs in one central location. The PINs are then protected with a single password. When you use One Step Update, you enter just one password to access all financial institutions.

Tip   You must have online account access or online payment set up with two or more institutions to use the PIN Vault feature.

Setting Up the PIN Vault

Choose Online | PIN Vault | Setup. The PIN Vault Setup window appears. It provides some introductory information. Click next to continue. The first window of the EasyStep tab of the PIN Vault Setup appears.

You have two ways to proceed:

- Follow the instructions in the EasyStep tab.
- Click the Summary tab to enter information.

I'll walk you through the EasyStep procedure.

In the first EasyStep tab, shown here, choose the name of a financial institution for which you want to enter a PIN and then click Next:

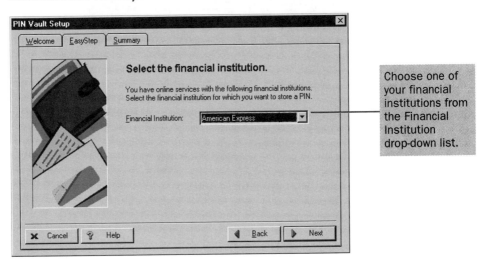

Choose one of your financial institutions from the Financial Institution drop-down list.

The next EasyStep window prompts you to enter the PIN for the selected financial institution twice. You enter it twice because the characters you type do not appear onscreen; this is a secure way of making sure you enter the same thing both times. When you're finished, click Next.

The next EasyStep tab asks if you want to enter additional PINs for other institutions. Select the Yes or No option button and click Next. What happens next depends on which option you selected:

- **Yes** takes you back to the first EasyStep tab window, where you can select another financial institution. Follow the preceding instructions.
- **No** displays a window like the following one. Use it to enter a PIN Vault password twice.

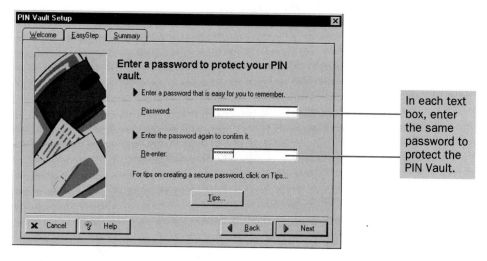

When you click Next, the Summary tab of the PIN Vault Setup window appears. It displays a list of your financial institutions and indicates whether a PIN has been stored for each one.

Click Change Vault Password to change the password for the PIN Vault.

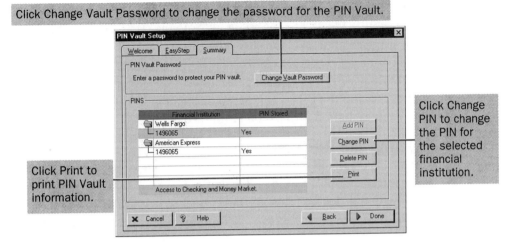

Click Change PIN to change the PIN for the selected financial institution.

Click Print to print PIN Vault information.

You can use buttons in this dialog box to change or delete a selected PIN, print all PINs, or change the Vault password. When you're finished working with the window's contents, click Done. Quicken creates the PIN Vault.

Using the PIN Vault

Using the PIN Vault is easy. Simply choose Online | One Step Update or click the One Step Update button at the top of the window. The PIN Vault Password dialog box appears. Enter your password and click OK. Then continue using One Step Update in the usual way with one difference: You don't have to enter PINs for any of the financial institutions for which a PIN has been entered in the PIN Vault.

Tip You can also use the PIN Vault in conjunction with the Update/Send button in the Online Financial Services Center window. Open that window and then choose Use Pin Vault from the Options menu on the Button bar. The Pin Vault Password dialog box appears for any financial institution you want to update.

Editing the PIN Vault

Once you've created a PIN Vault, you can modify it to change PINs or add PINs for other files. Choose Online | PIN Vault | Edit. In the PIN Vault Password dialog box that appears, enter the password that protects the PIN Vault and click OK.

The Modify PIN Vault dialog box appears. It looks and works much like the Summary tab of the PIN Vault Setup dialog box. Use it to make changes to the PIN Vault as desired. When you're finished, click Done.

Deleting the PIN Vault

You can delete the PIN Vault if you decide you no longer want to use the PIN Vault feature. Choose Online | Pin Vault | Delete. Then click Yes in the confirmation dialog box that appears. Quicken deletes the PIN Vault. From then on, you'll have to enter PINs for institutions when you use One Step Update.

Saving Money on Big-Ticket Items

This part of the book tells you about the Quicken and Quicken.com features you can use to save money on big-ticket items such as income tax, insurance, a home, and a vehicle. In these three chapters, you'll see how using Quicken to help you make big financial decisions can save you money:

Chapter 16: Saving Money at Tax Time

Chapter 17: Insurance

Chapter 18: Buying a Home or Car

Part Four

Saving Money at Tax Time

In This Chapter:

- *Tax Planning Basics*

- *Including Tax Information in Categories*

- *The Tax Center*

- *Tax Planner*

- *Deduction Finder*

- *Capital Gains Estimator*

- *Tax Reports*

- *Quicken.com Tax Features*

Chapter 16

345

Tax time is no fun. It can force you to spend hours sifting through financial records and filling out complex forms. When you're done with the hard part, you may be rewarded with the knowledge that you can expect a refund. But it is more likely that your reward will be the privilege of writing a check to the federal, state, or local government—or worse yet, all three.

Fortunately, Quicken can help. Its reporting features can save you time. Its planning features can save you money and help you make smarter financial decisions. By using the tax tools that are part of Quicken or available on Quicken.com, the next tax season may be a little less depressing. In this chapter, I show you how.

The Importance of Tax Planning

Don't underestimate the importance of tax planning. Doing so can cost you time and money. In this section, I explain why tax planning is important and give you some tips on what you can do to plan for tax time.

Why Plan for Tax Time?

Use the following scenarios to get yourself thinking about how a little planning now can save you time and money later.

Mary's Interest Expense Lesson

Mary is a homeowner who has been using her credit cards a little more than she should. She decides to cut up most of the cards and is now reducing her debt by paying a little more than the minimum monthly payment on each credit card account. Mary never considered the tax benefit of using a home equity loan, with tax-deductible interest, to pay off her credit card debt. Silly Mary doesn't even realize that the home equity reserve's interest rate might even be half the rate she pays the credit card company.

John's Capital Gains Lesson

John invests in the stock market. He's been holding shares in Company A for five years, in Company B for a year and a half, and in Company C for a few months. All three investments have been doing well. Now John wants to buy a new car. He needs to liquidate some of his investments for the down payment.

Because selling all shares of Company C would give him just the right amount of money, he sells them. What John didn't consider is that the gain on the sale of Company C is recognized as a short-term capital gain. If he'd sold some shares of Company A or B, he could have recorded a long-term capital gain, which is taxed at a lower rate.

Jean's Record-Keeping Lesson

Jean's young daughter has a serious medical problem that requires frequent trips to a big city hospital fifty miles away and other trips to doctors all over the state. Jean drives her there in the family car or, if her teenage son needs the car for work, she takes a cab. Her daughter's condition has improved greatly and the prognosis is good. But Jean's family health insurance doesn't cover all the transportation costs for the hospital and doctor visits. She was just told by a friend that she can deduct the cost of medical transportation from her income taxes. She's spent hours trying to compile a list of the dates of all those long drives and she wishes she'd asked for cab ride receipts.

Pete's Estimated Tax Lesson

Pete is a freelance writer who is having a very good year. By the end of June, he estimated that he'd already earned twice as much as he did the previous year. To celebrate, he bought a new car and took a two-week vacation in Peru. He also invested heavily in a mutual fund with good returns and a high front-end load. He feels great to have finally made the big time. But the estimated tax payments Pete has been making this year aren't nearly enough to cover his April 15 tax bill. He never considered increasing the payments to reduce his year-end tax bill, investing in a tax-deferred annuity or tax-free municipal bond to reduce his taxable income, or even saving some of his cash for April 15.

Learn from Their Mistakes, Not Yours

Mary, John, Jean, and Pete may as well be real people—I'm sure plenty of people find themselves in their situations every year. These examples illustrate the point: understanding the tax rules and planning ahead for tax time can save you time and money.

What You Can Do

Unless you're a tax accountant, you probably don't know all the tax laws. Fortunately, you don't need to know all the laws, just the ones that can affect you. Then, with the knowledge of what you can include on your tax returns, you can take steps to make smart decisions and keep track of items you can deduct.

Learning About Tax Rules

At tax time, people fall into two categories: Those who do their own taxes and those who find (and probably pay) someone else to do their taxes for them.

If you do your own taxes, you can learn a lot about tax laws by reading the tax forms and publications for your return. If you pay a tax preparer, you can really get your money's worth by asking him or her about how you could save money. Any good tax preparer should be able to tell you.

Either way, you can also learn tax rules, and get tips and advice by consulting the Tax Center within Quicken Deluxe or the Tax Department at Quicken.com. You learn about these resources throughout this chapter.

Saving Receipts and Recording Transactions

When you know what items are deductible, make a special effort to save receipts and record them in the proper Quicken categories. The receipts provide documentation for the expenditures, especially the date and amount. Recording them in the right account makes it possible to quickly generate reports of tax-deductible expenditures when it's time to fill out your tax returns. It also enables you to display up-to-date deduction information in the Tax Center window.

Analyzing All Options Before Making a Decision

Many people make decisions based on limited information—or worse yet, no information at all. As a Quicken user, you have access to all kinds of information and decision-making tools. Use Quicken.com to learn about finance-related opportunities. Go the extra step to research how an opportunity could affect your tax bill. Finally, use Quicken's built-in tools—such as the Tax Planner, Deduction Finder, and Capital Gains Estimator (all of which are discussed in this chapter)—to help you make an informed decision.

Tax Information in Accounts and Categories

As discussed briefly in Chapter 2, Quicken accounts and categories can include information that will help you at tax time. In this section, I'll tell you more about this feature, including why you should use it and how you can set it up.

Why Enter Tax Information?

By including tax information in Quicken accounts and categories, you make it possible for Quicken to do several things:

- **Prepare tax reports.** These reports summarize information by tax category or schedule.
- **Display tax information in the Tax Center.** This window shows an up-to-date summary of your tax situation.
- **Save time using the Tax Planner.** This feature of Quicken Deluxe can import information from your Quicken data file based on tax information you enter.
- **Distinguish between taxable and nontaxable investments.** This enables you to create accurate reports on capital gains, interest, and dividends.

 SAVE TIME   By spending a few minutes setting up tax information for your accounts and categories, you can save hours compiling information for your tax returns.

Including Tax Information in Accounts

You enter an account's tax information in the Tax Schedule Information dialog box for the account. Choose Lists | Accounts, or press CTRL-A, to open the Account List window. Select the account for which you want to enter tax information. Click Edit. In the Edit Account dialog box that appears, click the Tax button to display the Tax Schedule Information dialog box, which looks like this:

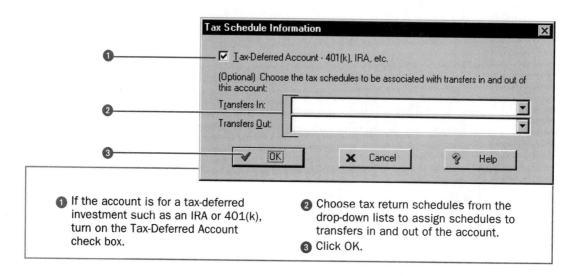

❶ If the account is for a tax-deferred investment such as an IRA or 401(k), turn on the Tax-Deferred Account check box.

❷ Choose tax return schedules from the drop-down lists to assign schedules to transfers in and out of the account.

❸ Click OK.

Set tax-related options in this dialog box as desired. The Transfers In and Transfers Out drop-down list enable you to map account activity to specific lines on a wide variety of tax return forms and schedules. When you're finished, click OK. Then click Done to dismiss the Edit Account dialog box. Repeat this process for all accounts for which you want to enter tax information.

Tip For a 401(k) account, set the Transfers In schedule to W-2 Salary. This ensures accurate reporting of 401(k) transactions throughout Quicken.

Including Tax Information in Categories

You have two ways to enter tax information for Quicken categories:

- Enter tax form and schedule information for a single category in the Edit Category dialog box.
- Match multiple categories to tax forms and schedules with the Tax Link Assistant.

Using the Edit Category Dialog Box

The Edit Category dialog box is handy when you need to check or set tax information for just one or two categories. Choose Lists | Category/Transfer, or press CTRL-C, to open the Category & Transfer List window. Select the category for which you want to enter tax information. Then click Edit to display the Edit Category dialog box, shown here:

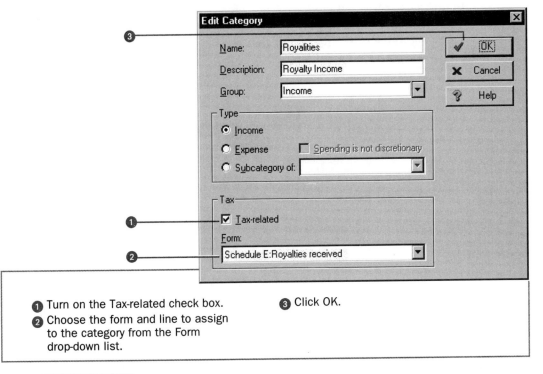

❶ Turn on the Tax-related check box.
❷ Choose the form and line to assign to the category from the Form drop-down list.

❸ Click OK.

Shortcut Quicken automatically sets tax information for many of the categories it creates automatically. You can identify tax-related categories by the **T** that appears in the Tax column in the Category & Transfer List window. Concentrate on the categories without the **T**; some of these may require tax information, depending on your situation.

If the category's transactions should be included on your tax return as either income or a deductible expense, turn on the Tax-related check box. Then use the Form drop-down list to select the form or schedule and line for the item. When you're finished, click OK. Repeat this process for all categories that should be included on your tax return.

Tip You can also enter tax information when you first create a category. The Summary tab of the Set Up Category dialog box looks and works very much like the Edit Category dialog box.

Using the Tax Link Assistant

The Tax Link Assistant offers a quick and easy way to set tax information for multiple categories, all in one place. Choose Features | Taxes | Set Up for Taxes. The Tax Link Assistant appears. Use this dialog box to match your Quicken categories to tax form or schedule line items. Follow Steps 1 through 3 below for each category you want to set up for taxes.

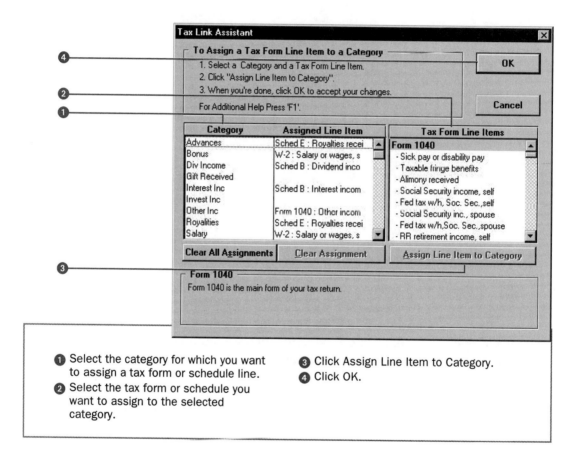

1. Select the category for which you want to assign a tax form or schedule line.
2. Select the tax form or schedule you want to assign to the selected category.
3. Click Assign Line Item to Category.
4. Click OK.

It is not necessary to match all categories—just the ones that should appear on your tax return. When you're finished, click OK to save your settings. The information is recorded in the Edit Category dialog box for each category.

Tax Center

Quicken's Tax Center should be your first stop for tax planning information and tools. Choose Features | Centers | Tax Center or click the Tax button near the top of the Home Page. The window will look something like the one shown in Figure 16-1. The following sections provide a quick tour of the things you can find in this window.

Tip If you access the Web with Quicken, the Tax Center window is automatically updated. Don't panic if your window doesn't offer exactly the same options as the one shown here.

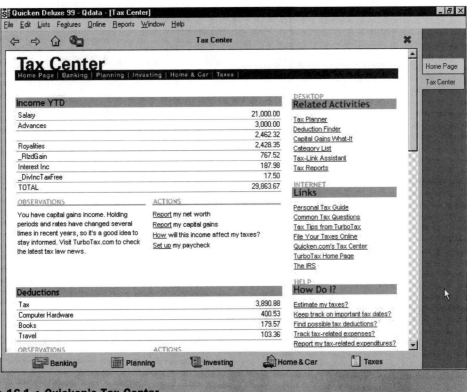

Figure 16-1 • Quicken's Tax Center

Current Information

The Tax Center window is chock-full of information you can use to keep track of your tax situation.

- **Income YTD** displays your year-to-date income. This area displays only tax-related categories, so make sure you properly set up any custom income categories that are taxable. For example, my Quicken data file includes income categories for Advances and Royalties. I manually set these up as tax-related so they would appear.

- **Deductions** displays your year-to-date deductible expenses. Because this area displays only tax-related categories, make sure you properly set up any custom expense categories that are deductible. My Quicken data file, for example, includes expense categories for Computer Hardware, Books, and Travel. I manually set these up as tax-related so they would appear.

- **Tax Calendar** displays upcoming tax deadlines, such as estimated tax payment dates, extension deadlines, and return due dates.

- **Projected Tax** displays estimated tax information based on your entries in Tax Planner, which is covered under "Quicken Tools," later in this chapter. Before you use Tax Planner, this area of the window isn't very informative, so you might want to put Tax Planner at the top of your planning to-do list.

Tools for Planning and Decision-Making

The Tax Center window also contains links to a number of built-in tools you can use to help you plan your taxes and make good tax-related decisions. The Related Activities area is a good example. It offers access to Quicken tools that you can use to plan your taxes, including the Tax Planner, Deduction Finder, Capital Gains Estimator, Category List, Tax Link Assistant, and Tax Reports.

Links for Learning More

If you have access to the Internet, you can click links in the Tax Center window to connect to Quicken.com and other sites for additional tax-related information.

- **Links** offers links to reference information at Quicken.com and other Web sites. These links include Common Tax Questions, Personal Tax Guide, Tax Law Changes, TurboTax Home Page, and the IRS.

- **How Do I?** provides links for a variety of help topics. Click a question to display a Quicken Help topic with the answer.
- **Did You Know?** offers links to timely, tax-related information, articles, and tips.

Quicken Tools

Quicken includes four main tools for planning and filing your taxes. You can access all of them by clicking links in the Tax Center window.

Tax Planner

Tax Planner includes features from Intuit's TurboTax product to help you estimate your federal income tax bill for 1998 and 1999. The information you enter into Tax Planner appears in the Projected Tax area of the Tax Center window.

To open Tax Planner, click the Tax Planner link on the Tax Center window or choose Features | Taxes | Tax Planner. The Tax Planner window appears. Here's what it might look like when completed:

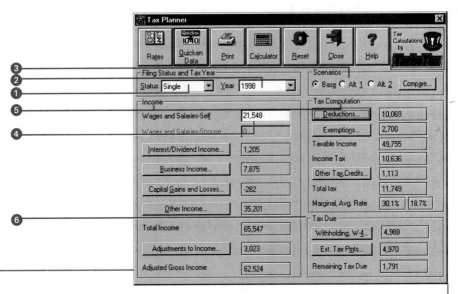

❶ Choose your filing status from the Status drop-down list.

❷ Choose the tax year for which you want to estimate taxes from the Year drop-down list.

❸ Select a scenario for which to enter data.

❹ Enter your expected annual income in the Income text box(es).

❺ Click buttons to display dialog boxes for entering income, deductions, and other information.

❻ View the estimated tax due information in the Tax Due area.

Entering data into the Tax Planner is pretty straightforward and easy to do. You can click buttons for various tax return categories and enter values into text boxes. You might want to have some tax records on hand when you do this to help ensure accuracy. You can always reopen the Tax Planner window and make changes later if new information becomes available. All calculations are performed automatically for you based on your entries.

Shortcut   To quickly enter data based on your current Quicken data file, click the Quicken Data button. Tax Planner collects Quicken information based on the tax information settings for each category. It then enables you to import the data directly into Tax Planner. This is a real time-saver!

When you click the Close button, the information you entered is saved and automatically summarized in the Tax Center window.

Deduction Finder

The Deduction Finder uses another TurboTax feature to help you learn which expenses are deductible. Its question-and-answer interface gathers information from you and then provides information about the deductibility of items based on your answers.

--- **Quicken Quote** ---

"Deduction Finder is a great feature. I had a clear understanding of what was tax-deductible even before I went to the accountant. In fact, I was able to print out a report of all the things necessary for him to review our taxes."

Pauline Schuman, Carmel, NY

To open the Deduction Finder, click the Deduction Finder link in the Tax Center window or choose Features | Taxes | Deduction Finder. An Introduction dialog box may appear. Read its contents to learn more about Deduction Finder and then click OK. The Deduction Finder window appears. Here's what the Deductions tab of that window says about the Godiva chocolates I sent my clients for the holidays last year:

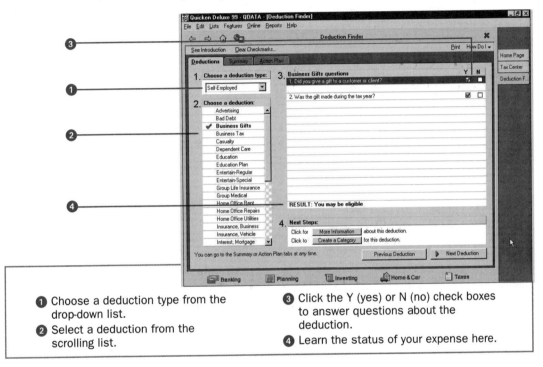

❶ Choose a deduction type from the drop-down list.

❷ Select a deduction from the scrolling list.

❸ Click the Y (yes) or N (no) check boxes to answer questions about the deduction.

❹ Learn the status of your expense here.

As you can see, the Deductions tab uses clearly numbered steps to walk you through the process of selecting deduction types and deductions and then answering questions. It's easy to use. You don't have to answer questions about all the deductions—only the deductions you think may apply to you. When you're finished answering questions about a deduction, a green check mark appears beside it. You can then move on to another deduction.

The Summary tab of the window, shown next, summarizes the number of deductions available in each category, the number for which you answered questions, and the number for which you may be eligible to take deductions based on your answers to the questions.

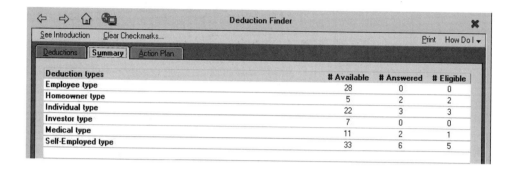

When you're finished answering questions, you can click the Action Plan tab to get more information about the deductions and the things you need to do to claim them. Here's what the Action Plan tab looks like:

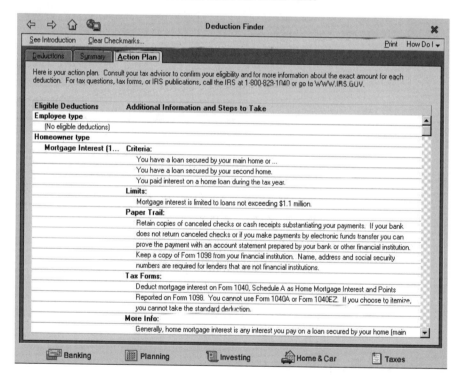

Quicken Quote

"I am looking forward to the money I will save! The Deduction Finder is very easy to use, and I will use it often. I pay my accountant something like $120 per hour at the end of the year, so the more thorough job I do sorting out my deductions, the less time he spends doing it for me."

Marni Johnston, Nehalem, OR

Although you can read this Action Plan information onscreen, if you answered many questions, you may want to use the Print button in the Button bar to print the information for reference.

Capital Gains Estimator

If you're interested in liquidating an investment, don't do a thing until you use the Capital Gains Estimator. This Quicken feature can help you decide which investment to liquidate based on the tax rules that apply to capital gains.

Tip   It's vital that you track investment purchases by lot if you plan to use this feature. You learn about recording investment transactions in Chapter 7.

To open the Capital Gains Estimator, click the Capital Gains Estimator link in the Tax Center window or choose Features | Taxes | Estimate Capital Gains. The Capital Gains Estimator Window appears. It displays proposed sales in the top half of the window, and your current holdings in taxable accounts in the bottom half of the window. Here's an example with four proposed sales:

Click Add to add a proposed sale for the holding selected in the bottom of the window.

Click Remove to remove the selected proposed sale in the top of the window.

Click Current Prices to enter the current (or estimated) security price as the Sale Price.

Click a Scenario tab to work with different proposed sale scenarios.

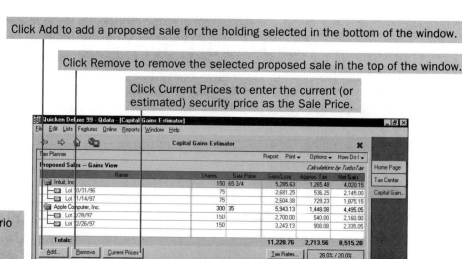

This illustration shows the power of the Capital Gains Estimator. The first two proposed sales, for Intuit stock, represent a long-term and a short-term sale. The purchase prices of both lots were very close—less than a dollar different. (You can see this in the bottom half of the window.) The difference between the two capital gains is less than $50, but the after-tax capital gain difference is about $180. Clearly, in this instance I can pay less taxes and keep more of my capital gain by selling the older lot. The proposed sale of Apple stock in the top half of the window also illustrates how I can save tax dollars by selling older lots.

GET SMARTER The Capital Gains Estimator helps you make informed investment decisions. By using it before you sell an investment, you can select the sale that helps you best achieve your goals.

Tax Reports

Quicken offers several different tax reports that can make tax time easier by providing the information you need to prepare your taxes. All three of these reports are based on the tax information settings for the accounts and categories in your Quicken file.

Tip You can learn more about Quicken's reporting feature in detail in Chapter 8.

Open the Create Report window by clicking the Tax Reports link in the Tax Center window. Click the Taxes tab to display options for tax-related reports.

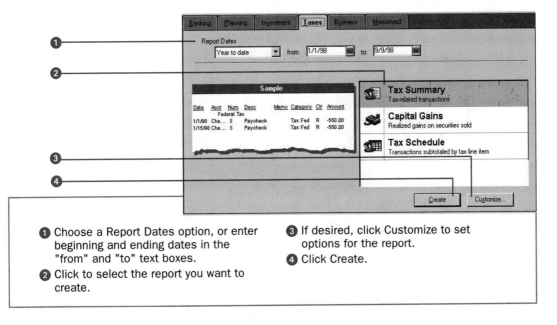

1 Choose a Report Dates option, or enter beginning and ending dates in the "from" and "to" text boxes.

2 Click to select the report you want to create.

3 If desired, click Customize to set options for the report.

4 Click Create.

To create a report, set the report dates at the top of the window. Then select a report and click Create. You have three tax reports to choose from:

- **Tax Summary** summarizes tax-related transactions, organized by category and date.
- **Capital Gains** summarizes gains and losses on the sales of investments, organized by the term of the investment (short or long) and the investment account.
- **Tax Schedule** summarizes tax-related transactions, organized by tax form or schedule and line item.

SAVE MONEY If you pay a tax preparation specialist, be sure to furnish him or her with an accurate Tax Schedule report from Quicken. Doing so may reduce your tax preparation bill for the time you save the preparer.

Quicken.com Resources

If you have access to the Internet, you also have access to the tax resources available at Quicken.com and other Web sites. Figure 16-2 shows what the main page for the Quicken.com Taxes department looks like.

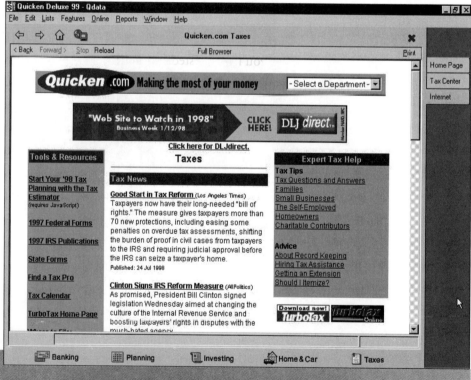

Figure 16-2 • The main page of the Quicken.com Taxes department

You have two ways to access this information:

- Follow links on the Tax Center window to go directly to the resources listed there.
- Choose Online | Quicken on the Web | Quicken.com to go to Quicken's Home Page. Then choose Taxes from the Select a Department drop-down list at the top of the page to go to the Taxes deparment main page.

The next few sections provide information about the resources you can find on the Taxes deparment main page for Quicken.com.

Tools & Resources

The Tools & Resources area includes useful information about tax forms, IRS publications, and tax filing locations. It also includes links to the Web versions of features found in Quicken Deluxe, including a Tax Estimator (like the Tax Planner) and a Tax Calendar. If you're looking for a tax professional to provide advice or help you prepare your taxes, the Find a Tax Pro link can make your search a lot easier. Or, if you're interested in using your computer to prepare your taxes, be sure to follow the TurboTax Home Page link to learn more about this great Intuit product.

More on Taxes

This area offers a link to a Web page full of other tax sites. These are the Quicken.com top picks—not amateur sites you might find using an Internet search engine. As this book went to press, links included the Armchair Millionaire Tax Center '98, Essential Links to Taxes, and the IRS Digital Daily.

SAVE TIME   Don't use Internet search engines to find sites to help with your taxes. Follow the links in the Taxes page on Quicken.com. These sites are prescreened for value so you don't waste time wading through information you can't use.

Tax News

The Tax News area offers brief summaries with links to recent tax-related news stories. Learn more about tax issues as they surface in the press. These stories prove that tax legislation is developed throughout the year—not just during the few weeks before April 15.

Tax Tip of the Week

The Tax Tip of the Week provides useful tips for tax planning and preparation. Check this area weekly to learn what you can do to minimize your tax bill. If you miss a week, don't worry. There's also a link to the Tax Tip archive, so you can review past tips.

Expert Tax Help

The Expert Tax Help area is a great feature for all taxpayers. Its Tax Tips links offer tips for various taxpayer categories, as well as a Questions and Answers page with commonly asked tax questions and their answers. The Advice links provide solid tax advice to help you make good tax-related decisions. This is expert advice without paying an expert. But if you think you need an expert, there's advice for hiring one, too!

Tax Bulletin Boards

The Tax Bulletin Boards put you in touch with other taxpayers who deal with the same tax rules and issues you do. Clicking one of the topical links enables you to read messages posted by other Quicken users, reply to messages, or post your own new messages. Ask questions, give advice. Let others help you while you help them. Some hot topics as this book went to press included Avoiding & Surviving an Audit, Tax Shelters, Changes in the Tax Code, Preparation & Planning, and Capital Gains.

Tip   For an idea of what's being discussed in one of the bulletin boards, check the People Are Talking About area right above the Tax Bulletin Boards area. You'll see a quote from a message board participant with a link to the message board in which the message appeared.

Insurance

In This Chapter:

- *Learning Insurance Basics*

- *Evaluating Your Insurance Needs*

- *Shopping for Insurance*

- *Finding Other Insurance Resources*

Chapter 17

As your assets, family, and responsibilities grow, so does your need for insurance. Insurance can protect you from financial loss in the event of loss, theft, or damage to your assets. It can help you cover medical costs and make ends meet if illness or injury requires extensive medical care or prevents you from working. It can provide for your family if something happens to you.

Quicken's InsureMarket feature and Insurance department at Quicken.com can help you meet your insurance needs in a number of ways:

- They provide basic insurance information to help you understand what the various types of insurance are and what they can do for you.
- They help you evaluate your insurance needs so you obtain enough—but not too much—insurance.
- They allow you to shop for insurance online, where the most up-to-date information, coverage, and pricing is available twenty-four hours a day.

In this chapter, I tell you about the features of InsureMarket and the Insurance department page of Quicken.com and explain how you can use them to save time, save money, and make informed insurance decisions.

Tip Because InsureMarket and the Insurance department on the Quicken.com Web site are Web-based, they can change from day to day. The options and features I discuss in this chapter may vary from what you see when you explore them online.

InsureMarket

InsureMarket is an online feature of Quicken Deluxe that provides a wealth of information, tools, and links for learning about and shopping for insurance. Although you can access it by choosing a command within Quicken, you need an Internet connection to take full advantages of the features it offers.

To open the InsureMarket main window, choose Online | Quicken on the Web | InsureMarket. The InsureMarket window appears:

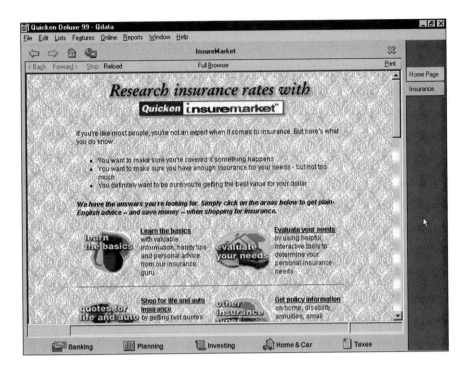

Tip   The InsureMarket main page within Quicken Deluxe has a different appearance than the one accessible directly through Quicken.com. Unless otherwise specified, the main page discussed in this chapter is the one within Quicken Deluxe.

Learning Insurance Basics

If insurance is a mystery to you—or even if you know something about it but want to know more, start by clicking the Learn the Basics link in the InsureMarket window. The window changes to display a long list of topical links. The next few sections summarize some of the topics you can learn more about.

A Quick and Easy Overview

A Quick and Easy Overview displays basic information about InsureMarket, including the kinds of things it can do for you. It also provides a general description of what insurance is, with two examples of how it can help you.

Speaking Cool Insurance Terms

To speak intelligently with an insurance agent, you must be able to speak his or her language. That's what this link is all about. If you don't know a deductible from a convertible, follow this link to learn. It defines a dozen or so important insurance terms, many of which refer to policy types, such as term life, variable life, and whole life. Links within some definitions provide even more information about the term.

Auto Insurance Basics

Auto insurance covers specific auto-related losses you may incur during the term of the insurance policy. Auto Insurance Basics explains this, as well as why you need auto insurance, who and what is covered by auto insurance, what affects your auto insurance rates and what you can do to reduce them, and what your auto insurance policy really means.

If the declarations page for your auto insurance policy has you scratching your head, you definitely want to click the link to the Auto Policy Educator. This displays a split-screen Web page, which looks something like this:

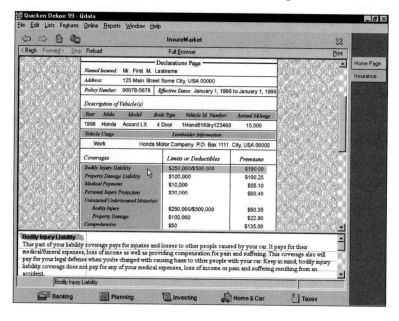

At the top of the page is a declarations pane, and at the bottom is a description pane. You click a line item in the declarations page to view a description of the item in the description pane. This neat, informative tool should clear up any questions you have.

Home Insurance Basics

Home insurance covers financial losses caused by theft, storms, fires, and other similar occurrences that could cause loss or damage to your home and property. It also covers damages resulting from injuries to other people for which you are held legally responsible.

Home Insurance Basics explains all of this, as well as what the various types of home insurance are—homeowner's, renter's, and condo or co-op owner's—and what they cover. It also explains what affects your home insurance rates and what you can do to reduce them.

Life Insurance Basics

Life insurance is money that an insurance company pays to your named beneficiary when you die. Life Insurance Basics explains why you need life insurance, what the different types of life insurance are—term life, whole life, variable life, universal life, and universal variable life—and which one is best for you, how much life insurance you need, and how you can get a term life quote. Links throughout this page provide additional information about many of the topics.

Annuity Basics

An annuity is a contract between you and an insurance company in which you pay a premium and, in return, the insurance company promises to make benefit payments to you or to another named beneficiary.

Annuity Basics tells you more about what an annuity is, whether an annuity is right for you, what the different types of annuities are—immediate or deferred and fixed or variable—and what payout options are available.

Disability Income Insurance Basics

Disability income insurance covers a percentage of your lost income if you cannot work because you are disabled. Disability Income Insurance Basics explains this, as well as whether you need disability income insurance, what determines if you are disabled, how much coverage you need, what policy features are available, what affects your rates, and how you can get coverage.

Long Term Care Insurance Basics

Long term care insurance covers the cost of long term care, which includes custodial care to help with the activities of daily life, whether at home or in a nursing home.

Long Term Care Insurance Basics tells you this, as well as whether you need long term care insurance, what to look for in your policy, how much coverage you need, what affects your rates, and how you can get coverage.

Medical Insurance Basics

Medical or health insurance covers the cost of medical care. Medical Insurance Basics explains this and tells you what different types of coverage are available.

Umbrella Liability Insurance Basics

As you'll learn in Umbrella Liability Insurance Basics, this type of insurance may indeed cover you for injuring someone with your umbrella. But that's not its only purpose. It covers injuries to other people or damage to their property for which you are legally responsible. It's an expansion of the basic liability coverage of your auto and home insurance.

Umbrella Liability Insurance Basics explains this, tells you whether you need umbrella liability insurance, and how much coverage you need.

Business Continuation Insurance Basics

Business continuation insurance protects your company from financial loss caused by the death or the long-term disability of a key employee.

Business Continuation Insurance Basics tells you this, as well as whether you need business continuation insurance, and what the different types are—business overhead expense (BOE), key person disability, and key person life.

Determining Your Insurance Needs

Determining Your Insurance Needs displays the Insurance Planner, which can help you determine which kinds of insurance you need. I tell you more about this tool a little later in this chapter.

Ways to Save

Ways to Save displays links with tips for saving money on auto, home, and life insurance. For example, Ways to Save on Auto Insurance offers tips like the following:

- Comparison shop
- Ask for a higher deductible

- Drop collision and/or comprehensive coverage on older cars
- Buy a "low-profile" car

These are just a few tips for one type of insurance; this area provides many more. It also explains what each tip means and how it can benefit you. A link to the Risk Evaluator, which I tell you about later in this chapter, shows you how much risk there is to owning your type of car in your part of the country.

Becoming an Insurance Guru

Becoming an Insurance Guru explains how you can become an insurance "guru"—someone who sees insurance as a tool of defensive financial planning and who uses insurance to share or transfer financial risks to insurance companies. Links on this page provide advice for attaining guru status.

Glossary of Terms

Glossary of Terms provides a complete index of all insurance terms used in InsureMarket, with links to definitions. Links from these terms to definitions appear in InsureMarket text, too, so it's easy to find out what a term means, right from within the article that uses it.

InsureMarket's Resident Insurance Pro

Much of InsureMarket's Insurance Basics and Glossary information is provided by Ben G. Baldwin, the author of two insurance-related books. This link tells you more about Ben and provides links to information about his books.

 GET SMARTER Before you start shopping for insurance— whether you shop online with InsureMarket or by phone with a phone book—be sure you know the basic information about the type of insurance you want to buy. Understanding insurance options is the only way to be sure you are purchasing all the insurance coverage you need, without being sold extra coverage for the benefit of an insurance company or commissioned salesperson.

Evaluating Your Insurance Needs

Once you know what types of insurance are available and have a general idea of which ones apply to you, it's time to evaluate your needs. That's where the Evaluate Your Needs link on the InsureMarket main window can help. Clicking the link displays a number of links to tips and tools you can use to get a better idea of how much insurance you need, as shown in the following illustration:

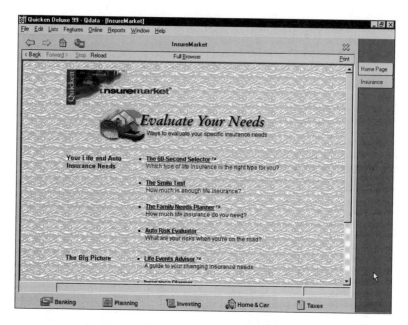

Here's a description of what each of these links offers.

The 60-Second Selector

The 60-Second Selector is a tool for determining what type of life insurance is best for you. It works by offering statements that you can click to logically progress through a decision tree. Click the statement that best describes your situation to eventually arrive at a decision.

For example, the first two statements are as follows:

- "I want a basic and inexpensive life insurance policy."
- "I want my life insurance policy to also serve as a tax-deferred cash value account."

Clicking the second statement provides additional information and displays the following statements:

- "I'm generally a conservative investor. I want a steady, even if modest, return on my money."
- "I'm generally an aggressive investor. I'm willing to take some risk in pursuit of a higher return on my money."

Clicking the first of these two statements displays more information and two more statements. This process continues until some advice appears, based on your selections.

The Smile Test

The Smile Test provides instructions for using your beneficiary's reaction to your life insurance coverage. If it's too much, the beneficiary will smile too much. If it's not enough, he'll frown. While whimsical, this approach does give you some insight into how some people decide on the right level of coverage. You may find the link on this page to the Family Needs Planner, which I tell you about next, a bit more valuable.

Family Needs Planner

The Family Needs Planner helps you figure out how much life insurance you need. By entering information in two worksheets—Your Family's Peace of Mind worksheet and Your Family's Lifestyle worksheet—you can determine how much life insurance you need to provide for your family's immediate and long-term expenses in the event of your death. Filling out Your Family's Peace of Mind worksheet takes about 20 minutes, but it's well worth the time if you're having trouble quantifying your life insurance requirements.

Auto Risk Evaluator

The Auto Risk Evaluator can tell you, based on statistics for your auto and location, just how risky it is to own or drive your car. As shown here, you can get answers for a number of risk-related questions:

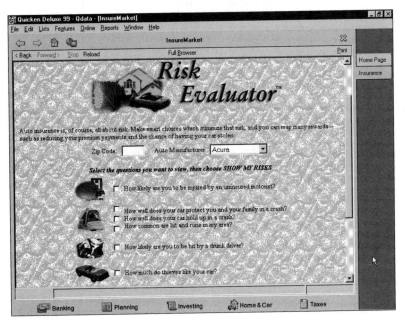

All you have to do is enter your zip code, provide information about your car (such as its make and model), and turn on the check boxes for the questions you want answered. InsureMarket provides the answers in a printable report.

Life Events Advisor

The Life Events Advisor can help you evaluate various insurance needs based on events in your life, such as marriage, birth of a child, relocation, retirement, and death of a spouse. Click one of the life events listed down the left side of the Life Events Advisor main window to get started. Life events about which you can find information include:

- Buying a car
- Buying a home
- Marriage
- Divorce
- Becoming a parent
- Changing jobs
- Retirement

Insurance Planner

The Insurance Planner enables you to assess your insurance needs in as little as ten minutes. By answering questions about yourself, your health and job, your home, and your automobiles, Quicken can tell you what insurance types you need and provide a personalized plan of action.

The process begins with the creation of a Personal Insurance Portfolio, which you protect with a user ID and password you provide. The information you enter and your action plan will be saved there for future reference or modification. From there, you answer questions by selecting options. It's all self-explanatory and easy to do. When you're finished, the Insurance Planner lets you view your action plan, provides information about why it made its recommendations, and offers links for shopping for the type of insurance you need, as shown here:

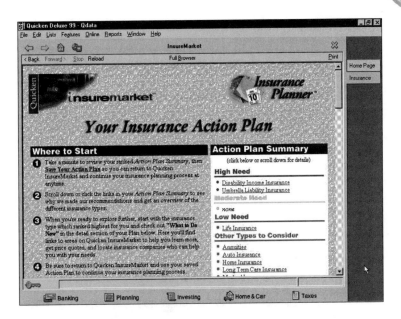

Shopping for Insurance

The InsureMarket main page also offers links you can use to shop for auto and term life insurance online and learn more about the policies available to you.

GET SMARTER   Two worksheets at the end of this chapter help you compare the costs and benefits of insurance policies: the Term Life Insurance Worksheet and the Auto Insurance Worksheet. Use these worksheets to take notes about the policies you research. They'll help you compare apples to apples to see which policy comes out on top.

Using EasyQuote

EasyQuote provides up-to-date insurance quotes for term life insurance and auto insurance. As this book went to press, online auto insurance quotes were only available for some states, but information about companies that provide coverage in all states was available.

Quicken Quote

"InsureMarket is a great way for me to compare rates. It helped me double my insurance coverage for the same cost."

Walt Button, *Orange Park, FL*

To get a quote or insurance information from EasyQuote, begin by clicking the Shop for Life and Auto Insurance link on the InsureMarket main page. A page like the one shown here appears:

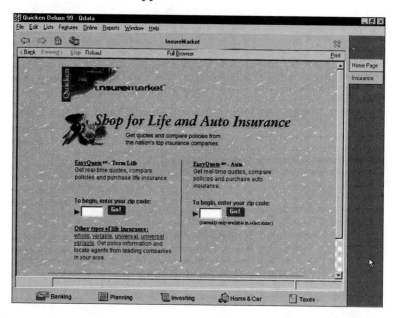

Click the EasyQuote link beside the type of insurance for which you want a quote. Then follow the instructions that appear onscreen to enter your zip code and other information to get insurance quotes and insurance company information.

Getting Other Policy Information

To learn more about other types of insurance policies and get lists of the companies and agents that offer them in your area, click the Get Policy

Information link on the InsureMarket main page. A page listing different kinds of insurance policies appears. Click the type of policy that interests you. Then follow the onscreen instructions to enter your zip code, which generates a list of companies offering that type of insurance in your area.

Contacting Insurance Companies Directly

If you prefer to contact insurance companies directly, you can find a list of them at the bottom of the InsureMarket main page. Companies are organized by the type of insurance they offer. For each company, you'll see its name and logo and a link to an ad on the InsureMarket Web site. For many of the companies, you'll also see a toll-free phone number so you can call them directly.

Tip   The list of insurance companies and their contact information is especially useful if you want to shop for insurance but don't have an Internet connection.

Quicken.com Resources

You can access InsureMarket and other insurance resources directly through Quicken.com. Choose Online | Quicken on the Web | Quicken.com to go to Quicken's home page. Then choose Insurance from the Select a Department drop-down list at the top of the page to go to the Insurance department main page, which looks like this:

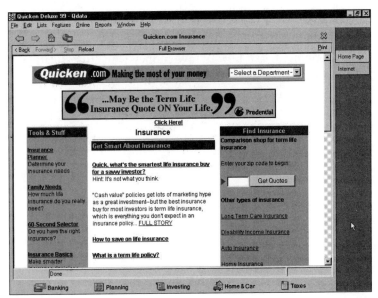

The following sections explain some of the resources you can find on the Insurance main page for Quicken.com.

Tools & Stuff

The Tools & Stuff area includes links to some of the features and information already discussed in this chapter, such as the Insurance Planner, the Family Needs Planner, the 60-Second Selector, and Insurance Basics.

More on Insurance

This area offers a link to a Web page full of other insurance sites. These are the Quicken.com top picks, which are all high-quality sites. As this book went to press, links included Insurance Industry Internet Network, Insurance News Network, and SafeTnet.

 SAVE TIME   Don't use Internet search engines to find sites for insurance information. Follow the links in the Insurance page on Quicken.com. These sites are prescreened for value so you don't waste time.

Get Smart About Insurance

The Get Smart About Insurance area provides useful tips for insurance planning and shopping. Learn how to save money while investigating the ins and outs of the insurance world. Links to current articles about insurance topics provides new content in this area every week.

Find Insurance

The Find Insurance area offers the same insurance shopping features you can access from the InsureMarket main page: EasyQuote for term life and auto insurance and information about companies in your area that offer other types of insurance. There's also a link to the Quicken InsureMarket home page, which may differ in appearance from the main page I showed you near the beginning of this chapter.

People & Chat

The People & Chat area puts you in touch with other people who deal with the same insurance needs and issues you do. Clicking one of the topical links enables you to read messages posted by others, reply to messages, or post your own new messages. Ask questions, give advice. Let others help you while you help them. The hot topic as this book went to press was "How do you feel about life insurance?" Other topics are constantly emerging, waiting for you to join in the discussion.

Worksheets

Use the following two worksheets to help you compare and evaluate different insurance policies.

Term Life Insurance Worksheet

Basic Information

Instructions: Enter information and values for each policy, one per column.

Company Name			
Agent Name			
Phone Number			
Policy Name			
Coverage Amount			
Annual Premium			
Comments			

Features and Options

Instructions: Check off the features and options Included with each policy. If a feature or option is not included, leave the space blank. If it is available as an option for which you must pay more, enter an O (for option) or the additional amount you must pay. You can enter additional features and options at the bottom of the form.

Guaranteed Level Premium			
Guaranteed Renewable			
Guaranteed Convertible			
Accelerated Death Benefit			
Disability Waiver Option			
Accidental Death Option			
Child Rider			
Other Insured Option			

Auto Insurance Worksheet (page 1)

Basic Information

Instructions: Enter information for each policy, one per column.

Company Name			
Agent Name			
Phone Number			
Comments			

Coverage and Cost

Instructions: Enter the limits and/or deductibles for each category of coverage in one column and the corresponding premium cost in the other. You can enter additional coverage options at the bottom of the section. Be sure to subtotal the Premiums column.

Standard Coverage	Limits or Deductibles	Premiums	Limits or Deductibles	Premiums	Limits or Deductibles	Premiums
Bodily Injury Liability		$		$		$
Property Damage Liability						
Medical Payments						
Personal Injury Protection						
Uninsured/ Underinsured Motorist: • Bodily Injury • Property Damage						
Comprehensive						
Collision						

Auto Insurance Worksheet (page 2)					
Additional Coverage Options					
Rental Reimbursement		$		$		$
Towing/ Labor					
Emergency Road Service					
Electronic Equipment Protection					
Sound Reproducing/ Tapes and Compact Disks					
Auto Loan/ Lease Gap					
Premium Total	$		$		$	

Auto Insurance Worksheet (page 3)			

Discounts

Instructions: Enter discounts offered by each insurance company. You can enter additional discounts at the bottom of the section. Be sure to total the discounts.

Multi-policy	$	$	$
Multi-car Coverage			
Safety Equipment			
Good Driver			
Anti-Lock Brakes			
Anti-Theft System			
Driver Training			
Discount Total	$	$	

Policy Cost

Instructions: Subtract the discount total from the premium total to arrive at the total cost of the policy with the options you selected.

Policy Cost	$	$	$

Buying a Home or Car

In This Chapter:

- *Types of Loans*

- *Loan Considerations*

- *Tracking a Loan in Quicken*

- *Home & Car Center*

- *Quicken.com Mortgage and Borrowing Resources*

Chapter 18

387

Possibly the biggest purchase you'll ever make is the purchase of a new home or car. These aren't the kinds of things you buy on a whim. They require research and planning. It's not only important to find the right living space or vehicle, it's important to get the right financing. You want the best deal on a loan, with a low interest rate and monthly payments that won't stretch your budget.

In this chapter, you learn about the tools within Quicken and on Quicken.com that you can use to determine what you can afford, research lending rates, and even apply for a loan online. Along the way, I provide useful information about the types of loans that are available to make major purchases, as well as some of the things to consider when comparing loans. I also tell you how to set up a loan account in Quicken so you can track loan balances as you make monthly payments.

Mortgage and Loan Basics

Before you start shopping for a loan—or for a home or car, for that matter—it's a good idea to have an understanding of loan basics. What kinds of loans are there? What are their benefits and drawbacks? Which is the right one for your purchase? What things are important when comparing one loan to another? In this section, I answer all of these questions and more.

Types of Loans

There are several types of loans, some of which are designed for specific purposes. Here's a quick summary of what's available, along with their pros and cons.

Mortgage

A *mortgage* is a long-term loan secured by real estate. Most mortgages require a 10% or more down payment on the property. Monthly payments are based on the term of the loan and the interest rate applied to the principal. The interest you pay on a mortgage for a first or second home is tax-deductible. If you fail to make mortgage payments, your house could be sold to pay back the mortgage.

A *balloon* mortgage is a special type of short-term mortgage. Rather than make monthly payments over the full typical mortgage term, at the end of the fifth, seventh, or tenth year, you pay the balance of the mortgage in one big "balloon" payment. Some balloon mortgages offer the option of refinancing when the balloon payment is due.

Home Equity Loans or Lines of Credit

A *home equity loan* or *second mortgage* is a line of credit secured by the equity in your home—the difference between its market value and the amount of outstanding debt. Your equity rises when you make mortgage payments or property values increase. It declines when you borrow against your equity or property values decrease. A home equity loan lets you borrow against this equity.

There are two benefits to a home equity loan: Interest rates are usually lower than other credit, and interest is tax-deductible. For these reasons, many people use home equity loans to pay off credit card debt, renovate their homes, or buy cars, boats, or other recreational vehicles. But, like a mortgage, if you fail to pay a home equity reserve, your house could be sold to satisfy the debt.

Reverse Equity Loans

A *reverse equity loan* provides homeowners who own their homes in full with a regular monthly income. Instead of you paying the loaner, the loaner pays you. This type of loan is attractive to retirees who live on a fixed income. The loan is paid back when the home is sold—often after the death of the homeowner. (You can imagine how the next of kin feel about that.)

Car Loans

A *car loan* is a loan secured by a vehicle such as a car, truck, or motor home. Normally, you make a down payment and use the loan to pay the balance of the car's purchase price. Monthly payments are based on the term of the loan and the interest rate applied to the principal. Interest on car loans is not tax-deductible.

Personal Loans

A *personal loan* is an unsecured loan—a loan that requires no collateral. Monthly payments are based on the term of the loan and the interest rate applied to the principal. You can use a personal loan for just about anything. Some people use them to pay off multiple smaller debts so they have only one monthly payment. Interest on personal loans is not tax-deductible.

Loan Considerations

When applying for a loan, a number of variables have a direct impact on what the loan costs you now and in the future. Be sure to ask about all these things before applying for any loan.

Interest Rate

The *interest rate* is the annual percentage applied to the loan principal. Several factors affect the interest rate you may be offered:

- **Your credit record.** A borrower with a good credit record can usually get a better rate than one with a bad credit record. Of course, if your credit record is really bad, you might not be able to borrow money at any rate.
- **The type of loan.** Generally speaking, personal loans have the highest interest rates, whereas mortgages have the lowest. From highest to lowest between these two types are a used car loan, a new car loan, and a home equity reserve or line of credit.
- **The loan term.** The length of a loan can vary the interest within a specific loan type. For example, for car loans, the longer the term, the lower the rate.
- **The amount of the down payment.** The more money you put down on the purchase, the lower the rate may be.
- **Your location.** Rates vary from one area of the country to another.
- **The lender.** Rates also vary from one lender to another. Certain types of lenders have lower rates than others.

Two kinds of interest rates can apply to a loan: fixed and variable.

- **Fixed rate** applies the same rate to the principal throughout the loan term.
- **Variable rate** applies a different rate to the loan throughout the loan term. For example, the loan may start with one rate and, each year, switch to a different rate. The rate is usually established by adding a certain number of percentage points to a national index, such as treasury bill rates. A cap limits the amount the rate can change. Mortgages with this type of rate are referred to as *adjustable rate mortgages,* or *ARMs.*

SAVE MONEY   When we purchased our first home, in the mid 1980s when interest rates were high, we selected an ARM. When interest rates dropped, so did the rate on our mortgage. If we'd selected a fixed-rate mortgage when we bought that home, we would have had to refinance to get the same savings. But because rates were much lower when we bought our current home, we selected a fixed rate to protect us from possible rate increases in the future.

Term

A loan's *term* is the period of time between the loan date and the date payment is due in full. Loan terms vary depending on the type of loan.

- Mortgage loan and home equity reserve loan terms are typically 10, 15, 20, or 30 years.
- Balloon mortgage loan terms are typically 5, 7, or 10 years.
- Car loan terms are typically 3, 4, or 5 years.

Down Payment

A *down payment* is an up-front payment toward the purchase of a home or car. Most mortgages require at least 10% down; 20% down is preferred.

SAVE MONEY   If you make only a 10% down payment on a home, you may be required to pay for the cost of private mortgage insurance. This protects the lender from loss if you fail to pay your mortgage, but increases your monthly mortgage payments.

Application Fees

Most lenders require you to pay an application fee to process your loan application. This usually includes the cost of obtaining a property appraisal and credit report. These fees are usually not refundable—even if you are turned down.

Mortgage Closing Costs

In addition to the application fee and down payment, many other costs are involved in securing a mortgage and purchasing a home. These are known as *closing costs*. Here's a brief list of the types of costs you may encounter. Because they vary from lender to lender, they could be a deciding factor when shopping for a mortgage. Note that most of these fees are not negotiable.

- **Origination fee** covers the administrative costs of processing a loan.
- **Discount or "points"** is a fee based on a percentage rate applied to the loan amount. For example, 1 point on a $150,000 mortgage is $1,500.
- **Appraisal fee** covers the cost of a market-value appraisal of the property by a licensed, certified appraiser.
- **Credit report fee** covers the cost of obtaining a credit history of the prospective borrower(s) to determine credit worthiness.
- **Underwriting fee** covers the cost of underwriting the loan. This is the process of determining loan risks and establishing terms and conditions.
- **Document preparation fee** covers the cost of preparing legal and other documents required to process the loan.
- **Title insurance fee** covers the cost of title insurance, which protects the lender and buyer against loss due to disputes over ownership and possession of the property.
- **Recording fee** covers the cost of entering the sale of a property into public records.
- **Prepaid items** are taxes, insurance, and assessments paid in advance of their due dates. These expenses are not paid to the lender but are due at the closing date.

GET SMARTER The Real Estate Settlement Procedures Act of 1974 requires that your lender provide a Good Faith Estimate of closing costs. This document summarizes all the costs of closing on a house based on the mortgage the lender is offering. If you're not sure what a fee is for, check the Mortgage Glossary available at the Quicken Mortgage Web site, which I tell you about later in this chapter.

Planning for Your Purchase

Whether you're buying a home, car, or recreational vehicle, you'll need to do some planning before you make your purchase. In this section, you learn about what information a lender wants to know about you, as well as how you can determine how much you can afford to spend.

Gathering Financial Fitness Information

Before anyone lends you money (except maybe Big Louie, who works out of the back room of a bar on the bad side of town), they need to assure themselves that you can pay it back, with interest, within the allotted time. Before a potential lender starts examining your financial fitness, you should. Then you'll know in advance what the lender will discover, and if there are problems, you can fix them.

Your Net Worth

Start by taking a look at your net worth. If you've been faithfully recording all your financial information in Quicken, this is easy. Choose Reports | Planning | Net Worth. The Create Report window appears with the Planning tab and Net Worth Report selected, as shown in Figure 18-1.

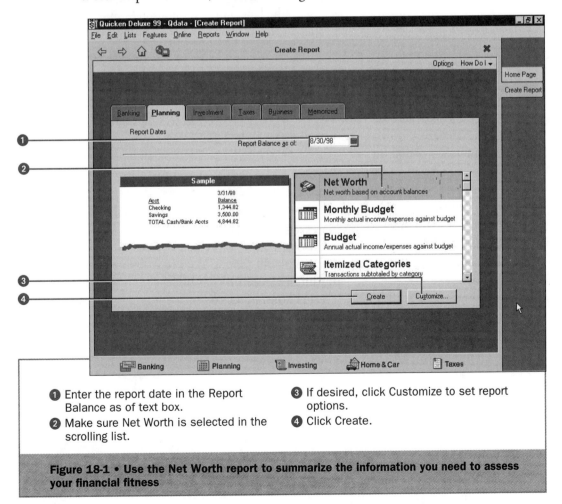

❶ Enter the report date in the Report Balance as of text box.

❷ Make sure Net Worth is selected in the scrolling list.

❸ If desired, click Customize to set report options.

❹ Click Create.

Figure 18-1 • Use the Net Worth report to summarize the information you need to assess your financial fitness

Set options in the window as desired and click Create. Quicken prepares a Net Worth Report that shows all of your assets and liabilities. The difference between these two is your net worth. The bigger this number is, the better off you are.

Not all of the numbers on your Net Worth report will interest a lender. They're interested primarily in cash, cars, real estate, investments, credit card balances, and other debt. If your home inventory values your T-shirt collection at $5,000, so what? T-shirts aren't easily exchanged for cash to make mortgage payments.

Debt Reduction

If all of your assets and liabilities have been recorded in Quicken and your net worth is a negative number, stop right here! No one (except maybe Big Louie) will loan you money, because too many others already have. Turn to Chapter 21, where I cover saving money and reducing debt. You'll need to follow the advice and instructions there before you can even think about applying for a loan. You might also find Chapter 9, "Budgeting and Forecasting," helpful to get your spending under control.

Credit Report

A lender is also going to be very interested in your credit history. Credit reports are created and maintained by third-party credit monitoring organizations such as Experian, Equifax, and Trans Union. They know everything about your finances—sometimes even things that aren't true. Before you apply for a loan, you may want to see what a credit report says about you. If there are errors, you can get them fixed before someone uses them to form a bad opinion of you.

Quicken Deluxe users can obtain a free credit report as part of a trial offer from CreditCheck. Choose Features | Planning | Credit Check. The CreditCheck main window appears. It provides basic information about reports available to you and how you can obtain them. If you have Internet access, you can click the Order Now button to connect to the Internet and order your credit report. If you don't have Internet access, you can click a link to get a toll-free number to call for the report.

Getting Current Interest Rates

Before you can estimate the monthly payments on a loan, you need a good idea of what the current interest rates are. You have three ways to research this information: check the newspaper, call banks, or look it up on Quicken.com.

Caution   Interest rates change often, sometimes on a daily basis. Although short-term variations are usually small, rates over a few weeks or months old usually aren't very accurate.

Checking a Recent Newspaper

Many banks and other lenders advertise their rates in the financial pages of the newspaper. Some newspapers summarize this information for you. For example, the big paper in my area, the *Arizona Republic*, has a weekly listing of organizations offering mortgages, complete with rates and phone numbers.

Checking with Local Banks

Get out the phone book and call a few banks in your area. Ask them what their rates are. Most banks will provide this information over the phone.

Looking Up Rates on Quicken.com

Quicken.com offers up-to-date rates on all kinds of loans. All you need is an Internet connection to check them for yourself. Choose Online | Quicken on the Web | Quicken.com. Your computer connects to the Internet and displays the Quicken.com home page. How you proceed depends on the type of loan for which you want a rate.

For mortgage rates, choose Home & Mortgage from the drop-down list near the top of the page. This displays the Home and Mortgage main page (see Figure 18-2), which displays national average mortgage rates.

For home equity, car, and personal loans, scroll down the Quicken.com home page to the Today's Rates area. Choose the type of loan that interests you from the drop-down list and click the Go button beside it. The page that appears shows rates for various states. You can get rates for your state by choosing it from the drop-down list and clicking the Start button.

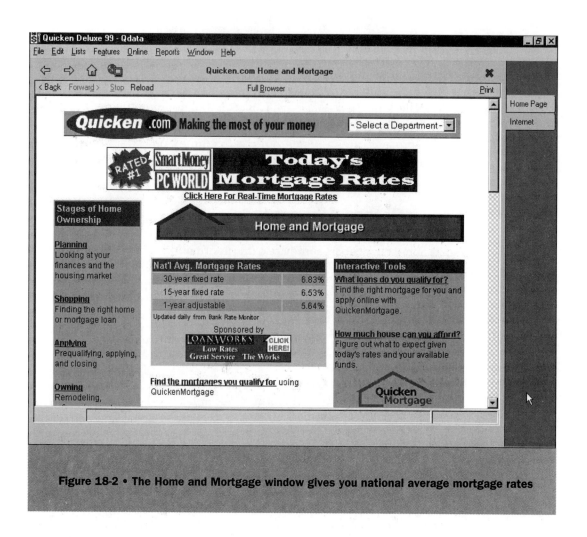

Figure 18-2 • The Home and Mortgage window gives you national average mortgage rates

Loan Calculator

Once you have a rate, you can use Quicken's Loan Calculator to determine how much a loan will cost you. Choose Features | Planning | Financial Calculators | Loan. The Loan Calculator dialog box appears:

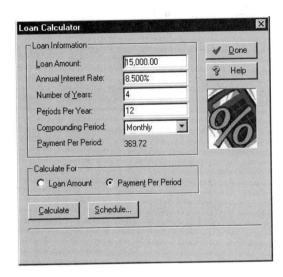

- To calculate the amount of loan you can afford, select the Loan Amount option button. Then you can enter an affordable monthly payment in the Payment Per Period text box.
- To calculate the periodic payment, select the Payment Per Period option button. Then you can enter the amount of the loan in the Loan Amount text box.

Enter values in the text boxes. When you're finished, click Calculate. The calculated value appears. You can try different values to play "what-if" until you have a good idea of how the loan could work for you. With the information this provides, you should be able to tell whether you can afford the home or car you have your eye on; or if you haven't started looking yet, how much you can afford to spend.

Refinance Calculator
If you already own a home and are thinking about refinancing, you can try the Refinance Calculator. Choose Features | Planning | Financial Calculators | Refinance. The Refinance Calculator dialog box shown next appears. Enter values in the text boxes to calculate your monthly savings with the new mortgage. You can even enter closing costs and points to calculate how many months it will take to break even after paying these fees.

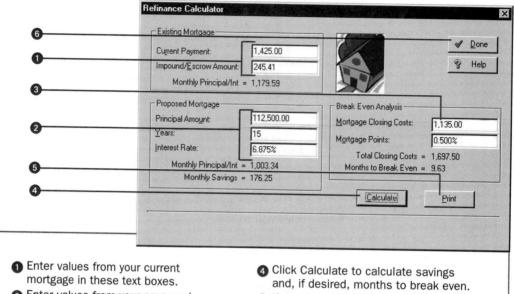

❶ Enter values from your current mortgage in these text boxes.

❷ Enter values from your proposed mortgage in these text boxes.

❸ If desired, enter closing costs and points in these text boxes.

❹ Click Calculate to calculate savings and, if desired, months to break even.

❺ If desired, click Print to print the results.

❻ When you're finished, click Done.

Tracking a Loan in Quicken

Quicken makes it easy to track the principal, interest, and payments for a loan. Once you set up a loan and corresponding liability or asset accounts, you can make payments with Quicken using QuickFill, scheduled transactions, or online payments. The Loan feature keeps track of all the details so you don't have to.

Setting Up a Loan

Choose Features | Bills | Loans, or press CTRL-H. The View Loans window appears. It displays information about your loans.

Click the New button in the Button bar to display the Loan Setup main window. Follow the instructions in this window and subsequent EasyStep windows to enter information for your loan.

Shortcut You can click the Summary tab to display and enter all loan information in a series of Summary tab windows.

First, you're prompted for the type of loan. You have two options:

- **Borrow Money** is for loans for which you're borrowing money from a lender, such as a car loan, mortgage, or personal loan. Quicken sets up a liability account to record the loan.
- **Lend Money** is for loans for which you're the lender. Quicken sets up an asset account to record the money owed from the borrower.

Next, you're prompted to enter the account for the loan. Again, you have two options:

- **New Account** enables you to set up a brand-new account for the loan.
- **Existing account** enables you to select one of your existing accounts for the loan. This option is only available if you have already created the appropriate type of account for the loan.

Subsequent windows ask for information about the loan creation, amount, and payments. Select options and enter values as prompted. Quicken can calculate some of the values—such as the loan balance and monthly payments—for you. When you're finished, a series of Summary tab windows displays entered and calculated values. Here's what the final Summary tab window looks like for a $132,000, 15-year mortgage started on 10/1/97:

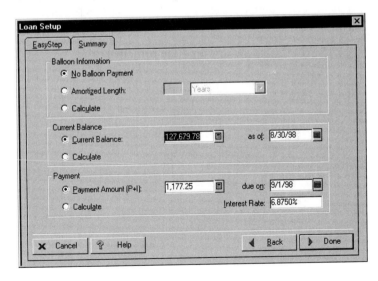

Setting Up Payments

When you set up a loan, Quicken automatically prompts you to set up payment information by displaying the Set Up Loan Payment dialog box:

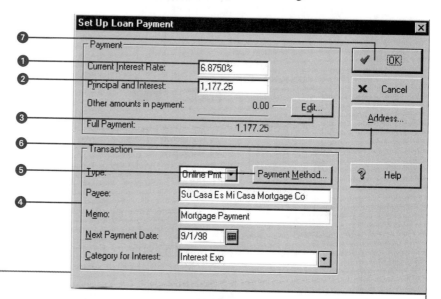

❶ Enter the current interest rate.
❷ Enter the amount of the principal and interest.
❸ Click the Edit button to enter additional amounts to be included in the payment, such as property taxes and insurance.
❹ Enter transaction information.

❺ Click the Payment Method button to select a payment method.
❻ For a Print Check transaction, click the Address button to enter an address for the payee.
❼ Click OK.

Enter information in this dialog box to set up the payment. If the total payment should include additional amounts for property taxes, insurance, or other escrow items, click the Edit button. This displays the Split Transaction window, which you can use to enter categories, memos, and amounts to be added to the payment.

In the Transaction area of the Set Up Loan Payment dialog box, you can specify the type and method for the transaction. For type, there are three options on the drop-down list:

• **Payment** is a transaction recorded in your account register only. You must manually write and mail a check for payment. This is covered in Chapter 4.

- **Print Check** is a transaction recorded in the Write Checks dialog box and account register. You can use the Print Check command to print the check, and then mail it for payment. This is also covered in Chapter 4.
- **Online Pmt** creates a payment instruction to be processed by your financial institution for use with online payment. This is covered in Chapter 12.

For payment method, click the Payment Method button. The Select Payment Method dialog box appears:

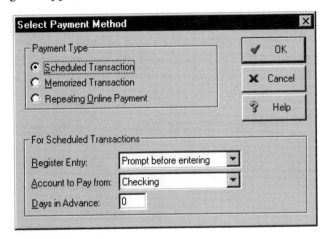

This dialog box offers three Payment Type options:

- **Scheduled Transaction** is a transaction scheduled for the future. If you select this option, you must also choose options and enter values to specify how Quicken should enter the transaction, which account should be used to pay, and how many days in advance it should be entered and paid. All this is covered in Chapter 5.
- **Memorized Transaction** is a transaction memorized for use with QuickFill or the Quicken Financial Calendar. This is also covered in Chapter 5.
- **Repeating Online Payment** is a recurring online payment instruction processed by your financial institution. If you select this option, you must also select a repeating online payment transaction from a drop-down list. (If you have not already created a transaction to link to this loan payment, select one of the other options and return to this dialog box after you have created the required transaction; consult the section titled "Linking a Loan Payment to a Repeating Online Payment" later in this chapter.) Repeating online payments are discussed in Chapter 12.

Click OK to accept your settings in the Select Payment Method dialog box. Then click OK to save your settings in the Set Up Loan Payment dialog box.

Creating an Associated Asset Account

Next, Quicken displays a dialog box asking if you want to create an asset to go with the loan. This enables you to set up an asset account for the full purchase price of your new home or car. Click Yes to create a new account; click No if you have already created one.

Follow the steps in the EasyStep tab of the Create Asset window to create the asset account. I explain how to create accounts in Chapter 2, so I won't repeat the instructions here. When you're finished entering information, Quicken displays it in the Summary tab of the Create Asset window. It might look something like this:

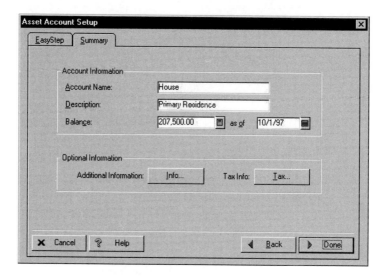

Click Done to save the account.

Reviewing Your Loan Information

If you've followed these instructions to the letter, the View Loans window for your loan should appear. It displays information about your loan in three tabs:

Loan Summary   Loan Summary summarizes the loan information.

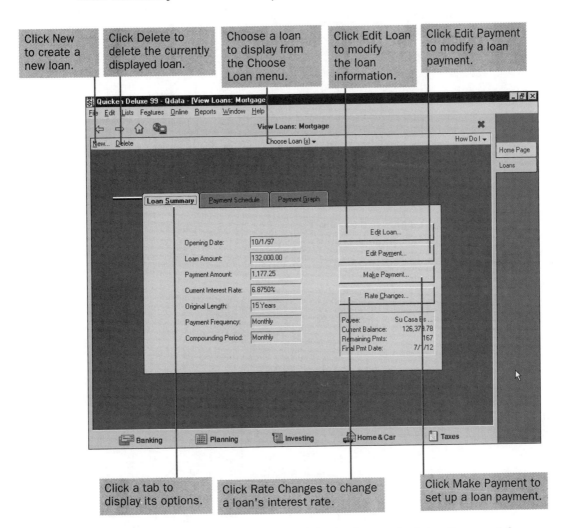

Click New to create a new loan.

Click Delete to delete the currently displayed loan.

Choose a loan to display from the Choose Loan menu.

Click Edit Loan to modify the loan information.

Click Edit Payment to modify a loan payment.

Click a tab to display its options.

Click Rate Changes to change a loan's interest rate.

Click Make Payment to set up a loan payment.

Payment Schedule   Payment Schedule displays a schedule of past and future payments. You can turn on the Show Running Total check box to display cumulative totals, rather than individual payment information.

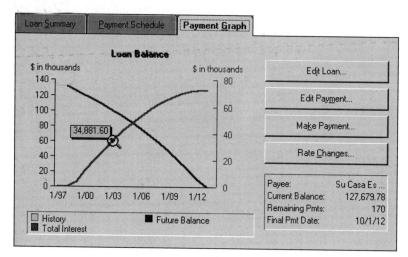

Pmt	Date	Principal	Interest	Balance
Bal	10/1/97	Opening Bal		132,000.00
Bal	8/30/98	4,320.22		127,679.78
	9/1/98	Rate - 6.87...	New Pmt -	1,177.25
1	9/1/98	445.75	731.50	127,234.03
2	10/1/98	448.31	728.94	126,785.72
3	11/1/98	450.87	726.38	126,334.85
4	12/1/98	453.46	723.79	125,881.39
5	1/1/99	456.05	721.20	125,425.34
6	2/1/99	458.67	718.58	124,966.67
7	3/1/99	461.30	715.95	124,505.37
8	4/1/99	463.94	713.31	124,041.43
9	5/1/99	466.60	710.65	123,574.83

Payment Graph   Payment Graph displays a graph of the loan payments. Where the two lines meet indicates the point at which you start paying more toward the loan principal than for interest. You can click on one of the graph lines to display its value.

Other Loan Setup Tasks

Once you've created a loan, you can modify it as necessary to record corrections, changes in the interest rate, or changes in payment methods. Here are a few tasks you might need to perform over the life of a loan.

Changing Loan Information

You modify a loan's information using options in the View Loans window.
Choose Features | Bills | Loans to display the window. Then, if necessary, choose
the loan account's name from the Choose Loan menu in the Button bar to
display the information for the loan you want to modify.

Click the Edit Loan button. A series of Edit Loan windows enable you to
change just about any information for the loan. Modify values and select
different options as desired. Click Done in the last window to save your changes.

Changing the Interest Rate

If you have an adjustable rate mortgage, periodically you'll have to adjust the rate
for the loan within Quicken to match the rate charged by the lender. Choose
Features | Bills | Loans to display the Loans window. If necessary, choose the loan
account's name from the Choose Loan menu in the Button bar to display the
information for the loan whose rate you want to change.

Click the Rate Changes button. The Loan Rate Changes window appears.
It lists all the loan rates throughout the history of the loan, as shown here:

Click New to insert a new interest rate.

Click Edit to modify the selected rate.

Click Delete to delete the selected rate.

Loan Rate Changes

New   Edit   Delete   Close

Date	Rate	Principal and Interest
9/1/98	6.875%	1,177.25
10/1/99	6.75%	1,172.67

To insert a rate change, click the New button in the window's Button bar.
The Insert an Interest Rate Change dialog box appears:

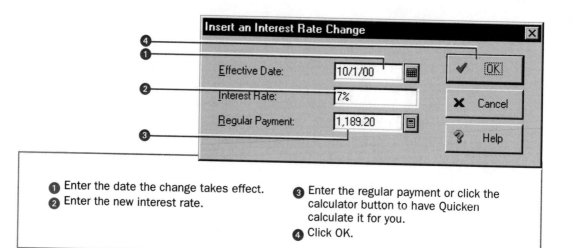

❶ Enter the date the change takes effect.
❷ Enter the new interest rate.

❸ Enter the regular payment or click the calculator button to have Quicken calculate it for you.
❹ Click OK.

When you enter rate information and click OK, the rate appears in the Loan Rate Changes window. Click the Close button to dismiss the window.

Linking a Loan Payment to a Repeating Online Payment

If you use Quicken's online payment feature, you probably realize that repeating online payments are perfect for making loan payments. After all, loan payments are the same every month and must be paid by a certain date. You can set up a repeating online payment instruction, send it to your financial institution, and let Quicken and your bank make the payments automatically every month for you.

To use repeating online payments with a loan, you must set up the repeating online payment first. I explain how in Chapter 12. When creating the payment instruction, don't worry about all the categories that are part of a loan payment transaction. Choose the loan account as the category; when you link the transaction to the loan, Quicken will make the necessary adjustments.

When the payment instruction is complete and has been saved, choose Features | Bills | Loans to display the Loans window. If necessary, choose the loan account's name from the Choose Loan menu in the Button bar to display the information for the loan for which you want to use the payment instruction.

Click the Edit Payment button to display the Edit Loan Payment dialog box. Click the Payment Method button. In the Select Payment Method dialog box, select Repeating Online Payment. Then choose the repeating online payment instruction you created from the Repeating Payment drop-down list. It might look something like this:

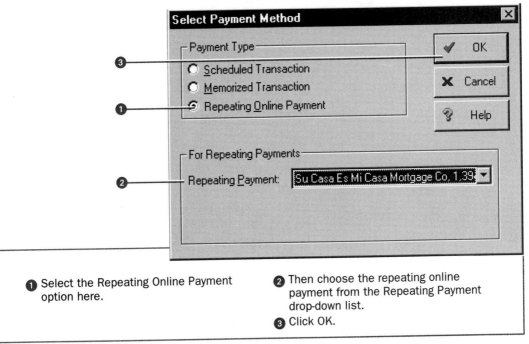

❶ Select the Repeating Online Payment option here.

❷ Then choose the repeating online payment from the Repeating Payment drop-down list.

❸ Click OK.

    Click OK in each dialog box to dismiss it. Quicken links the loan payment to the repeating online payment instruction. It makes changes to the payment instruction, if necessary, to match the payment categories and split information. The next time you connect to your financial institution, the instruction will be sent and payments will begin.

Home & Car Center

Quicken's Home & Car Center displays information about your assets, loans, and cars, as well as links to other tools and information you might find useful when setting up or researching loans. To open this window, choose Features I Centers I Home & Car, or click the Home & Car button near the top of the Quicken Home Page. It should look something like the window shown in Figure 18-3.

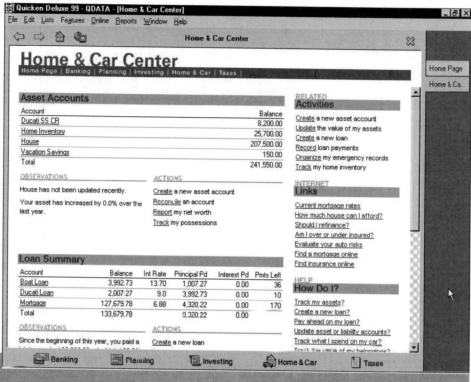

Figure 18-3 • The Home & Car Center provides information about your assets and loans, as well as information on researching loans

In this section, I provide a brief description of what you can expect to find.

Tip   If you access the Web with Quicken, the Home & Car Center page is automatically updated. Don't be surprised if your page doesn't offer the same options as the one shown here.

Current Information

Most of the Home & Car window displays current information from some of your Quicken accounts.

- **Asset Accounts List** displays a list of all your assets and their values. This includes not only your home and car (if asset accounts exist for them) but assets you may track with Quicken's Home Inventory feature, which I discuss in Chapter 10. You can click on any asset account name to open the account register for that asset.

- **Loan Summary** displays a list of all your loans and their balances. You can click on any loan account name to open the account register for that loan.
- **Auto Expenses** lists the total expenditures in the Auto category and its subcategories. It also provides totals for the month and monthly averages.

The Observations and Actions lists within each of these areas provide additional information about your finances and offer links to access Quicken features.

Access to Quicken Commands

The Activities area offers links to commands you might find useful when working with assets and loans.

- **Create a new asset account** displays the Create New Account window so you can create a new asset account.
- **Update the value of my assets** displays the account register window so you can change the value of an asset.
- **Create a new loan** displays the Loan Setup window so you can create a new loan.
- **Record loan payments** displays the account register window so you can record a loan payment.
- **Organize my emergency records** displays the Emergency Records Organizer so you can enter information useful in the event of an emergency.
- **Track my home inventory** opens Quicken Home Inventory, so you can add, modify, or remove home inventory items.

Links for Tools and Information

Other areas in the Home & Car window offer links to tools and information available on Quicken.com. You need Internet access to take advantage of some of these links.

- **Links** includes links to information about current mortgage and loan rates, advice on buying a home, and other useful information from Quicken.com.

- **How do I?** provides information for completing specific tasks within Quicken. Click a question to display a Quicken Help window with instructions.
- **Did You Know?** displays questions about mortgages, with brief answers. Clicking a link takes you to a Quicken.com Web page with more information.

Quicken.com Resources

The mother lode of mortgage and loan resources is Quicken.com. You can find links to tools and information in at least three places: the Home and Mortgage department, the Banking and Borrowing department, and the QuickenMortgage Mortgage Center.

Home and Mortgage

Home and Mortgage, as the name implies, offers a wealth of information about buying a new home, refinancing or renovating the home you have, and obtaining a mortgage.

Open Quicken.com by choosing Online | Quicken on the Web | Quicken.com. Your computer connects to the Internet and displays the Quicken.com home page. Choose Home & Mortgage from the drop-down list near the top of the page. The Home and Mortgage main page, shown earlier in Figure 18-2, appears. This page offers links to information and other tools.

Stages of Home Ownership

The Stages of Home Ownership area offers links for each stage in the process of buying or owning a home: Planning, Shopping, Applying, and Owning. Other links take you to the Refinance Center, the Credit Center, Home Listings, and the Guide to Home Ownership. All of these links offer valuable resources for buying and owning a home.

Nat'l Avg. Mortgage Rates

Nat'l Avg. Mortgage Rates, which I discuss earlier in this chapter, displays the current average mortgage rates for several types of mortgages. A link to QuickenMortgage enables you to search for mortgages for which you qualify, and a link to Bank Rate Monitor enables you to get any mortgage rate you want.

News and Features

News and Features offers links to Daily Mortgage News, Daily Real Estate News, recent news stories, and questions and answers about real estate and mortgages.

Interactive Tools

Interactive Tools offers links to useful QuickenMortgage tools for planning and shopping for a mortgage:

- **What Loans Do You Qualify For?** takes you to QuickenMortgage, where you can get information about the loans you qualify for and even apply for a mortgage online.

- **How Much House Can You Afford?** displays a form you can fill in with information about your personal financial situation. Enter your income, monthly debt, cash available for a down payment, and (optionally) information about a loan you're considering. Click the Calculate button to see the maximum amount you can spend on a house.

- **Should You Refinance Now?** displays a form you can fill in with existing and proposed mortgage information. Click the Calculate Now button to see whether refinancing can save you money on monthly payments and long-term costs.

- **What Are Today's Rates in Your State?** displays a form on which you can choose your state and the type of mortgage in which you are interested. Click the Show Today's Rates button to see the current rates in your area.

- **Guest Columnists** offers timely articles about topics such as New Homes, Your Apartment, and Starting Out. These are written by experts in the real estate and housing field and are full of tips for making the most of your housing dollars.

- **Money Talk** offers access to a live chat room and message boards for discussing real estate. Learn what's on the minds of other people like you. Share your thoughts and insights with them. Learn from their experiences and mistakes.

Banking & Borrowing

Banking & Borrowing offers links to information about the world of banking and borrowing money. This area is especially useful for learning about auto loans and other types of financing.

Open Quicken.com by choosing Online | Quicken on the Web | Quicken.com. Your computer connects to the Internet and displays the Quicken.com home page. Then choose Banking & Borrowing from the drop-down list near the top of the page. The Banking & Borrowing main page appears, as shown in Figure 18-4.

Banking Topics

The Banking Topics area includes links related to banking and loans:

- **Find a Bank** helps you locate a bank in your area, including local branches and Intuit banking partners.
- **Online Banking** tells you about online banking. It offers guidance, deals, and free software.
- **Credit Report** provides information about credit reports, including how you can protect, obtain a copy of, and fix yours.

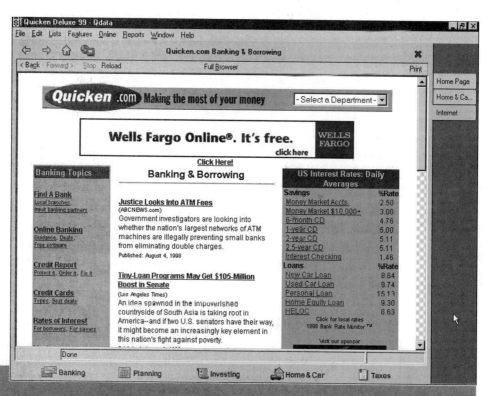

Figure 18-4 • You'll find more information about auto loans and other financing in the Banking & Borrowing area

- **Credit Cards** offers information about credit cards, including the types of credit cards and some good credit card deals.
- **Rates of Interest** gives you access to current interest rates for borrowers and savers.
- **Mortgages** takes you to the Home and Mortgage main page, which I tell you about earlier in this chapter.
- **Checking & ATMs** provides information about checking accounts and automated teller machines (ATMs), including a checking account guide and ATM fee information.
- **Intuit Banking** offers links to sites where you can learn about Quicken, QuickBooks, and BankNOW.

More on Banking & Borrowing

This area offers a link to a Web page full of other banking and borrowing sites. These are the Quicken.com top picks, full of useful information. As this book went to press, links included Bank Rate Monitor, BanxQuote Virtual Banking & Finance Center, and Experian.

Articles

The middle of the page offers links to timely articles related to banking and borrowing. Another link takes you to a page full of banking news.

US Interest Rates: Daily Averages

This area displays the current rates on savings and loans, including CDs, money market accounts, new and used car loans, personal loans, and home equity reserves. You can click the name of a rate to go to a page where you can look up your local rate.

Resources and Guides

The resources and guides area offers links to obtain a free credit report as well as to two extremely useful online guides:

- **Loan Application Guide** tells you everything you need to know about applying for a loan, including the documents you'll have to provide and the questions you'll have to answer at an interview. This is an excellent resource for anyone applying for any kind of loan for the first time.
- **Credit Report Guide** tells you what you need to know to understand, protect, and fix your credit report.

Mortgage Center

The Mortgage Center takes you to QuickenMortgage, a Web site full of information about mortgages. It includes many of the resources mentioned for the Home and Mortgage page discussed earlier in this chapter. It also offers links you can use to apply for a loan online.

Choose Online | Quicken on the Web | Mortgage Center. The QuickenMortgage introduction page appears. Click the "Let's get started" button. Your computer connects to the Internet and displays the QuickenMortgage main page (see Figure 18-5). Follow links to navigate through the topics the site has to offer.

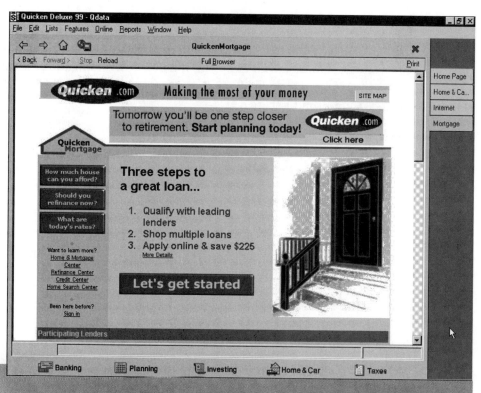

Figure 18-5 • QuickenMortgage includes links for applying for a loan online

Worksheets

Use the following two worksheets to help you compare and evaluate different loans or mortgages.

Loan Comparison Worksheet			
Basic Information			
Instructions: Enter information for each loan, one per column.			
Lender Name			
Contact Name			
Phone Number			
Comments			
Amount of Loan			
Rates and Fees			
Instructions: Enter rate and fee values for each loan.			
Application Fee			
Other Fees			
Term (in months)			
Annual Interest Rate			
Payment Calculations			
Instructions: Calculate the monthly payments. Use the Loan Calculator within Quicken for accuracy (choose Features I Planning I Calculators I Loan). Then calculate the total of all payments and fees.			
Monthly Payment			
Total Payments (monthly payment × number of months)			
Total Payments Plus Fees			

Mortgage Comparison Worksheet (page 1)		

Basic Information

Instructions: Enter information for each mortgage, one per column. Note: You can get most of this information from the Good Faith Estimate the lender should provide.

Lender Name			
Contact Name			
Phone Number			
Comments			

Purchase Price and Down Payment Information

Instructions: Enter the purchase price, down payment, and loan amount for each mortgage. For the best comparison, these should be the same.

Purchase Price			
Down Payment	% \$	% \$	% \$

Basic Loan Information

Instructions: Enter values for each mortgage. Then calculate monthly payments. Use the Loan Calculator within Quicken for accuracy (choose Features | Planning | Calculators | Loan). Total the monthly payments for the life of the mortgage.

Annual Interest Rate						
Term (in years)						
Fixed or Variable						
If Variable, Adjustment Period and Cap	Period	Cap	Period	Cap	Period	Cap
Monthly Payments						
Total Monthly Payments (Term × 12 × Monthly Payments)						

Mortgage Comparison Worksheet (page 2)

Closing Costs

Instructions: Enter expected closing costs for each loan. Do not include prepaid amounts that are due at closing. Not all of these fees may apply; use space at the bottom of this section to enter other fees not listed here.

Origination Fee	%	$	%	$	%	$
Discount Fee (Points)	%	$	%	$	%	$
Credit Report Fee						
Lenders Inspection Fee						
Tax Service Fee						
Application Fee						
Underwriting Fee						
Courier Fee						
Settlement Fee						
Document Preparation Fee						
Notary Fee						
Administration Fee						
Title Insurance Fee						
Recording Fee						
City/County Tax Stamps						
State Tax Stamps						
Recordation Tax						

Mortgage Comparison Worksheet (page 3)			
Loan Program Fee			
Pest Inspection Fee			
Final Inspection Fee			
Total Closing Costs	$	$	$

Total Mortgage Costs

Instructions: Add the Total Monthly Payments to the Total Closing Costs to arrive at the total cost of each mortgage.

Total Mortgage Costs	$	$	$

Achieving Your Goals

This part of the book focuses on how you can use Quicken to help make your dreams come true. It has three chapters:

Chapter 19: *Maximizing Investment Returns*

Chapter 20: *Planning for Retirement*

Chapter 21: *Saving for the Future*

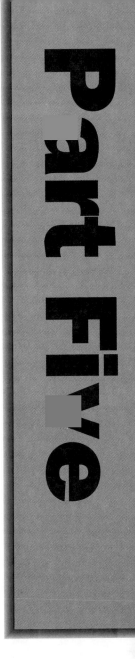

Maximizing Investment Returns

Chapter 19

423

If you're good at managing your finances, you probably have a little left over every month. If you're concerned about risk and don't mind relatively low returns, the savings accounts and certificates of deposit offered by your local bank may be just the place for your money. But if you don't mind a little risk for the possibility of greater financial rewards, there's a good chance you've discovered Wall Street and investing.

In this chapter, I provide some basic information about investing, as well as what you can do to get started. I also tell you about the tools within Quicken and on Quicken.com that can help you research your investments to make smart financial decisions.

Tip If you think Wall Street and its risks are just for high rollers, skip this chapter for now and move ahead to Chapter 21. That's where I tell you about savings and the type of low-risk accounts you can open with your local bank.

Investment Basics

An investment is a security you purchase with the hope that it rises in value, pays you interest or a dividend, or both. Investments differ from savings in several ways:

- An investment is somewhat more difficult to redeem for cash, thus making it less liquid.
- An investment's value varies depending on the market—what another investor is willing to pay for it—thus giving it the potential to be worth far more (or less) than you paid for it.
- An investment is not insured against loss, thus making it more risky.

In this section, I provide the basic information you need to understand what investments are available, what you need to know before deciding on a specific investment type, and the things you can do to get started as an investor.

Types of Investments

There are many types of investments and each one has its pros and cons. Following is a summary of the most common types of investments.

Money Market Funds

A *money market fund* or *account* is an investment in short-term debt instruments such as certificates of deposit, commercial paper, banker's acceptances, treasury bills, and discount notes. Although you can open a money market account with your local bank, it is not insured by the FDIC (Federal Deposit Insurance Corporation) as are most other bank accounts. The rate of return and value is not guaranteed. Money market funds earn income for investors by paying dividends.

Treasury Bills

A *treasury bill* (or *T-bill*) is a short-term government security, sold through the Federal Reserve Bank by competitive bidding. T-bills are the most widely used of all government debt securities. They are backed by the full faith and credit of the U.S. government. T-bills earn money for investors by paying interest.

Stocks

A *stock* is part ownership of a corporation. Sold as shares through stock exchanges throughout the world (as well as privately, in the case of private corporations), their market values fluctuate daily. Thousands or millions of shares of any given stock can change hands each day. Stocks earn money for investors by paying dividends or rising in value.

Bonds

A *bond* is essentially a loan made by the investor to a company or government entity. Bonds earn money for investors by paying interest. The actual interest rate paid often depends on the stated interest rate and the purchase price of the bond.

Mutual Funds

A *mutual fund* is a group of securities held by a group of investors. When you invest in a mutual fund, your investment dollars are pooled with other investors. A fund manager buys and sells securities to maximize the fund's return. Mutual funds earn money for investors by paying dividends (which can often be automatically reinvested in the fund) or rising in value. In return for his or her services, the fund manager is paid a fee. Other fees may include *loads,* which can be applied when you invest or sell mutual fund shares.

There are thousands of mutual funds, each with its own "mix" of investment types. Investors—especially novice investors—find mutual funds attractive because an investment professional can make decisions for them.

Investment Considerations

When evaluating an investment, you should consider several important factors: return, risk, goal, and taxability.

Return

An investment's return is what it earns for the investor. Most investments earn money by paying interest, paying dividends, or rising in value.

Interest   Interest is a rate applied to the face or par value of a security that is then paid to the investor in cash. Treasury bills and bonds pay interest. Money market accounts pay dividends, although amounts are calculated like interest and often referred to as interest on bank statements.

Dividends   Dividends are per share payments to shareholders. There are two types: cash and stock.

- **Cash dividends** pay a certain cash amount per share to each stockholder. For example, a $1 per share cash dividend pays each stockholder $1 for each share held. Cash dividends are normally paid by large companies; smaller companies need cash to grow.

- **Stock dividends** pay a certain number of stock shares per share to each stockholder. A stock split is a type of stock dividend. For example, a 2-for-1 stock split doubles the number of shares each stockholder owns. Although this cuts the per share value in half, the value is expected to rise again over time.

Capital Gains   A stock's price indicates what another investor is willing to pay for it. When the stock's price is higher than what you paid, you have a gain on your investment. When the stock's price is lower than what you paid, you have a loss on your investment. A capital gain (or loss) can be realized or unrealized:

- **Realized gains (or losses)** are the gains or losses you can record when you sell an investment. If an investment is taxable, the realized gain or loss must be reported on your tax return.

- **Unrealized gains (or losses)** are the gains or losses based on your purchase price and the current market value for investments you have not yet sold. Because the investment has not been sold, the gain is not realized and does not have to be reported on your tax return.

Risk

Risk is your chance of making or losing money on an investment. Although all investments have some element of risk involved, some investments are more conservative (less risky) than others.

There is a direct relationship between risk and return. The higher the potential return, the higher the risk. The lower the risk, the lower the potential return. For example, money market accounts and T-bills are considered relatively conservative investments. On July 31, 1998, they earned an average of 2.5% and 5.2% respectively. Stocks, on the other hand are considered more risky. On July 31, 1998, the rates of return for a one-year investment in Intuit, Microsoft, and Apple were 100.4%, -17.2%, and 48.9%, respectively. As these examples show, you can make more money in the stock market, but you can also lose some.

Caution   These examples are for illustrative purposes only. Exact accuracy is not guaranteed. I am neither recommending nor advising against an investment in any of these securities.

Goal

Goal refers to your goal as an investor. You should choose an investment based on its ability to meet your goals. There are two main goals: income and growth.

- **Income investments** generate income for investors in the form of dividends and interest. Investors get regular cash payments. Income investments are popular with investors who are retired and living on fixed incomes. Income investments include money market accounts, T-bills, bonds, stocks of larger ("blue chip") companies, and some mutual funds.
- **Growth investments** grow in market value. Growth investments are popular with younger people who want to build a "nest egg" for their later years. Growth investments include stocks of smaller companies and some mutual funds.

Taxability

The taxability of an investment refers to how it is taxed. This matters most to individuals in high tax brackets. Generally speaking, investments fall into three categories: taxable, nontaxable, and tax-deferred:

- **Taxable investments** are fully taxed by the federal and local government. You must report and pay taxes on interest and dividend income, as well as capital gains. Capital losses can be deducted from income (within certain limitations) to reduce your tax bill. Visit the Taxes department on Quicken.com or talk to your tax advisor for more information.

- **Nontaxable investments** are not taxed by the federal government. They may, however, be taxed by local governments such as your state government. Examples of nontaxable investments include municipal bonds.

- **Tax-deferred investments** are investments for which income is not taxed until it is withdrawn. An example is an investment set up as a tax-deferred annuity. In this case, you invest as much as you like. Income, when earned, is automatically reinvested into the account but is not taxed at that time. The value of the account continues to grow. When you're 59½ years old you can begin withdrawing money from the account. Income on the investment is taxed then, when you're likely to be in a lower tax bracket.

Getting Started

If you've never invested money before, the following sections outline some things you might want to consider doing to get started on the right track.

Doing Your Research

Would you go grocery shopping blindfolded? Groping around on the shelves for beef stew, only to wind up with dog food? Poking meat packages for porterhouse steak, only to wind up with bacon ends?

Investing without research is like shopping blindfolded. You spend money but don't know what you've purchased until it's paid for. Even then, you may not know—until it's too late and you've lost money.

The Investment Research feature available in Quicken Deluxe and the Investment department on Quicken.com offer literally hundreds of resources you can tap into to get almost any information you can imagine about a company. Even if you don't know where to start, these features can help you search for stocks and mutual funds that meet criteria you specify. You can get news, price histories, and ratings. You can get financial results. You can even participate in message boards to see what other investors think is hot.

If you're not sure what you should be looking for, the Investment Research feature and the Investment department can help, too. They offer links to basic information that goes far beyond the basics I provided at the beginning of this chapter. Spend a few hours learning about the types of investments that interest you. Then check out the individual investments themselves. Gather information before you make a decision.

Remember, it's your money. Put it where it'll work hardest for you.

Finding a Broker

If you decide to invest in stocks and bonds, you need a broker. (It's a lot cheaper than buying a seat on the stock exchange.) A stockbroker or brokerage firm can handle the purchases and sales of securities. Nowadays, there are three kinds of brokers:

- **Full service brokers** can buy and sell securities for you, based on your instructions. But these people also research investments for you and tell you about the ones they think are hot. They also keep an eye on the securities you own and tell you when they think one of them may lose value. Based on their recommendations, you can buy or sell. Fees for full service brokers are higher than any other—a typical stock purchase or sale could cost well over $100 in commissions. But you're getting more service for your money— you're paying someone to do investment research for you. If you decide to use a full service broker, track his or her performance carefully; if your broker is not meeting your expectations, you might want to find another broker.

- **Discount brokers** can buy and sell securities for you, too. They usually don't offer any advice, though. They're much cheaper than full-service brokers—a typical stock purchase or sale could be $30 to $60.

- **Deep discount brokers** can also buy and sell securities for you. They don't offer advice either. They're dirt cheap—I've seen fees as low as $8 per trade.

You have two main ways to contact your broker to buy or sell stock:

- **Telephone trading** enables you to give buy or sell instructions by phone, either by speaking to someone at the brokerage firm or by entering information using your telephone keypad.

- **Online trading** enables you to enter buy or sell instructions using your computer and Internet connection. This is fast, convenient, and cheap. In fact, companies that offer both telephone and online trading usually offer online trading for less money.

Tip I've been using online trading for over a year now and I'm very happy with it. I can do more trades for less money. My brokerage firm can process orders within 60 seconds of receiving them. They even allow me to trade on margin and pay interest on any cash balance in my account!

If you're interested in telephone trading, you can find a broker the same way you'd find a bank: ask your friends or check your local phone book. Or ask your bank—some banks offer brokerage services or are connected with brokerage firms. You can also find broker information on Quicken.com.

If you're interested in online trading, your first stop should be Quicken.com. It provides information and links to a number of online brokerage firms. See what each one has to offer and select the one with the best deal for you.

 GET SMARTER When shopping for a broker, use the Broker Comparison Worksheet at the end of this chapter to take notes about and compare different services and fees.

Getting Advice from a Pro

If you don't want a full service broker but you do want investment advice, find a financial advisor. Many banks have financial advisors on staff and they can usually provide good, objective advice about investing. They often even handle investment transactions for you (which really makes them a full service broker).

The trick (I think) is finding an advisor who is objective. Most of the ones I've spoken to deal only with certain types of investments or certain fund families. While these might be great investments, the fact that the advisor doesn't even deal with others makes me wonder how objective he or she can be.

Quicken.com also offers information and links for finding a financial advisor. If you can't get a good recommendation from a knowledgeable friend, be sure to tap into Quicken.com's online resources to see what's out there.

Remember to Diversify!

I'm not a financial planner and, in this lawsuit-crazy era we live in, I don't like to give advice. But here's a one-word piece of advice I must share, one that can help minimize your investment risks: diversify.

I can explain with my version of an old story. Farmer Joe has chickens. Every day, he takes a wicker basket to the hen house and collects the eggs. One day, on his way back from the hen house, the basket breaks, dropping the eggs all over the farmyard. As you can imagine, almost every egg breaks. That day, Farmer Joe learned the hard way that he should never put all of his eggs in one basket.

The eggs and basket story applies to your finances, too. If all your investment dollars are in one security and that security fails, you're liable to lose a lot of money. Now take that a step further. If all your investment dollars are in the stock market and the stock market takes a turn for the worse, you're also liable to lose money.

I'm not saying that you shouldn't have "favorite" investments or that you shouldn't invest in the stock market. I'm saying that you should spread your investment dollars among multiple securities and types of investments. If you don't put your eggs in one basket, you can't lose them all.

Quicken Tools

Quicken offers many ways to track and evaluate your investments. Most of them are covered in other chapters throughout this book.

Investment Tracking Features

If you read Chapters 7, 14, and 15, you should already know that Quicken Deluxe is stuffed with features for people who are serious about investing. The ones you'll use most are investment accounts, the Portfolio View window, and—if you have access to the Internet—online quotes and news. I discuss these and other features in those chapters; if you skipped them, what are you waiting for? Go back and read them now!

Decision Making Features

Quicken also includes the Capital Gains Estimator, which I discuss in detail in Chapter 16. This tool enables you to estimate capital gains or losses and their related tax implications *before* you sell a security. The information it provides can help you make an informed decision about which security to sell.

To get started with the Capital Gains Estimator, choose Features | Investing | Estimate Capital Gains. Check Chapter 16 for more information.

Investment Reports

One built-in Quicken investing feature that I didn't discuss in detail yet is investment reports. Reports can help you get a better understanding of the value of your investments and their performance. Quicken offers five standard investment reports:

- **Portfolio Value** reports the value of your investment portfolio on a specific date. The report includes the security name, number of shares, current price, cost basis, unrealized gain or loss, and balance for each security in your portfolio.

- **Investment Performance** reports the internal rate of return of investments during a specific period. The report includes dates, actions, transaction descriptions, investments, returns, and average annual return on investment. This report offers a good way to compare the performance of one security to another.

- **Investment Income** reports the income and expenses from investments during a specific period.

- **Capital Gains** reports capital gains (and losses) from the sale of investment securities for a specific period. The report includes the security name, number of shares, purchase and sale dates, selling price, basis, and gain or loss.

- **Investment Transactions** provides a summary of all investment-related transactions for a specific period. The report includes the date, account, action, security name, category, price, number of shares, commission, cash amount, investment value, and net transaction value for each transaction.

To create a report, choose Reports | Investment to display the Investment submenu. Then choose the name of the report you want. The Create Report window, shown in Figure 19-1, appears. Use it to select a report and enter date options. When you click the Create button, the report appears onscreen.

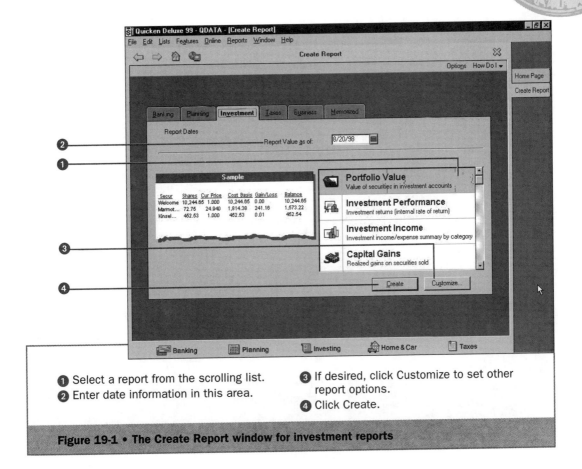

① Select a report from the scrolling list.
② Enter date information in this area.
③ If desired, click Customize to set other report options.
④ Click Create.

Figure 19-1 • The Create Report window for investment reports

Investing Center

Quicken's Investing Center displays information about your investments, as well as links to other tools and information you might find useful when setting up or researching investments. To open this window, choose Features | Centers | Investing, or click the Investing button near the top of the Quicken Home Page. It should look something like the window shown in Figure 19-2.

In this section, I provide a brief description of what you can expect to find.

Tip   If you access the Web with Quicken, the Investing Center window is automatically updated. Don't be surprised if your window doesn't offer the same options as the one shown here.

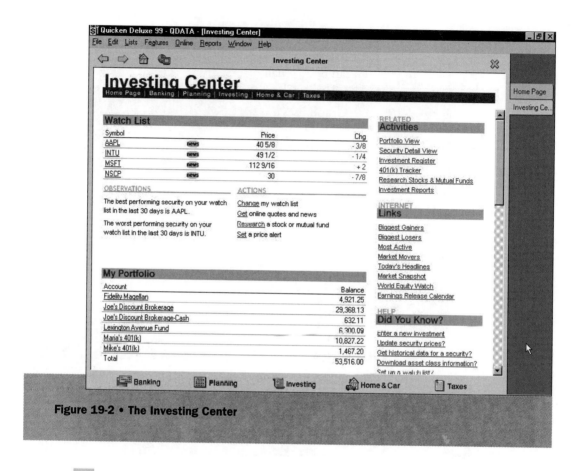

Figure 19-2 • The Investing Center

Current Information

Most of the Investing Center window displays current information about your Watch List and investments.

- **Watch List** displays the securities in your Watch List. The prices that appear are the ones most recently entered or downloaded into your Quicken data file. I explain how to set up Watch List items in Chapter 7, and how to download quotes in Chapter 14. Links in this area enable you to get quotes and news, change your Watch List, view your portfolio, or research a stock or mutual fund.

- **My Portfolio** displays the current items in your portfolio and their values. Values are based on the most recently entered or downloaded quotes. Links in this area enable you to add an investment, see more detail, or get quotes and news.

- **Asset Allocation** uses a pie chart to illustrate the distribution of investment types within your portfolio. This information comes from the asset class for the security, which can be manually entered or downloaded into Quicken. I tell you about asset class in Chapter 7.
- **Investment Return Graph** uses a columnar chart to illustrate your internal rate of return for each investment account. A horizontal line across the graph indicates the average internal rate of return for all of your investment accounts.

Access to Quicken Commands

The Activities area offers links to commands you might find useful when working with investments.

- **Portfolio View** displays the Portfolio View window. Use it to get information about your entire portfolio.
- **Security Detail View** displays the Security Detail View window. Use it to get detailed information about one security.
- **Investment Register** displays the Investment Register window. Use it to enter or edit investment transactions.
- **Investing Reports and Graphs** displays the Create Report window. Use it to create one of the reports I discussed earlier in this chapter.

Links to Tools and Information

Other areas in the Investing Center window offer links to tools and information available on Quicken.com. You need Internet access to take advantage of these links.

- **Links** includes links to today's headlines and other news of interest to investors.
- **How Do I?** provides help information for working with investment accounts.
- **Did You Know?** provides links to investment-related articles and advice.

Investment Research

The Investment Research area is also available from Quicken Deluxe, but you need Internet access to take advantage of all of its features. Start by choosing

Features | Investing | Investment Research. The Quicken Investment Research main window appears (see Figure 19-3). It offers quick access to research tools for stocks and mutual funds.

Stocks

Investment Research offers three stock research tools: Stock Screener, Popular Searches, and Quotes Plus. All three tools can help you identify potential stock investments.

Stock Screener

Stock Screener enables you to search for stocks based on specific performance criteria you specify. Click the Stock Screener link to display a selection form like the one shown in Figure 19-4. Enter criteria in the form and click the Submit Search button.

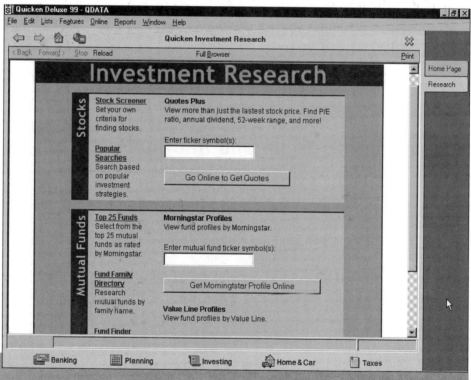

Figure 19-3 • Quicken Investment Research main window

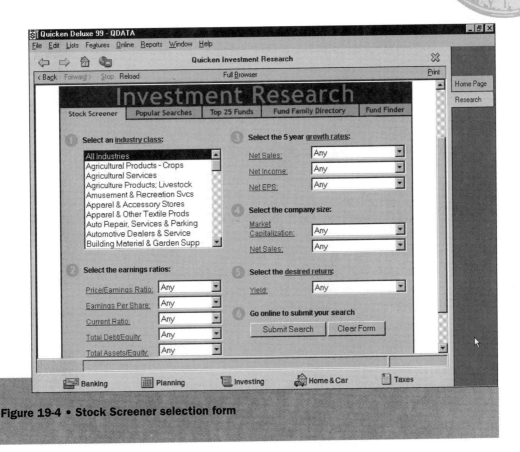

Figure 19-4 • Stock Screener selection form

When you click the Submit Search button, Quicken connects to the Internet, searches a database for stocks matching your criteria, and displays a list of results. You can then click the name of a company to get additional information about it.

Popular Searches

What if you haven't got a clue about what to enter in the fields on the Stock Screener form? That's when Popular Searches can come in handy. Click the link to display a list of predefined searches based on popular investment strategies:

- **Growth** searches for stocks that have had higher-than-average growth over the last five years.
- **Yield** searches for stocks that have produced high dividend yields for stockholders.

- **Valuation** searches for stocks that may be undervalued or overvalued, based on the P/E (price/earnings) ratio.
- **Earnings Strength** searches for stocks that have shown strong earnings both historically and in their current annual report.

When you click a link for any of the predefined searches, Quicken connects to the Internet, searches a database for stocks matching the criteria, and displays a list of results. You can then click the name of a company to get additional information about it.

Quotes Plus

Quotes Plus offers quotes and other market information for any stock. Enter the stock's ticker symbol in the Enter ticker symbol(s) text box in the Quicken Investment Research main window (refer to Figure 19-3). Then click the Go Online to Get Quotes button. Quicken connects to the Internet and displays a page with quote information for the stock. Figure 19-5 shows what Intuit looked like on August 20, 1998—not a particularly good day for any stock market investor.

What's great about Quotes Plus is that a wealth of information about a company is just a click away. Use links along the left side of the window to learn more or to discuss the stock with others in a message area dedicated to it.

Mutual Funds

Investment Research offers four mutual fund research tools: Top 25 Funds, Fund Family Directory, Fund Finder, and Fund Profiles. These tools can help you find mutual funds to meet your needs or check the performance of specific mutual funds.

GET SMARTER   Use the Mutual Funds Comparison Worksheet at the end of this chapter to take notes on mutual funds. It enables you to compare multiple funds, side-by-side, so you can make a better investment decision.

Top 25 Funds

The Top 25 Funds area enables you to search for the top 25 mutual funds in a variety of Morningstar categories. (Morningstar is one of the leading mutual fund rating services.) Click the link to display a search page like the one shown in Figure 19-6. Enter criteria and click the View Top 25 Funds button.

Enter another ticker symbol and click
Get Quote to get another stock quote.

Click the
Symbol
Lookup link
to look up a
ticker symbol.

Click a link to get
more information
about the stock.

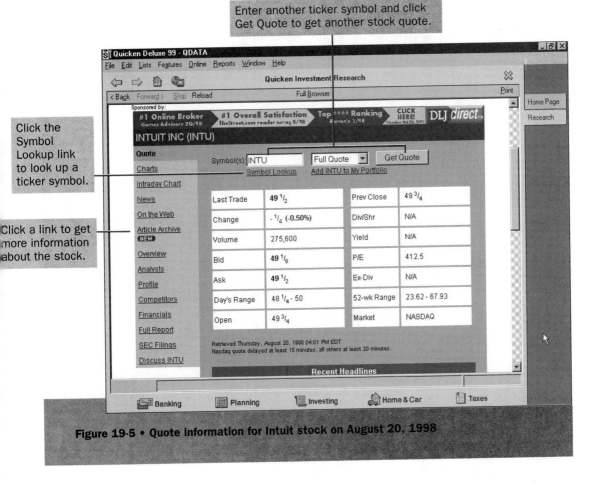

Figure 19-5 • Quote information for Intuit stock on August 20, 1998

When you click the View Top 25 Funds button, Quicken connects to the
Internet, searches a database for the top 25 mutual funds matching the criteria
you entered, and displays a list of results. You can then click one of the links in
the Links column of the list to get additional information about a fund.

Fund Family Directory

The Fund Family Directory enables you to get information about a specific
family of funds. When you click the link, a simple form with a list of fund
families appears. Select the name of the fund family that interests you, and then
click the Visit Fund Family button. Quicken connects to the Internet and
displays a list of all the funds in that family, including the fund name, ticker
symbol, and links to more information.

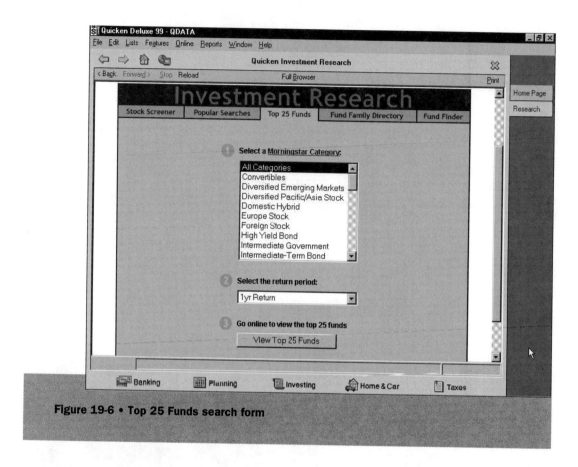

Figure 19-6 • Top 25 Funds search form

Fund Finder

The Fund Finder enables you to find mutual funds that match criteria you enter. Click the link to display a form like the one shown in Figure 19-7. Enter criteria into fields and click the Submit Search button.

When you click the Submit Search button, Quicken connects to the Internet, searches a database for the mutual funds that match the criteria you entered, and displays a list of results. You can then click links in the Links column of the list to get additional information about a fund.

Fund Profiles

If you're interested in a particular fund and you know its ticker symbol, you can use the Fund Profiles feature to get either its Morningstar or Value Line profile. (Value Line is another mutual fund rating service.)

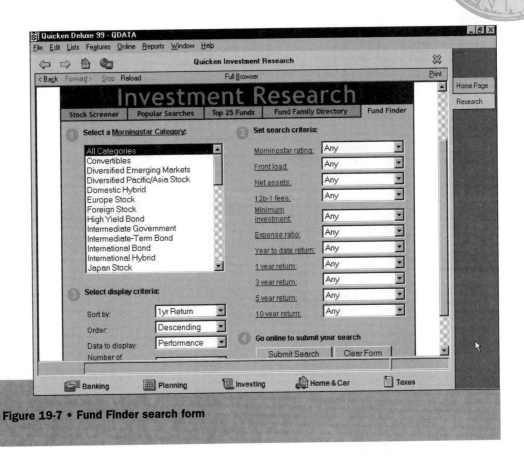

Figure 19-7 • Fund Finder search form

Enter the fund's ticker symbol in the Enter mutual fund ticker symbol(s) text box under Morningstar Profiles or Value Line Profiles in the second pane of the Quicken Investment Research main window. Then click the Get Morningstar Profile Online or Get Value Line Profile Online button. Quicken connects to the Internet and displays a page with the mutual fund's profile.

Quicken.com Resources

Quicken Investment Research is part of Quicken.com's investment resources. A small part. There's a lot more where that came from.

Choose Online | Quicken on the Web | Quicken.com. Quicken connects to the Web and displays the Quicken.com Home Page. Choose Investments from the drop-down list near the top of the window. After a moment, the Investments main page appears, as shown in Figure 19-8.

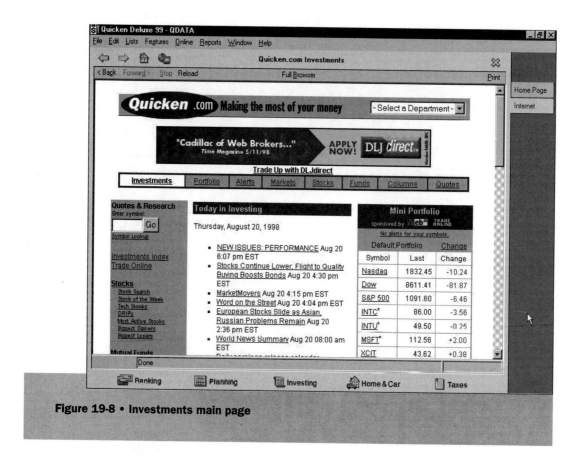

Figure 19-8 • Investments main page

In this section, I'll introduce you to Quicken.com's investing resources so you know what you can find online.

Navigation Bar

A navigation bar with links to categories of information appears near the top of the Investment main page. Use this bar to move quickly to the areas that interest you most:

- **Investments** displays the Investments main page.
- **Portfolio** either displays your Quicken portfolio (if you are logged in to Quicken.com) or displays a screen you can use to log in or register. You can customize this portfolio using the Portfolio Export feature I discuss in Chapter 15 or by clicking links in the Portfolio window.

- **Alerts** displays alerts you have set up for securities. Alerts can either be downloaded from Quicken to Quicken.com using One Step Update or created manually by clicking the "change options" link on the page.
- **Markets** displays a page with charts for the current day's market activity, as well as links to news articles and investing indices.
- **Stocks** displays the Stocks page, which is an area devoted entirely to stocks. On it, you'll find tools to obtain quotes and links to news, articles, and other stock-related information.
- **Funds** displays the Mutual Funds page, which is an area devoted entirely to mutual funds. On it, you'll find tools to obtain quotes, research resources, news, articles, and other information.
- **Columns** displays the Investing Columns page, with links to a variety of articles written by investment experts.
- **Quotes** displays the Quotes page, which enables you to get quotes, charts, news, and overviews for companies and mutual funds.

Quotes & Research

The Quotes & Research area offers a form to get stock quotes, as well as links to other areas on the Quicken.com site:

- **Stocks** displays the Stocks page. Links beneath it offer access to Stock Search, Stock of the Week, Tech Stocks, DRIPs, and other stock-related information.
- **Mutual Funds** displays the Mutual Funds page. Links beneath it offer access to Fund Finder, Top 25 Funds, Fund Q & A, and fund profiles.
- **Basics** displays the Investing Basics page. This is a great destination for novice investors because it provides a wealth of basic information and timely articles. You can even find discussion boards that cover basic investing topics.
- **Columns** displays the Investing Columns page, with links to articles written by investment experts.
- **Bonds** displays the Bonds Home Page, the main page for an area about bonds. That's where you can get market quotes, read commentaries, and learn more about bonds.
- **Retirement** takes you to the Retirement main page. I tell you about that in Chapter 20.
- **Tools** offers links to a number of interactive tools for planning: Retirement Planner, College Planner, Roth IRA Calculator, and Debt-Reduction Planner. I tell you about these tools in Chapters 20 and 21.

More on Investments

This area offers a link to a Web page full of other investing sites. These are the Quicken.com top picks, which are all high-quality sites. As this book went to press, links included Choosing a Discount Broker, CNNfn, and Hoover's Online.

 SAVE TIME   Before you use Internet search engines to find sites for investing information, check the More on Investments link on the Investments main page. The sites you'll find listed are prescreened for value so you don't waste time.

News

The middle of the Investments main page is devoted to market and investing news:

- **Today in Investing** provides clickable market summary headlines for current events of interest to investors. Learn about the biggest gainers and losers, read the "Word on the Street," and get market commentary from Briefing.com.
- **New This Week** provides links to articles about top investing issues for the week.

Mini Portfolio

The Mini Portfolio is an abbreviated version of your stock portfolio. If you are not logged in to Quicken.com, it displays the default portfolio's securities and indices. If you are logged in and have created a custom portfolio, it displays the securities in your portfolio. You can use the Change link to change the default portfolio if desired.

Investing Basics

The Investing Basics area offers links to information of interest to novice investors. You'll find definitions, advice, tips, and answers to frequently asked investing questions.

Talk Back

The Talk Back area offers access to investing message boards, where you can read, write, and reply to messages about investing topics. As this book went to press, topics included Talk to Beginning Investors and Stocks A–Z.

Worksheets

Use the following two worksheets to help you compare and evaluate brokerage firms and mutual funds.

Broker Comparison Worksheet (page 1)			

Basic Information

Instructions: Enter information for each brokerage firm, one per column.

Company Name			
Agent Name			
Phone Number			
Type of Brokerage Firm (circle one)	Full / Discount	Full / Discount	Full / Discount
Comments			

Trading Fees

Instructions: Enter fees for each of the services listed. If fees vary based on the number of shares in the transaction, base the fee on 1,000 shares. If a service is not available, enter N/A. If a service is free, enter $0. Enter additional trading fees at the end of each section if necessary.

Broker-assisted telephone trading			
Market Orders			
Limit Orders			
Options (per trade)			
Options (per contract)			
Bonds			
Treasury Bills			
Mutual Funds			
Touch-tone telephone trading			
Market Orders			
Limit Orders			
Options (per trade)			
Options (per contract)			
Bonds			
Treasury Bills			
Mutual Funds			

Broker Comparison Worksheet (page 2)		
Online Trading		
Market Orders		
Limit Orders		
Options (per trade)		
Options (per contract)		
Bonds		
Treasury Bills		
Mutual Funds		

Other Fees

Instructions: Enter fees for each of the services listed. Enter additional fees at the end of this section if necessary.

Real-time Quotes		
Return Check Fee		
Wire Transfer Fee		
Stock Certificate Issuance Fee		
Check Writing Fee		
Stock Transfer Fee		
Cash Transfer Fee		

Interest Rates

Instructions: Enter the interest rate charged or paid for the following items.

Margin Rates (for <$50,000)		
Account Cash Balance Rates		

Mutual Funds Comparison Worksheet

Basic Information

Instructions: Enter information for each fund, one per column.

Family Name			
Phone Number			
Fund Name			
Ticker Symbol			
Manager Name			
Manager Tenure			
Category			
Goal			
Minimum Initial Purchase			
Comments			

Ratings

Instructions: Enter ratings information from the fund's Morningstar profile.

Stars			
Return			
Risk			

Returns

Instructions: Enter the current average returns for each period listed. You can get this information from the fund's profile.

3 Months			
Year to Date			
1 Year			
3 Years			
5 Years			
10 Years			

Fees

Instructions: Enter values for the expense ratio and each of the fees charged by the fund.

Expense Ratio			
Front Load			
Deferred Sales Charge			
Redemption Fee			
12b-1 Fee			

Planning for Retirement

Chapter 20

451

Throughout your life, you work and earn money to pay your bills, buy the things you and your family need or want, and help your kids get started with their own lives. But there comes a day when it's time to retire. Those regular paychecks stop coming and you find yourself relying on the money you put away for retirement.

Retired people live on fixed incomes. That's not a problem—*if* the income is fixed high enough to support a comfortable lifestyle. You can help ensure that there's enough money to finance your retirement years by planning and saving now. In this chapter, you learn about planning and financing your retirement, and how Quicken and Quicken.com can help.

Planning for Retirement

Retirement planning is one of the most important financial planning jobs facing individuals and couples. In this section I tell you about the importance of planning, and offer some planning steps and a word of advice based on personal experience.

The Importance of Planning

Poor retirement planning can lead to catastrophic results—imagine running out of money when you turn 75. Or having to make a lifestyle change when you're 65 just to accommodate a much lower income.

Planning is even more important these days as longevity increases. People are living longer than ever. Your retirement dollars may need to support you for twenty years or more, at a time when the cost of living will likely be much higher than it is today.

With proper planning, it's possible to properly finance your retirement years without putting a strain on your working years. By closely monitoring the status of your retirement fund and periodically adjusting your plan and acting accordingly, your retirement years can be the golden years they're supposed to be.

Planning Steps

Retirement planning is much more than deciding to put $2,000 a year in an IRA. It requires careful consideration of what you have, what you'll need, and how you can make those two numbers the same.

Tip Quicken's Retirement Calculator and Retirement Planner, which I discuss later in this chapter, can help you perform many of the calculations you need to come up with a good retirement plan.

Assess What You Have

Take a good look at your current financial situation. What tax-deferred retirement savings do you already have? A pension? An IRA? Something else? What regular savings do you have? What taxable investments do you have? The numbers you come up with will form the basis of your final retirement funds—like a seed you'll grow.

Be sure to consider property that can be liquidated to contribute to retirement savings. For example, if you currently live in a large home to accommodate your family, you may eventually want to live in a smaller home. The proceeds from the sale of your current home may exceed the cost of your retirement home. Also consider any income-generating property that may continue to generate income in your retirement years or can be liquidated to contribute to retirement savings.

Tip Your savings, investments, and other assets are part of your net worth. If you use Quicken to track all of your assets, you can use its reporting feature to generate a Net Worth report. Choose Reports | Planning | Net Worth, and then click the Create button in the Create Reports window that appears.

Determine What You'll Need

What you'll need depends on many things. One simple calculation suggests you'll need 80% of your current gross income to maintain your current lifestyle in your retirement years. You may find a calculation like this handy if retirement is still many years in the future and you don't really know what things will cost.

Time is an important factor in calculating the total amount you should have saved by retirement day. Ask yourself two questions:

- **How long do you have to save?** Take your current age and subtract it from the age at which you plan to retire. That's the number of years you have left to save.
- **How long will you be in retirement?** Take the age at which you plan to retire and subtract it from the current life expectancy for someone your age and gender. That's the number of years you have to save for.

When I did this math, I learned that I have only 23 years left to save for a 28-year retirement. I'm glad I've been saving!

Develop an Action Plan

Once you know how much you need, it's time to think seriously about how you can save it. This requires putting money away in one or more savings or investment accounts. I tell you about your options a little later in this chapter.

Stick to the Plan!

The most important part of any plan is sticking to it. For example, if you plan to save $5,000 a year, don't think you can just save $2,000 this year and make up the $3,000 next year. There are two reasons: First, you can't "make up" the interest lost on the $3,000 you didn't save this year. Second, you're only kidding yourself if you think you'll manage to put away $8,000 next year.

If you consider deviating from your plan, just think about the alternative: making ends meet with a burger-flipping job in the local fast food joint when you're 68 years old.

Don't Wait! Act Now!

I remember when I first began thinking about retirement. I was 30 or 31 and had been self-employed for about three years. I didn't have a pension or 401(k) plan with my former employer. I didn't have much saved. I only had $2,000 in an IRA. Up until that point, I never worried about retirement. But one day, something just clicked and retirement became something to think about.

I've done a lot of retirement planning and saving since then. While I admit that I don't have a perfect plan (yet), I've certainly come a long way in five years. But when I consider how much more I could have saved if I'd begun five years earlier, I could kick myself for waiting.

See for yourself. Table 20-1 shows how $1,000, $2,000, and $5,000 per year contributions to a tax-deferred retirement account earning 8% a year can grow. (These calculations do not take into consideration tax benefits or inflation.)

Retirement Funds

There are many different kinds of retirement funds. In this section, I'll tell you about the most common: social security, pension plans, tax-deferred savings and investments, and other savings and investments.

		Savings at Age 62		
Start Age	**Years of Saving**	**$1,000/year**	**$2,000/year**	**$5,000/year**
60	2	$2,080	$4,160	$10,400
55	7	$8,923	$17,846	$44,614
50	12	$18,977	$37,954	$94,886
45	17	$33,750	$67,500	$168,751
40	22	$55,457	$110,914	$277,284
35	27	$87,351	$174,702	$436,754
30	32	$134,214	$268,427	$671,068
25	37	$203,070	$406,141	$1,015,352
20	42	$304,244	$608,487	$1,521,218

Table 20-1 • An Example of How Your Savings Can Grow

Social Security

Social security is the government's way of helping us fund our retirement. If you work, you make mandatory contributions to the social security system. When you reach age 62, you can begin to collect benefits in the form of a monthly check. You don't have to collect social security until you reach the age of 70½; the longer you wait, the more your monthly benefit will be. One thing is relatively certain, however: Your monthly benefit will probably not be enough to fund your retirement.

Tip You can find out how much you'll get from social security when you retire by obtaining a Personal Earnings and Benefit Estimate Statement (PEBES) from the Social Security Administration. Call 800-772-1213 to request your free copy.

Pension Plans

Pension plans are among the most common—and most traditional—methods of retirement funding. They reward loyal employees by guaranteeing a specific amount of benefits upon retirement. There are several types of pension plans, including company pension plans and 401(k) and 403(b) plans.

Company Pension Plan

In a company pension plan you and your employer contribute regularly to a pension fund. This is commonly referred to as a *defined benefit plan,* because the final benefit can always be calculated using a formula that usually includes your years of service, final salary, and a fixed percentage rate. Benefits are usually paid monthly from your retirement date, for the rest of your life.

Most pension funds are insured by the Pension Benefit Guaranty Corporation (PBGC), a government agency that protects employer-sponsored defined benefit plans. That means the money will be there when you retire.

Company pension plans cannot be transferred from one employer to another. If you leave a job where you had a pension plan, your benefits stay with the plan until you turn 65, when you can start collecting benefits.

Here's a quick, real-life story. Uncle Gerry, who is now 80, collects three pensions. How? By working hard. He was in the army for 20 years. Then he worked for the U.S. Postal Service for 20 years. Then he worked in the mailroom at a bank for almost 10 years. When he finally retired, he began collecting pension money from each of his employers. He gets social security benefits, too. He and Aunt Rose are doing just fine.

401(k) and 403(b) Plans

A 401(k) plan is a tax-deferred investment and savings plan that works like a personal pension fund for employees. It allows a company's employees to save and invest for their own retirement. The employee authorizes a pre-tax payroll deduction that is invested in one of the investment options offered by the plan. Some companies may match the employee's contribution by paying 25% to 100% into the plan.

There are two tax benefits to a 401(k) plan:

- **Reduction in taxable income.** Because the contribution comes from pre-tax earnings, it reduces the amount of taxable income, thus reducing the employee's income tax.

- **Taxes are deferred until money is withdrawn.** The contributions and earnings grow tax-deferred until withdrawal, when they are taxed as ordinary income. Because funds are normally withdrawn at retirement when the employee is in a lower tax bracket, the tax hit is reduced.

One of the benefits of a 401(k) plan over a company pension plan is portability. If you leave your job, you can take your 401(k) plan's funds to your new employer's plan or roll it over into an IRA.

A 403(b) plan is basically the same as a 401(k) plan, but it is designed for the employees of certain types of tax-exempt organizations.

Tax-Deferred Savings and Investments

You can take advantage of a number of tax-deferred savings and investments if you don't have a pension or want to supplement one. These plans all have one thing in common: They enable you to save money for retirement without paying taxes on interest or investment earnings until they are withdrawn.

IRAs

The most well-known type of tax-deferred savings is an Individual Retirement Account (IRA). An IRA is a tax-deferred investment and savings account that acts as a personal retirement fund for people with employment income. You hear a lot about these accounts around tax time because the government allows you to deduct contributions for many types of IRAs from your taxable income, thus reducing your taxes. Here's a summary of the different types of IRAs currently available:

- **IRA** contributions (up to $2,000) can be deductible or nondeductible; earnings are tax-deferred until withdrawn after the age of 59½, when they are taxed as ordinary income. There are two types of IRAs: regular and spousal. A regular IRA is designed for an individual whereas a spousal IRA is designed for married couples in which only one person has employment income.
- **Roth IRA** contributions (up to $2,000) are not tax-deductible. The contributions and earnings, however, can be withdrawn *tax-free* after the age of 59½. The idea is to provide an alternative for people who expect to be in a

high tax bracket when they retire. You can contribute to a Roth IRA for as long as you like.

- **SEP-IRA,** or **Simplified Employee Pension IRA**, is provided by sole proprietors of small businesses to employees (including themselves). The employer can contribute up to 15% of the employee's compensation, up to $24,000. The SEP-IRA is subject to the same other rules as an IRA. Employees with SEP-IRAs can also contribute to regular IRAs.

- **SARSEP-IRA,** or **Salary Reduction SEP-IRA**, is provided by sole proprietors of businesses with less than 25 employees. Contributions, which can be made by both employer and employee, are tax-deductible. The SARSEP-IRA is subject to the same other rules as an IRA. New SARSEP-IRA accounts can no longer be started; this type of savings and investment plan has been replaced by the SIMPLE-IRA.

- **SIMPLE-IRA** or **Savings Incentive Match Plan for Employees-IRA** replaced the SARSEP-IRA in 1997. It's basically the same as the SARSEP-IRA, but can be used by companies with up to 100 employees, and allows maximum contributions of $6,000 for the employee plus the employer share. The SIMPLE-IRA is subject to the same other rules as an IRA. Employees with SIMPLE-IRAs can also contribute to regular IRAs.

Keoghs

A Keogh plan is a tax-deferred retirement plan for self-employed individuals, including sole proprietors who report income on Schedule C, and partners who report income on Schedule E. Contributions and earnings are tax-deferred until withdrawn after the age of 59½. There are two kinds of Keogh plans:

- **Profit-Sharing Keogh** plans allows contributions of up to 13.04% of your self-employment income, with a maximum of $30,000. The contribution percentage can be adjusted annually.

- **Money-Purchase Keogh** plans allows contributions of up to 20% of your self-employment income, with a maximum of $30,000. The contribution percentage you select must be the same from year to year.

Tax-Deferred Annuities

A tax-deferred annuity enables you to make contributions (that are not tax-deductible) toward an investment for which the earnings are tax-deferred until withdrawal, after the age of 59½. Annuities are sponsored by insurance companies and other financial institutions and are commonly available through agents, banks, stockbrokers, and financial planners. There are two types of annuities:

- **Fixed annuities** have a guaranteed rate of return.
- **Variable annuities** have a rate of return that varies based on the performance of the securities in which annuity funds are invested.

Other Savings and Investments

Any type of savings or investment can be used to fund your retirement: stocks, bonds, mutual funds, savings accounts, certificates of deposit, money market accounts, and so on. I tell you about these things in Chapters 19 and 21.

Unlike the tax-deferred savings and investments discussed in this chapter, taxable savings and investments can be liquidated or withdrawn and spent at any time. This is a two-edged sword. Although the money will always be available in the event of an emergency, you may find it a tough source of funds to resist when a new car or boat is on your mind. To me, the main benefit of retirement funds is that they're almost untouchable. In my mind, my retirement funds don't even belong to me right now—I'm not tempted to spend them.

You shouldn't overlook the tax benefits of tax-deferred retirement funds, either. Your money will grow more quickly when earnings aren't taxed.

Quicken Tools

Quicken Deluxe includes two tools to help you plan your retirement: the Retirement Calculator and the Quicken Financial Planner.

Retirement Calculator

The Retirement Calculator can help you calculate some of the numbers you need to plan for your retirement. To open it, choose Features | Planning | Financial Calculators | Retirement. The Retirement Calculator appears:

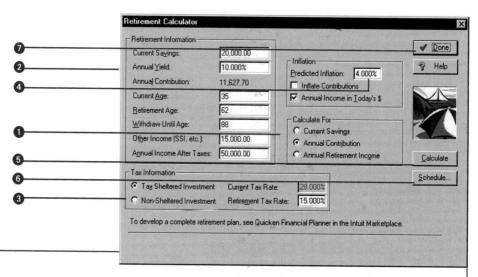

❶ Select a Calculate For option.
❷ Enter retirement information.
❸ Select a Tax Information option, and then enter rates as necessary at right.
❹ Enter the expected average annual inflation rate and select inflation options.

❺ Click Calculate.
❻ If desired, click Schedule to view a schedule of savings, income, and balances.
❼ When you are finished, click Done.

Select What You Want to Calculate

Begin by selecting one of the three Calculate For options:

- **Current Savings** calculates the amount of money you should currently have saved based on the values you enter.

- **Annual Contribution** calculates the minimum amount you should contribute to a retirement account based on the values you enter.

- **Annual Retirement Income** calculates the annual amount of retirement income you'll have based on the values you enter.

Enter Retirement Information Values

Next, enter values in the Retirement Information area. Here's a quick list of the information you'll have to provide:

- **Current Savings** is the amount you currently have in savings or a retirement plan. (This value is calculated for you when you select the Current Savings option in the Calculate For area.)
- **Annual Yield** is the percent return you expect to earn on your money.
- **Annual Contribution** is the amount you expect to contribute to a retirement account each year. (This value is calculated for you when you select the Annual Contribution option in the Calculate For area.)
- **Current Age** is your current age. (Don't lie like I did in the illustration.)
- **Retirement Age** is the age at which you plan to retire.
- **Withdraw Until Age** is the age at which you expect to either die or win a lottery jackpot. (With my luck, that's the year I'll do both.)
- **Other Income** is other annual income from sources such as a pension, social security, or income property.
- **Annual Income After Taxes** is the post-tax annual income you can expect when you retire. (This value is calculated for you when you select the Annual Retirement Income option in the Calculate For area.)

Enter Tax Information

Your retirement funds can be invested in taxable or tax-deferred investments. The type you select will make a big difference in the calculated amounts:

- **Tax Sheltered Investment** is for tax-deferred retirement accounts, such as the ones discussed earlier in this chapter. If you select this option, enter your expected tax rate for your retirement years.
- **Non-Sheltered Investment** is for other types of investments, like the ones I discuss in Chapter 19. If you select this option, enter your current tax rate and the expected tax rate for your retirement years.

Set Inflation Options

Enter inflation options in the Inflation area:

- **Predicted Inflation** is the predicted average annual inflation rate. Quicken uses a default of 4%, but you can change the value in the text box if you're feeling more optimistic or pessimistic about the economy's future.
- **Inflate Contributions** applies the inflation rate to the annual contributions.
- **Annual Income in Today's $** displays the Annual Income After Taxes value in today's dollars, ignoring inflation.

Calculating and Viewing the Results

Once all the information has been entered and options have been selected, click the Calculate button to calculate the selected value. Hopefully, the result is good news. You can get details about the contributions by clicking the Schedule button. Here's what it looks like for my example:

Age	Deposit	Income	Balance
0	0.00	0.00	20,000.00
35	11,627.70	0.00	33,627.70
36	11,627.70	0.00	48,618.17
37	11,627.70	0.00	65,107.69
38	11,627.70	0.00	83,246.16
39	11,627.70	0.00	103,198.47
40	11,627.70	0.00	125,146.02
41	11,627.70	0.00	149,288.32
42	11,627.70	0.00	175,844.85
43	11,627.70	0.00	205,057.04
44	11,627.70	0.00	237,190.44

Deposit Schedule — Print — Close. This deposit schedule assumes that your retirement income keeps pace with a 4.0% annual inflation rate. Note that income is in future, pre-tax dollars.

Quicken Financial Planner

While the Retirement Calculator is a good tool for quick retirement funding calculations, the Quicken Financial Planner covers every aspect of retirement planning, from your personal information, savings, and investments to an action plan that really works. It uses a simple, step-by-step approach for gathering information, and then performs calculations and generates reports that are easy to understand and use.

To open the Quicken Financial Planner, choose Features | Add-Ons | Quicken Financial Planner. The Quicken Financial Planner program launches. Its first window, which looks like the cover of a spiral-bound notebook, appears. Click the Open button to begin. The Welcome page of the introduction, shown here, provides information about using the Quicken Financial Planner:

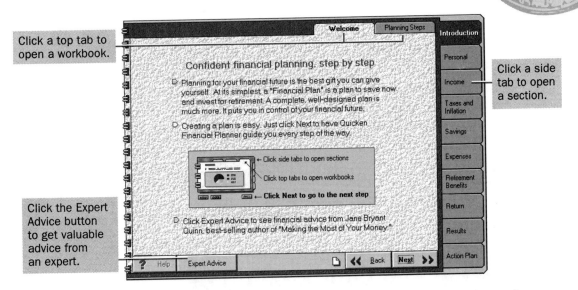

Click a top tab to open a workbook.

Click a side tab to open a section.

Click the Expert Advice button to get valuable advice from an expert.

Using the Quicken Financial Planner takes some time but not much—perhaps 10 minutes. Its instructions are extremely easy to understand and follow, so I won't take you through them. However, here's a summary of each section, just so you know what to expect:

- **Introduction** explains how to use the Quicken Financial Planner and provides an overview of the planning process.
- **Personal** enables you to enter information about yourself and your spouse, such as your name, date of birth, gender, and desired retirement age.
- **Income** prompts you to enter income information.
- **Taxes and Inflation** enables you to enter information about your tax bracket and expected inflation.
- **Savings** enables you to enter information about tax-deferred and taxable savings and investments.
- **Expenses** prompts you to enter expected living expenses after retirement.
- **Retirement Benefits** enables you to enter information about pension and social security benefits to which you are entitled.

- **Return** enables you to enter your expected rate of return on investments before retirement.
- **Results** displays the results of your entries using text, numbers, and charts. You can print most of the result windows. You can also change assumptions and recalculate the results.
- **Action Plan** displays and enables you to print a complete plan of action for achieving your retirement planning goals.

Tip If you have the full plan version of Quicken Financial Planner, you can include more financial information in your plan. You can upgrade the version that comes with Quicken Deluxe by calling a toll-free number that appears on your screen.

Quicken.com Resources

Choose Online | Quicken on the Web | Quicken.com. Quicken connects to the Web and displays the Quicken.com home page. Choose Retirement from the drop-down list near the top of the window. The Retirement main page appears, as shown in Figure 20-1.

In this section, I'll introduce you to Quicken.com's retirement resources so you know what you can find online.

Links to Information and Tools

The Contents area of the page offers links to information about different retirement options, including the 401(k), the IRA, and pensions. It also offers links to useful planning tools, including the Quicken Retirement Planner and the Roth IRA Planner.

Quicken Retirement Planner

Clicking the Build Your Plan link gives you access to the online version of the Quicken Retirement Planner, which is similar to the Quicken Financial Planner I discuss earlier in this chapter. Following the links to start the planner launches your Web browser to display the Retirement Planner window shown in Figure 20-2. Follow the instructions that appear onscreen to complete the planner.

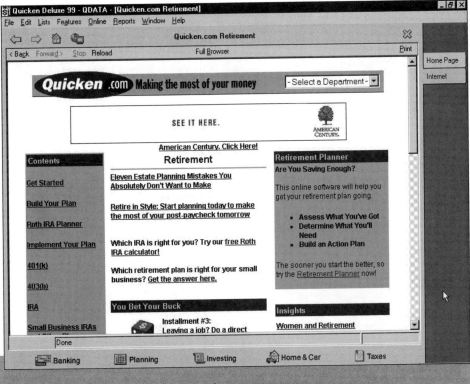

Figure 20-1 • The Retirement department main page

SAVE TIME Because the Quicken Financial Planner does almost the same thing and is already installed on your hard disk (if you have Quicken Deluxe), I recommend using that instead. It runs much faster because it doesn't rely on downloading information from the Internet.

Roth IRA Planner

The Roth IRA Planner enables you to evaluate which is better for you: a traditional IRA or a Roth IRA. The Roth IRA Planner's Introduction window is shown in Figure 20-3. Follow the instructions that appear onscreen to enter

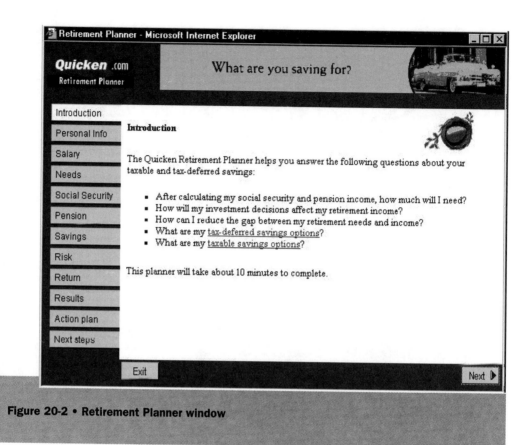

Figure 20-2 • Retirement Planner window

values. Results are calculated automatically and displayed using text, numbers, and charts.

More on Retirement

The More on Retirement area's link displays a page full of links to other retirement-related sites. These are the sites selected by Quicken.com and there isn't a dud among them. As this book went to press, sites on the list included Benefits Link, Financial Pipeline, and Lifenet.

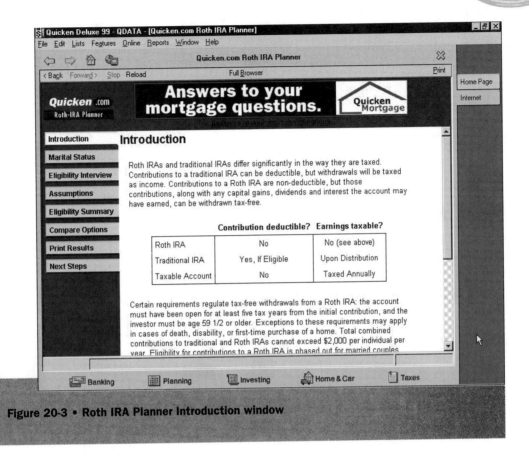

Figure 20-3 • Roth IRA Planner Introduction window

SAVE TIME Don't use Internet search engines to find sites about retirement topics. Start at Quicken.com's Retirement page and follow links from there. You won't waste time wading through junk to find a few treasures; all the sites you can link to from Quicken.com are full of information and packed with value.

Articles

Most of the Retirement page includes links to articles covering timely retirement topics. The articles change regularly, so be sure to check in at least once every few weeks to see what's new. A number of areas on the page offer specific features:

- **You Bet Your Buck** offers advice for saving money and avoiding penalties.
- **Insights** offers articles about topics that affect specific groups of people. For example, as this book went to press, one article covered women's retirement issues.

News Links

The Retirement Newstracker area offers links to current articles about retirement planning, inflation, and asset allocation. These articles can help you plan your retirement by offering tips, providing inflation trend data, and helping you understand how asset allocation can affect your retirement investments.

Saving for the Future

In This Chapter:

- *The Importance of Saving*

- *Types of Savings Accounts*

- *Setting Up Savings Goals*

- *Using Financial Calculators*

- *Reducing Debt*

- *The Planning Center*

- *Quicken.com Resources*

Chapter 21

Saving money is an important part of financial management. Savings enable you to take vacations and make major purchases without increasing debt, help your kids through college, and handle emergencies. In this chapter I tell you about saving for the future and how Quicken and Quicken.com can help. If you're in debt and can't even think about saving until you dig your way out, this chapter can help you, too. It also covers Quicken tools for reducing your debt.

Tip   If you don't mind risk and want to earn higher income on your savings, consult Chapter 19. It discusses investments, including stocks, bonds, and mutual funds.

Saving Basics

Remember when you got your first "piggy bank"? It may not have looked like a pig, but it had a slot for slipping in coins and, if you were lucky, a removable rubber plug on the bottom that made it easy to get the coins out when you needed them. Whoever gave you the bank was trying to teach you your first financial management lesson: save money.

As an adult, things are a little more complex. In this section, I explain why you should save, provide some saving strategies, and tell you about the types of savings accounts that make your old piggy bank obsolete.

Why Save?

Most people save money so there's money to spend when they need it. Others save for a particular purpose. Still others save because they have so much they can't spend it all. Here's a closer look at why saving makes sense.

Saving for "Rainy Days"

When people say they are saving for a rainy day, they probably aren't talking about the weather. They're talking about bad times or emergencies—situations when they need extra cash.

For example, suppose the family car needs a new transmission. Or your beloved dog needs eye surgery. Or your daughter manages to break her violin three days before the big recital. In the "rainy day" scheme of things, these might be light drizzles. But your savings can help keep you dry.

Here are a few other examples. Suppose your employer goes bankrupt and closes up shop. Or after a three-martini lunch with a customer, you get back to the office, tell your boss what you really think of him, and quit on the spot. Or after being poked one too many times in the butt by a bull, you find it impossible to continue your career as a rodeo clown. If your paychecks stop coming, do you have enough savings to support yourself or your family until you can get another source of income? On the "rainy day" scale, this could be a torrential downpour. Your savings can be a good umbrella.

Saving for a Goal

Planning for your future often includes planning for events that affect your life—and your wallet. Saving money for specific events can help make these events memorable for what they are, rather than what they cost.

For example, take a recently engaged couple, Sally and Joe. They plan to marry within a year and buy a house right away. Within five years, they plan to have their first child. That's when Sally will leave her job to start the more demanding job of mother and homemaker. Someday, they hope their children will go to college and they want to help cover the expenses. They also want to be able to help pay for their children's weddings. Eventually, they'll retire. And throughout their lives, they want to be able to take annual family vacations, buy a new car every six years or so, and get season tickets for the Arizona Diamondbacks.

All of these things are major events in Sally and Joe's lives. Saving in advance for each of these events will make them possible—without going into debt.

Saving for Peace of Mind

Some people save money because events in their lives showed them the importance of having savings. Children who lived through the Depression or bad financial times for their families grow up to be adults who understand the value of money and try hard to keep some available. They don't want to repeat the hard times they went through. Having healthy savings accounts gives them peace of mind.

Saving Strategies

There are two main ways to save: when you can or regularly.

Saving When You Can   When money is tight, saving can be difficult. People who are serious about saving, however, will force themselves to save as much as possible when they can. Saving when you can is better than not saving at all.

Saving Regularly   A better way to save money is to save a set amount periodically. For example, save $25 every week or $200 every month. Timing this with your paycheck makes sense; you can make a split deposit for the check. A savings like this is called an *annuity*, and you'd be surprised at how quickly the money can accumulate. The following table shows some examples based on a 4.5% annual interest rate.

Month	Weekly Contributions				Monthly Contributions				
	$25	$50	$75	$100	$50	$100	$200	$300	$400
1	$100	$200	$300	$401	$50	$100	$200	$300	$400
2	$226	$452	$677	$903	$100	$200	$401	$601	$801
3	$327	$653	$980	$1,307	$151	$301	$602	$903	$1,205
4	$428	$856	$1,284	$1,712	$201	$402	$805	$1,207	$1,609
5	$555	$1,110	$1,665	$2,220	$252	$504	$1,008	$1,511	$2,015
6	$657	$1,314	$1,971	$2,628	$303	$606	$1,211	$1,817	$2,423
7	$759	$1,519	$2,278	$3,038	$354	$708	$1,416	$2,124	$2,832
8	$888	$1,776	$2,664	$3,552	$405	$811	$1,621	$2,432	$3,242
9	$991	$1,982	$2,974	$3,965	$457	$914	$1,827	$2,741	$3,654
10	$1,095	$2,190	$3,284	$4,379	$509	$1,017	$2,034	$3,051	$4,068
11	$1,225	$2,449	$3,674	$4,899	$560	$1,121	$2,242	$3,363	$4,483
12	$1,329	$2,658	$3,987	$5,316	$613	$1,225	$2,450	$3,675	$4,900

Types of Savings Accounts

There are different types of savings accounts, each with its own benefits and drawbacks.

Tip   All the accounts discussed in this chapter (except where noted) should be insured by the FDIC (Federal Deposit Insurance Corporation). This organization covers savings deposits up to $100,000 per entity (person or company) per bank, thus protecting you from loss in the event of a bank failure.

Standard Savings Accounts   All banks offer savings accounts and most accommodate any balance. Savings accounts pay interest on your balance and allow you to deposit or withdraw funds at any time.

Holiday Clubs   A "holiday club" account is a savings account into which you make regular, equal deposits, usually on a weekly basis. Many banks offer these accounts, along with an option to automatically withdraw the deposit funds from your regular savings or checking account. The money stays in the account, earning interest until the club ends in October or November. The idea behind these accounts is to provide you with cash for the holidays, but there are variations on this theme, such as vacation club accounts that end in May or June.

Credit Union Payroll Savings   A bank isn't the only place where you can open a savings account. If your company has a credit union, it also offers a number of accounts. These accounts often offer the option of payroll savings deductions. This is a great feature for people who have trouble saving money, because the money comes out of their paycheck before they see (and can spend) it. It's as if the money never existed, when in reality it's accumulating in an interest-bearing account. In case you're wondering, the withdrawn funds are included in your taxable income.

Tip   I had a payroll savings account with the credit union of my last employer. Every time I got a raise, I increased the amount of the savings withdrawal so my take-home pay was almost the same. Before I left that job, I was saving $100 a week and I didn't miss a penny of it. Not bad!

Certificates of Deposit   A certificate of deposit, or CD, is an account, normally with a bank, that requires you to keep the money on deposit for a specific length of time. As a reward for your patience, your earnings are based on a higher, fixed interest rate than what is available for a regular savings account. The longer the term of the deposit and the more money deposited, the higher the rate. At the CD's maturity date, you can "roll over" the deposit to a new account that may have a different interest rate, or you can take back the cash. If you withdraw the money before the CD's maturity date, you pay a penalty, which can sometimes exceed the amount of the interest earned.

Money Market Accounts   A money market account is actually a form of investment, but it should be included here because it is offered by many banks. It has a higher rate of return than a regular savings account but is not insured by the FDIC. It is considered a conservative investment and can be treated just like a savings account for depositing and withdrawing money.

Interest-Bearing Checking Accounts   Many banks offer interest-bearing checking accounts. They usually have minimum balance requirements, however, forcing you to keep a certain amount of money in the account at all times. Although it's nice to earn money on checking account funds, the interest rate is usually so low that it's better to have a regular checking account and keep your savings in a savings account or money market account.

Reducing Your Debt

It's not easy to save money if most of your income is spent paying credit card bills and loan payments. If you're heavily in debt, you might even be having trouble keeping up with all your payments. If that's the case, stop thinking about saving for a moment and start thinking about reducing your debt.

Consumer credit is a huge industry. It's easy to get credit cards—sometimes too easy. And it's a lot easier to pay for something with a piece of plastic than with cold, hard cash. The "buy now, pay later" attitude has become an acceptable way of life. It's no wonder that many Americans are deeply in debt.

Those credit card bills can add up, however. And paying just the minimum payment on each one only helps the credit card company keep you in debt—and paying interest—as long as possible. I've been there, so I know. Unfortunately, it took two experiences to set me straight. I hope you can learn your lesson the first time.

Don't despair. There is hope. Here are a few things you can do to dig yourself out of debt.

GET SMARTER   Use Quicken's Debt Reduction Planner to develop a complete plan for reducing your debt. I tell you about it later in this chapter.

Breaking the Pattern

Your first step to reducing debt must be to break the pattern of spending that got you where you are. For most people, that means cutting up credit cards. After all, it's tough to use a credit card if you can't hand it to a cashier at the check-out counter.

Before you take out the scissors, however, read this: You don't have to cut up *all* of your credit cards. Leave yourself one or two major credit cards for emergencies like car trouble or unexpected visits to the doctor. The cards that should go are the store and gas credit cards. They can increase your debt, but they can only be used in a few places.

Here's the logic behind this strategy. If you have 15 credit cards, each with a credit limit of $2,000, you can get yourself into $30,000 of debt. The minimum monthly payment for each card may be $50. That's $750 a month in minimum credit card payments. If you have only two credit cards, each with a credit limit of $2,000, you can only get yourself into $4,000 of debt. Your monthly minimum payment may be only $100. This reduces your monthly obligation, enabling you to pay more than the minimum so you can further reduce your debt.

Shopping for Cards with Better Interest Rates

Yes, it's nice to have a credit card with your picture on it. Or one that's gold, platinum, or titanium. Or one with your college, team, club, or association name on it. A friend of mine who breeds horses showed off a new Visa card with a picture of a horse on it. She told me it was her favorite. I asked her what the interest rate was and she didn't know.

The purpose of a credit card is to purchase things on credit. When you maintain a balance on the account, you pay interest on it. The balance and interest rate determine how much it costs you to have that special picture or name on a plastic card in your wallet. Is it worth 19.8% a year? Or 21%? Not to me!

Tip   Here's a reality check exercise: Gather together all of your credit card bills for the most recent month. Now add up all the monthly finance fees and interest charges. Multiply that number by 12. The result is an approximation of what you pay in interest each year. Now imagine how nice it would be to have that money in your hands the next time you went on vacation or needed a down payment on a new car or home.

Low-interest credit cards are widely available. Sometimes you don't even have to look for them—offers arrive in the mail all the time. They promise low rates—usually under 10% a year. But you must read these offers carefully before you apply for one of these cards. Most offer the low rates for a short, introductory period—usually no longer than six months. (I got one the other day that offered 0% for the first 25 days. Big deal.) Some offer the low rate only on new purchases, while others offer the low rate only on balance transfers or cash advances. Be sure to find out what the rate is after the introductory period.

Here are two strategies for using a low-interest card:

- Consolidate your debt by transferring the balances of other credit cards to the new card. For this strategy, select a card that offers a low rate on balance transfers. When you transfer the balances, be sure to cut up the old cards so you don't use them to add more to your debt.
- Make purchases with the low-interest card. Make the new card your emergency credit card. Be sure to cut up your old emergency card so you don't wind up using both of them.

Tip   If you really like that special picture or name on the card in your wallet, call the credit card company and ask if they can give you a better interest rate. In many instances, they can.

Consolidating Your Debt

Consolidating your debt is one of the best ways to dig yourself out. By combining balances into one debt, whether through balance transfers to a single credit card or a debt consolidation loan, you're better able to pay off the balances without causing financial hardship. This is sometimes the only option when things have gotten completely out of control and you can't meet your debt obligations.

Tip   If you own a home, consider a home equity loan to consolidate your debt. The interest rate is usually lower than any credit card or debt consolidation loan and the interest may be tax-deductible. I tell you more about home equity loans in Chapter 19.

Using Charge Cards, Not Credit Cards

There's a difference between a credit card and a charge card:

- **Credit cards** enable you to buy things on credit. If each month you pay less than what you owe, you pay interest on your account balance. Most major "credit cards" are true credit cards. MasterCard, Visa, and Discover are three examples. Most store "charge cards" are also credit cards.
- **Charge cards** enable you to buy things on credit, too. But when the bill comes, you're expected to pay the entire balance. You don't have to pay any interest, but if you don't pay the entire balance on time, you may have to

pay late fees and finance charges. American Express is an example of a charge card.

The benefit of charge cards is that they make it impossible to get into debt. How can you owe the charge card company money if you must pay the balance in full every month? Using these cards prevents you from overspending. Every time you use the card to make a purchase, a little accountant in the back of your head should be adding the charge to a running total. You should stop spending when that total reaches the limit of your ability to pay.

Tip   Chapters 6 and 13 explain how you can use Quicken to track credit card balances manually or online. This includes charge cards. If you use Quicken to keep track of expenditures, you won't need that little accountant in the back of your head.

If you don't want an American Express card (for whatever reason), use another major credit card as a charge card. Just pay the entire balance each time you get a bill. If you don't carry a balance you won't pay interest.

If You Can't Stop Spending, Get Help

Many people who are deeply in debt may have a spending problem. They can't resist buying that fifth pair of running shoes or that trendy new outdoor furniture. They don't need the things they buy, but they buy them anyway. There's nothing wrong with that if your income can support your spending habits, but if your net worth is less than $0, it's a real problem—one that might require counseling to resolve.

The next time you make a purchase, stop for a moment and think about what you're buying. Is it something you need? Something you can use? Something you can justify spending the money on? If you can't answer yes to all of these questions, don't buy it. If you have to buy it anyway, it's time to seek professional help.

Living Debt-Free

It is possible to live debt-free—and you don't have to be rich to do it. Just learn to stop relying on credit cards to make your purchases and to spend only what you can afford to.

I've been debt-free for the past two years. With the exception of my mortgage, I have no debt. I do have major credit and charge cards, but I pay their balances in full every month, along with the bills I get for utilities and other living expenses. My trick: I only spend what I can afford to. I'm able to save whatever money I don't spend, and I don't pay a penny of nondeductible interest. Compared to the feeling I had (twice) when I was drowning in debt, being debt-free feels great! Try it sometime and see for yourself.

Quicken Saving and Debt-Reduction Tools

Quicken offers a number of features you can use to help you save money, plan for events, and reduce your debt, including Savings Goals, financial calculators, and the Debt Reduction Planner.

Savings Goals

Quicken's Savings Goals feature helps you save money by "hiding" funds in an account. You set up a savings goal and make contributions to it using the Savings Goals window. Although the money never leaves the source bank account, it is deducted in the account register, thus reducing the account balance in Quicken. If you can't see the money in your account, you're less likely to spend it.

Tip This really works. I used this technique with a paper check register years ago. Not only did it help me save money, but it prevented me from bouncing checks in the days when I kept a dangerously low checking account balance.

Open the Savings Goals window by choosing Features | Planning | Savings Goals. Figure 21-1 shows what the window looks like with one savings goal already created.

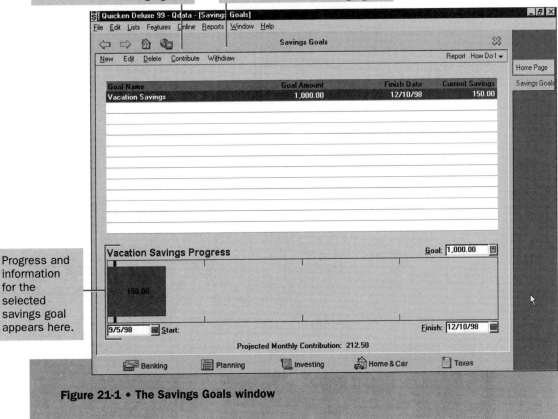

Click Contribute to add funds to the selected savings goal.

Click Withdraw to remove funds from the selected savings goal.

Progress and information for the selected savings goal appears here.

Figure 21-1 • The Savings Goals window

Creating a Savings Goal

To create a savings goal, click the New button on the Button bar in the Savings Goals window. The Create New Savings Goal dialog box appears:

Enter the information for your savings goal in the text boxes. The name of the savings goal cannot be the same as any Quicken category or account. For the Finish Date, enter the date by which you want to have the money saved. For example, if you're using savings goals to plan for a vacation, the Finish Date should be shortly before the date you want to start the vacation. When you're finished, click OK to add the savings goal to the list in the Savings Goals window.

Contributing Funds to a Savings Goal

To contribute funds to a savings goal, select the savings goal in the Savings Goals window and click the Contribute button in the Button bar. The Contribute to Goal dialog box appears. Use it to specify an amount and source account for the contribution:

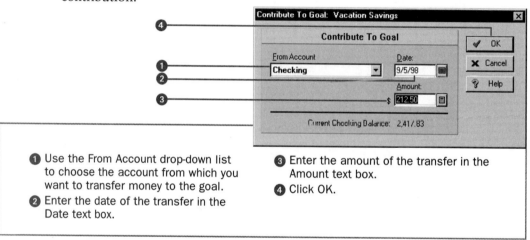

1. Use the From Account drop-down list to choose the account from which you want to transfer money to the goal.
2. Enter the date of the transfer in the Date text box.

3. Enter the amount of the transfer in the Amount text box.
4. Click OK.

As shown in the next illustration, Quicken creates an entry in the account register of the account from which the money was contributed. It also updates the progress bar and information in the Savings Goals dialog box.

| 9/5/98 | | Contribution towards goal | 150 | 00 | | | | 2,417 | 83 |
| | | [Vacation Savings] | | | | | | | |

Tip   When you create a savings goal, Quicken creates an asset account to record the goal's transactions and balance. To automate contributions to the goal, you can create a scheduled transaction to periodically transfer money from one of your bank accounts to the savings goal asset account. I tell you about scheduled transactions in Chapter 5.

Meeting Your Goal

Once you have met your savings goal, you can either withdraw the funds from the savings goal so they appear in a Quicken account or delete the savings goal to put the money back where it came from.

Withdrawing Money   In the Savings Goals window, select the savings goal from which you want to withdraw money. Click the Withdraw button on the Button bar. The Withdraw From Goal dialog box appears. Use this dialog box to remove funds from the savings goal and put them back into the account from which they were contributed:

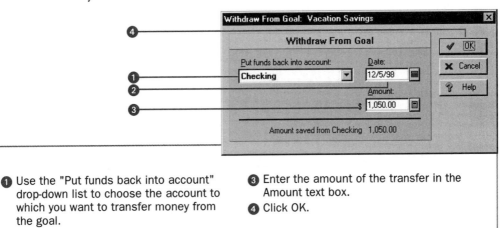

❶ Use the "Put funds back into account" drop-down list to choose the account to which you want to transfer money from the goal.

❷ Enter the date of the transfer in the Date text box.

❸ Enter the amount of the transfer in the Amount text box.

❹ Click OK.

Deleting a Savings Goal   In the Savings Goals window, select the savings goal you want to delete and click the Delete button on the Button bar. A dialog box like the following one asks if you want to keep the savings goal account for your records. Click the appropriate button.

Click Yes to transfer funds back to the original account(s) and keep the savings goal account.

Click No to transfer funds back to the original account(s) and delete the savings goal account.

Financial Calculators

Quicken includes two financial calculators that you can use to help yourself save money: the Investment Savings Calculator and the College Calculator.

Investment Savings Calculator

The Investment Savings Calculator enables you to calculate savings annuities. Choose Features | Planning | Financial Calculators | Savings. The Investment Savings Calculator appears:

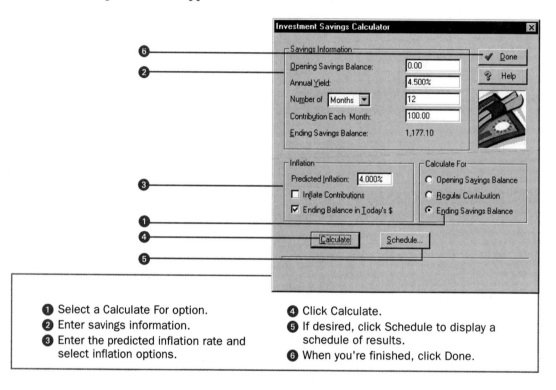

① Select a Calculate For option.
② Enter savings information.
③ Enter the predicted inflation rate and select inflation options.

④ Click Calculate.
⑤ If desired, click Schedule to display a schedule of results.
⑥ When you're finished, click Done.

Select a Calculate For option, and then enter or select values and options throughout the dialog box. The Calculate For option affects which value is calculated by Quicken. Most options are pretty straightforward and easy to understand. The Inflation options enable you to enter a predicted inflation rate, and then apply that rate to the contributions and to the calculation of the present value of the final balance. When you click Calculate, Quicken displays the results. You can click the Schedule button to see a printable list of deposits, with a running balance total.

College Calculator

The College Calculator enables you to calculate savings for the cost of a college education. Choose Features | Planning | Financial Calculators | College. The College Calculator appears:

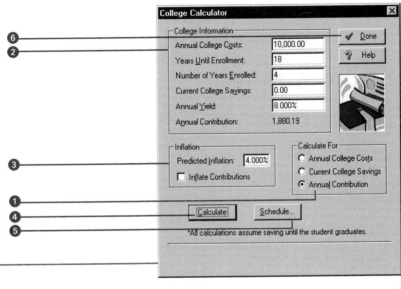

❶ Select a Calculate For option.
❷ Enter college information.
❸ Enter the predicted inflation rate and, if desired, turn on the Inflate Contributions check box to apply the rate to the savings contributions.

❹ Click Calculate.
❺ If desired, click Schedule to display a schedule of results.
❻ When you're finished, click Done.

Select a Calculate For option, and then enter or select values and options throughout the dialog box. The Calculate For option affects which value is calculated by Quicken. Most options are pretty straightforward and easy to understand. When you click Calculate, Quicken displays the results. You can click the Schedule button to see a printable list of deposits and tuition expenses, with a running balance total.

Debt Reduction Planner

The Debt Reduction Planner is a tool for helping you reduce your debt. You enter information about your financial situation and Quicken develops a debt reduction plan for you.

Choose Features | Planning | Debt Reduction Planner. If you have explored this feature before, the Debt Reduction window appears with a chart showing the information you previously entered. If you have never used it before, the Debt Reduction planner window appears, enabling you to create a new debt reduction plan.

Creating a New Debt Reduction Plan

If necessary, click the New Plan button on the Button bar of the Debt Reduction window. If a dialog box warns that you will overwrite your current plan, click Yes. The Debt Reduction planner window appears, displaying its Welcome screen. Insert your Quicken Deluxe CD in your CD-ROM drive and click the Next button to continue. An introductory movie plays to tell you what the Debt Reduction Planner can do for you. When it is finished, click the Next button to begin.

Entering Debt Information

When you click the Next button after viewing the movie, the Debts tab of the window appears. It should look something like this:

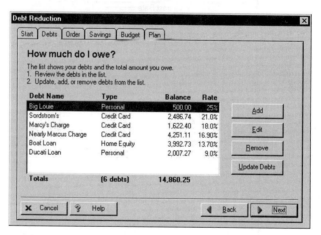

This window lists all your current debts. Use the buttons to the right of the list to modify it:

- If the debt list is not complete, click the Update Debts button to import current debt information from your Quicken data file.
- To add a debt that you do not track in Quicken, click the Add button. The Edit Debt Reduction dialog box, shown next, appears. Use it to enter information about the debt and click OK to add it to the list.

- To modify information about a debt, select it and click the Edit button to display the Edit Debt Reduction dialog box, shown in the following illustration. Make changes as desired and click OK to save the changes.

- To remove a debt from the list, select it and click the Remove button. In the confirmation dialog box that appears, click Yes. This removes the debt from the Debt Reduction Planner, but does not remove it from your Quicken data file.

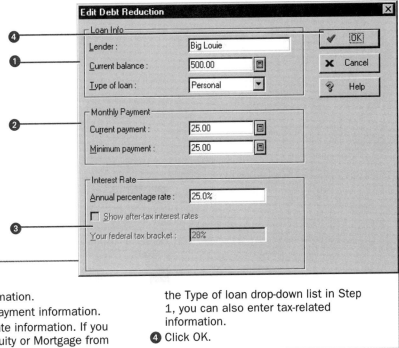

❶ Enter loan information.
❷ Enter monthly payment information.
❸ Enter interest rate information. If you chose Home Equity or Mortgage from

the Type of loan drop-down list in Step 1, you can also enter tax-related information.
❹ Click OK.

When the debt list shows all of your debts, click the Next button to continue.

Tip   If required information is missing from one or more debts, Quicken will tell you, and then display the Edit Debt Reduction dialog box for each debt so you can update the information. You must complete this process before you can continue.

Next, Quicken tells you about your current debt situation, including your total debt, your total monthly payments, and a projection of when you will be debt-free based on the debt information you provided. Click Next to continue.

Setting the Order of Debts

The Order tab of the Debt Reduction planner window puts your debts in the order of cost, with the highest at the top. Read the instructions that appear onscreen and click Next when prompted to view the ordered list. It might look something like this:

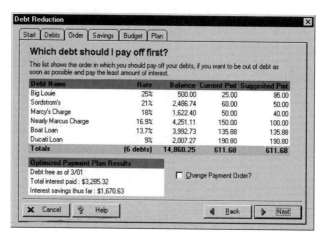

This window sets the debt payoff order so that the most expensive debt is paid off first, thus saving you interest charges. The Suggested Pmt column offers a suggested payment amount; following the suggestion makes it possible to pay off the debts faster without increasing your monthly payments. If desired, you can turn on the Change Payment Order? check box to change the order in which debts are paid off—this, however, will cost you more and increase the payoff time. Click Next to continue.

If you turn on the Change Payment Order? check box, when you click the Next button, the window changes to enable you to change the order of debts. Click a debt to select it, and then click the Move Up or Move Down button to change its location in the list. When you're finished, click Next.

Using Savings to Pay Off Debt

The Savings tab begins by playing a movie that tells you why you might want to use savings and investments to pay off your debt. Listen carefully—the movie is full of good information! When the movie is finished, click Next.

Quicken displays a window summarizing your current savings and investments, and enables you to specify how much of your savings should be applied to your debt.

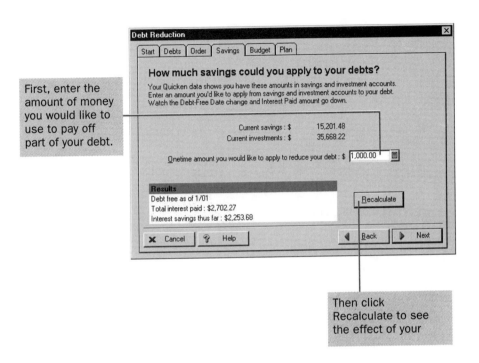

First, enter the amount of money you would like to use to pay off part of your debt.

Then click Recalculate to see the effect of your

Enter a value in the text box and click the Recalculate button. The Results area shows the effect of your change. Click Next to continue.

Adjusting Your Budget

The Budget tab offers options for helping you reduce your spending which can, in return, help you reduce your debt. It begins by displaying a movie with tips and instructions. When the movie is finished, click Next to continue.

Quicken displays a list of your top four expenses, with text boxes for entering the amount by which you can cut back on each one each month:

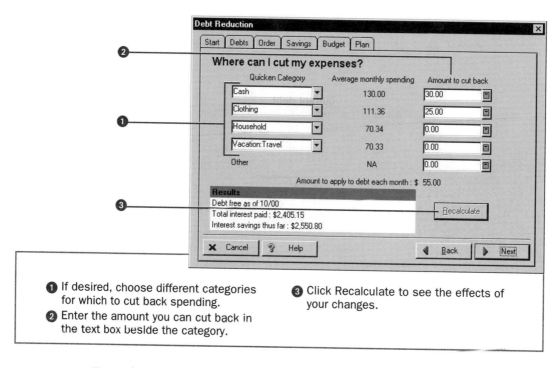

❶ If desired, choose different categories for which to cut back spending.

❷ Enter the amount you can cut back in the text box beside the category.

❸ Click Recalculate to see the effects of your changes.

Enter the amounts by which you can cut back for the categories that appear or on different categories you select from the drop-down lists. Quicken automatically suggests that you apply the savings to the debt, thus adjusting the Results area for your entries. Click Next to continue.

Reviewing the Plan

The Plan window displays your custom debt reduction action plan:

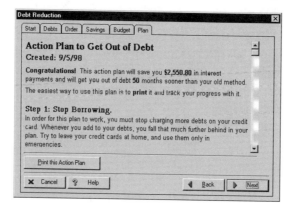

Scroll through the debt reduction plan to see what it recommends. Better yet, click the Print this Action Plan button to print a copy you can refer to

throughout the coming months. Click Next to continue, and then click Done to
view a graph of your debt reduction plan in the Debt Reduction window. It
might look something like this:

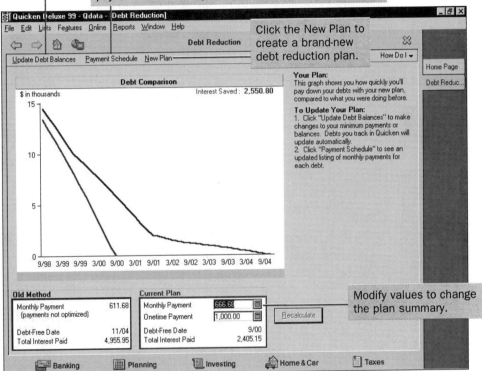

Click Update Debt Balances to import current debt
balances into the Debt Reduction Planner.

Click Payment Schedule to view a printable schedule of
payments to reduce your debt according to the plan.

Click the New Plan to
create a brand-new
debt reduction plan.

Modify values to change
the plan summary.

Modifying the Plan

Once you have a debt reduction plan, you can modify it in a number of ways:

- Click the Update Debt Balances button in the Button bar to import the
  current balances of your debt into the Debt Reduction Planner.
- Enter new values in the Current Plan area at the bottom of the Debt
  Reduction window.
- Click the New Plan button in the Button bar to create a new plan
  from scratch.

No matter which method you choose, Quicken will automatically revise the graph and other information to reflect your changes.

Planning Center

Quicken's Planning Center window offers a variety of information and links to commands and tools you can use for planning—whether it's to save money or reduce debt. Choose Features | Centers | Planning Center to display the Planning Center window (see Figure 21-2).

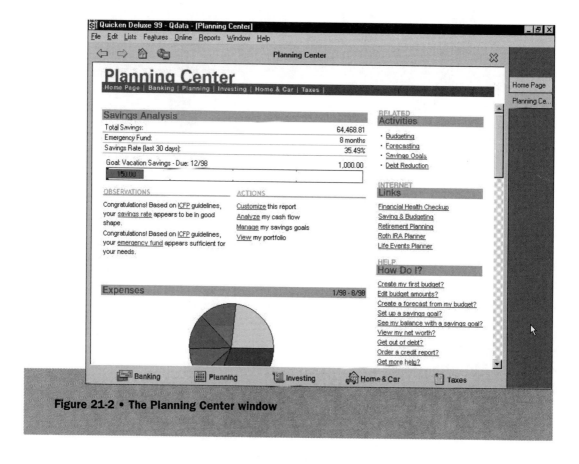

Figure 21-2 • The Planning Center window

Current Information

Most of the Planning Center window is filled with information about your current financial situation. You can customize what's displayed to meet your needs.

Savings and Expense Summaries

The Planning Center window displays four main summaries of financial information:

- **Savings** summarizes your savings, including savings goals, and your savings rate. The Emergency Fund area tells you how long your emergency funds would last based on your minimum monthly spending. Links enable you to customize the report, analyze your cash flow, manage your savings goals, and view your portfolio.
- **Expenses** displays a pie chart of your major expense items. Links enable you to customize the graph, analyze your spending, and help change your spending by setting up alerts.
- **Budgets** summarizes your budget for the month, including budgeted and actual amounts. Progress bars indicate your spending in different budget category groups. Links enable you to customize the report, analyze your spending, change your budget, and help change your spending by setting up alerts.
- **Net Worth** displays a combination chart that shows your assets and liabilities as bars, and your net worth as a line. Links enable you to customize the graph, analyze your net worth, view your accounts, and forecast your future growth.

Customizing the Savings Display

To customize the savings information displayed and set up an emergency fund, click the Customize link in the Savings area of the window. This displays the Customize Savings dialog box:

Click Savings to specify the accounts, categories, and classes to be included as savings.

Click Income to specify the accounts, categories, and classes to be included as income.

Customize Savings

To Customize the Savings Display

1. Click on the buttons below to specify which accounts and categories you want Quicken to use for each calculation.

2. Enter the approximate minimum amount you need to spend each month.

✔ OK

✗ Cancel

? Help

Accounts and Categories

Savings...   Income...   Emergency Fund...

Emergency Fund

Minimum Monthly Spending: 1,500.00

Enter the minimum amount you must spend each month in the Minimum Monthly Spending text box.

Click Emergency Fund to specify the accounts, categories, and classes to be included in the emergency fund.

For each button you click, a dialog box appears, enabling you to select the accounts, categories, and classes to be included in Savings, Income, or Emergency Fund. Set options for each of these areas. For example, Savings may include only bank and investment accounts for all categories and classes. Income may include only income categories for certain accounts and classes. Emergency Fund may include only savings and non-tax-related investment accounts for all categories and classes. When you're finished setting options for these areas, enter the minimum amount you must spend each month in the Minimum Monthly Spending text box. Then click OK. The Savings and Expense areas in the Planning Center window change to reflect your modifications.

Other Resources

Other areas on the Planning Center page offer links to Quicken features, as well as information, tools, and resources on Quicken.com.

Activities

The Activities area offers links to open Quicken feature windows, including Budget, Forecasting, Savings Goals, and Debt Reduction windows.

Links

Links offers links to tools and resources on the Quicken.com Web site. I tell you more about the saving and debt reduction tools you can find on Quicken.com a little later in this chapter.

How Do I?

The How Do I? area displays frequently asked questions as links to Quicken's online Help feature. Click a question to learn the answer.

Did You Know?

The Did You Know? area displays information about one or more planning-related articles, with links to the articles on the Web.

Quicken.com Resources

The Quicken.com Web site also offers resources for saving and reducing debt. Choose Online | Quicken on the Web | Quicken.com to connect to the Internet and open the Quicken.com home page. Choose Saving & Spending from the drop-down list near the top of the page. The Saving and Spending department's main page appears, as shown in Figure 21-3.

This section provides a quick summary of some of the resources available from the Saving and Spending department's main page.

Tip The Banking & Borrowing department's main page also offers saving- and debt-related information—including current rates on savings accounts, money market accounts, and CDs. Open it by choosing Banking & Borrowing from the drop-down list near the top of the Quicken.com home page window. I tell you about its resources in Chapter 18, so consult that chapter to learn more about what you can find there.

Resources & Tools

The Saving and Spending department offers links to a variety of resources and interactive tools you can use to get more information about saving and spending.

Frugal Features

The Frugal Features link takes you to the Frugal Features page, full of information, tips, and articles about saving money by being frugal. On this page, you'll find links to help you save money by spending less. Remember: A penny saved is a penny earned.

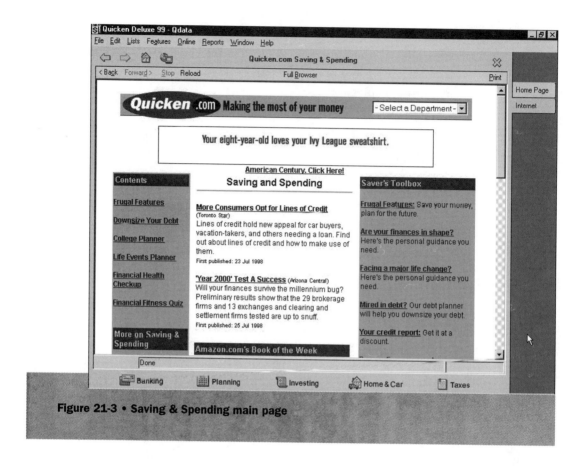

Figure 21-3 • Saving & Spending main page

Downsize Your Debt

The Downsize Your Debt link gives you access to the online version of the Debt Reduction Planner. This works very much like the Debt Reduction Planner within Quicken Deluxe, which I discuss in detail earlier in this chapter.

SAVE TIME If you have Quicken Deluxe, use its Debt Reduction Planner, rather than the online version. It'll run much faster on your computer.

College Planner

The College Planner link gives you access to the College Planner, which you can use to calculate how much you need to save each year to cover the cost of a college education. It's similar to the College Calculator, which I discuss earlier in this chapter, but it has many more features, including a database of colleges and their costs, estimates for financial aid, and the ability to generate an action plan. Using the College Planner is easy; just follow the instructions that appear onscreen. Its introductory window looks like this:

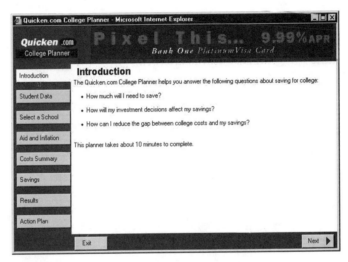

Life Events Planner

The Life Events Planner enables you to plan for major life events, such as marriage, the purchase of a new home, additions to your family, college, divorce or separation, illness, retirement, and your estate. Its main window is shown in Figure 21-4.

To use the Life Events Planner, click the tab for the event that interests you most. Then follow the instructions that appear onscreen to enter information. It's easy to use and informative. It includes links to many other Quicken.com and Web features, making it an extremely useful planning tool.

Financial Health Checkup

The Financial Health Checkup offers a unique way to test your financial "fitness." You answer a series of questions about things such as investments, debt management, and retirement planning. Then the Checkup tells you how you are doing and offers tips for doing better in the future. The process takes about 20 minutes to complete, but can provide valuable advice well worth the time spent.

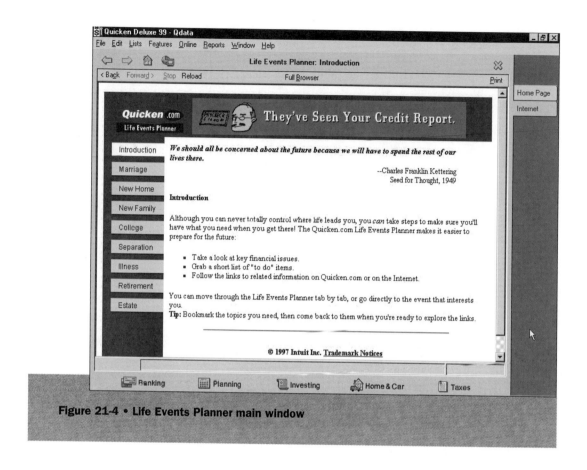

Figure 21-4 • Life Events Planner main window

Financial Fitness Quiz

The Financial Fitness Quiz offers ten multiple-choice questions you can answer about your finances. Submitting your answers displays a score, along with tips on how you can improve your finances. The process takes about three minutes to complete and the tips are useful and full of links to learn more.

Articles

The Saving and Spending department also offers links to timely articles covering saving and spending issues. As this book went to press, articles covered consumer lines of credit and Year 2000 testing by brokerage firms. Article links change regularly, so check in at least once a week to see what's new.

More on Saving & Spending

The More on Saving & Spending area's Other Web Sites link displays a page full of Quicken.com-reviewed Web sites. As this book went to press, links on that page included BizRate Guide: World Wide Where to Shop, Compare Net: The Interactive Buyer's Guide, and The Fat Cat Cafe.

 SAVE TIME   When you're searching for useful Web sites for saving money and reducing debt, start with the Other Web Sites links on Quicken.com. They'll take you right to valuable sites, without wading through lists of "matches" generated by Internet search engines.

People & Chat

Want to learn what other people are doing to save money? The People & Chat area of the Saving and Spending department's main page offers links to a number of bulletin boards where you can read, write, and reply to messages composed by people just like you. Get and share saving tips. Current bulletin board topics as this book went to press included Savvy Saving, Debt Downsizing, Borrowing, and Smart Spending.

Managing Quicken Files

In This Appendix:

- *Backing Up and Restoring Data Files*

- *Importing and Exporting Data*

- *Performing other File Management Tasks*

- *Password-Protecting Quicken Data*

Appendix A

501

All the data you enter in Quicken is stored in a Quicken data file. This file includes all account and category setup information, transactions, and other data you have entered into Quicken.

Commands under Quicken's File menu enable you to perform a number of file management tasks, including backing up, restoring, importing, exporting, renaming, and deleting data files. In this appendix, I cover all of these tasks.

Caution   Technically speaking, your Quicken data file really consists of a number of files with the same name and different extensions. Manipulating these files without using Quicken's file management tools can cause errors.

Backing Up Your Quicken Data File

Imagine this: You set up Quicken to track all of your finances and you record transactions regularly so the Quicken data file is always up-to-date. Then one evening, when you start your computer to play your favorite shoot-'em-up action game, you find that your hard drive has died. Not only have your plans for the evening been ruined, but your Quicken data file is also a casualty of your hard drive's untimely death.

If you back up your Quicken data as regularly as you update its information, the loss of your Quicken data file would be a minor inconvenience, rather than a catastrophe. In this section, I explain how to back up your Quicken data file and how to restore it if the original file is lost or damaged.

Tip   May 1, 1993, is the day I lost a hard drive. I learned a valuable lesson about backing up data that day. Heed my warning: Back up your data! Don't learn the hard way about the importance of backing up data.

Backing Up

Quicken makes it very difficult to forget backing up. Every third time you exit the Quicken program, it displays the Automatic Backup dialog box (shown at the top of the next page), which prompts you to back up your data file.

Click Backup to back up
your Quicken data file.

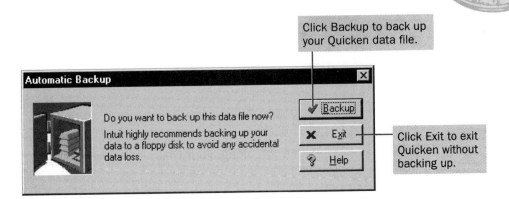

Click Exit to exit
Quicken without
backing up.

Tip   You can also begin the backup process by choosing File I Backup or
pressing CTRL-B at any time while using Quicken.

When this dialog box appears, click the Backup button. Another dialog box
appears, telling you that you need to have a formatted floppy disk and label
available. It also recommends that you alternate between two disks for backup
purposes. This means you'll always have two versions backed up, in case one
version is bad.

Click the Yes button to continue. The Select Backup Drive dialog box shown
here appears next:

Tip   You don't have to back up to a floppy disk. You can back up to any
disk, including a Zip disk or other removable media. Do not back up to
your hard drive. Doing so defeats the purpose of backing up!

Insert your disk in the disk drive and choose the drive designation letter from the Backup Drive drop-down list. Then select one of the two File to Back Up options:

- **Current File** backs up just the currently open Quicken data file. This is the option you'll probably select most often.
- **Select From List** enables you to select the Quicken data file you want to back up from a list of data files. This option is only useful if you have more than one Quicken data file.

After making your selection, click the OK button. Quicken backs up the data to the disk. It displays a status window as it works. The Quicken data file may disappear from screen momentarily. When the backup is complete, a dialog box tells you that the file has been backed up successfully. Click the OK button.

Tip   If your Quicken data file is too large to fit on one disk, Quicken will prompt you to insert additional formatted disks until the backup is complete. Follow the instructions that appear onscreen to complete the backup.

Restoring

In the event of loss or damage to your data file, you can restore from backup. Start Quicken, and then choose File | Restore Backup File. The Select Restore Drive dialog box appears:

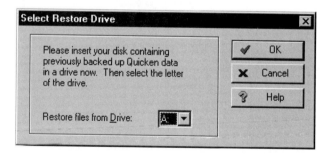

Choose the drive designation letter for the drive containing the backup files from the Restore files from Drive drop-down list. Click OK to continue. The Restore Quicken File dialog box appears next:

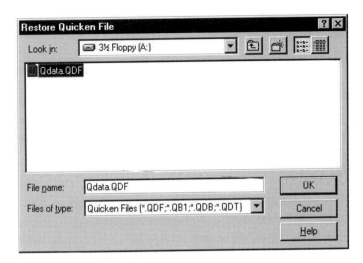

Use this dialog box to locate and select the data file that you want to restore. Then click OK. If the file has the same name as the Quicken file currently in use, a dialog box appears, asking if you want to overwrite the file in use. To replace the current file with the backup copy, click OK.

Quicken restores the file from the backup copy. It places a copy of the restored file in the QUICKENW directory on your hard disk, displaying a status window as it works. When it's finished, it displays a dialog box telling you that the file has been restored successfully. Click OK.

Importing and Exporting Data

Quicken supports its QIF format for importing data from other versions of Quicken to Quicken 99, or exporting Quicken 99 for Windows data for use with other versions of Quicken.

Importing Quicken Data

You can import data saved in Quicken QIF format into Quicken 99 for Windows. You might find this useful when converting Quicken for Macintosh or QuickBooks files to Quicken format. Simply use the program's Export command to create the QIF format file. Then import the data into Quicken.

Tip   Quicken 99 can automatically open files created with previous versions of Quicken for Windows (.QDF extension), Quicken for DOS versions 3 through 8 (.QDF extension), or Microsoft Money (.MNY extension). You don't need to use the Import command for these files; use the Open command instead. Quicken automatically handles any conversions for you. Converters for Quicken for DOS versions 1 and 2 are available on the Quicken technical support Web site, http://www.intuit.com/support/quicken/. That's also where you can find additional details about converting Quicken for Macintosh data files.

Before you import a QIF format file into your Quicken data file, back up the data file. Remember, Quicken automatically saves all changes to a data file. If something goes wrong with the import, your original data file could be damaged or could contain some incorrect transactions. I explain how to back up a data file earlier in this appendix.

To import a QIF format file, choose File | Import | QIF File. The QIF Import dialog box appears. Click the Browse button to display the Import from QIF File dialog box:

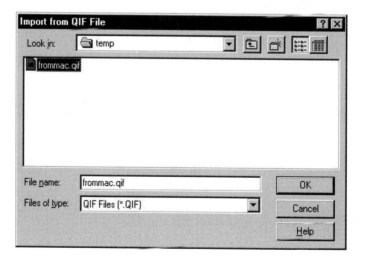

After you locate and select the QIF format file that you want to import, click OK to go back to the QIF Import dialog box, which looks like this:

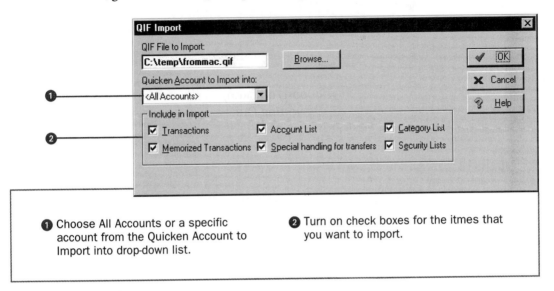

① Choose All Accounts or a specific account from the Quicken Account to Import into drop-down list.

② Turn on check boxes for the itmes that you want to import.

Set options as desired in the QIF Import dialog box. If you are importing into a brand-new Quicken file that does not include any accounts or categories, be sure to turn on the Account List, Category List, and Security List check boxes. When you are finished, click OK to begin the import.

Quicken displays an account list as it imports the data. You can watch balances change as data is imported. Occasionally, a dialog box may ask if you want to import transactions into a specific account or create a specific category. Answer Yes or No as appropriate. A dialog box tells you when the import is finished. Click OK. You can then begin working with the revised data file.

Exporting Quicken Data

You can also export Quicken data to QIF format. Choose File | Export to display the QIF Export dialog box:

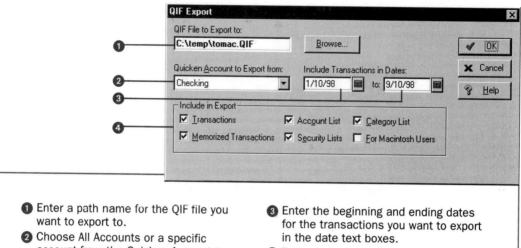

① Enter a path name for the QIF file you want to export to.

② Choose All Accounts or a specific account from the Quicken Account to Export from drop-down list.

③ Enter the beginning and ending dates for the transactions you want to export in the date text boxes.

④ Turn on check boxes for the items that you want to export.

Set options in the dialog box as desired. Each option changes the amount of data exported. When you have the options set the way you want them, click OK. Quicken exports the data, creating a file with the name you specified.

Tip You can also use options in the Print dialog box to save report data as a file on disk. The file can then be imported into other applications such as word processors, spreadsheets, or databases. I explain how to use the Print command to save data to a file in Chapter 8.

Other File Management Tasks

The File Operations submenu under Quicken's File menu enables you to perform several other tasks with Quicken data files. Here's a quick summary of each command, with tips for when you may find them useful.

Copying the Current Data File

The Copy command enables you to copy the current data file to a different disk or save a copy with a different name. When you choose File | File Operations | Copy, the Copy File dialog box, shown next, appears. Use it to set transactions for the copy, and then click OK to save the copy on disk.

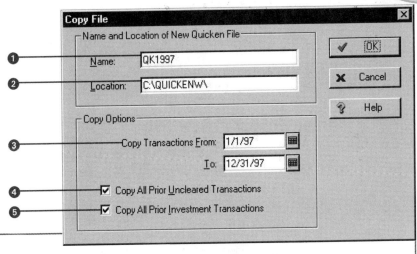

- ❶ Enter a name for the data file copy.
- ❷ Enter the directory path for the data file copy.
- ❸ Enter transaction range dates in the Copy Transactions To and From text boxes.
- ❹ To copy all uncleared transactions prior to the date range, turn on the Copy All Prior Uncleared Transactions check box.
- ❺ To copy all investment transactions prior to the date range, turn on the Copy All Prior Investment Transactions check box.

Deleting a Data File

The Delete command enables you to delete a data file. When you choose File | File Operations | Delete, the Delete Quicken File dialog box, shown next, appears. Use it to locate and select the data file you want to delete.

Delete Quicken File

Look in:	🗀 Quickenw

🗀 03001	🗀 Hpinvest	⧉ frommac.QDF
🗀 03101	🗀 Hpplan	⧉ Qdata.QDF
🗀 07776	🗀 Hptax	Qdata2.qdf
🗀 Hpbank	🗀 Inet	
🗀 Hpcar	🗀 sounds	
🗀 Hphome	⧉ ~qw~link.qdt	

File name: Qdata2.qdf

Files of type: Quicken Files (*.QDF;*.QDB;*.QDT)

OK   Cancel   Help

When you click OK, another dialog box appears, asking you to confirm that you want to delete the file. You must type in **Yes** to delete the file.

Caution Deleting a Quicken data file permanently deletes all of its data, so use this command with care!

Renaming a Data File

The Rename command enables you to rename a data file. When you choose File | File Operations | Rename, the Rename Quicken File dialog box shown next appears. Use it to select the file you want to rename and enter a new name. When you click OK, Quicken changes the name of the main data file you selected and all of its support files.

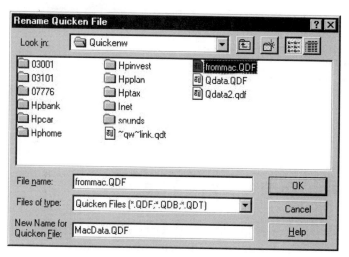

Tip This is the best way to rename a data file. Renaming files in Windows Explorer could cause information to be lost.

Checking the Integrity of a Data File

The Validate command enables you to check the integrity of a Quicken data file. This command is particularly useful if you believe that a file has been damaged. When you choose File | File Operations | Validate, the Validate Quicken File dialog box appears. It looks very much like the Delete Quicken File dialog box illustrated earlier in this chapter. Use it to locate and select the file you want to validate. When you click OK, Quicken checks its integrity and reports back to you with one of the following dialog boxes:

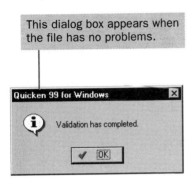

This dialog box appears when the file has no problems.

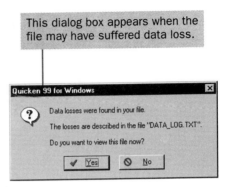

This dialog box appears when the file may have suffered data loss.

Making a Year-End Copy of a Data File

The Year-End Copy command enables you create two different types of file copies suitable for year-end data storage: Archive and Start New Year. When you choose File | File Operations | Year-End Copy, the Year-End Copy dialog box, which is shown next, appears. Select a Year-End Action and click OK.

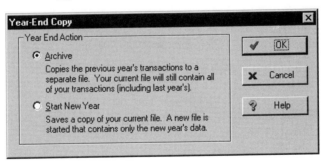

Creating an Archive

An *archive* is a copy of the previous year's transactions saved in a separate file. All transactions remain in the current file. Use this if you want a separate record of a year's transactions but you want to continue working with the data in your current data file.

When you choose this option, the Archive File dialog box appears:

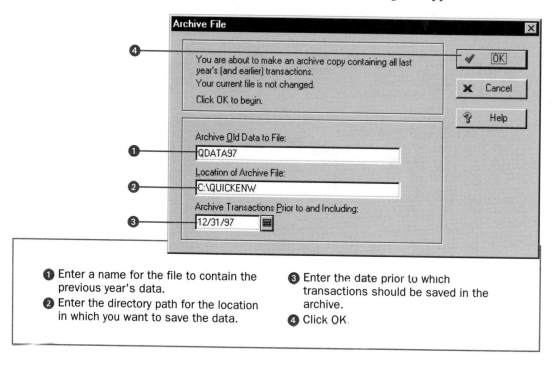

① Enter a name for the file to contain the previous year's data.

② Enter the directory path for the location in which you want to save the data.

③ Enter the date prior to which transactions should be saved in the archive.

④ Click OK.

Set options in the dialog box and click OK. Quicken creates the archive file as specified. When it's finished, it displays a dialog box that enables you to select the file you want to work with: the Current file or the Archive file. Select the option button for the file you want and click OK to continue working with Quicken.

Creating a New Year File

The Start New Year option in the Year-End File dialog box saves a copy of the current file, and then creates a new file with just the transactions from the current year. Use this if you want to keep your current file small.

When you choose this option, the Start New Year dialog box appears:

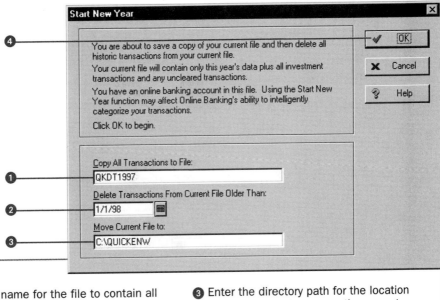

Start New Year

You are about to save a copy of your current file and then delete all historic transactions from your current file.

Your current file will contain only this year's data plus all investment transactions and any uncleared transactions.

You have an online banking account in this file. Using the Start New Year function may affect Online Banking's ability to intelligently categorize your transactions.

Click OK to begin.

Copy All Transactions to File:
QKDT1997

Delete Transactions From Current File Older Than:
1/1/98

Move Current File to:
C:\QUICKENW

✓ OK
✗ Cancel
? Help

❶ Enter a name for the file to contain all of the data.
❷ Enter the date prior to which transactions should be deleted from the current file.
❸ Enter the directory path for the location in which you want to save the current file.
❹ Click OK.

Set options in the dialog box and click OK. Quicken copies the current file and saves it with the name you specified. It then deletes all prior year transactions and saves the file as the current file. When it's finished, it displays a dialog box that enables you to select the file you want to work with: the Old file or the File for the New Year. Select the option button for the file you want and click OK to continue working with Quicken.

Password-Protecting Quicken Data

Quicken offers two types of password protection for your data: file passwords and transaction passwords. In this section, I tell you how these options work.

Protecting a Data File

When you password-protect a data file, the file cannot be opened without the password. This is the ultimate in protection—it prevents unauthorized users from even seeing your data.

Setting Up the Password

Choose File | Passwords | File to display the Set Up Password dialog box, which is illustrated next. Enter the same password in each text box, and then click OK.

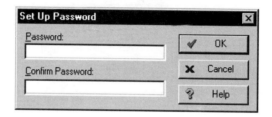

Opening a Password-Protected Data File

When you open a data file that is password-protected, the Quicken Password dialog box appears:

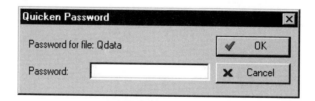

You must correctly enter your password to open the file, and then click OK.

Protecting Existing Transactions

When you password-protect existing transactions, the transactions cannot be modified unless the password is properly entered. This prevents unauthorized—or accidental—alterations to data.

Setting Up the Password

Choose File | Passwords | Transaction to display the Password to Modify Existing Transactions dialog box, shown next. Enter the same password in the top two text boxes, enter a date before which the transactions cannot be modified, and then click OK.

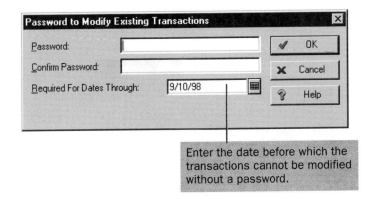

Enter the date before which the transactions cannot be modified without a password.

Modifying a Password-Protected Transaction

When you attempt to modify a transaction that is protected with a password, the Quicken Password dialog box shown next appears. You must correctly enter your password to modify the transaction, and then click OK.

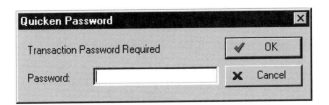

Password Tips

Here are a few things to keep in mind when working with passwords:

- Passwords can be up to 16 characters in length and can contain any character, including a space.
- Quicken does not distinguish between uppercase and lowercase characters.
- If you forget your password, you will not be able to access the data file. Write your password down and keep it in a safe place—but not on a sticky note attached to your computer monitor.
- To change or remove a password, choose File | Passwords | File; or choose File | Passwords | Transactions. The Change Password dialog box or the Change Transaction Password dialog box appears. To change the password, enter the old password in the first text box and the new password in the second and third text boxes. To remove the password, enter the existing password in the first text box and leave the next two text boxes empty. When you click OK, the password is removed or changed.

Remember, your data file is only as secure as you make it. Quicken's password protection can certainly help prevent unauthorized access to your Quicken data files.

Index

U

V